The Psychology of Rights and Duties

The LAW AND PUBLIC POLICY: PSYCHOLOGY AND THE SOCIAL SCIENCES series includes books in three domains:

Legal Studies—writings by legal scholars about issues of relevance to psychology and the other social sciences, or that employ social science information to advance the legal analysis;

Social Science Studies—writings by scientists from psychology and the other social sciences about issues of relevance to law and public policy; and

Forensic Studies—writings by psychologists and other mental health scientists and professionals about issues relevant to forensic mental health science and practice.

* * *

The Right to Refuse Mental Health Treatment
Bruce J. Winick
Violent Offenders: Appraising and Managing Risk
Vernon L. Quinsey, Grant T. Harris, Marnie E. Rice, and Catherine A. Cormier
Recollection, Testimony, and Lying in Early Childhood
Clara Stern and William Stern; James T. Lamiell (translator)
Genetics and Criminality: The Potential Misuse of Scientific Information in Court
Edited by Jeffrey R. Botkin, William M. McMahon, and Leslie Pickering Francis
The Hidden Prejudice: Mental Disability on Trial
Michael L. Perlin
Adolescents, Sex, and the Law: Preparing Adolescents for Responsible Citizenship
Roger J. R. Levesque
Legal Blame: How Jurors Think and Talk About Accidents
Neal Feigenson
Justice and the Prosecution of Old Crimes: Balancing Legal, Psychological, and Moral Concerns
Daniel W. Shuman and Alexander McCall Smith
Unequal Rights: Discrimination Against People With Mental Disabilities and the Americans With Disabilities Act
Susan Stefan

Treating Adult and Juvenile Offenders With Special Needs
Edited by José B. Ashford, Bruce D. Sales, and William H. Reid
Culture and Family Violence: Fostering Change Through Human Rights Law
Roger J. R. Levesque
The Legal Construction of Identity: The Judicial and Social Legacy of American Colonialism in Puerto Rico
Efrén Rivera Ramos
Family Mediation: Facts, Myths, and Future Prospects
Connie J. A. Beck and Bruce D. Sales
Not Fair! The Typology of Commonsense Unfairness
Norman J. Finkel
Competence, Condemnation, and Commitment: An Integrated Theory of Mental Health Law
Robert F. Schopp
The Evolution of Mental Health Law
Edited by Lynda E. Frost and Richard J. Bonnie
Hollow Promises: Employment Discrimination Against People With Mental Disabilities
Susan Stefan
Violence and Gender Reexamined
Richard B. Felson
Determining Damages: The Psychology of Jury Awards
Edie Greene and Brian H. Bornstein
Protecting Society From Sexually Dangerous Offenders: Law, Justice, and Therapy
Edited by Bruce J. Winick and John Q. La Fond
Treating Chronic Juvenile Offenders: Advances Made Through the Oregon Multidimensional Treatment Foster Care Model
Patricia Chamberlain
Juvenile Delinquency: Understanding the Origins of Individual Differences
Vernon L. Quinsey, Tracey A. Skilling, Martin L. Lalumière, and Wendy M. Craig
Lawyer, Know Thyself: A Psychological Analysis of Personality Strengths and Weaknesses
Susan Swaim Daicoff
The Psychology of Rights and Duties: Empirical Contributions and Normative Commentaries
Edited by Norman J. Finkel and Fathali M. Moghaddam

The Psychology of Rights and Duties

EMPIRICAL CONTRIBUTIONS AND NORMATIVE COMMENTARIES

EDITED BY

Norman J. Finkel

Fathali M. Moghaddam

AMERICAN PSYCHOLOGICAL ASSOCIATION

WASHINGTON, DC

Published by
American Psychological Association
750 First Street, NE
Washington, DC 20002
www.apa.org

To order
APA Order Department
P.O. Box 92984
Washington, DC 20090-2984
Tel: (800) 374-2721; Direct: (202) 336-5510
Fax: (202) 336-5502; TDD/TTY: (202) 336-6123
Online: www.apa.org/books/
E-mail: order@apa.org

In the U.K., Europe, Africa, and the Middle East, copies may be ordered from
American Psychological Association
3 Henrietta Street
Covent Garden, London
WC2E 8LU England

Typeset in Goudy by Stephen McDougal, Mechanicsville, MD

Printer: Edwards Brothers, Inc., Ann Arbor, MI
Cover Designer: Berg Design, Albany, NY
Technical/Production Editor: Emily Leonard

Library of Congress Cataloging-in-Publication Data

The psychology of rights and duties : empirical contributions and normative commentaries / edited by Norman J. Finkel and Fathali M. Moghaddam.
p. cm. — (The law and public policy)
Includes bibliographical references and index.
ISBN 1-59147-166-4
1. Obedience (Law) 2. Duty. 3. Culture and law. 4. Human rights—Philosophy. I. Finkel, Norman J. II. Moghaddam, Fathali M. III. Series.

K258.P78 2005
342.08'5'01—dc22 2004007720

British Library Cataloguing-in-Publication Data
A CIP record is available from the British Library.

Printed in the United States of America
First Edition

To Marilyn and Maryam
Fair and wise, they balance rights and duties in our lives,
And give to us not equal measure, but rather a more ample treasure.

CONTENTS

CONTRIBUTORS

Enid Chung, MA, Department of Psychology, George Washington University, Washington, DC

Willem Doise, PhD, Professor, Faculty of Psychological and Educational Sciences, University of Geneva, Switzerland

Norman J. Finkel, PhD, Professor, Department of Psychology, Georgetown University, Washington, DC

Rom Harré, DLitt, Fellow, Linacre College, Oxford University, England; Department of Psychology, Georgetown University, Washington, DC

Thomas L. Haskell, PhD, Samuel G. McCann Professor of History, Department of History, Rice University, Houston, TX

Siegfried Hoppe-Graff, PhD, Professor, Department of Education, University of Leipzig, Germany

Hye-On Kim, PhD, Associate Professor, Department of Education, Mokpo National University, Chonnam, South Korea

Winnifred R. Louis, PhD, Post-Doctoral Fellow, School of Psychology, University of Queensland, St. Lucia, Australia

Fathali M. Moghaddam, PhD, Professor, Department of Psychology, Georgetown University, Washington, DC

Philip J. Moore, PhD, Associate Professor, Department of Psychology, George Washington University, Washington, DC

Cara Joy Riley, BA, Research Associate, Department of Psychology, Georgetown University, Washington, DC

Stephanie Spernak, JD, PhD, Professor, Department of Psychology, George Washington University, Washington, DC

Dario Spini, PhD, Associate Professor, Department of Social and Political Sciences, PaVie Center, University of Lausanne, Switzerland

Thomas A. Spragens Jr., PhD, Professor, Department of Political Science, Duke University, Durham, NC

Donald M. Taylor, PhD, Professor, Department of Psychology, McGill University, Montreal, Quebec, Canada
Tom R. Tyler, PhD, Professor, Department of Psychology and School of Law, New York University, New York City
Stephen Worchel, PhD, Professor, Department of Psychology, University of Hawai'i, Hilo

PREFACE

Rights and *duties*, two foundational concepts of justice correlatively yoked and long studied by the normative disciplines, are basic to civic virtue, the social contract, and the life of the law. When rights are respected, duties are fulfilled, and the two are balanced, relationships between individuals, groups, and the government generally function well enough, such that these concepts tend to remain out of awareness. But when rights are not respected, duties are not fulfilled, or when the two are markedly out of balance, then a founding father such as Jefferson, may urge citizens to nullify the law (British law), declare independence, and claim in the Declaration of Independence that "it is their right, it is their duty" to do so.

Rights and duties are our topic in this book, in part because empirical research from psychology particularly on the topic of duty came to an abrupt halt following the bystander intervention studies three decades ago. But we are renewing this empirical research in a much wider and deeper way here and for a more pressing reason because on September 11, 2001, the world got a wake-up call. In the wake of the World Trade Center towers' tragic falling, the question of rights and duties once again jumped into consciousness as the very ontology of those terms shifted within a dramatically changing world.

A "war on terrorism" was declared by President George W. Bush. Whereas in the past, the Chief Executive might have said it is his duty to protect the safety of the citizens, now the claim was framed as a right to do so; as the terms seemed not only to dilate but also to interchange, the right extended to hunting down terrorists wherever they may be, even crossing the borders of other nation states if necessary, with the rights of other nations having to apparently yield to our "higher" rights or duties. If a new right waxed, certain due process rights waned, for in the United States, the 342-page Patriot Act shifted rights and duties significantly. The President, invoking a newly claimed executive duty, declared certain individuals, some of them U.S. citizens, "enemy combatants." As a result, many detainees were held several years without charge and without seeing a lawyer, and some who saw lawyers had their conversations monitored.

Two years later, however, the tide began to change in this ebb and flow of rights and duties. As more citizens became aware of which rights were "given away" in the period following September 11, 2001, over 150 jurisdictions symbolically nullified parts of the Patriot Act; courts began to question the administration's claim that judges could neither look behind the government's allegations that someone was an enemy combatant nor review executive decisions; and "friendly countries" began to complain about the detention of their citizens and about the United States' skirting international law and violating fundamental rights and duties. This topic is clearly timely, yet change had been coming for some time. At the community level, a series of human tragedies starting with the 1964 murder of Kitty Genovese in New York—when 38 neighbors heard her screams for help yet no one came to her rescue or called the police—finally moved eight states to enact Good Samaritan laws. These laws require either a duty to report or a duty to rescue, which transform a civic and moral duty into a legal duty. But the debate is just heating up because a number of legal scholars believe that these laws are Bad Samaritan laws, vague and problematic.

At a national level and within the criminal law, the picture used to be much simpler with a defendant who had certain rights at trial and the state that had a duty to prosecute alleged crimes. But victims and the families of victims add new players and claims of rights, creating confusion and conflict over rights and duties. Going still further, many parents see their children as "potential victims" and want them protected from pedophiles and sex offenders, and legislatures and courts have responded. The passage of the Jacob Wetterling Crimes Against Children and Sexually Violent Offender Registration Act, Megan's Law, Internet postings of information about convicted pedophiles for anyone to see, and even the involuntary commitment of those who have completed their prison sentence are just some of the responses that have greatly restricted the rights of those in this designated class in favor of the duty to protect the many. At the same time, the question of who is a married person brings gay marriages before the country and the law; an Alabama Supreme Court justice and his Ten Commandments statue and right to religious expression both exit from the law; and the French pass a law banning religious garb and emblems worn by students in schools. Everywhere we turn, it seems rights and duties are now at the forefront of community, national, and international challenges.

The idea for this work began at Georgetown University as we, the two editors, one coming from a psycholegal perspective of commonsense justice and fairness and the other from a perspective of intergroup relations, culture, and conflict, realizing our common interest in matters of justice, began a series of conversations that grew into regular meetings. Our focus began to narrow on the topic of rights and duties, so central in law, philosophy, and political science, yet an area that had received scant empirical study within psychology. Our aim for this book was to get as contributors the leading researchers in this area, and we believe we have. Some of our authors do cross-cultural work; others are in the area of intergroup relations; and still others do psycholegal research.

When Rom Harré, a renowned philosopher from Oxford who has been teaching at Georgetown each spring semester, joined our conversations, we took the opportunity of adding the normative perspective. The additional conceptual clarity Rom brought to our discussions of terms and his knowledge of the historical background that had preceded our initial wrestling with these knotty issues made us realize that we of the empirical persuasion were the new kids on the block. The idea of normative commentaries, a rather exciting but risky proposition, was taking shape: Our empirical researchers would expose their work to a moral philosopher, an intellectual historian, and a political scientist, and the normative commentators would have the freedom to comment critically on these chapters and use them as a springboard for discussion. Our twofold aim was to make future empirical work as well as our present work conceptually sounder, substantively richer, and more informative.

This book fills a vitally important gap in the scholarship of psychology and justice, and in this way, we think it will be particularly useful to psychology students and professors in courses on intergroup relations, social justice, psychology and law, ethnic relations and multiculturalism, cross-cultural and cultural psychology, and social psychology. This book brings together those who meet at the empirical and normative nexus over the common ground of rights and duties at the professional and scholarly level and is likely to appeal to those who study this topic; they may come from backgrounds of psychology, philosophy, political science, history, law, sociology, anthropology, and more, for this topic cuts across many disciplinary lines.

This book, to our knowledge, is novel and innovative. It is certainly a different sort of book for the Law and Public Policy: Psychology and the Social Sciences book series. For that, we would like to thank our acquisitions editor at the American Psychological Association (APA), Susan Reynolds, for getting behind this unusual project; Bruce Sales, the editor of the series, who recognized the new ground we were trying to break and made constructive suggestions along the way; Judy Nemes, editorial supervisor, and Emily Leonard, production editor, at APA Books; and those reviewers who helped in the honing and harnessing of this work. And finally, we sincerely thank both our empirical chapter authors and our normative chapter authors for their openness to the other, for their willingness to meet at the empirical and normative nexus and inform one another, and for bringing their fresh perspectives and cutting-edge work on rights and duties to this project.

The Psychology of Rights and Duties

1

HUMAN RIGHTS AND DUTIES: AN INTRODUCTION

NORMAN J. FINKEL AND FATHALI M. MOGHADDAM

It was early morning, March 13, 1964, when a young woman named Kitty Genovese was attacked on her way from her car to her apartment in a middle-class neighborhood of Queens, New York. Her screams for help awakened many neighbors (Rosenthal, 1964/1999, p. 68). During the estimated 35-minute attack, her attacker was scared away, but only temporarily, for when he realized that nobody was coming to the victim's aid, he returned to attack her again. This scream–flight–return pattern was repeated until the victim died from knife wounds in a pool of blood as her assailant "then lay down on her body to ejaculate" (p. ix). What brought this case to national and international attention was the police's finding that at least 38 people heard the disturbance, but none came forward to intervene directly. The only help was from a lone bystander who got an elderly neighbor to make a call. Casting this as an "apathy story" as *The New York Times* initially did, we believe, failed to capture the deeper story, the failure to act on a civic duty, which is one of the prompts for this book.

The Genovese tragedy triggered promising psychological research on "bystander intervention" (Latané & Darley, 1970). Findings from this research emphasized "pluralistic ignorance" and "diffusion of responsibility" factors that could account for why Genovese's neighbors did nothing. Furthermore, researchers showed that when an emergency situation was highlighted and when pluralistic ignorance and diffusion of responsibility were minimized, participants were more likely to see a personal duty to provide help to others in need. Yet this promising empirical line died out, failing to expand to a consideration of other duties such as the duties of individuals to the larger community.

Thirty-four years after the tragedy of Kitty Genovese, the case of David Cash, a Berkeley student, made headlines. Cash found himself a bystander in the women's restroom of the Primadonna Casino in Nevada where he witnessed his friend Jeremy Strohmeyer raping, brutalizing, and killing a 7-year-old girl, yet he did not intervene to stop the crimes (Hammer, 1998; Kelly, 1998). This case is instructive in light of research findings on bystander intervention and in the way Cash's situation contrasted with that of the Genovese bystanders. Cash's sense of emergency was highlighted, for he saw what was happening up close, literally at arm's length. In addition, his situation reduced pluralistic ignorance and diffusion of responsibility because he was the lone bystander. Moreover, unlike the bystanders who were strangers to Genovese, Cash had a special relationship, that of best friend, with the assailant. On the basis of bystander intervention findings, these are the conditions in which someone is likely to believe that he or she has a personal duty to intervene on the victim's behalf and to pull a friend back from the criminal brink, but Cash did not intervene. Social critics saw Cash's failure as indicative that the sense of duty among citizens had changed not a whit since the Genovese tragedy.

AN ERA OF RIGHTS?

One approach to explaining cases such as Genovese and Cash is to point to the supremacy of rights over duties (e.g., Dworkin, 1978; Glendon, 1991). *Rights talk*, the clarion for this era's collective movements (e.g., human rights, Black rights, women's rights, gay rights, children's rights, the rights of the mentally ill, disabled persons' rights, and patients' rights), was the standard under which groups marched into battle for their rights, although we hear no correlative slogans and see no banners for duties. At the level of rhetoric, rights talk clearly has hegemony, as the very idea of *duties talk* sounds dissonant or archaic. But deeper than talk and at a more ingrained level, rights are codified in national constitutions. We have celebrated one sacred document's endurance in a bicentennial of the Bill of Rights, for which eminent scholars wrote *The Bill of Rights in the Modern State* (Stone, Epstein, & Sunstein, 1992) and which contained, interestingly, no entry for duty in its index. And in the United Nations Universal Declaration of Human Rights (see Appendix for full text), as the chapter by Spini and Doise (see chap. 2, this volume) makes clear, one has to look hard for duties, for after wading through generations of rights, duties are mentioned last as something of an endnote.

Still, we are left with empirical questions. Does this predominance of rights talk actually mean that there is a neglect of duties? Does talk in fact translate into problematic action for the citizenry such that people fail to act on duties to other people, to groups, and toward the government, and vice versa?

Some scholars came to believe that rights talk had already translated into problematic actions, and these critics painted a rather pathological picture of the individual within society. For example, in Christopher Lasch's (1979) jeremiad, *The Culture of Narcissism*, the historian perceived a trend in which individuals (enough, we presume, to generalize to "culture") were turning inward, focusing decidedly and pathologically on the self, while in the 1980s, communitarians (e.g., Etzioni, 1993) and other social theorists highlighted the decline in the commitment to community. In Allan Bloom's (1987) howl over lost civility in *The Closing of the American Mind*, the only absolute he found was relativism. By the late 1990s, the general opinion seemed to be that Americans were "bowling alone" (Putnam, 1995) and were giving priority to individual rights and freedoms (derived from a skewed view of individualism and autonomy), rather than to duties to others (Mitchell, 1998; Spragens, 1999; Taylor, 1989).

This imbalanced and negative portrait is supported at the anecdotal level by the etiquette book literature and Miss Manners-like columns (e.g., Caldwell, 1999) that have been featuring more and more instances of incivility and by civil duties on the roads that are being blown away in increasing incidents of road rage. Failures to follow customary social duties and civilities are also occurring in some unlikely places. For example, an editorial in *The Washington Post* entitled a "House Divided" (2003) tells of one Republican congressman taking "the extraordinary step of summoning the Capitol police to roust the Democrats from the library." Another Republican congressman told a Democrat to "shut up," whereon the Democrat said, "You think you are big enough to make me, you little wimp? Come on. Come over here and make me. I dare you. You little fruitcake" (p. A20). One's reaction has to be, "So much for *Robert's Rules of Order*." We also see the dissents in Supreme Court cases turning more bitter and biting, and in academia, a president of the American Psychological Association (Sternberg, 2003) opined on the apparent breakdown of the duty to be civil in reviewing journal articles noting an increase in "nasty ad hominem remarks" (p. 5). These analyses and anecdotes suggest that things seem to be changing for the worse. Still, the questions remain: How sound and substantive is the evidence for these claims regarding the waning of duties and the waxing of rights, and are the claimants seeing the whole picture in the proper context?

Historical Evidence for a Shift Toward Rights?

Other writers offer historical reminders that once upon a time in America, the balance between rights and duties was different. Gary Wills (1999) claimed that at the creation of the United States, there was no severe imbalance between rights and duties: The federalists and founding fathers and the foundational doctrines (e.g., Declaration of Independence, The Federalist Papers, Constitution) they debated and created clearly spoke of both.

Consider, as an illustration, a sentence from Thomas Jefferson's Declaration of Independence in which both right and duty appear:

> But when a long train of abuses and usurpations, pursuing invariably the same Object evinces a design to reduce them under absolute Despotism, *it is their right, it is their duty* [italics added], to throw off such Government, and to provide new Guards for their future security.

Note that Jefferson's use of duty is neither the logical correlative of right nor a mere redundancy, for it conveys a distinct and independent meaning from his "it is their right" phrase, a point we shall return to shortly.

Barry Shain (1994), in *The Myth of American Individualism*, presented evidence suggesting that early America was community and duty based and that the "aggregate needs of the public over the arbitrary ones of the particular individual" (p. 116) generally prevailed. An 1831 observation by Alexis de Tocqueville (Pierson, 1938) also makes plain that the neglect of duty was not always so:

> The second thing I envy this people is the ease with which they do without government. Each man here regards himself as interested in public security and in the functioning of the laws. Instead of counting on the police, he counts only on himself. It results that, on the whole, public force is everywhere without ever showing itself. It's really an incredible thing, I assure you, to see how this people keeps itself in order through the single conviction that its only safeguard against itself lies in itself. (p. 161)

These reminders and illustrations, however, speak to the past; at present the issue is whether the rhetoric, thinking, and actions of citizens today have become rights imbalanced for the worse.

More to the point is Haskell, one of our normative commentators (see chap. 11, this volume), who makes a subtler rejoinder. He notes that

> the rhetorical dominance of rights talk in America means that rights march down the middle of main street to the clash of cymbals and the beat of drums, inspiring the applause of the crowd, while duties, no matter how powerfully they may shape conduct, generally trudge along in the shade, unaccompanied and unnoticed. But we know that rhetoric and appearance are often deceptive. Even the most rights-oriented cul-

> tures cannot help being chock-full of duties, for in practice, rights and duties normally develop more or less in tandem, simultaneously doing away with certain constraints in the lives of rights bearers, while introducing new constraints, new duties of forbearance, for instance, into the lives of everyone else. (p. 247)

From Haskell's viewpoint, things may not be as bad as they sound and seem, for duties often reside in the penumbra with a muted voice. More important, it is action that counts most, and when it comes to action, Haskell believes that duties generally develop in tandem with rights. But for his tandem point, Haskell relies heavily on Feinberg's (1969) "logical correlativity," that for every right there is a duty and for every duty there is a right. But two questions arise. First, even if we accept the tandem notion, do rights nonetheless have primacy, being up-front on this tandem bicycle, steering the course? And second, is this tandem notion, in fact, correct?

In *Taking Rights Seriously*, Dworkin (1978) recognized that different political theories can be generated based on the primacy of goals, duties, or rights. Although Dworkin himself favored a rights-based approach, he nonetheless used an illustration to expose the logic of the separateness of rights and duties when he asked us to consider two rights-versus-duties propositions:

> There is a difference between the idea that you have a duty not to lie to me because I have a right not to be lied to, and the idea that I have a right that you not lie to me because you have a duty not to tell lies. (p. 171)

In the first proposition, the right is primary and the duty is derivative; but in the second proposition, the duty is primary and the right is derivative.

But there is another possibility that ruptures the rights-and-duties tandem entirely. As Feinberg (1969) has made clear, rights and duties can be independent; as the moral philosopher Harré (see chap. 10, this volume) shows through his analysis of the ontology of duties and rights, these entities derive from different root sources (i.e., powers and vulnerabilities, respectively), such that the alleged correspondence or symmetry between them is not conceptual. In Thomas Jefferson's usage of the two terms, he may have been invoking two different root sources in summoning quite different and independent reasons for overthrowing such a government. If this independence is so, then rights may walk down the center of the street while duties stroll down a different part of town. But quite apart from the logic of the connection, there is the matter of citizens' commonsense understandings (Finkel, 1995) of these terms and their connections, for the pragmatic lessons of history tell us that rights won in name may not be honored in fact; thus, the logic of logical correlativity does not answer the empirical question of whether rights and duties are independent or dependent in the minds and actions of people in the real world.

The real world, however, extends far beyond America's apparent rights-dominant shores, and this fact leads us to ask: Have we seen the alleged imbalance problem through our own provincial myopia, missing the bigger picture? For instance, a contrary claim could certainly be offered by cross-cultural researchers (e.g., Miller, Bersoff, & Harwood, 1990; Shweder, 1991) who could easily point out cultures in which duties are predominant and rights discourse is neglected or nearly silent. This cross-cultural reminder brings us up short, for what we apparently see in America today is not the picture everywhere.

Interim Summary

We hear the hegemony of rights talk in rhetoric and the argument put forth in some quarters that this imbalance has translated into action and problems for individuals and society, but the empirical evidence for the latter does not satisfy. Nor do we know what we will find when we empirically examine citizens' concepts of rights and duties and how these concepts develop here and abroad. Our own view is that if the imbalance is tilted sharply toward duties, the picture may be no more pleasing than if the imbalance tilts sharply toward rights. When people are yoked to duties, the spirit may be broken, and thinking out loud about rights (and how life might be otherwise) may get them imprisoned or killed (e.g., Moore, 1978). In such duties-dominant societies, rights thinking becomes suppressed, no longer necessary for setting one's moral compass or reflecting on one's conscience, for that is done for you rather than by you. It would seem, then, that a severe imbalance in either direction is likely to be problematic. But as one of our normative commentators, Spragens reminds us (see chap. 12, this volume), this is a "theory-laden" assumption, an empirical question that needs to be tested, which is yet another reason for writing this book.

THE NEED FOR EMPIRICAL INPUT

Is there an imbalance? Are things changing and in what direction? And what is the picture in other countries and cultures? With many questions unanswered, the reader will not be surprised to learn that we intend to reopen an empirical line of investigation. But still, why now? What has changed in both our landscape and language that produces this urgency? And what can empirical researchers cultivate that normative scholars haven't already mined? We will begin our answers at the disciplinary level of psychology. We then broaden our answers by focusing on where and how the discipline of psychology meets the more normative disciplines. And then we widen our answer to the international level, to a world radically changed by the events of September 11, 2001, and to a consideration of how rights and duties are affected.

Psychology's Contribution

We begin by highlighting the need for more psychological research on rights and duties. Our proposition is that citizens' conceptions of rights and duties are fundamentally psychological because they arise out of shared perceptions of human social relations. However, we find that very little attention has been given to rights and duties in psychological research. One of the editors of this volume (Moghaddam), a social and cross-cultural psychologist who studies intergroup conflict, finds that the topic of duties is not discussed in most of social psychology's classic texts (e.g., Brown, 1966; McDougall, 1908), in its modern best sellers (e.g., Myers, 1998), in its newer culturally oriented texts (including his own, Moghaddam, 1998), or in its recent handbooks of social psychology (e.g., Gilbert, Fiske, & Lindzey, 1998). The other editor (Finkel), whose field is psychology and law, finds that a 20-year review (Ogloff, 1999) of the articles in that field's main journal, *Law and Human Behavior*, gives nary a mention to the topic of duties, and even though rights and duties are centrally situated in the Supreme Court's analyses of cases before it, the field fails to study how citizens understand these foundational concepts. Given that psychologists are devoted to understanding human behavior, this topic needs to be addressed adequately.

The fundamental psychological nature of peoples' concepts makes the need for research even more acute. We observe that rights and duties animate the everyday lives of people, and yet we do not know the very basics: the length, breadth, and depth of our topic, so to speak. The old research into bystander intervention involved a duty between individuals, but there are duties between individuals and a group, between in-groups and out-groups, between citizens and the state, and between states, all of which need investigating. Moreover, the very meaning (i.e., ontology) of these duties may vary among people and by culture, political system, power distance, and social life. The development (i.e., ontogeny) of these rights and duties also needs investigating, and this may differ significantly by culture. Furthermore, we may assume that certain fundamental rights and duties are universal, and the United Nations Universal Declaration of Human Rights may declare them so, but are they in fact so?

When citizens speak about rights and duties, they are generally not engaging in a normative discourse about rights or duties floating among Platonic ideals. What individuals typically construe is a particular right or duty perceived in an interpersonal and social context with a cast of characters that may include individuals, groups, and government representatives. Each of these entities has roles and responsibilities, and individuals make inferences, attributions, and judgments about the motives, culpability, rights and duties of the various actors, what Haney (2002) called "a contextual model of justice." The complexities of the situation being perceived, the various vantage points from which to view the actions and the actors, and the various predilections and biases of the one doing the perceiving are all sources of variance capable of producing very different views of rights and duties.

Many of the chapters in this volume illustrate and analyze these complexities. For example, in chapter 7 by Finkel, duties more than hold their own in clashes with rights, being highly nuanced with citizens adjudicating these disputes by using a commonsense moral analysis rather than a legal analysis, leading in some cases, to disparate verdicts from Supreme Court decisions. In chapter 4, Moghaddam and Riley make the case that turn taking is how a child begins to learn about duty, and that this occurs long before rights and rights talk take hold. Yet there seems to be a developmental shift that occurs across the age span in the different cultures they examine as rights eventually become dominant. In chapter 3, Hoppe-Graff and Kim note sharp perspectival differences between German and Korean adolescents in how they understand the origins and meaning of rights and duties, either as something given and imposed or as something learned as part of the development of the self. This perspectival point is also made in chapter 8, in which Moore, Spernak, and Chung address patients' rights and physicians' duties, with the predominance of rights or duties dependent on which model of the patient–physician relationship (e.g., the paternalistic model, expert model, consumer model, or partnership model) is upheld.

A number of chapter authors postulate that whether individuals give priority to rights or duties depends on their group membership and power status. Approaching the issue from an intergroup perspective, Louis and Taylor argue in chapter 5 that whether you stress the right or the duty may also depend on whether you are a member of the in-group or of the out-group. In chapter 4, Moghaddam and Riley propose that those with less power, such as children in relation to parents and as members of minority groups in relation to members of majority groups, give priority to rights, whereas those who enjoy more power give priority to duties. In chapter 9, Worchel adds further complexity by showing that both individuals and groups in their interrelationship have rights and duties to one another, which are in turn affected by culture. But the primacy of rights is challenged in chapter 6 by Tyler, in which he offers a deference-based perspective on duty and shows that people will empower the government to solve certain social problems by giving up their rights. Yet in terms of the social representations that people have, Spini and Doise in chapter 2 show that the generations of rights from the United Nations Declaration do find some endorsement across the peoples from the many nations they tested, although citizens differ as to whether individuals or governments bear the responsibilities for effecting these rights.

Psychological Findings and the Nexus With More Normative Disciplines

Psychological findings about ordinary citizens' notions of rights and duties are important beyond their basic knowledge value for psychology, for these views affect judges, as Justice Oliver Wendell Holmes Jr. knew and expressed in *The Common Law* (1881/1963):

> The felt necessities of the time, the prevalent moral and political theories, intuitions of public policy, avowed or unconscious, even the prejudices which judges share with their fellow-men, have had a good deal more to do than the syllogism in determining the rules by which men should be governed. (p. 1)

Holmes also believed that the "first requirement of a sound body of law is, that it should correspond with the actual feelings and demands of the community" (p. 35).

In the U.S. Supreme Court's 2003 term, the Court ruled 6 to 3 in *Lawrence & Garner v. Texas* (2003), a homosexual sodomy case, to reverse its ruling in *Bowers v. Hardwick* (1986). Justice Kennedy, writing for the majority, widened the right of privacy, given the "emerging awareness" that "the liberty protected by the Constitution allows homosexual partners the right to choose to enter upon relationships in the confines of their homes and their own private lives and still retain their dignity as free persons"(slip op. at p. 2). Yet Justice Scalia, writing for the dissent, attacked this so-called emerging awareness as a "product of a law-profession culture, that has largely signed on to the so-called homosexual agenda." Scalia, far from rejecting the intrusion of community sentiment into the decision, clearly preferred the old sentiment, the "societal reliance" on the principles confirmed in *Bowers* that the current Court discarded.

Community sentiment about rights and duties also entered the affirmative action cases of *Grutter v. Bollinger* (2003) and *Gratz v. Bollinger* (2003). In those cases, although there were normative questions aplenty about rights (e.g., the minority students' rights, the majority students' rights, and the university's rights) and duties (e.g., whose duties? was promoting diversity a duty?), community sentiment in the form of amicus briefs not only weighed in but also was cited in the Court's opinions, such that some subset of community sentiment clearly affected the law. If there is an ongoing interplay between the community's sense of rights and duties and those of black-letter law, then empirical investigations of the former would certainly be informing for the latter.

Empirical and normative scholars, who usually work on opposite sides of the *is–ought* divide, also wind up working in the same areas. For instance, there are two fields of nonnormative ethics (Beauchamp, 1978, p. 2), "the *scientific study of morality*, which is a factual investigation of moral behavior," in which anthropologists, sociologists, historians, and psychologists may study "whether moral attitudes and codes differ from society to society," and *meta-ethics*, a field usually (but not invariably) pursued by philosophers, in which scholars seek "to analyze the meanings of crucial ethical terms such as 'right,' 'obligation,' and 'responsibility.'" The methods that empirical psychologists use and the "firmness" of their findings may be of particular value here.

The Post-September 11, 2001, World and Rights and Duties

John Rawls (1999, p. 13; see also Rousseau, 1950) attempted to create a "realistic utopia" for a pluralistic society that contained multicultural views of "liberal democratic peoples (and decent peoples)," paying full homage to the psychological reality by taking "men as they are." His basic principles were replete with duties, but his approach invited empirical investigation to anchor these lofty principles to ground with facts. But September 11, 2001, brings home the shattering fact that we live in a much wider world in which basic values regarding rights and duties are not shared by all, and terrorism (Moghaddam & Marsella, 2003) is a fact of life. Countries may claim a right or a duty to send armed forces into another country to hunt for terrorists or weapons of mass destruction or to stop genocide or internecine wars, although the invaded countries may recognize no such right or duty. With seemingly fundamental disagreements about rights and duties, not only between nations at odds but also among traditional allies, are we further than we have ever been from "international law"?

Change has been a theme running throughout this introduction. We see examples of this change in the discourse in which governmental duties have been recast as "officers' rights" (Orren, 2000). Not long ago a president might have said it is his duty to protect the national security, but now we hear that duty is being recast as our right to protect. In chapter 4 by Moghaddam and Riley, they call this "replaceability," that is, what one person calls a right another can perceive as a duty, suggesting that citizens' ontologies may be dilating, obfuscating, or shifting with perspective changes. This movement between rights and duties, waiving the former and then reclaiming the former, can be fluid, as Tyler points out in chapter 6. Not long ago Congress overwhelmingly passed the USA Patriot Act (2001), which restricts certain rights, but now we see a backlash, a taking back of those ceded rights, with over 100 jurisdictions passing ordinances to nullify the Patriot Act (Nieves, 2003). This is a new and changed world in which fluidity is evident and the once normatively fixed notions of rights and duties seem to slip and slide in the empirical world of rhetoric and action, creating uncertainty about our foundational values. This is another important reason for this book, which features empirical contributions on the topic of rights and duties.

THREE GOALS

This book has three major goals. The first goal is to bring together critical research contributions by leading psychologists from around the world to achieve a better understanding of rights and duties. This volume includes critical discussions of and references to the main psychological research studies relevant to rights and duties. The intention is to provide a platform for future research in terms of both empirical findings achieved thus far and theoretical orientations for the future.

A second goal of this volume is to strengthen dialogue between empirical psychological research and the normative disciplines. One of the strengths of this book is that we have normative commentators who read an earlier, lengthier introduction and all of the empirical chapters. They were asked to offer their opinions on the chapters and to use these chapters as a springboard to develop their own ideas about the empirical–normative interface. It is rare that empirical researchers expose their work to normative critique, and we thank the empirical contributors for their willingness to submit their work to such scrutiny. We thank our normative colleagues who were willing to venture beyond their customary confines to provide us with their conceptual insights and point us toward issues and ways of investigating issues that would inform the debate and enhance future research.

For the editors who wanted to reopen an empirical line of investigation, this was the kind of empirical–normative interchange we sought to promote and that we rarely see. Rights and duties and their relationship are topics central to and crossed by many disciplines on both sides of the *is–ought* divide. In this work, we hope that the words of Kant from *The Critique of Pure Reason* (Greene, 1957, p. 57) that "thought without content is empty, intuitions without concepts are blind" can be exemplified.

A third major goal of this volume is to identify promising questions for future research. Toward this goal, we provided our empirical contributors with three sets of questions and asked them to address at least one set, although they often did more. The purpose of these questions was not only to stimulate discussions in the present volume but also to encourage future research. Some of the research questions we posed are not directly addressed in this volume, but we believe they are worthy of attention in future research.

The first set of questions raises basic issues about the origins and universality of rights and duties, their justifications, the influences of culture and law on them, and their subjective understanding by citizens.

1. What are the duties (and rights) in everyday life?
2. How do citizens around the world construe duties (i.e., their commonsense notions), and are their conceptions broader or more limited than rights?

3. Do citizens' commonsense notions of duties cover more ground than formal, black-letter law duties or those expressed in international declarations?
4. How do children come to acquire notions relating to duties and rights?
5. Are there universals (or only locals) regarding rights and duties, and if there are universals, what is the source?
6. What influence do social life, laws, cultures, political systems, and power distance between majority and minority status have on rights and duties, and does the influence go both ways?

The second set of questions involves the relationship between rights and duties.

7. Are duties the complement or corollary of rights?
8. Are duties primary, such that rights are derivative or the corollary, rather than the other way around?
9. If primacy varies, then where, when, and with what justification does one become primary and the other derivative?
10. If there is greater independence between rights and duties, then are duties a parallel discourse to rights?
11. If it is a parallel discourse, how are duties different from rights in meaning, scope, origins, and consequences?
12. Are duties more local and rights more universal, such that the former are more bound to legal, cultural, ethnic, religious, group, or role status than the latter?
13. Is there evidence for an independent discourse between duties and rights?

Our third set of questions presumes some findings of independence.

14. Do citizens perceive a greater weight for a duty, for though we can create parallel locutions (e.g., we can speak of a right to vote and a duty to vote or a right to attend class and a duty to attend class), does the parallelism not break down given that the duty conveys an *ought* that the right does not?
15. Is there an origins distinction between rights and duties because rights are often linked to our very being, as in inalienable rights, whereas duties seem to stem from relationships—person to God, person to society, person to person, person in role?
16. Are their social duties (e.g., a duty to take turns while conversing, a duty to be civil with others) and supererogatory duties (e.g., duties to the environment, to the land, air, water, flora, and fauna), which are not only distinct from legal duties but also independent of any right?

17. What are we to make of the affective distinction between rights that are generally happily embraced by individuals who have them and duties that seem imposed and even burdensome?
18. How is it that rights need not be exercised (e.g., voting) or can be waived (e.g., my rights to a trial by my peers and to counsel), whereas waiving duties is not so easily done?
19. And when rights and duties appear to conflict or clash, how do ordinary citizens reconcile such clashes, and are these reconciliations different from the solutions and reasons offered by judges and justices?

CONCLUDING COMMENT

The interpersonal, national, and international situations all strongly suggest a need for a better understanding of human rights and duties. Psychological researchers are in a privileged position to take on this challenge because the understandings people have about rights and duties are fundamentally psychological. However, it is important that in conducting empirical research on the commonsense notions of rights and duties, psychologists keep in touch with and are guided by the insights of normative scholars. These scholars remind us that the concepts of rights and duties have normative values and a rich history that provides context and nuance to empirical endeavors. It is with this empirical–normative link in mind that we designed this book. But this book also looks to the future by posing research questions that can only in part be addressed at present. For this empirical line of research to flourish, other researchers must be stimulated to take on the many open questions that remain.

REFERENCES

Beauchamp, T. L. (1978). Ethical theory. In T. L. Beauchamp & L. Walters (Eds.), *Contemporary issues in bioethics* (pp. 1–5). Belmont, CA: Wadsworth.

Bloom, A. (1987). *The closing of the American mind.* New York: Simon & Schuster.

Bowers v. Hardwick, 478 U.S. 186 (1986).

Brown, R. (1966). *Social psychology*. New York: Free Press.

Caldwell, M. (1999). *A short history of rudeness: Manners, morals, and misbehavior in modern America.* New York: Picador.

Dworkin, R. (1978). *Taking rights seriously*. Cambridge, MA: Harvard University Press.

Etzioni, A. (1993). *The spirit of community: Rights, responsibilities, and the communitarian agenda.* New York: Crown Publishers.

Feinberg, J. (1969). The nature and value of rights. *Journal of Value Inquiry*, *4*, 243–257.

Finkel, N. J. (1995). *Commonsense justice: Jurors' notions of the law*. Cambridge, MA: Harvard University Press.

Gilbert, D. T., Fiske, S. T., & Lindzey, G. (Eds.). (1998). *The handbook of social psychology* (4th ed., Vols. 1–2). New York: McGraw Hill.

Glendon, M. A. (1991). *Rights talk: The impoverishment of political discourse*. New York: Free Press.

Gratz v. Bollinger, No. 02-516 (U.S. June 23, 2003).

Grutter v. Bollinger, No. 02-241 (U.S. June 23, 2003).

Greene, T. M. (Ed.). (1957). *Kant selections*. NewYork: Scribner.

Hammer, J. (1998, October 19). Shunned at Berkeley. *Newsweek*, p. 70.

Haney, C. (2002). Making law modern: Toward a contextual model of justice. *Psychology, Public Policy, and Law*, *8*, 3–63.

Holmes, O. W. (1963). *The common law* (M. D. Howe, Ed.). Cambridge, MA: Harvard University Press. (Original work published 1881)

House divided. (2003, July 21). *The Washington Post*, p. A20.

Kelly, M. (1998, September 9). Somebody else's problems. *The Washington Post*, p. A19.

Lasch, C. (1979). *The culture of narcissism*. New York: Norton.

Latané, B., & Darley, J. M. (1970). *The unresponsive bystander: Why doesn't he help?* Englewood Cliffs, NJ: Prentice-Hall.

Lawrence & Garner v. Texas, No. 02-102 (U.S. June 26, 2003).

McDougall, W. (1908). *Introduction to social psychology*. London: Methuen.

Miller, J. G., Bersoff, D. M., & Harwood, R. L. (1990). Perceptions of 'social responsibility' in India and in the United States: Moral imperatives or personal decisions? *Journal of Personality and Social Psychology*, *58*, 33–47.

Mitchell, L. E. (1998). *Stacked deck: A story of selfishness in America*. Philadelphia: Temple University Press.

Moghaddam, F. M. (1998). *Social psychology: Exploring universals across cultures*. New York: Freeman.

Moghaddam, F. M., & Marsella, A. J. (Eds.). (2003). *Understanding terrorism: Psychosocial roots, consequences, and interventions*. Washington, DC: American Psychological Association.

Moore, B., Jr. (1978). *Injustice: The social bases of obedience and revolt*. White Plains, NY: M. E. Sharpe.

Myers, D. (1998). *Social psychology* (6th ed.). New York: McGraw Hill.

Nieves, E. (2003, April 21). Local officials rise up to defy the Patriot Act. *The Washington Post*, pp. A1, A8.

Ogloff, J. R. P. (1999). Reflecting back and looking forward. In J. R. P. Ogloff (Ed.), The first 20 years of *Law and Human Behavior* [Special issue]. *Law and Human Behavior*, *23*, 1–8.

Orren, K. (2000). Officers' rights: Toward a unified field theory of American constitutional development. *Law & Society Review*, *34*, 873–909.

Pierson, G. W. (1938). *Tocqueville in America*. Baltimore: Johns Hopkins Press.

Putnam, R. D. (1995). Bowling alone: America's declining social capital. *Journal of Democracy*, *6*, 65–78.

Rawls, J. (1999). *The law of peoples*. Cambridge, MA: Harvard University Press.

Rosenthal, A. M. (1999). *Thirty-eight witnesses: The Kitty Genovese case*. Berkeley: University of California Press. (Original work published in 1964)

Rousseau, J. J. (1950). *The social contract and discourses* (G. D. N. Cole, Trans.). New York: Dutton.

Shain, B. (1994). *The myth of American individualism: The Protestant origins of American political thought*. Princeton, NJ: Princeton University Press.

Shweder, R. (Ed.). (1991). *Thinking through cultures: Expeditions in cultural psychology*. Cambridge, MA: Harvard University Press.

Spragens, T. A., Jr. (1999). *Civic liberalism: Reflections on our democratic ideals*. Lanham, MD: Rowman & Littlefield.

Sternberg, R. J. (2003, July/August). To be civil. *Monitor on Psychology*, *34*, p. 5.

Stone, G. R., Epstein, R. A., & Sunstein, C. R. (Eds.). (1992). *The Bill of Rights in the modern state*. Chicago: University of Chicago Press.

Taylor, C. (1989). *Sources of the self: The making of the modern identity*. Cambridge, MA: Harvard University Press.

USA Patriot Act, Pub. L. No. 107-56 (2001).

Wills, G. (1999). *A necessary evil: A history of American distrust of government*. New York: Simon & Schuster.

I

EMPIRICAL CONTRIBUTIONS ON RIGHTS, DUTIES, AND CULTURE

2

UNIVERSAL RIGHTS AND DUTIES AS NORMATIVE SOCIAL REPRESENTATIONS

DARIO SPINI AND WILLEM DOISE

A basic idea on which this chapter is grounded is that mutual interactions and communications between humans generate normative social representations. While interacting with each other, individuals know that their fate will be affected by that interaction, at least in certain domains, to a certain extent, and at a certain cost. Normative representations exist about what these mutual effects should be. As there are many kinds of interactions characterized by all sorts of differences in status, purpose, forms of interdependence, and degree of formality (Deutsch, 1985), there are different mod-

The social representations of human rights program was funded by the Swiss National Science Foundation (Grants 1114-037604.93 and 1113-043160.95). The data used in the research by Spini (1997) was collected by Daniel Roselli (Argentina); Velina Topalova (Bulgaria); Victor Espinoza, Isabell Kempf, and Pablo Salvat Bologna (Chile); Danilo Pérez Zumbado (Costa Rica); Yapo Yapi (Côte d'Ivoire); Maaris Raudsepp (Estonia); Eva Green (Finland); Joane Cotasson and Elena Lozano (France); Jyoti Verma (India); Luisa Campanile and Annamaria Silvana de Rosa (Italy); Araceli Otero de Alba (Mexico); Cecilia Gastardo-Conaco (Philippines); Aliou Sall (Senegal); Alex Amati and William Onzivu (Uganda); Glynis Breakwell (United Kingdom); and Gordana Jovanovic (Yugoslavia). The Société Académique de Genève provided financial support for this study. We are grateful to the editors of this book, Norman Finkel and Fathali Moghaddam for their valuable comments, to Erika Hofmann for her editorial assistance, and to Ian Hamilton for stylistic corrections and partial translations.

els of acceptable relationships, of explicit or implicit models of contracts that govern these relationships, and of prototypes of fair and just relationships. These guiding principles for evaluating relationships are part of human nature and constitute normative social representations.

Human rights and duties are considered here to be part of such principles. They should, at least by intention, organize our social interactions. For historical (i.e., economic, political, military, religious, and also scientific) reasons, Western societies, and later almost all countries around the world, were led to organize relationships not only within national and cultural boundaries but also across such boundaries. The declarations of rights in the 18th century and the Universal Declaration of Human Rights (see Appendix for full text) adopted by the General Assembly of the United Nations Organization in 1948 are clear expressions of principles that should govern the interactions between individuals and the state. One can of course argue about the content, priority, and validity of the rights and duties set forth in the Universal Declaration of Human Rights, but a discussion of the limits of any universal statement is not the focus of this chapter.

We start from the idea that the relationship between the individual and the state is nowadays potentially universal; it is an incontestable reality that human rights are universally declared and widely known all over the world (Bobbio, 1992, p. 21). On this basis, one can consider that human rights and duties constitute a shared set of guiding principles of life in society, of which the diverse declarations are formal expressions. This starting assumption does not mean that human rights and duties are consensual pieces of knowledge. On the contrary, the model of social representations on which we have constructed the work presented here states as a second assumption that individuals position themselves on the basis of these shared meanings (see Doise, Clémence, & Lorenzi-Cioldi, 1993) and in accordance with their social anchorings (Doise, 1990). The theory of social representation on which this chapter is grounded was first proposed by Moscovici (1961/1976) on the basis of the work of Durkheim (1898) and is concerned with the circulation of theories, ideas, and concepts in the public sphere and particularly the relationship between expert scientific knowledge and lay theories.

The first part of this chapter contains a short analysis of how human rights and duties have been constructed since the 18th century from a historical, political, and legal point of view. In order to have a counterpart to this expert knowledge on human rights and duties, the second part presents the research program initiated by Doise and colleagues on the social representations of human rights (see Doise, 2002), in order to spell out some guiding principles of the lay theories on human rights and duties.

Comparing and contrasting these two types of knowledge gives some insight into the functions of the discourses on human rights and duties. In particular, we argue that human rights and duties are fundamental pillars of the social contract that defines the role and limits of action of individuals and the state. In this respect, agreed definitions of human rights and duties have a twofold effect. On the one hand, they are guiding principles for organizing society and they are buffers against the power of the state, which has shown at various times that it can easily become an oppressor. On the other hand, definitions of rights and duties are not symmetrical, as they depend on two basic ideologies that defend either the primacy of the community, emphasizing the concrete duties of the individual, or the primacy of the rights of the individual, stressing the duties of the state.

HISTORICAL ANCHORS OF UNIVERSAL RIGHTS AND DUTIES

Debates on the issue of rights and duties and the various declarations that ensued led to the creation at the end of the 17th and 18th centuries of the modern state, particularly in England with the Bill of Rights in 1689, in the United States of America with the Declaration of Independence in 1776 and the Bill of Rights in 1789, in France with the successive declarations of the rights and duties of man and the citizen from 1789 to 1795, and after the World War II with the founding of the United Nations. These two historical periods were of the utmost importance in defining and establishing the relationship between these two concepts in political philosophy.

The Debate During the French Revolution

The debate on duties and rights opposed the principles of nature and society. On the one side, there were conceptions of natural rights, which had their roots in the philosophies of the Enlightenment. On the other side, the primacy of the individual's duties to the community was considered necessary to ensure public and social order. These two lines of argument are fundamentally different. The first affirms the primacy of the natural and inalterable rights of individuals against any social systems and in particular against oppressors. The second affirms the supremacy of public order over the freedom of individuals. However, the two cannot be refuted easily. The revolutionaries were themselves surprised by the difficulties they had created in their desire to define a solid new foundation for their nation. When they had to decide whether duties should be added to the declaration of rights, 433 voted in favor and 570 against (Gauchet, 1989, p. 70). In fact, the tension between the individual and society created by the discovery of universal rights and duties is the political domain itself. More than a choice between tradition and progress, that vote was the victory of those who defend the individual against the oppressor over those who defend the collective order in opposition to individualism (Gauchet, p. 91). In this regard, Articles I and II of the Declaration of 1789 considered the rights of freedom, equality, property, security, and resistance to oppression as the foundations of a new definition of collective power and as the limits of this power over individuals.

THE UNIVERSAL DECLARATION OF HUMAN RIGHTS

The process of industrialization in the 19th century and its excesses with regard to the condition of workers, the communist revolution in Russia, the two world wars, and the realization of the horrors of the Holocaust created conditions and a need for the discussion of new rules among nations and a new definition of the social contract between the state and the individual. These are the crucial events in human history that have to be kept in mind to understand the debate on rights and duties that took place in 1948 when the Universal Declaration of Human Rights was drafted.

The strongest divergence concerned the types of rights to be included in the Declaration. The ideological division of the world at the end of the World War II, which would subsequently give rise to the Cold War, was also at the origin of an accentuation of the differences between first- and second-generation rights (Weston, 1992). First-generation rights are based on the idea that there are fundamental freedoms of the individual that have to be protected against the state. Included in this first generation are such claimed rights as freedom from discrimination; the right to life, liberty, and the security of the person; freedom from torture, slavery, and arbitrary arrest; the right to a fair and public trial; freedom of thought, conscience, religion, and movement; and the right to own property. Articles 3 to 21 of the Universal Declaration include these rights of the first generation, also known as civil and political rights. Second-generation rights are based on the duty of the state to supply conditions for the basic needs of the individuals to be respected. Here we find such rights as the right to social security, to an adequate standard of life for self and family, to work, and to education. These "positive" rights, also known as economic, social, and cultural rights, are listed in Articles 22 to 27 of the Universal Declaration. Again, we find here the duality between rights and duties. On the one hand, the individual's rights are considered to be the basis and goal of political and economic development. On the other hand, the community or the state, which is considered to be responsible for providing conditions for basic economic needs to be met, takes on primary importance, and individuals have to fulfill their duties to share in the benefits of development. It is worth noting that this predominance of the common good over the individual also finds support among developing countries, where communal systems of justice and power and collectivist values are more prevalent than in industrialized or postmodern societies (Inglehart, 1990; Triandis, 1995).

As a compromise, the Universal Declaration proclaimed rights of both the first (fundamental rights, Articles 1 and 2; civil and political rights, Articles 3 to 21) and the second (Articles 22 to 27) generations. And what about duties? The debate about duties took place from the time of the first drafts of the Universal Declaration onward. The opinion that individuals had duties to fulfill toward society was shared by the various members of the drafting committee. However, duties did not find a prominent place in the Declaration. Rights won again, partly because of the shadow of the Holocaust and the war, which demonstrated that states were capable of denying the most fundamental rights of individuals.

The duties of individuals to the community have been, and are still nowadays in some parts of the world, a very powerful structuring principle of fascist, communist, military, or fundamentalist religious states. These ideologies often use "efficient" systems of control and sanctions based on propaganda, exclusion of minorities, and social or police control to limit individuals' rights. Under such conditions, there is no doubt that the dignity and interests of the weakest can be defended by claims of human rights. This argument was overriding for the experts who drafted the Universal Declaration. As a consequence, the article mentioning duties was placed at the end of the Universal Declaration (Article 29). It is composed of three parts:

> 1. Everyone has duties to the community in which alone the free and full development of his personality is possible; 2. In the exercise of his rights and freedoms, everyone shall be subject only to such limitations as are determined by law solely for the purpose of securing due recognition and respect for the rights and freedoms of others and of meeting the just requirements of morality, public order and the general welfare in a democratic society; 3. These rights and freedoms may in no case be exercised contrary to the purposes and principles of the United Nations. (Lawson, 1991, p. 1659; see Appendix, Art. 29)

It is evident that the reference to duties is not very strong and that the reference to duties toward the community is not really clear. (The reference to the state was avoided for reasons mentioned earlier.)

Recent Trends

Since the fall of the Berlin Wall and the end of the Cold War, there has been a trend toward the universalization of liberalism, which is a mixture of economical and political principles such as democracy, free trade, social order in domestic affairs, and human rights in the international sphere. In most democratic societies, the constitution details individuals' rights and duties and provides institutional protection of these rights through the courts. Liberalism in its purest form asserts that fundamental rights and in particular freedoms are respected when the state does not interfere in private affairs. This individualistic ideology is gaining ground nowadays in the most industrialized countries, leading to the gradual curtailment of state monopolies and the idea of public service.

The paradox of liberalism is that rights are proclaimed, but this does not mean that duties disappear. On the contrary, the question of duties, central to liberalism, is masked (Madiot, 1998). If the state should not work as a welfare system, then individuals still have the duty to take care of themselves and their close circle. If they do not conform to this model, then the state has the duty and the means to sanction or control them.

To this powerful trend there are of course reactions, coming in particular from the least industrialized countries and minorities who defend what is sometimes called third-generation or collective rights. These rights are based on the idea that communities and in particular minorities also have rights that should be respected (see Herrera & Doise, 2001). These third-generation rights include claims for a redistribution of power, wealth, and other important values; the right to political, economic, social and cultural self-determination; the right to social and economic development; the right to participate in and benefit from the common heritage of mankind (resources, scientific and technical progress, cultural traditions, etc.); the right to peace; and the right to a healthy and balanced environment and to humanitarian disaster relief (Weston, 1992, pp. 19–20). The emergence of an organized civil society supporting these new rights and of problems that go beyond the state's ability to decide and to act could also gradually change the distribution of power and the responsibility for the application of human rights and duties (e.g. Ekins, 1992; Mendlovitz & Walker, 1987).

RIGHTS, DUTIES, AND SOCIAL PSYCHOLOGY

This brief incursion into the history of rights and duties indicates that duties and rights lie at the core of the social contract linking individuals to the community. But until now we have combined historical, political philosophy, and legal issues. What explanations and descriptions can social psychology add to these? Are duties and rights a subject of study for social psychology?

Looking at the table of contents of most handbooks on social psychology, we have to admit that rights and duties are not directly mentioned. But this does not mean that they have not been a subject of concern to social psychologists. The relationship between the individual and the community has been a key element in the theories developed by prominent figures in social psychology. For instance, Solomon Asch, Leon Festinger, Kurt Lewin, Stanley Milgram, Serge Moscovici, Muzafer Sherif, and Henri Tajfel devoted at least part of their scientific work to understanding how social conditions characteristic of war, holocaust, and fascist or racist regimes could lead individuals to deny the rights of others.

In this connection, the research by Milgram (1974, see also Haney & Zimbardo, 1977; Meeus & Raijmaakers, 1986) has profoundly changed our understanding of the individual's ability to comply with a sense of duty when an order aimed at violating the basic rights of another person is given by an institutional authority. The cases of Kitty Genovese and David Cash described by Finkel and Moghaddam (see chap. 1, this volume) are other instances of the various situations studied extensively by social psychologists, which show that numerous conditions may lead an individual to deny others' rights or to behave in an antisocial way. Research on intergroup relations shows that ethnocentrism and in-group favoritism (Tajfel & Turner, 1986) are among the fundamental characteristics of this type of relationship. Duties to the in-group and denial of others' rights are a well-known result of this dynamic, and the behavior of a soldier in war is probably the most prototypical example of such antagonism (Tajfel, 1978). However, more sophisticated manifestations of ethnocentrism can be found in the fact that condemnation of human rights violations is more straightforward when they occur in a non-Western out-group than when they occur in an in-group (see Moghaddam & Vuksanovic, 1990), and more generally, one can consider that human rights issues provide evaluative criteria for citizens of Western democracies to enhance the differentiation between their countries and nondemocratic countries (Staerklé, Clémence, & Doise, 1998).

Another theoretical line is rooted in the work of Piaget (1932) and Kohlberg (1981, 1984) on different stages of moral development and had a great impact on the reasoning of such influential scholars as Jürgen Habermas and John Rawls. Similar constructivist ideas have also inspired a vast amount of research on the idea of social justice (Deutsch, 1975; Lind & Tyler, 1988; Thibaut & Walker, 1975).

The examples we have just quoted show that many findings in social psychology can be related to rights or duties (see Clémence & Doise, 1995). Of course the works in question did not tackle directly the question of the links between rights and duties, and in this respect, the research we present now is not very different. Its primary intent was to study how the idea of human rights is represented in the public sphere. However, on several occasions, notions such as responsibility in relation to rights were also studied.

STUDYING THE SOCIAL REPRESENTATIONS OF HUMAN RIGHTS: A RESEARCH PROGRAM IN GENEVA

In a series of investigations, Doise and colleagues studied the social representations of human rights. This program mainly explored how violations are interpreted in lay thinking (Clémence, Doise, De Rosa, & Gonzalez, 1995; Doise, Dell'Ambrogio, & Spini, 1991), how cultural minorities position themselves with respect to human rights (Herrera, Lavallée, & Doise, 1998), how advancement in school degrees goes together with a more institutionalized definition of human rights (Doise, Staerklé, Clémence, & Savory, 1998), and how students from various countries position themselves in relation to the rights and duties included in the Universal Declaration of Human Rights (Doise, Spini, & Clémence, 1999; Spini, 1997).

This research was developed in the framework of social representation theory (for a general presentation, see Breakwell & Canter, 1993; Deaux & Philogène, 2001; Farr & Moscovici, 1984). Social representation theory analyzes the intervention of patterns of social regulations and communications in the way individuals describe and explain social issues they are confronted with (Moscovici, 1961/1976; Doise, 1990). One purpose of the social representation approach is thus to study commonsense knowledge about scientific or expert theories when they become a debated stake in a specific context (Clémence, 2001; Moscovici & Hewstone, 1983). This approach has developed a large array of studies and methodologies to study the social representations of diverse themes such as intelligence (Mugny & Carugati, 1985), physical and mental illness (e.g., Comby, Devos, & Deschamps, 1993; Flick, 1992; Joffe, 1995), economic matters (e.g., Duveen & Shields, 1985; Emler & Dickinson, 1985), politics (e.g., Catellani & Quadrio, 1991; Echebarria & Castro, 1993; Moodie, Markovà, & Plichtovà, 1995), and new technologies (e.g., Galli & Nigro, 1987; Wagner & Kronberger, 2001). Compared with other approaches in social psychology, social representation theory can be described as a systemic development of the theory of attitudes (McGuire, 1986), as the main object of the theory of social representations is to study the relationship between the individual cognitive, emotional, or conative systems and the social and relational systems in which they are embedded (Doise, 1993).

In this framework, the work of Doise and colleagues is based on the idea that social representations are defined as organizing principles of symbolic relationships between individuals and groups. One central idea followed by this research group is that individuals and groups structure meaningful images of their social environment following very general explicit or implicit guiding principles or "themata" (see Moscovici, 2001, pp. 31–32) to position themselves in the social relationships they are involved in. In this regard, a specificity of social representations is that they are not necessarily to be found within individuals. The individual who takes a position with regard to any object does not do so in a social vacuum. For example, when someone smokes, this may be construed as an individual attitude and explained at an individual level. This is, of course, a worthwhile enterprise. However, in the framework of social representation theory, researchers are more interested in the social functions of this attitude. Asking the question of function refers here to the meaning of this attitude for an individual who does not stand in isolation but who is in a communicative relationship with other individuals and groups or institutions with expert knowledge and lay theories. In this communicative realm, values, norms, groups, and institutions—in a word, society—exist prior to the individual. This means that in many ways, attitudes are not within the individual but between individuals, anchored and objectified in communicative processes. At least this is what the social qualification of representations stands for (Moscovici, 1961/1976, p. 75). In complement to the study of the subject–object relationship characteristic of social cognition research, social representation theory explores the system of subject–object relationships embedded in social relationships.

On the basis of these assumptions, Doise et al. (1993) developed a three-step methodology for the quantitative analysis of social representations. A first assumption on which this methodology is grounded is that various members of a population under study share common views about a given social issue. Social representations are generated in systems of communication that necessitate common frames of reference for individuals and groups. A first phase in the study of social representations is thus to describe the common image or shared cognitive structure of the object at stake in a given system of communication.

However, sharing common references does not imply that individuals or groups necessarily hold the same position. A second assumption of this method is that differences in individual positioning are organized on structured and structuring dimensions. Individuals may differ according to the strength of their adherence to various opinions, attitudes, or stereotypes. This means that this second step implies a search for the organizing principles of individual differences that structure the image of the object.

The third assumption is that these systematic differences are anchored in collective symbolic realities (e.g., cultures, institutions, social categories, and groups), in social psychological experiences (e.g., experiences of injustice), and in beliefs about different aspects of social reality (e.g., beliefs in a just world, Lerner, 1977) or values (Rokeach, 1973; Schwartz, 1992).

First Evidence of a Common Field and of Organizing Principles in Human Rights Representations

The first hypothesis of a common field, defined as shared contents of meaning (but not consensual meanings, see Doise, 1993), in the social representation of human rights has received considerable support in past research (see Doise, 2002). Of special importance here is a study by Clémence et al. (1995) carried out in four countries (Costa Rica, France, Italy, and Switzerland) in which participants were asked if instances of limitations of individual rights were to be considered violations of human rights. For this purpose, participants were invited to answer 21 questions presenting various situations involving violations or limitations of individual rights. Some of these situations (e.g., situations of racial discrimination, imprisonment without trial or legal assistance, and starvation) corresponded to classical definitions of human rights as contained in the Universal Declaration. Others, involving the rights of children or family affairs, were less explicitly related to articles of the Universal Declaration. And last, some situations concerning economic inequality or health matters (e.g., prohibition of smoking and hospitalization in case of contagious illness) were apparently not covered by official definitions of human rights.

The results of this study were very clear. For the various situations, the order of frequency with which they were related to human rights violations shows a convergence in the application of criteria across countries. In this sense, we can speak of a significant amount of common understanding. This does not mean that there was a complete consensus among participants about human rights. However, if consensus is defined as a majority view, it was reached for 17 (out of 21) situations. Opinion was divided about parents who oblige their children to attend church services, and only minorities consider that enforcing hospitalization on contagiously ill people, unequal salaries, or prohibition of smoking may be or are violations of human rights.

Further Cross-Cultural Evidence for the Hypothesis of a Common Field

This first set of results shows that the idea that there exists a shared organization in the image of human rights and duties is plausible. Another research strategy, which we report in more detail, has been to directly ask students from 35 countries in the five continents to evaluate the 30 articles of the Universal Declaration (Doise et al., 1999; Doise, Spini, Jesuino, Ng, & Emler, 1994). An analysis of the answers resulted repeatedly in the division of the articles into two main clusters, one of social (Articles 12, 13, and 15 to 27) and basic individual rights (Articles 3 to 5) and the other of civil and political rights (Articles 6 to 11 and 14), basic principles (Articles 1 and 2), and the last articles of the Declaration (28 to 30) proclaiming the duties of individuals to the community. In this clustering, categories of rights are found again that were already used by René Cassin when he presented the structure of the Universal Declaration to the United Nations General Assembly in 1948 (see Johnson & Symonides, 1994). Furthermore, it appears that duties toward society defined in Article 29 are linked to the cluster of basic principles and individual rights. A multivariate profile analysis confirms that these clusters remain valid across various countries.

Let us now proceed to a more detailed report of a study (Spini, 1997) from which results confirmed this organization of the image of rights and duties. This study involved a standardized questionnaire containing different positional scales for judging nine articles of the Universal Declaration (Articles 1, 3, 10, 13, 16, 18, 23, 25, and 29) and one question concerning human rights in general. The choice of these articles was designed to represent the clusters of rights obtained by Doise et al. (1994, 1999). The positioning of participants with respect to the articles and human rights in general was assessed using eight scales dealing with the issue of personal and government involvement (see a description of their content below). Data were collected in the years 1996–1997. The sample was composed of university students, mainly of psychology and law. In choosing the countries, an attempt was made to obtain samples from five different cultures or geographical areas (Hofstede, 1983) presenting differences concerning their human development in the classification devised by the United Nations Development Programme (UNDP, 1996). The following 16 countries were included in the study reported here (the Human Development Index, which includes the GNP per capita, the degree of literacy, and the life expectancy at birth, being reported as the first number in parentheses after each country): (a) African countries: Ivory Coast (357, n = 195), Senegal (331, n = 158), and Uganda (326, n = 200); (b) Asian countries: India (442, n = 200) and the Philippines (665, n = 206); (c) Eastern European countries: Bulgaria (773, n = 210), Estonia (749, n = 210), and Yugoslavia (not calculated by UNDP in 1996, n = 200); (d) Latin American countries: Argentina (885, n = 226), Chile (882, n = 129), and Costa Rica (884, n = 104); and (e) Western European countries: Finland (935, n = 256), France (935, n = 181), Great Britain (924, n = 117), Italy (914, n = 129), and Switzerland (926, n = 182). The whole sample was composed of 2,903 respondents.

To obtain a shared picture of the way their judgments assessed differences and similarities between rights, researchers performed a hierarchical cluster analysis on a matrix composed of mean answers having the 10 types of rights in rows and the eight scales in columns, using Ward's method and squared Euclidean distances. The result of this procedure for the total sample of respondents is displayed in Figure 2.1. The cluster analysis produces three classes of rights. The first class is composed of three rights: "men and women of full age, without any limitation due to race, nationality and religion, have the right to marry and to found a family (. . .)" (Article 16); "everyone has the right to freedom of thought, conscience and religion (. . .)" (Article 18); and "everyone has duties to the community (. . .)" (Article 29). The finding of the previous study that duties to the community are clearly linked to the first generation of human rights (civil and political rights, rights of the individual; see Johnson & Symonides, 1994) is corroborated. This cluster is labeled *individual rights*.

The second class contains four rights. Two are traditionally categorized as socioeconomic rights: "the right to work, to free choice of employment, to just and favorable conditions of work, and to protection against unemployment (. . .)" (Article 23) and "the right to a standard of living adequate for the health and well-being of himself and of his family, including food, clothing, housing, and medical care and necessary social services, and the right to security in the event of unemployment, sickness, disability, widowhood, old age, or other lack of livelihood (. . .)" (Article 25). The two other rights are the right to "a fair and public hearing by an independent and impartial tribunal" (Article 10) and "the freedom of movement and residence within the borders of each State" and the right to "leave any country, including his own,

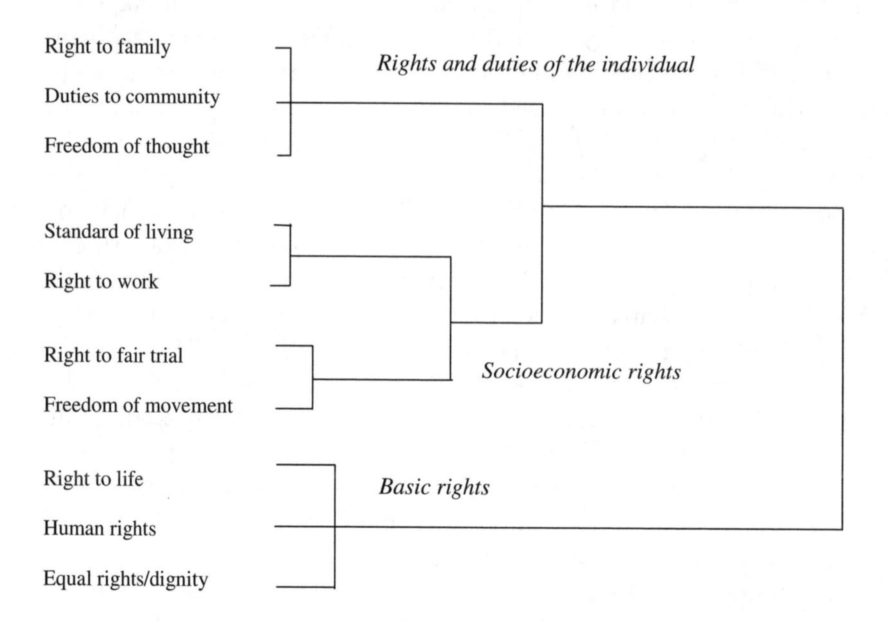

Figure 2.1. Graphic representation (dendogram) of the hierarchical analysis of distances between averaged responses to nine articles of the Universal Declaration of Human Rights and the general question of human rights.

and to return to his country" (Article 13). The rights to work and to a standard of living belong to the second generation of economic, social, and cultural rights (Johnson & Symonides, 1994). However, they also provide a vehicle for conceptions about relationships with important features of the state like borders, courts, and judicial authorities. Hence, we think that they also can be considered as linked to the second generation of rights. This class of rights is thus labeled *socioeconomic rights*.

The third class, separated from the other two classes of rights, includes what could be termed basic rights. First, the question of human rights in general, which was used to detect the most prototypical articles of the definition of human rights, is situated here. Two articles accompany it: the right to "life, liberty, and security of person" (Article 3) and the recognition that "all human beings are born free and equal in dignity and rights. They are endowed with reason and conscience and should act towards one another in a spirit of brotherhood" (Article 1). These rights belong to the basic rights (Article 1) and rights of the individual (Article 3) consistent with the classical categories (see Johnson & Symonides, 1994). As they are linked to the basic values of freedom, equality, and brotherhood at the basis of the Declaration, this class, also including the "human rights in general" item, is labeled *basic rights*.

To assess the stability of this solution, and especially to check if the link between duties and rights is similar in the different samples under study, researchers performed the same cluster analysis for each of the five cultural areas separately. A synthesis of the results is reported in Table 2.1. As can be seen, the result for each of the five groups of countries is very similar to that presented for the whole sample or in Doise et al. (1999) and shows that rights and duties included in the Universal Declaration of Human Rights can be divided into three basic types: basic human rights, rights and duties of the individual, and socioeconomic rights. There is indeed a common pattern of rights that can be extracted from judgments about one's own and the government's involvement in the enforcement of human rights that discriminates the three types of rights mentioned, and for all samples studied, duties proclaimed in the Universal Declaration occupy a similar place in this shared-meaning structure.

Positions Regarding Individual and Government Responsibility in Enforcing Human Rights

As mentioned earlier, the subgroups of rights in the social representation studies correspond closely to the subgroups contained in expert definitions drawn up 50 years ago. Why is this so? A plausible explanation would be that the organizing principles on which the understanding of human rights is founded may be common to both lay and expert representations. This leads us to the second step of the quantitative analysis of social representations, which focuses on the extraction of the organizing principles of position taking.

We saw in the historical section that in expert thinking, a basic issue concerns the relative role and responsibility of the individual and the government in defending people's basic rights. But is this differentiation between citizens' and governments' duties also a guiding principle in lay thinking?

The importance of studying the expressions of views on individual and government efficacy in the enforcement of human rights became evident after the results of the cross-national study conducted by Doise et al. (1999). Students were asked to evaluate the 30 articles of the Universal Declaration on eight scales concerning the degree of agreement with the stated right; the importance of the right; the understanding of the content of the right; the relevance of the right to the participant's life; the efficacy of self, of political parties, and of government in enforcing the right; and the readiness to join other people in defending the given right. Of these eight scales, two explain the largest part of interindividual differences, namely, the scales concerning self- and government efficacy. The participants can be meaningfully classified into four subgroups. Members of the first group had the highest score on all scales. They can be regarded as *advocates* of the idea of human rights.

TABLE 2.1
Correspondence Between Ten Rights and Three Categories of Rights in the Total Sample and by Cultural Groups

	Total	Africa	Asia	Eastern Europe	Latin America	Western Europe
Freedom of thought	I	I	I	I	I	I
Right to family	I	I	I	I	I	I
Duties to community	I	I	I	I	I	I
Right to work	S	S	S	S	S	S
Level of life	S	S	S	S	S	S
Fair trial	S	S	X	S	S	S
Freedom of movement	S	I	X	S	I	S
Human rights	B	B	B	I	B	B
Right to life	B	B	B	B	B	B
Equality	B	B	B	B	B	B

Note. I = rights and duties of the individual, S = socioeconomic rights, B = basic rights, X = distinct category of rights.

Another group felt that they were personally concerned with human rights but that it was not very easy for governments to do anything about them. This response pattern can be described as *personalist*. The third group can be called pessimists or *skeptics*. These had the lowest score on all scales. The last group felt that they were rather powerless to ensure respect for their rights but considered the government more efficient in doing so. This response pattern is typical of *governmentalists*.

An examination of the links among these four positions (personalists, governmentalists, skeptics, and advocates) and the participants' value choices or their experience of social injustice led us to conclude that (a) strong support for the values of universalism and social harmony and agreement with a societal explanation of social injustice were systematically related to more favorable human rights attitudes as expressed by advocates and personalists, whereas opposite value choices resulted in skepticism or more governmentalist attitudes; and (b) characteristic of personalists, and to a lesser extent of skeptics, was also a positioning shaped by personal experience of, and concern about, various forms of discrimination and injustice considered to be inevitable products of human nature and economic relations and linked with less concern about happiness. Conversely, those who are relatively more concerned about happiness are often to be found among governmentalists and advocates.

These four kinds of positioning were not represented in the same proportion over all the countries studied. It was found that skeptics were relatively more numerous in Japan and India, whereas personalists were more often found in countries with serious human rights problems (according to the ratings by Humana, 1992) and human development problems (according to the ratings of the United Nations Development Programme, 1996) and governmentalists in more developed countries or countries that had recently changed to a democratic regime.

In another study, Spini and Doise (1998) added a second opposition to the personal-versus-governmental dimensions: the distinction between what can or should be done and what is actually done. These two new principles are referred to as abstract-versus-applied judgments in reference to Jackman's (1978, 1981) work on judgments about racial equality. These four principles (personal vs. governmental and abstract vs. applied) were crossed to measure four distinct dimensions. Moreover, each dimension was measured by two scales: (a) Personal–Abstract: "I can(not) do a great deal (anything) for the enforcement of this right" and "I (don't) have a share of responsibility for the enforcement of this right;" (b) Personal–Applied: "I am (not) sufficiently committed to the enforcement of this right" and "I am (not) involved practically in the enforcement of this right;" (c) Governmental–Abstract: "My government can(not) do a great deal (anything) for the enforcement of this right" and "My government has (doesn't have) a share of responsibility for the enforcement of this right;" and (d) Governmental–Applied: "My government is (not) involved practically in the enforcement of this right" and "My government is (not) sufficiently committed to the enforcement of this right."

It is worth noting at this point that these questions introduce a new level of duties. At the first level, we find the duties listed in parallel to rights within the various declarations. The questions we introduced concerning the abstract or applied responsibility for the enforcement of the rights and duties included in the Universal Declaration are also treated here as duties as they refer to a more abstract and "moral" or to a more concrete and applied duty of the individual and the government. The concept of duty is used in these diverse ways below and the term *responsibility* is used as a synonym of duty.

To compare the answers concerning these four organizing principles of position taking (personal-versus-governmental combined with abstract-versus-applied involvement), Spini (1997) computed the mean answer per type of right—basic rights, individual rights and duties, and socioeconomic rights—across the groups of countries. The right to freedom of movement was discarded from the subsequent analyses as it was unstable in the cluster analyses. Cronbach's alpha for these new scales has a mean value of 0.71 (minimum = 0.63; maximum = 0.77), a reasonable value for three-item scales.

A multivariate analysis of variance was then computed with the five groups of countries as independent variables and two within-subject dependent variables: the mean individual answers to each cluster of rights on three levels, basic, individual, and socioeconomic, and the dimensions of judgment about involvement in human rights identified as principles on four levels, personal abstract, personal applied, governmental abstract, and governmental applied.

As in the study of Doise et al. (1999), the results of this analysis show strong main effects in terms of statistical significance, which is why we are relying more on the effect size than on the probabilities of effects. The first observation is that the effects of the rights, $F(2, 5764) = 405.14$, $p < .001$, $\eta 2 = 0.123$; of the principles, $F(3, 8646) = 2187.97$, $p < .001$, $\eta 2 = 0.432$; and their interaction, $F(6, 17292) = 539.97$, $p < .001$, $\eta 2 = 0.158$ are stronger than their corresponding second- and third-order effects, which include the interaction with countries: $F(8, 5764) = 11.66$, $p < .001$, $\eta 2 = 0.016$ for Rights × Countries; $F(8, 5764) = 107.45$, $p < .001$, $\eta 2 = 0.130$ for Principles × Countries; and $F(24, 17292) = 24.40$, $p < .001$, $\eta 2 = 0.033$ for Rights × Principles × Countries. We should, however, point out that the simple effect of countries, $F(4, 2882) = 147.77$, $p < .001$, $\eta 2 = 0.170$, is also substantial and indicates that there are differences in the judgments about personal and government involvement in human rights and duties among the groups of countries, but these differences do not strongly interact with the judgments on the different dimensions of judgment. Thus, we focus our comments on the effects of the rights and principles and, in particular, on their interaction, $F(6, 17292) = 539.97$, $p < .001$, $\eta 2 = 0.158$. The means corresponding to this interaction effect are presented in Figure 2.2.

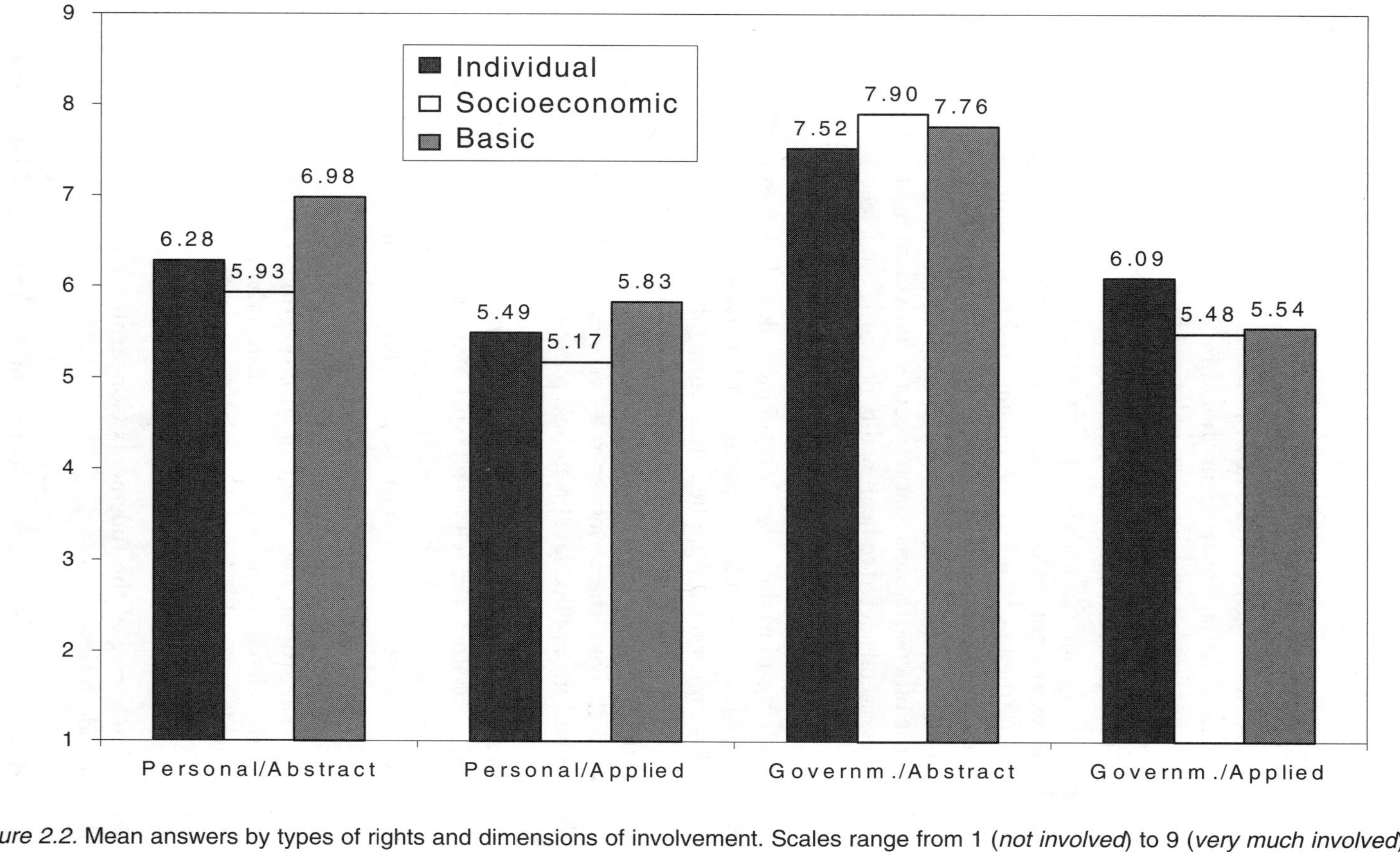

Figure 2.2. Mean answers by types of rights and dimensions of involvement. Scales range from 1 (*not involved*) to 9 (*very much involved*).

The interaction between different types of involvement is due to greater differences within the personal abstract type of involvement, $F(2, 5774) = 991.24$, $p < .001$, $\eta 2 = 0.256$, than within the governmental applied dimension, $F(2, 5772) = 443.82$, $p < .001$, $\eta 2 = 0.133$, or the personal applied dimension, $F(2, 5774) = 380.16$, $p < .001$, $\eta 2 = 0.116$. The governmental abstract judgments are the most consensual, $F(2, 5772) = 218.17$, $p < .001$, $\eta 2 = 0.070$, as already observed by Spini and Doise (1998): Individuals in general consider that government should be the first actor in the enforcement of human rights and duties, as indicated by the very high means for the three types of rights, and values that are much higher than those attributed to self. This significant effect, however, indicates that the government should be concerned primarily with socioeconomic and basic rights. At the applied level, the respondents judge their governments more severely, particularly in reference to the basic and socioeconomic rights, for which they indicate a low practical involvement. Concerning individual rights and duties, the judgments indicate that governments are slightly more involved in these rights than in the others. It seems that respect for individual rights, as well as societal duties, is considered to be in reality primarily an object of governmental concern, even if respondents expect the government to be rather more concerned with other families of rights, namely, basic and socioeconomic rights.

With regard to the judgments on individual dimensions, there are two main considerations. First, the pattern of involvement concerning the types of rights is similar for the applied and abstract dimensions. Respondents feel that they themselves should be, and are in fact, more involved in the basic human rights than in the individual rights and duties or the socioeconomic rights, which have the lowest scores. Second, the difference between the abstract and the applied level is far less pronounced than in the case of the judgments concerning the government.

In short, most critical judgments concern the government. First, they should do more than the self for all types of rights than they actually do. But they should also be more involved in socioeconomic rights, whereas in practice they are most involved in the respect of individual rights and duties. It is clear that expectations about the role of the government are very high, and generally governments do not live up to these expectations, although they seem to some extent more efficient in protecting traditional rights of the bourgeoisie related to the duties of citizenship than in protecting socioeconomic rights and rights involving relations with the judiciary and national institutions.

Social Anchoring of the Judgments Concerning Human Rights and Duties

A final result of the research program concerns the social anchoring of the positions taken by individuals with respect to the duties of the self and the government (third step of the quantitative analysis of social representations). Are the positions already described, such as personalist or governmentalist, related to specific values or practices?

The studies by Doise et al. (1999), Spini (1997), and Spini and Doise (1998) showed, using the Rokeach Value Survey (Rokeach, 1973) and the Schwartz Value Survey (Schwartz, 1992), that individuals who regard universalistic or self-enhancement values as most important also consider that governments do not take concrete action in the protection of human rights and duties and express a relatively high personal involvement at both abstract and applied levels. The opposite pattern is true for individuals who defend conservative, traditional, and security values.

Judgments concerning involvement in human rights also have a strong link with social activism, religious practice, and political ideology. In their study, Spini and Doise (1998) found evidence in Switzerland that more socially committed and nonreligious students, who tended to be at the left of the political spectrum, were more inclined to be personally involved in the enforcement of human rights and to consider that their government should be highly involved in it. But when they were asked to evaluate the concrete action taken by the government, they were more critical than right-wing students, who were less socially committed or were practicing Catholics.

These anchorings of attitudes toward human rights have now been found repeatedly in different studies (Clémence et al., 1995; Diaz-Veizades, Widaman, Little, & Gibbs, 1995; Moghaddam & Vuksanovic, 1990). Values of conservation, related to tradition, security, and religious practices or right-wing political preferences, lead individuals to consider that individual rights may be restricted in order to guarantee the functioning of society and to positive evaluations of the action of the institutions. Universalistic or self-enhancement values and practices devoted to social change correspond to a personal concern for human rights and a critical evaluation of one's own government. The effects of these oppositions among value types are not peculiar to human rights and can be found in other types of evaluations, such as trust in institutions (Devos, Spini, & Schwartz, 2002). It is also worth mentioning at this point the obvious correspondence between these basic ideological oppositions and the oppositions concerning the content of the various declarations of human rights and duties described previously in the historical section.

CONCLUSION

A Shared Definition of Rights and Duties

In this chapter, we defend the argument that the natural environment of rights and duties in history as well as in contemporary social representations is not individuals but the relationship between citizens and the state. Duties and rights are embedded in the so-called social contract between the community and individuals, between the nation-state and the citizen.

In our research on social representations of human rights, the issue of duties was not initially on the agenda. However, rights cannot be studied in a societal vacuum, and when we analyzed the positioning of individuals in relation to human rights and their violations, it became evident that we could not disregard notions related to the semantic field of responsibility or duty. Of course, our exploratory interview studies (Doise et al., 1991) had already drawn our attention to this aspect of the social representation of human rights.

Philosophers, such as Rousseau or Kant, could consider the individual, in a kind of prepolitical state, as endowed with inalienable rights and freedoms, and such a stand was also expressed by the vote of the Assembly of the French people in 1789. It remains nevertheless true that the definition, and especially the defense, of basic rights is to a great extent a matter of state intervention. The participants in our research were aware of this fact, even if they differed among themselves in the amount of responsibility they attributed to individuals and authorities and to citizens and government, respectively.

They also admitted that although some rights are inalienable, many can be limited by institutions or the state (see Doise et al., 1991). This is also the official position as expressed in the European Convention for the Protection of Human Rights and Fundamental Freedoms. It is important to consider that several fundamental rights proclaimed in this convention are not to be considered absolute rights in the sense that they should be respected in all circumstances. Article 15, which ends the listing of the rights, stipulates the following:

> In time of war or other public emergency threatening the life of the nation, any High Contracting Party may take measures derogating from its obligations under this Convention to the extent strictly required by the exigencies of the situation, provided that such measures are not inconsistent with its other obligations under international law. (p. 502)

One also has to note that the different dimensions used to measure judgments about personal and governmental responsibilities for the enforcement of human rights and duties throw some light on the shared classification of rights in expert and lay knowledge. Presenting the Universal Declaration to the respondents brought us back to the expert classification of rights and duties. First, there are fundamental rights for which both the individual and the government have duties, then individual rights and duties that should primarily concern the self, and finally socioeconomic rights that mainly correspond to duties of the state. This classification of rights is in line with the expert theories, which distinguish rights of the first and second generation

(Weston, 1992). This concordance, found in very different samples and in two cross-cultural studies (Doise et al., 1999; Spini, 1997), confirms the hypothesis of a common, shared categorization of rights and duties in expert and lay knowledge, a typical hypothesis of the social representation theory (Doise et al., 1993). In this regard, if there is a potentially universalistic reality in our results concerning the origin of rights and duties (see the first set of questions in chap. 1, this volume), it is the shared definition of the social contract composed of different types of rights and duties that define the role of the citizen and the state.

The Limits of the Rights of the State and of the Duties of the Individual

In her book on controlling the abuse of reason-of-state arguments, Delmas-Marty (1989) lists the rights that have to be considered as absolute following the European Convention for the Protection of Human Rights and Fundamental Freedoms:

> When all is said and done, fully protected rights are only the interdiction of torture and inhuman or degrading treatment (Art. 3) as well as the interdiction of collective expulsions (Art. 4 additional Protocol n° 4) or the multiplication of prosecutions or penal sanctions for the same violation (Art. 4 additional Protocol n° 7). As for other rights, they may sometimes benefit from a quasi-absolute protection, more than often only from a relative protection." For these rights to be protected in all circumstances, one should probably add the right defined in article 4 of the Convention "No one shall be held in slavery or in servitude." (p. 12)

These limitations are anchored in the very conception of the democratic state. The Preamble to the European convention states clearly that fundamental freedoms are best maintained "by an effective political democracy." Exceptions to the respect of these freedoms cannot be envisaged to protect the state per se (which is often the interpretation advanced by the notorious reason-of-state argument) but to safeguard a democratic system, which should at all times "keep the State at reason," in the words of Delmas-Marty (1989, p. 24).

Depending on one's viewpoint, that of the individual or that of the state, the asymmetry in the conception of rights will be tilted in one direction or another. Conventionally enough, we find on one side those who defend the primacy of the community and of the duties of individuals and on the other those who advocate the rights of the individual vis-à-vis the community. This is particularly clear in the described empirical studies from the social anchoring of the positions taken toward the duties of the individual and the government.

Another illustration of this asymmetry is the case in which an individual wants to defend his or her rights against an institution or a state. The procedure is usually very long, complicated, and expensive. But when a government deems that there is a threat to public (often meaning social) order, it can very quickly and legally restrict the freedom of individuals or declare a state of emergency. What is evident here is that there is a clear asymmetry between duties and rights, which is an asymmetry of power between the state and the individual. The state can define and invoke duties specified by the law, whereas individuals have rights specified in the constitution or declarations at a very general but not necessarily efficient level. Such asymmetry is certainly not confined to the citizen–state relationship but can be generalized to the relationships between individuals and groups or communities. In this respect the relationships between children and parents and between employees and employers are not very different.

Duties of the Individual and the State

Institutions such as the state usually define and apply rights and duties at the level of individuals. For example, the law is based on the general assumption that there is an individual responsibility to respect it. Rights are usually expressed by the law or the various declarations of human rights at a very abstract level, whereas codes of obligations or duties are more concrete and are accompanied by norms and penalties. If this observation is correct, it can be said that there is an asymmetric relationship between the community and the individual, with the state emphasizing the rights and duties of the individual in its positive law and masking the duties of the community to the individual.

A good example of this mechanism is provided by the duties listed in the 1948 American Declaration on Human Rights and Duties. In this text, we find, for example, duties to receive instruction, to vote, to pay taxes, to obey the law, and to serve the community and the nation. The relationship between rights and duties is also detailed in Article 27 of the African Charter on Human and Peoples' Rights (adopted in 1981), which indicates perfectly this focus on individual responsibility for social order:

> 1. Every individual shall have duties towards his family and society, the State and other legally recognized communities and the international community. 2. The rights and freedoms of each individual shall be exercised with due regard to the rights of others, collective security, morality and common interest. (Lawson, 1991, p. 15)

This logic of duties of the individual to the community is most common in the official documents on human rights and duties.

But the logic of the authorities may be different to that of its citizens. A government may legitimize the imposition of duties on the individual by arguments based on societal order, whereas individuals may press for more concrete action by the state to enforce socioeconomic rights. The "new" citizen, represented by the students who answered our surveys, tends precisely to indicate that the government should apply a different logic. There is a general claim that governments should take more concrete action to enforce socioeconomic rights in particular. Whether this claim is common to other countries or other populations is of course not clear. Our results suggest that this demand for government duties may be stronger in industrialized countries than in poorer ones, where the personalist logic may be stronger. This second asymmetry emphasizes the differential role of the self (which should be responsible for individual rights and duties) and the government (which should be practically engaged in enforcing socioeconomic rights) and emerges consistently from the various surveys we conducted. In taking these positions, respondents highlight and identify the duties of the state. In place of the emphasis on the duties and rights of the individual upheld by states and by the law, the citizens propose a new definition with specific duties for both the state and the individual.

As to the second question of the relationship of rights and duties raised by Finkel and Moghaddam (see chap. 1, this volume), we feel we have presented some evidence that

1. The statist logic gives some primacy to rights over duties in declarations. This asymmetry is very important as it puts a rein on oppression of the individual by the community. The idea of human rights is a very powerful one that has given rise to much progress and is now internationally widespread.
2. There is an asymmetry between rights and duties. Historically, this may appear to derive from the fact that rights have prevailed over duties in official declarations. But there is another asymmetry, which is due to the fact that rights are defined in very abstract terms, whereas duties are specified in positive law. Moreover the duties are supervised by various state institutions, which can sanction the individual. Conversely, it is very difficult for an individual to struggle against the state.
3. The respondents to our surveys indicate that the apportionment of duties between the state and the individual could or should be different, with greater practical involvement of the state in particular in socioeconomic rights rather than in individual rights and duties.

Rights and Duties as Normative Social Representations

One important task for social psychologists is to document and understand how ideologies function and circulate within society (e.g., Billig, 1991; Tetlock, Peterson, & Lerner, 1996) and how common sense assimilates and accommodates scientific revolutions and changes in ideological discourse (e.g., Jovchelovitch, 2001; Moscovici & Hewstone, 1983). This is precisely the aim not only of social representation theory but also of other fields of social psychology such as the study of social influences and clashes between majorities and minorities in power (e.g., Moscovici, Mugny, & van Avermaet, 1985; Reicher, 2001).

Research on rights and duties is of prime importance as they are not just talk. Rights and duties are concrete concepts with concrete effects. They are at the heart of any social contract linking the individual to the state. In this regard they can be studied as normative social representations that simultaneously define and are defined by the symbolic and practical relationships between the state and the citizen, the institutions and the individual, the groups and their members.

REFERENCES

Billig, M. (1991). *Ideology and beliefs*. London: Sage.

Bobbio, N. (1992). *L'età dei diritti* [The age of rights]. Turin, Italy: Einaudi.

Breakwell, G. M., & Canter, D. V. (Eds.). (1993). *Empirical approaches to social representations*. London: Surrey University Press, with Academic Press and Harcourt Brace Jovanovich.

Catellani, P., & Quadrio, A. (1991). Ideal and real in the representation of politics. *Revue Internationale de Psychologie Sociale, 4*, 231–255.

Clémence, A. (2001). Social positioning and social representations. In K. Deaux & G. Philogène (Eds.), *Representations of the social* (pp. 83–95). Oxford, England: Blackwell.

Clémence, A., & Doise, W. (1995). La représentation sociale de la justice: Une approche des droits dans la pensée ordinaire [The social representation of justice: An approach of the rights in the ordinary thought]. *L'Année Sociologique, 45*, 371–400.

Clémence, A., Doise, W., De Rosa, A. S., & Gonzalez, L. (1995). La représentation sociale des droits de l'homme: Une recherche internationale sur l'étendue et les limites de l'universalité [The social representation of human rights: International research on the range and limits of universality]. *International Journal of Psychology, 30*, 181–212.

Comby, L., Devos, T., & Deschamps, J.-C. (1993). Représentations sociales du sida et attitudes à l'égard des personnes séropositives [Social representations of AIDS and attitudes in regard to seropositive people]. *Cahiers internationaux de psychologie sociale, 17*, 6–33.

Deaux, K., & Philogène, G. (2001). *Representations of the social*. Oxford, England: Blackwell.

Delmas-Marty, M. (1989). *Raisonner la raison d'état* [To reason the reason of state]. Paris: Presses Universitaires de France.

Deutsch, M. (1975). Equity, equality and need: What determines which value will be used as the basis of distributive justice? *Journal of Social Issues, 31*, 137–149.

Deutsch, M. (1985). *Distributive justice*. New Haven, CT: Yale University Press.

Devos, T., Spini, D., & Schwartz, S. H. (2002). Conflicts among human values and trust in institutions. *British Journal of Social Psychology, 41*, 481–494.

Diaz-Veizades, J., Widaman, K. F., Little, T. D., & Gibbs, K. W. (1995). The measurement and structure of human rights attitudes. *Journal of Social Psychology, 135*, 313–328.

Doise, W. (1990). Les représentations sociales [Social representations]. In R. Ghiglione, C. Bonnet, & J.-F. Richard (Eds.), *Traité de psychologie cognitive: Tome 3. Cognition, représentation, communication* (pp. 112–173). Paris: Dunod.

Doise, W. (1993). Debating social representations. In G. M. Breakwell & D. V. Canter (Eds.), *Empirical approaches to social representations* (pp. 157–170). Oxford, England: Clarendon.

Doise, W. (2002). *Human rights as social representations*. London: Routledge.

Doise, W., Clémence, A., & Lorenzi-Cioldi, F. (1993). *The quantitative analysis of social representations*. London: Harvester Wheatsheaf.

Doise, W., Dell'Ambrogio, P., & Spini, D. (1991). Psychologie sociale et droits de l'homme [Social psychology and human rights]. *Revue Internationale de Psychologie Sociale, 4*, 257–277.

Doise, W., Spini, D., & Clémence, A. (1999). Human rights as social representations in a cross-national context. *European Journal of Social Psychology, 29*, 1–29.

Doise, W., Spini, D., Jesuino, J. C., Ng, S. H., & Emler, N. (1994). Values and perceived conflicts in the social representations of human rights: Feasibility of a cross-national study. *Swiss Journal of Psychology, 53*, 4, 240–251.

Doise, W., Staerklé, C., Clémence, A., & Savory, F. (1998). Human rights and Genevan youth: A developmental study of social representations. *Swiss Journal of Psychology, 57*, 86–100.

Durkheim, E. (1898). Représentations individuelles et représentations collectives [Individual representations and collective representations]. *Revue de Métaphysique et deMorale, 6*, 273–302.

Duveen, G., & Shields, M. (1985). Children's ideas about work, wages and social rank. *Cahiers de Psychologie Cognitive, 5*, 411–412.

Echebarria, A., & Castro, J. L. G. (1993). Social representations of democracy, attitudes and the prediction of voting. *Revue Internationale de Psychologie Sociale, 2*, 23–45.

Ekins, P. (1992). *A new world order: Grassroots movements for global change*. London: Routledge.

Emler, N., & Dickinson, J. (1985). Children's representation of economic inequalities: The effect of social class. *British Journal of Developmental Psychology, 3*, 191–198.

Farr, R. M., & Moscovici, S. (Eds.). (1984). *Social representations*. Cambridge, England: Cambridge University Press and Paris: Maison des Sciences de l'Homme.

Flick, U. (1992). *La perception quotidienne de la santé et la maladie: Théories subjectives et représentations sociales* [The everyday perception of health and sickness: Subjective theories and social representations]. Paris: L'Harmattan.

Galli, I., & Nigro, G. (1987). The social representation of radioactivity among Italian children. *Social Sciences Information, 26*, 535–549.

Gauchet, M. (1989). *La révolution des droits de l'homme* [The revolution of human rights]. Paris: Gallimard.

Haney, C., & Zimbardo, P. G. (1977). The socialization into criminality: On becoming a prisoner and a guard. In J. L. Tapp & F. L. Levine (Eds.), *Law, justice and the individual in society: Psychological and legal issues* (pp. 198–223). New York: Holt.

Herrera, M., & Doise, W. (2001). Représentations sociales des droits de l'homme et des droits des peuples autochtones chez des membres de la nation montagnaise ou innu du Québec [Social representations of human rights and the rights of the aboriginal people among members of the Montagnais or Innu nation in Quebec]. *Canadian Journal of Political Science, 34*, 739–761.

Herrera, M., Lavallée, M., & Doise, W. (1998). Représentations sociales des droits de l'homme auprès de diverses communautés culturelles au Québec [Social representations of human rights attached to the diverse cultural communities of Quebec]. *Revue québécoise de psychologie, 19*(3), 151–187.

Hofstede, G. (1983). Dimensions of national cultures in fifty countries and three regions. In J. B. Deregowski, S. Dzivrawiec, & R. C. Annis (Eds.), *Expiscations in cross-cultural psychology* (pp. 335–355). Lisse, the Netherlands: Swets & Zeitlinger.

Humana, C. (1992). *World human rights guide* (3rd ed.). New York: Oxford University Press.

Inglehart, R. I. (1990). *Culture shift in advanced industrial society*. Princeton, NJ: Princeton University Press.

Jackman, M. R. (1978). General and abstract tolerance: Does education increase commitment to racial integration? *American Journal of Political Science, 22*, 302–324.

Jackman, M. R. (1981). Education and policy commitment to racial integration. *American Journal of Political Science, 25*, 256–269.

Joffe, H. (1995). Social representations of AIDS: Towards encompassing issues of power. *Textes sur les représentations sociales, 4*, 1, 29–40.

Johnson, G., & Symonides, J. (1994). *The Universal Declaration of Human Rights: 45th anniversary 1948–1993*. Paris: UNESCO.

Jovchelovitch, S. (2001). Social representations, public life, and social construction. In K. Deaux & G. Philogène (Eds.), *Representations of the social* (pp. 165–182). Oxford, England: Blackwell.

Kohlberg, L. (1981). *Essays on moral development. Vol. 1: The philosophy of moral development: Moral stages and the idea of justice*. New York: Harper & Row.

Kohlberg, L. (1984). *Essays on moral development. Vol. 2: The psychology of moral development: The nature and validity of moral stages*. New York: Harper & Row.

Lawson, E. (1991). *Encyclopedia of human rights*. New York: Taylor & Francis.

Lerner, M. J. (1977). The justice motive: Some hypotheses as to its origins and forms. *Journal of Personality, 45*, 1–52.

Lind, E. A., & Tyler, T. R. (1988). *The social psychology of procedural justice*. New York: Plenum Press.

Madiot, Y. (1998). *Considérations sur les droits et les devoirs de l'homme* [Considerations on human rights and duties]. Brussels, Belgium: Bruylant.

McGuire, W. J. (1986). The vicissitudes of attitudes and similar representational constructs in twentieth century psychology. *European Journal of Social Psychology, 16*, 89–130.

Mendlovitz, S. H., & Walker, R. B. J. (1987). *Towards a just world peace: Perspectives from social movements*. London: Butterworths.

Meeus, W. H., & Raijmaakers, Q. A. W. (1986). Administrative obedience: Carrying out orders to use psychological administrative violence. *European Journal of Social Psychology, 16*, 311–324.

Milgram, S. (1974). *Soumission à l'autorité* [Submission of authority]. Paris: Calman-Levy.

Moghaddam, F. M., & Vuksanovic, V. (1990). Attitudes and behavior toward human rights across different contexts: The role of right-wing authoritarianism, political ideology, and religiosity. *International Journal of Psychology, 25*, 455–474.

Moodie, E., Markovà, I., & Plichtovà, J. (1995). Lay representations of democracy: A study of two cultures. *Culture & Psychology, 1*, 423–453.

Moscovici, S. (1976). *La psychanalyse, son image, son public* [Psychoanalysis, its image, its public] (2nd ed.). Paris: Presses Universitaires de France. (Original work published 1961)

Moscovici, S. (2001). *Why a theory of social representations?* In K. Deaux & G. Philogène (Eds.), *Representations of the social* (pp. 8–35). Oxford, England: Blackwell.

Moscovici, S., & Hewstone, M. (1983). Social representations and social explanations: From the "naïve" to the "amateur" scientist. In M. Hewstone (Ed.), *Attribution theory, social and functional extensions* (pp. 98–125). Oxford, England: Blackwell.

Moscovici, S., Mugny, G., & van Avermaet, E. (Eds.). (1985). *Perspectives on minority influence*. Cambridge, England: Cambridge University Press.

Mugny, G., & Carugati, F. (1985). *L'intelligence au pluriel: Les représentations sociales de l'intelligence et de son développement* [Intelligence in the plural: Social representations of intelligence and its development]. Cousset, Switzerland: DelVal.

Piaget, J. (1932). *Le jugement moral chez l'enfant* [The moral judgement of the child]. Paris: Presses Universitaires de France.

Reicher, S. (2001). Crowds and social movements. In M. Hogg & S. Tindale (Eds.), *Blackwell handbook of social psychology: Group processes* (pp. 182–208). Oxford, England: Blackwell.

Rokeach, M. (1973). *The nature of human values*. New York: Free Press.

Schwartz, S. H. (1992). Universals in the content and structure of values: Theoretical advances and empirical tests in 20 countries. In M. P. Zanna (Ed.), *Advances in experimental social psychology* (Vol. 25, pp. 1–65). San Diego, CA: Academic Press.

Spini, D. (1997). *Valeurs et représentations sociales des droits de l'homme: Une approche structurale* [Values and social representations of human rights: A structural approach]. Unpublished manuscript, University of Geneva, Switzerland.

Spini, D., & Doise, W. (1998). Organising principles of involvement in human rights and their social anchoring in value priorities. *European Journal of Social Psychology, 28*, 603–622.

Staerklé, C., Clémence, A., & Doise, W. (1998). Representation of human rights across different national contexts: The role of democratic and non-democratic populations and governments. *European Journal of Social Psychology, 28*, 207–226.

Tajfel, H. (1978). *Differentiation between social groups: Studies in the social psychology of intergroup relations*. London: Academic Press.

Tajfel, H., & Turner, J. C. (1986). An integrative theory of intergroup conflict. In W. G. Austin & S. Worchel (Eds.), *The social psychology of intergroup relations* (pp. 7–24). Monterey, CA: Brooks/Cole.

Tetlock, P. E., Peterson, R. S., & Lerner, J. S. (1996). Revising the value pluralism model: Incorporating social content and context postulates. In C. Seligman, J. M. Olson, & M. P. Zanna (Eds.), *The psychology of values: The Ontario symposium* (Vol. 8, pp. 25–51). Mahwah, NJ: Erlbaum.

Thibaut, J., & Walker, L. (1975). *Procedural justice: A psychosociological analysis*. Hillsdale, NJ: Erlbaum.

Triandis, H. C. (1995). *Individualism and collectivism*. Boulder, CO: Westview Press.

United Nations Development Programme. (1996). *Human development report*. New York: Oxford University Press.

Wagner, W., & Kronberger, N. (2001). Killer tomatoes! Collective symbolic coping with biotechnology. In K. Deaux & G. Philogène (Eds.), *Representations of the social* (pp. 147–164). Oxford, England: Blackwell.

Weston, B. H. (1992). Human rights. In R. P. Claude & B. H. Weston (Eds.), *Human rights in the world community: Issues and action* (2nd ed., pp. 14–30). Philadelphia: University of Pennsylvania Press.

3

UNDERSTANDING RIGHTS AND DUTIES IN DIFFERENT CULTURES AND CONTEXTS: OBSERVATIONS FROM GERMAN AND KOREAN ADOLESCENTS

SIEGFRIED HOPPE-GRAFF AND HYE-ON KIM

Humans are social beings from the very beginning of life, but it is not until adolescence that the individual reflects about his or her relation to society and community. The growing awareness of the self being surrounded by and facing society—its structures, rules, and symbolic products—results from the interaction of two sources: one, the emergence of internal prerequisites like new acquisitions in self-reflective thinking (Moshman, 1999), perspective taking (Selman, 1980), and moral judgment (Kohlberg, 1984) and the other, increasing external expectations. Among other things, society and its members expect adolescents to take over new social roles, obligations, and responsibilities, while at the same time society grants them new rights, such as voting, concluding agreements, driving a car, and marrying. These rights, like all rights, necessarily include new duties.

More than 50 years ago, Robert Havighurst (1948) introduced the concept of age-specific developmental tasks for that kind of instigation for developmental processes from the growth of inner potentials and outer pressure. As one of the developmental tasks for the adolescent period, Havighurst mentioned explicitly the achievement of socially responsible behavior. Evidently, at the core of the achievement of this task is the subjective reconstruction of the self as a holder of both right and duties. During that process, the self has to take possession of society (in this case, rights and duties), and in turn, society takes possession of the young person.

To find out how this task is solved and how it is influenced by culture and context, we carried out a questionnaire study with German and South Korean adolescents between 12 and 16 years old. We asked these adolescents to (a) define right and duty in their own words, (b) think about their most important rights and duties, (c) tell us who lays down rights and duties, and (d) decide whether it is right or wrong that they do not have the same rights and duties as adults and teachers. To study context, the adolescents were instructed to reflect about their rights and duties in general or about their rights and duties as students.

This chapter is mainly based on observations from that study. But we start with conceptual work, fitting the issues of right and duty more precisely into the map of human development. In addition, we discuss the peculiarities of growing up in a collectivistic culture and society (Korea) or in an individualistic culture and society (Germany). After describing the methods of our study, we compare in detail the answers of the German and Korean participants. In the discussion section, we relate our data to some of the guiding questions of the editors (see chap. 1, this volume).

THE REPRESENTATION OF RIGHTS AND DUTIES IN ADOLESCENTS: DEVELOPMENTAL CONSIDERATIONS

Right and *duty* may be studied in developmental psychology from at least three perspectives (see also Hoppe-Graff & Kim, 2001). First, right and duty are concepts, and thus, may be studied as other cognitive structures (or knowledge structures) within the framework of cognitive development. For example, we may ask participants in a sentence completion task to define right and duty.

Second, different from other concepts like number or space (to mention some of Piaget's classical examples of concept development) right and duty are intrinsically moral categories. In everyday life, right talk and duty talk in most cases is normative talk. Thus, right and duty may also be studied from the perspective of moral development. For example, one may ask children and adolescents whether it is okay or not okay that they do not have the same rights and duties as adults.

Third, developmentalists may concentrate on the fact that with the child's construction of politics and society (Connell, 1971), a new dimension is introduced into the understanding of rights and duties both as concepts and moral categories. As long as the child does not grasp the sense of the political and legal system, he or she will not relate rights and duties to the community and the society, to government and law. The meaning and the normative implications of the concepts will be restricted to the interpersonal sphere. But with growing awareness of societal and political reality, these concepts will be elaborated in both extension and intension to include "the world out there."

According to studies by Adelson and his coworkers (Adelson, Green, & O'Neil, 1969; Adelson & O'Neil, 1966) the growth of the sense of community does not start before early adolescence (roughly between 13 and 15 years old). This fundamental change results from several factors, particularly the growth of abstract thinking and adolescents' experience of increased autonomy, but it is also deeply interwoven with the growing sense of community.

As far as we know, Adelson and his coworkers did not study the development of the ideas of right and duty. Research on the concept of right started with Melton (1980) who found three developmental stages in reasoning about rights. At Stage 1, children perceive rights in an egocentric manner in terms of the privileges that are bestowed or withdrawn on the whims of an authority figure. At Stage 2, rights are seen as based on fairness, maintaining social order, and obeying rules. At Stage 3, rights are recognized in terms of abstract universal principles. This progression is closely linked to the general principles of cognitive and moral development as laid down by Piaget and Kohlberg.

Ruck, Abramovitch, and Keating (1998) introduced the distinction between nurturance and self-determination rights and studied the development of 8- to 16-year-olds' understanding of nurturance and self-determination rights. They used semistructured interviews containing hypothetical vignettes in which a story character wished to exercise a self-determination right or nurturance right that conflicted with the wishes or practices of those in authority. Ruck et al. observed that reasoning about nurturance rights did not show an age-related progression from concrete to abstract, whereas reasoning about self-determination rights was more likely to exhibit such a progression.

The studies just reviewed have several weaknesses. First, none of the studies takes into account the distinction between cognitive and moral aspects of the understanding of right (or of law), which we introduced above. Second, Ruck et al. presupposed that young persons focus exclusively on nurturance and self-determination when they reason about rights. But it may be that other kinds of rights come into their mind, for example, respect and appreciation. Finally, the authors of all studies tacitly assume that the results may be generalized to other societies and cultures.

We took these weaknesses as starting points for our own work. But before we lay out in detail the goals and the strategy of our study, we consider cultural influences on young persons' understanding of rights and duties.

DIFFERENT CULTURAL BACKGROUNDS FOR THE UNDERSTANDING OF RIGHTS AND DUTIES

Since Hofstede's (1980) seminal study, *Culture's Consequences*, the dichotomy between individualism and collectivism has become the most popular basis on which to characterize (or classify) cultures. In *Culture's Consequences*, Hofstede proposed that a single bipolar individualism-versus-collectivism dimension is a useful construct for subsuming a complex set of differences between cultures.

Triandis (1995) lists four aspects that distinguish collectivistic-from-individualistic cultures:

1. Interdependent definition of the self in collectivism versus independent self-definition in individualism.
2. Close alignment of personal and communal goals in individualism versus no alignment in collectivism.
3. "Cognitions that focus on norms, obligations, and duties guide much of social behavior in collectivist cultures. Those that focus on attitudes, personal needs, rights and contracts . . . guide social behavior in individualistic cultures." (p. 44)
4. Emphasis on relationships, even when they are disadvantageous, in collectivistic cultures versus emphasis on rationalist advantages and disadvantages of maintaining relationship in individualistic cultures.

At least the third characteristic supposes that the concepts of right and duty may differ between adolescents from collectivistic and individualistic cultures. Of course, the orientation of a culture does not determine the attitudes, beliefs, concepts, and behaviors at the personal level. But in each culture there is a modal pattern with a characteristic distribution of individuals.

Several authors agree that modern Germany is an individualistic culture. According to Kuechler (1993), individualization took place in the 1970s. "In this process, ties of family, church, and community, as well as identification with social groups . . . became less important" (p. 37). As in France and the United States, German individualism is vertical. Vertical individualism (in contrast to horizontal individualism) includes placing a high value on freedom and a low value on equality. Individualism in any given culture is influenced by cultural looseness. Looseness is the opposite to tightness and refers to the extent that members of a culture agree about what constitutes a correct action, behave according to the norms of a culture, and suffer for or offer severe criticisms for even slight deviations from norms. Compared with the United States, Germany may be a relatively tight culture (within the individualistic syndrome), but compared with Korea it is surely a loose culture.

Korea is recognized in cross-cultural research as the prototypical case of a collectivistic culture. In a recent social psychological study of the Korean people from the perspective of the individualism-versus-collectivism continuum, Cha (1994) explored the modifications that collectivism in Korea has gone through in the 20th century. Among the specific features of collectivism in the traditional Korean culture is high respect for the following values: dependence, hierarchy, courtesy, heartfulness or fraternity, family line, filial piety, and loyalty. In particular, dependence includes a lack of the notion of individual rights, and at the behavioral level, intrusive actions and not accepting the others' rights. The high value of hierarchy is expressed in the attitudes of obedience and respect for parents, elders, and the *yangban* class (nobility, aristocratic class) and in obedient, loyal, and compliant behavior to authorities. Filial piety requires deference to parents.

The common thread behind respect for dependence, hierarchy, filial piety, and loyalty is the Confucian idea of propriety. In a recent article, we tried to explain the East Asian meaning of propriety to Western people in the following way: "First, you have to leave behind the assumption, that propriety is related to conformism or lack of independence. Next, you should concentrate on the following concepts: kindness, honesty, correctness (keeping to rules), wisdom, and sincerity. Then go to the center of the meaning space that is constructed by those concepts—there you will find a first approximation to the Confucian meaning of propriety" (Hoppe-Graff & Kim, 2000, p. 383).

In 1980, Cha presented results demonstrating that collectivism in Korea has declined and, at the same time, become different from traditional collectivism. Nevertheless, survey data of the beliefs and attitudes of younger and older generations of Koreans showed that in both age groups, Korean people were still collectivists. For example, the ideals of loyalty and filial piety were still important in Korean society (supported in the survey by 75% and 86% of the younger and older groups, respectively). These data reported by Cha were collected during the period from 1970 to 1980, and it remains open as to how far the turn to individualism among young Koreans has come at the beginning of the 21st century.

GOALS OF THE STUDY

Our review of the literature led to the conclusion that an extensive study of the understanding of rights and duties in adolescence does not exist. An extensive (if not comprehensive) study should (a) include the cognitive and the moral aspects of right and duty; (b) be sensitive to the distinction between the interpersonal and the societal, political, and legal aspects of rights and duties; (c) take into account that rights and duties may mean different things in different cultures; (d) also take into account that the concepts of right and duty may differ, when they are applied in different contexts; and (e) not restrict from the start the meaning of rights and duties to specific components (as to the nurturance and self-determination components in the study by Ruck et al., 1998).

For obvious reasons, the comprehensive character of the study excluded costly data collection procedures. We decided to carry out a questionnaire study with open-ended questions. It was structured as follows:

1. To include the cognitive aspect, we ensured that the questionnaire included a definition task and a question about the authority that lays down rights and duties. The normative (or moral) aspect was introduced by asking the participants about their most important rights and duties and about equal versus unequal rights and duties for adolescents and adults.
2. The issue of interpersonal versus social and legal interpretations of rights and duties was not brought into the study as an independent factor; instead we analyzed the answers with categories from both fields of interpretation.
3. Data collection was carried out with German and Korean adolescents of the same age and of comparable academic careers. The questionnaire was constructed in cooperation by the two authors, who represent the two cultures. Preliminary versions of the questionnaire were revised cooperatively. Thus, we assessed the right and duty concept in very different cultural frameworks, in both an individualistic and a collectivistic culture, but the assessment was carried out with parallel procedures.
4. Context was varied by asking parallel questions about rights and duties in general versus at school. In the following sections, we refer to this variation by use of the terms *general study* and *school study*. In both Germany and Korea, school is an institutional context with very specific rights and duties for the students and the teachers. Thus, by comparing the answers on "rights and duties as adolescents" with the answers on "rights and duties as students," we tried to find out how sensitive the adolescents are to changes in a context that is of great significance to their daily life.
5. None of the items in the questionnaire restricted the meaning of right or duty to one or the other component.

We were also interested in developmental changes of the concepts during adolescence. Therefore we compared the right and duty concepts in 12-, 14-, and 16-year-olds. But age differences were only of secondary importance, and for that reason the categories for the analysis of the participants' answers were created with the primary aim being to catch variations in content and not in complexity.

METHOD

Participants

Our goal was to compare German and Korean students who were at the same age levels. But the school year begins in Germany in September and in Korea in March, and Koreans enter school a half-year earlier than Germans. Therefore, we included German students from Grades 6, 8, and 10 and Korean students from Grades 7, 9, and 11 and collected data during the school years when the mean age of the participants was the same: approximately 12, 14, and 16 years. The general study and the school study were carried out in independent samples. The German subsamples consisted of forty 12-year-olds, forty-one 14-year-olds, and forty-four 16-year-olds in the general study and forty-five 12-year-olds, forty-five 14-year-olds, and forty-six 16-year-olds in the school study. For the Korean subsamples, the corresponding frequencies were 37, 39, and 40 in the general study and 40, 39, and 40 in the school study.

In each of the German subsamples, about half of the students attended high school and the other half secondary school. In Korea, the division between high school and secondary school starts in Grade 10. The subsamples included both male and female participants. Each of our measures (see next section) was analyzed for sex differences. But only a very few, unsystematic differences were found. Therefore, we excluded sex as an independent factor from further analysis.

Procedure

Questionnaire

The questionnaire included 13 items. This report is based on the analysis of 8 items, 4 right items and 4 corresponding duty items. The topic of the questionnaire was the understanding of adolescents' rights and duties, either in general or at school. To introduce the reader to the questions, we listed word-for-word each of the right and duty items in the general context.

Definition (Sentence Completion Task). Imagine that you should explain to someone who does not know anything about it what it means to have a right (duty). Please try to do this by completing the following sentence: "To have a right (duty) means . . . "

Most Important Rights (Duties). Each human being has certain rights (duties). This is true for adults as well as for children and adolescents. Please write down your rights (duties) one by one. Begin with the most important right (duty), continue with the second important right (duty), and so on.

Who Lays Down Rights (Duties)?

1. Who lays down your rights (duties)?
2. Who lays down the rights (duties) of adults?

The Same Rights (Duties) for Adolescents and Adults? Is it right or wrong that you do not have certain rights (duties)? Please explain by completing the following sentence: "It is (not) right, because. . ."

The meaning of the English word *right* is very similar to the Korean word *(Kuonri)* and the German word *Recht*. But neither duty nor responsibility is very close to the Korean *(Uimu)* or the German *Pflicht*. *Uimu* and *Pflicht* include both aspects, responsibility and duty.[1]

In the school context, the definition item was identical. For the other items, the phrase "students and teachers" replaced "adults and adolescents."

Data Collection

Data collection took place in the summer of 1999 in public schools in Leipzig (Germany) and Mokpo (South Korea). Leipzig is a city of about 500,000 inhabitants in the former German Democratic Republic. There has been much controversy about different attitudes in young people from the former "two Germanys." In a study on student–teacher conflicts that we carried out in 1996 in West and East Germany, we found no significant differences in the students' attitudes toward teacher authority and obedience (Hoppe-Graff, Latzko, Engel, Hesse, Mainka, & Waller, 1998). Therefore, we assume as a working hypothesis that right and duty concepts in adolescents from former West Germany will not be different from the Leipzig data.

Mokpo has about 200,000 inhabitants and is a harbor and university town in the Southwest edge of the Republic of Korea. We have no evidence of the representativeness of data from a city like Mokpo for South Korea in general. A Korean stereotype says that you have to always distinguish between Seoul (the capital) and the rest of the country. If this cliché carries truth for the issue of rights and duties, then we may expect that the data from Mokpo do not hold for adolescents from the capital but for young persons from other Korean provinces.

The data were collected by the authors' assistants at school during regular lessons. The students needed about 30–45 minutes to fill out the whole questionnaire. They did not fill in their name so that anonymity was preserved.

Data Analysis

Data analysis for each item started with the construction of categories to arrange and classify the individual data. This was done on the basis of a

[1]Thus, it is only for simplicity that throughout this chapter we use *duty* as the adequate English translation.

priori assumptions that were mainly derived from Hye-On Kim's knowledge of German and Korean culture. (Kim has lived for more than 30 years in Korea and more than 10 years in Germany.) Preliminary categories were applied to about 20% of the raw data and modified if necessary. The basic categories that grew out of that modification were applied to the data set in general. Ratings were carried out by student assistants. To determine interrater agreement, another 20% of the data were also rated. Kappa was computed as a measure of interrater agreement. For all items, kappa was consistently high, at least .80.

The number of categories per item ranged from 15 to 23. For clarity and conciseness, we created for each item out of the basic categories a smaller set of superordinate categories. In the next section we present data only at the superordinate level. Also for clarity, in most of the tables we omitted categories with frequencies less than 5% in all samples and in the category for remaining cases.

RESULTS

All tables include comparisons of category distributions for the different samples. Whenever it was possible, we added the results of chi-square comparisons to the descriptive data.

Definition (Sentence Completion Task)

Right

The top of Table 3.1 shows the results for the definition of holding a right. The table presents percentages for the defining characteristics that had been included in the definitions. The definition task was the same in the general and the school study; therefore, the data from both studies are included within one table.

Except for the category self-determination, the data patterns from the two studies are identical. In both studies, the general and the school, permission is the most salient feature of possessing a right for German adolescents (53% and 56%, respectively). In contrast, permission does not dominate the right concept of Korean adolescents. Permission is expressed either by the simple statement "to be allowed to do something" or by talking about legality. For example, one participant explained: "To have a right means that you can't be punished." Other typical definitions included "What you do is legal;" "It cannot be forbidden;" or "You can do something and it does not matter what someone else thinks about it."

For the German participants in the school study, when we compare the simple statements versus the "legality explanations" across the different age

TABLE 3.1
Definition of Right and Duty by German and Korean Adolescents: Comparison of Defining Characteristics Included in the Definitions

Defining characteristics	General study		School study	
	Germany	Korea	Germany	Korea
	Right			
Self-determination	41	43	29	**49**
"To do, what I want to do"	5	17**	7	16*
Autonomy, power	36	26	22	**33**
Permission	53	7***	56	17***
"To be allowed to do something"	18	4**	26	**12**
Legality	39	4***	33	5***
Obligation and responsibility	21	27	15	30**
To be respected and appreciated	9	24**	7	29***
Propriety or decency	1	16***	1	9**
	Duty			
Commitment "To have to do something"	67	24***	80	41***
Obligation and responsibility	27	28	16	33**
Enlargement of scope of one's actions	2	18***	2	21***
To be respected and appreciated	2	8	2	16***
Propriety	2	30***	2	12**

Note. All values represent percentages.
*$p < .05$. **$p < .01$. ***$p < .001$.

levels, we find significant age trends. Whereas the sentence completion "to have a right means to be allowed to do something" drops from 33% in 6th graders to 17% in 8th graders to 7% in 10th graders, definitions that point to legality grow from 8% in 6th graders to 31% in 8th graders to 71% in 10th graders.[2] By and large, a similar but nonsignificant age trend is found in the German sample for the right definitions in the general study.

The second significant difference between the German and Korean definitions lies in the Korean adolescents' emphasis on respect and appreciation as well as propriety or decency. Propriety or decency has been explained previously (see Different Cultural Backgrounds for the Understanding of Rights and Duties section); examples of definitions based on the criterion of respect or appreciation are "To have a right means to be accepted as a member of the society;" "It means dignity;" "It means shelter." As we explain in the discussion section that follows, the respect and appreciation and propriety or decency categories have in common that the essence of a right is an experience inside the person. Taken together, they are considered criteria for holding a right by about 40% of the young Koreans in both studies. In

[2]Note that the sum of the percentages from the subcategories is not equal to the percentage of the superordinate category because a subject who mentioned more than one subcategory was counted only once at the superordinate level.

contrast, propriety or decency is totally irrelevant for the Germans, and respect and appreciation are only rarely considered. No clear-cut, consistent age trends for propriety or decency and respect and appreciation were found in the Korean samples.

Although propriety or decency and respect and appreciation are those aspects of holding a right that are much more salient for Koreans than for Germans, they are not the most often used single category in Korea. About one out of two Korean adolescents points to self-determination when asked to explain holding a right. In the general study, the German young persons use this category at a similar rate, but in the school study the rate decreased so that only one out of three Germans talks about self-determination.

In Table 3.1 we have divided the self-determination category into two subcategories: (a) the single statement "to have a right means to do what I want to do" and (b) explanations with reference to autonomy and power (e.g., "I can decide by myself about my future;" "My voice will be heard;" and "I may have my own opinion"). For the definition "to do what I want to do," we found for neither the German nor the Korean samples any significant age trends. In contrast, there was a sharp increase with age in both Korean samples for the autonomy and power subcategory (from 25% to 42% to 40% in the general study and from 3% to 22% to 39% in the school study), but no age-related change for the German samples.

Duty

The bottom of Table 3.1 presents results for the definition of duty from the general and the school study. In both studies, the task for the participant was identical. They were asked to complete the sentence "To have a duty means . . ." The data patterns from the general study and the school study are very similar. The majority of the German adolescents (67% and 80%, respectively) define duty by pointing to its binding nature. Duty includes that you have to do something. The binding nature or commitment is expressed by the very same words "you have to do something" or by a similar phrasing. Those German participants who do not point to commitment consider duty to involve obligation and responsibility (e.g., "it means to accept responsibility" and "to be responsible").

In sharp contrast, there is much more diversity about the criteria that identify duty among the Koreans. In the general study, propriety (30%) is as important as the binding nature (24%) and obligation and responsibility (28%). But the strong emphasis on propriety has not been replicated in the school sample (only 12%). In that study, commitment was the most salient attribute of duty (41%), although not at the same rate as in the German sample (80%). The age-specific results show that in the school study commitment was particularly salient among 10th-grade students (59%), a fact the may be explained by the particular situation of 10th graders in Korea. Tenth graders much more than 6th and 8th graders are under strong pressure from families and teachers to learn from morning to night, to do homework and take tests, and to achieve at school. School success, depending on commitment, in fact means for Korean students to behave properly. It is through academic achievement that you "pay back" to your parents all that they have invested in you. Thus, we suppose that for Korean adolescents, the propriety and binding-nature aspects of duty are very similar in the school context, and therefore propriety matters less in the school study.

Unlike the German participants, about 20% of the Koreans perceive duty as involving an increase in the scope of one's action. They express that enlargement by saying, "Duty means that one can do something" or by pointing to the reciprocity between duty and right, "If you have a duty, then you also have a right." Finally, for a small subgroup in both the general and school studies of the Korean samples (8% and 16%, respectively), but not for the German peers, respect and appreciation is a criterion for duty. The categories "enlargement of the scope of one's actions" and "respect and appreciation" have in common that the participant focuses on an increase of the self, either in terms of the actions or in terms of the person, when he or she reflects about duty.

The only criterion that is common to right and duty is the reference to obligation and responsibility. It is not only common to both concepts but also mentioned by a considerable number of the subgroups of both the Germans and the Koreans. For 27% (general study) and 16% (school study) of the young persons from Germany and for 28% (general study) and 33% (school study) of the young Koreans, to have a duty means in the first place to be responsible or to have an obligation. It is surprising that obligation and responsibility is associated with right for a similar rate of participants (21% and 15% of the Germans and 27% and 30% of the Koreans).

The Most Important Right and Duty

Right

In the general study, the participants were asked to nominate one after the other their five most important rights, and in the school study, we asked them to write down the five most important rights they hold as students. We had discovered in a preliminary analysis that the frequency distributions for the categories that we used to classify important rights were very similar for the most important right and for a summary score across the five most important rights. Readers should bear in mind these facts when they analyze the results in Table 3.2.

Obviously, the nomination task pushes into the fore an aspect that is not in the participants' focus during the definition task. Two out of three German adolescents nominated a basic or civil right as his or her most important right. Examples include "to believe in God," "freedom of speech," "to be happy," "peace," "freedom," "equality," "labor," and "the right to a say

TABLE 3.2
The Most Important Right and Duty Nominated by German and Korean Adolescents in the General and the School Study

Most important right and duty	General study		School study	
	Germany	Korea	Germany	Korea
	Right			
Self-determination (general and specific)	19	47***	15	20
Nurturance	8	5	6	11
Basic and civil rights	66	30***	69	27***
To be respected and appreciated	2	9*	2	4
Propriety or decency	2	9*	1	36***
	Duty			
To keep to laws, norms, and rules	9	10	18	9*
Special duties (at home and in school)	30	5***	21	3***
School attendance	43	17***	37	12***
Learning and growth of personality	3	42***	11	53***
Nurturance and care	12	20	8	7
Responsibility (also, to act responsively)	2	3	1	3
Propriety or decency	1	5	0	4

Note. All values represent percentages.
*$p < .05$. **$p < .01$. ***$p < .001$.

in a matter." In the school study, the category includes, to a large degree, basic and civil rights that are applied to the school (e.g., "fair marks," "objectivity," "equality," "the teacher should not have any favorite students," "right to criticize the teacher," "freedom of speech during the classes," "right to stay at home when ill," and "the teacher should not be allowed to be violent against the students").

For Korean adolescents, basic and civil rights are of some importance in both the general and the school context (30% and 27%, respectively), but they do not stand out. In the general study, self-determination exceeds basic and civil rights, and taken together respect and appreciation and propriety or decency total 18%. In the school study, the most important right as a student is propriety (36%), which exceeds basic and civil rights, and together self-determination and nurturance rights total 31%, also exceeding basic and civil rights.

The comparison of the different age groups in the German sample demonstrates that basic and civil rights become the most important rights during adolescence. In the general context, there is a significant increase from 33% in Grade 6 to 78% in Grade 8 to 86% in Grade 10, and for the students' rights, this category increases from 59% to 61% to 77%. In contrast, no age trend was observed for basic and civil rights in the Korean samples. The only significant age-related changes in the Korean samples were an increase in self-determination (from 5% to 13% to 20%) and a decline in propriety from 45% in 12- and 14-year-olds to 20% in 16-year-olds.

In sum, there are two significant differences between Germans' and Koreans' ideas of the most important rights. First, they emphasize different rights, and second, as in the definition task, once again we observe much more diversity in the Korean samples.

Duty

The bottom of Table 3.2 includes the results on the most important duties. Responsibility and propriety or decency have been nominated only at a very low rate. Nevertheless, we have included them in Table 3.2 to illustrate the contrast with the definition task (see Table 3.1).

To understand the data in Table 3.2, we should bear in mind that both the German and the Korean samples consisted of adolescent students and that the studies were carried out during classes. But why is the most important duty in both contexts for Germans "school attendance" and for Koreans "learning and growth of personality"? At a quick glance, school attendance and learning and growth of personality seem to be similar. But in fact, the categories are very different. School attendance ("you have to go to school day by day") points to the fact that there is a law or rule that you have to keep to. Students are forced by an external condition, the existence of a black-letter law, to attend school. In this respect, school attendance is similar to the categories "to keep to laws, norms, and rules" and "particular duties" (e.g., "to keep to the school rules," "to write tests," "to do homework," "to clean my room," and "to do housework"). The similar meanings of school attendance and keeping to laws and particular duties may explain why (with one exception) the data patterns for all three categories look the same: They are considered much more important by the German than by the Korean participants (with the exception of keeping to laws, norms, and rules in the general study).

For Korean adolescents, learning and the growth of personality is the most important single duty in both contexts (42% and 53%, respectively). Some examples may demonstrate the difference between learning (and growth of personality) and school attendance. The most frequent nomination in the learning category is simply "to learn." Other illustrations are "to be good at school," "to learn so that my parents may be proud of me," "to concentrate at school," and "to make efforts." The growth of personality aspect of this category is included in nominations like "to stay healthy," "to become a nice person," and "to become a tolerant and patient person." The examples illustrate that learning and growth of personality refers to an inner attitude or orientation and not to the external fact that the student has to go to school day by day. Today, Korean children and adolescents are socialized to the idea that their parents have invested all their efforts for the academic career of their children and that the children, in turn, should make all efforts to return the parents' love, care, and engagement. The best way to fulfill this task is by school achievement and an academic career. At the same time, returning the parents' investment means to behave properly. The fact that the willingness to learn means proper behavior for Korean students may explain why the category propriety or decency is not frequently nominated as the most important duty; it is included in nominations of the learning category.

Who Lays Down Rights and Duties?

Right

The superordinate categories that we have constructed to classify the participants' answers to the items "Who lays down your rights?" (in the general study) and "Who lays down your rights as a student?" overlap to a large degree (although they are not identical). Therefore, we have included in Table 3.3 the data from both the general and the school studies.

The percentages in Table 3.3 add up to more than 100% because in particular the German participants mentioned more than one person or institution. Reflecting about rights in general, German adolescents attribute the power to lay down their rights to their parents and to the legal, political, and administrative system. Within this group, 75% nominate parents and about the same percentage mention the administration and the political and legal system. Thus, typical answers are "my parents and the constitution" or "my parents, the state and youth laws." When asked to think about their rights as students, parents do not count any longer. In the eyes of German adolescents, their rights as students are laid down on the one hand by teachers and the head of the school and on the other hand by the administration and the political and the legal system. Therefore, we often find answers like "the teachers and the state" or, even more often, "the head of the school and the school administration." In general, German adolescents do not perceive themselves or other persons (with the exception of their parents in the general context and teachers or the head of the school in the school context) as significant creators of their rights.

Korean adolescents perceive the establishment of their rights in quite a contrary manner. In the case of rights in general, they focus on themselves or the extended family (more than 80%). In some respect, the role of the parents for Germans and the role of the family for Koreans are comparable. Even today, young Koreans experience important decisions in their life and the life of other family members as a family affair. Grandfathers and grandmothers may have more authority than their parents. In the school study, one difference between German and Korean participants is that Germans attribute power to the head of the school and Koreans, in contrast, to teachers. What remains as a really basic difference in both contexts is that the Koreans perceive themselves as the other important source of their right, whereas the Germans attribute the power to define and restrict rights to the

TABLE 3.3
Distribution of Answers for the Questions: "Who Lays Down Your Rights (Duties)?" (General Study) and "Who Lays Down Your Rights (Duties) as a Student?" (School Study)

	General study		School study	
Who lays down your rights (duties)?	Germany	Korea	Germany	Korea
	Right			
I myself	12	53***	2	43***
Parents	75	18***		
Other persons (e.g., family) excluding parents	7	29***		
Other persons including parents			6	13
Teachers, head of the school	18	5**		
Teachers			27	45**
School, head of the school			41	10***
Institutions and administration	24	2***	51	5***
The state, government, and the law(s)	44	3***	34	1***
Society, tradition, and norms	11	11	2	8*
	Duty			
I myself	21	52***	2	52***
Parents	83	18***		
Other persons (e.g., family) excluding parents	8	28***		
Other persons including parents			14	13
Teachers, head of the school	25	5***		
Teachers			38	30
School, head of the school			43	14***
Institutions and administration	10	3*	41	6***
The state, government, and the law(s)	32	5***	24	2***
"Society", tradition, norms	11	12	2	10**

Note. All values represent percentages.
$^{*}p < .05$. $^{**}p < .01$. $^{***}p < .001$.

social world and its constructions (i.e., state, government, law, and administration). To summarize, German adolescents perceive the sources of their rights in the personal and institutional environment, and Koreans perceive the origin in other persons and in themselves.

Duty

The data for the establishment of duties look like a copy of the results for the right issue (see Table 3.3, bottom). The classification scheme is identical and, with a few negligible exceptions, the pattern of the results is very similar. For the most part, German adolescents assume that their duties in general are laid down both by their parents and by the state and law, public institutions, or the administration. In contrast, Koreans attribute their duties either to themselves (in the first place) or to parents and the family. When asked to think about their duties as students, the German students name teachers and the school and political and administrative forces, like the state, the government, school administration, and the law. Korean adolescents point primarily to themselves and secondarily to teachers and the school head.

In another item on the questionnaire, we asked the participants to tell us who lays down the rights and duties of adults and of teachers. The basic difference between the data for the German and Korean participants reoccurred. For rights in general, 91% of the German and only 7% of the Korean adolescents mentioned the political or legislative power or the administration, whereas 82% of the Korean and only 15% of the German participants answered "the adults themselves." The results looked very similar for the establishment of the rights of teachers and the duties of adults and teachers.

The Same Rights and Duties for Adolescents and Adults (for Students and Teachers)?

Rights and Duties in the General Study

When asked about rights and duties in general, 87% and 96% of the Germans agree that "It is okay that I do not have the rights (duties) of adults." In the Korean sample, the rate of agreement is 57% and 80%. We also asked the participants to give reasons why it is okay. The answers were categorized into the categories presented in the top of Table 3.4.

The main reason for Korean adolescents (60% and 47%, respectively) to find it all right that they do not have the same rights and duties as adults is the difference in age or status. Typical answers are "because I am too young," "because I am not grown up," "because there are things that young persons can do, but there are others that they should not do," and "because my parents demand it." In particular, the last example is not found in the German justifications, although some of them also mention age and status differences (see Table 3.4). For Koreans, to stick to age or status is an expression of propriety. Therefore, we may conclude that propriety justifies for Korean adolescents to a considerable extent why they should not hold the same rights and duties as adults.

About half of the German participants (47% and 57%, respectively) justify the differences between adults' and adolescents' rights and duties by pointing to the lack of competences (and resources). They argue that "I can not behave responsibly"; "I am too impulsive"; "I have no stable value orientation"; and "I have no income" (in the case of duties). Although the lack of competencies and resources is only the second most important reason for the Korean adolescents, they mention it as often as the Germans when justifying differences in rights. But in the case of duties, it is nominated twice as often by Germans as by Koreans. For Germans, the third most significant reason

TABLE 3.4
Distribution for the Reasons That Were Mentioned in the General Study and in the School Study (Bottom) to Justify Different Rights and Duties for Adolescents and Adults (Students and Teachers)

It is okay that I have not the same rights (duties) as adults (teachers) because...	Rights		Duties	
	Germany	Korea	Germany	Korea
General study				
Age or status differences (in Korea, propriety)	29	60***	17	47***
Lack of competencies and resources	47	45	57	25***
Negative consequences	27	6**	13	7
Reciprocity of rights and duties "because my duties (rights) also differ"	6	3	8	8
"Because I already have enough duties"			3	9
School study				
Age or status differences (in Korea, propriety)	6	26**	5	13*
Different tasks or roles of teachers versus students	16	37*	34	62***
Teachers' superior experiences and competences	11	23	16	10
Consideration of expediency	37	17***	4	1
Respect and appreciation	19	3***	2	1
Strains and restrictions for the student	9	0**	37	5***
Reciprocity of rights and duties "because my duties (rights) also differ"	11	9	5	8

Note. All values represent percentages. The distributions are based only on the subsamples of those participants who agreed that different rights for adolescents and adults (students and teachers) are okay.
$^{*}p < .05$. $^{**}p < .01$. $^{***}p < .001$.

why adolescents and adults should have different rights and duties is that negative consequences might occur if no distinctions were made. For rights, this category is used significantly more often by the German participants (27%) than by the Korean participants (6%).

In sum, Korean adolescents tend to refer to the rules of proper behavior to justify differences between adults' and adolescents' rights and duties, whereas their German peers more often consider the qualifications (competences and resources) or the consequences of equal rights and duties.

Rights and Duties in the School Study

In the school study 73% and 91% of the German participants agreed that "it is okay that students do not have the same rights (duties) as teachers." The rates of agreement in the Korean samples were significantly lower:

55% and 72%. The bottom of Table 3.4 gives an overview of the justifications for agreement.

The number of categories in Table 3.4 demonstrates that the reasons mentioned to justify different rights and duties for teachers and students are much more varied than the reasons for differences between adolescents' and adults' rights and duties in general. Still, the same basic distinction in the perspectives of Korean and German adolescents as in the general study can be seen.

In contrast to the Germans, the Koreans put much more emphasis on age and status, and they refer more often to the different roles or tasks that teachers and students have at school, which includes propriety (see the preceding discussion). These differences are consistent across rights and duties. Here are some examples for justifications by role, task, or status: "because we have to learn," "because the teacher has the right to teach us," "because I am only a student," and "because teachers have the right to teach us, and we have the right to learn." Two out of three Koreans give reasons like these examples when arguing about rights, and three out of four mention similar reasons for different duties.

To justify differences between adolescents' and adults' rights, German adolescents point to (a) consideration of expediency (37%) and (b) respect and appreciation of teachers (19%). Consideration of expediency is of some importance for Koreans (17%), but the rate is significantly lower (see Table 3.4). To illustrate the categories of expediency and respect and appreciation, we offer some examples for consideration of expediency: "otherwise learning would be impossible"; "because students cannot learn without pressure"; and "otherwise, chaos!" Following are examples for respect and appreciation of teachers: "because teachers should be respected," "because it must be possible for teachers to punish students when they have not done their homework," and "because teachers are respected persons." The examples illustrate that respect and appreciation does not mean that the students grant more rights to the teachers because they are in fact highly respected and appreciated. In most cases, it means that differences in rights are necessary to establish or guarantee the student's respect and appreciation for the teacher. Thus, respect and appreciation shares with consideration of expediency a focus on usefulness and appropriateness.

In justification of different duties for teachers and adolescents, the German students switch from expediency, respect, and appreciation to strains and restrictions that duties would bring along for them. Our data show that 37% argue from this point of view against equal duties (vs. 5% in Korean students).

Evidently, young persons from Korea take into consideration proper behavior and conventions (role and status) when they compare their own rights and duties with those of adults and teachers. Role and status is of some relevance for the German participants, too, in particular when they think about duties. But contrary to the Koreans, they also take into consideration the negative consequences of equal duties and the usefulness and appropriateness of unequal rights for students and teachers.

DISCUSSION

The Construction of Right and Duty in Different Cultures

At the center of our discussion is the question whether the concepts of right and duty are constructed in the same way by adolescents living in very different cultures. Although some of the conclusions for the right and duty concept are similar, we discuss them separately, starting with the right concept.

Right

Citizens around the world construe rights simultaneously in similar and different terms. This is the most impressive single result from our questionnaire study, at least if we generalize from citizens in Germany and Korea to citizens around the world. Our questionnaire study assessed four strictly different aspects of rights and duties: defining characteristics of the concepts, nomination of one's most important rights and duties, authority to lay down rights and duties, and reasons for unequal rights for adolescents (students) and adults (teachers). In each item, we not only found statistically significant differences but, what is much more important, we also observed enormous differences at the descriptive level.

Common to the understanding of rights in young persons from Korea and Germany are the concepts of self-determination and obligation and responsibility. Self-determination in our study relates to the experience of autonomy and power (in the sense of control) and to the simple statement, "To have a right means that I can do what I want to do." This category names an important aspect of the Koreans' concept, and it is of some importance to the Germans' concept. The understanding of right in both cultures also includes, to some degree, obligation and responsibility, a fact that indicates an awareness of the interrelation between rights and duties.

There is one constant, distinctive feature that separates the German idea qualitatively from the Korean concept. For Germans, right is connected to the outer conditions of one's actions. To hold a right, for the Germans, means in the first place to be permitted to do something, that their actions are legal, and that no one can therefore restrict their scope of action. The scope is guaranteed through basic and civil rights that are guaranteed or have been laid down by a legal, political, or administrative authority (or a person in charge of an institution).

For Koreans, on the other hand, the concept of right primarily relates to the inner experiences that derive from holding a right: the feelings of obligation and responsibility, the experience of being respected and appreciated, and feelings associated with the strongly internalized norm of propriety. As a reminder, we mention the outstanding fact that one out of three Korean students mentions as his most important right (!) at school to behave properly.

The different orientation of the view of rights, inward in Koreans and outward in Germans, fits into the different cultural backgrounds that we have described previously. In the individualistic culture of the West, the enhancement and development of the individual is highly respected. Rights are construed to protect this sphere of individual freedom and self-actualization. The emphasis on the outer conditions of one's actions may be understood as recognition of this sphere (or space) of freedom. Thus, we conclude that we have indeed observed a deep cultural difference in the understanding of rights between the so-called individualistic and collectivistic cultures and not only a difference between persons from two nations.

Duty

The differences between the duty concepts of German and Korean adolescents are even larger than between the right concepts. The sense of obligation and responsibility that is included for some of the participants in the understanding of duty is the only commonality between both groups. For the overwhelming majority of the Germans, duty means simply that you have to do something. This is similar to their understanding of rights, because the focus is on one's scope of action and its restriction from the outside, as we can see from the nomination of the most important duty. The German adolescents name school attendance, special duties at home, and the keeping of laws and rules; that is, they think of duties as a force that exists as a matter of law (school attendance) or by interpersonal expectations from parents or teachers (duties at home and at school).

Korean adolescents, on the other hand, put into the fore the inner experience that is connected with having a duty: obligation and responsibility, respect and appreciation, and propriety (feelings that derive from acting according to roles, norms, and expectations). There is one single duty that dominates in Koreans: the duty to learn. As we have already pointed out, the duty to learn is strictly different from the duty to attend school. Learning is more an obligation and responsibility than a duty because it is an attitude that derives from the effort to live in accordance with the value of filial piety.

The data on the question of who decides about one's duty support the dominant distinction between an inward gaze on one's rights and duties in a collectivistic culture like Korea and a view to the outward conditions on one's action in an individualistic country like Germany. About half of the Korean adolescents perceive themselves as establishers of their own rights and duties. This holds both in general and in the school context. In contrast, Germans focus on the outer forces that establish their duties and rights: the government, the law, and the administration, that is, on those authorities that in fact lay down the limits of their actions.

Are Commonsense Concepts of Rights and Duties More Than Copies of Formal Black-Letter Law Rights and Duties?

The plain conclusion that follows from our data is that commonsense notions both in the individualistic and in the collectivistic cultures indeed cover more ground than the formal black-letter concepts. At the same time, the overlap between black-letter concepts and commonsense ideas is much larger in the West than in East Asia. We once more focus on the issues of the most important rights and duties and on the establishment of rights and duties. Two out of three Germans nominate a basic or civil right as their most important, and if we include nurturance rights into the superordinate category of black-letter law, about three out of four Germans think about their top right in terms of the law. But the conclusion is different when we inspect the authorities that lay down the rights. In the case of general rights, parents are mentioned more often than the legal, societal, and political authorities. Turning from rights to duties, duties from law are often mentioned as the most important duties (to obey laws and school attendance). But the most important authorities in establishing duties are parents and teachers, and we do not think that parents and teachers are perceived as representatives of the law.

Black-letter rights, in the sense of basic and civil rights, come into mind for only a minority of the Korean adolescents as most important, and the same is true for black-letter duties. At least in the case of duties, the minor importance is not based on the fact that fewer black-letter duties exist for young Koreans. In fact, there are many more, in particular in the school context. Therefore, we may conclude that the minor salience of black-letter duties (and rights) results mainly from the fact that through the internalization of informal moral duties the Korean culture draws the attention away from black-letter law.

Contextual Influences

In the preceding paragraphs we have pointed to cultural influences on adolescents' understanding of rights and duties. Let us now turn to context influences that we have studied through the additional assessment of rights and duties in the school context. It is clear that the cultural differences occurred consistently in both contexts. This is evidence for the fundamental nature of cultural differences in the understanding of rights and duties. Context effects are, in general, smaller than cultural differences, and the context sharpened or leveled cultural differences. The sharpening effect is most evident in the reasons that the adolescents gave for unequal rights. The school context brings out very clearly that German adolescents argue against equal rights with rational, utilitarian arguments, whereas Koreans focus much more on the age, status, and role differences between student and teachers, that is, on arguments linked to proper behavior. Rationality and utility are the very ideas behind the legitimization of black-letter law in individualistic countries (see the description of individualism in Triandis, 1995).

CONCLUSION

The goals of our study were limited to description. Through the description of the ideas of right and duty in German and Korean adolescents we have shown that the commonsense concepts have different meanings for young Germans and Koreans. At least some of the differences may be related to cultural background, for example, to Confucian ideas of propriety and filial piety in the East Asian sample or to the rational and utilitarian understanding of laws and society in the West. Therefore, we assume that what we identified are cultural influences on the everyday understanding of right and duty. We have also demonstrated that intracultural context variations (general context vs. school context) are of minor importance as compared to culture. Only in passing have we mentioned some developmental data such as how the concepts change between 12 and 16 years of age. To explain how the culture-specific meanings enter into the individual meaning systems during ontogenesis, we need explanatory work, for example, longitudinal studies and microgenetic analysis (e.g., Case, 1998; Rogoff, 1998).

A similar limitation holds for the adolescents' task to integrate the early interpersonal concepts of rights and duties that have been acquired during childhood with the later awareness of rights and duties as important dimensions of the relationship between individuals and society. Our results demonstrate that both components, the interpersonal and the societal, are tacitly involved in German and Korean concepts, but at least at the surface, the social–institutional dimension is more salient for the German adolescents (e.g., see the data on the authority who establishes rights and duties). Again, the data that we have presented are only descriptive. Further research should concentrate on the very process of the integration of both the interpersonal and the societal aspects throughout childhood and adolescence.

Finally, the future study of the cultural acquisition of the concepts of right and duty during childhood and adolescence demands interdisciplinary work. Keeping in mind the very nature of Havighurst's concept of a developmental task, for a full understanding of the acquisition process we have to consider both the inner and the outer sources of development and to work on an integrated picture. The inner sources traditionally fall into the psychologists' domain, and the outer sources have been analyzed by ethnologists (e.g., Geertz, 1975), philosophers of law (e.g., Dworkin, 1986), and culture theorists (e.g., Taylor, 1989), but integrative ideas can only result from cooperation between disciplines.

REFERENCES

Adelson, J., Green, B., & O'Neil, R. (1969). Growth of the idea of law in adolescence. *Developmental Psychology, 1*, 327–332.

Adelson, J., & O'Neil, R. P. (1966). Growth of political ideas in adolescence: The sense of community. *Journal of Personality and Social Psychology, 4*, 295–306.

Case, R. (1998). The development of conceptual structures. In D. Kuhn & R. S. Siegler (Eds.), *Handbook of child psychology: Vol. 2. Cognition, perception, and language* (pp. 745–800). New York: Wiley.

Cha, J.-H. (1980). The personality and consciousness of the Korean people [*Hankukineo inseongkwa eosik*]. In S. B. Han, J. H. Cha, M.Y. Lee, C. Yang, B. M. Ahn, & Y. K. Shin (Eds.), *Studies of the continuity and change of a culture* (pp. 6–58). Seoul: Korean Social Science Research Council.

Cha, J.-H. (1994). Aspects of individualism and collectivism in Korea. In U. Kim, H. C. Triandis, C. Kagitcibasi, S.-C. Choi, & G. Yoon (Eds.), *Individualism and collectivism: Theory, methods, and applications* (pp. 157–174). London: Sage.

Connell, R.W. (1971). *The child's construction of politics*. Melbourne, Australia: Melbourne University Press.

Dworkin, R. (1986). *Law's empire*. Cambridge, MA: Harvard University Press.

Geertz, C. (1975). Common sense as a cultural system. *The Antioch Review, 33*, 5–26.

Havighurst, R. J. (1948). *Developmental tasks and education*. New York: McKay.

Hofstede, G. (1980). *Culture's consequences*. Beverly Hills, CA: Sage.

Hoppe-Graff, S., & Kim, H.-O. (2000). Verstehen, Konsens und Kenntnis der Lebenswelt im interkulturellen Diskurs [Understanding, agreement, and knowledge of the "Lebenswelt" in intercultural discourse]. *Ethik und Sozialwissenschaften, 11*, 382–384.

Hoppe-Graff, S. & Kim, H.-O. (2001). Struktur, Kultur und Entwicklung [Structure, culture, and development]. In S. Hoppe-Graff & A. Rümmele (Eds.), *Entwicklung als Strukturgenese* (pp. 333–360). Hamburg, Germany: Kovac.

Hoppe-Graff, S., Latzko, B., Engel, I., Hesse, I., Mainka, A., & Waller, M. (1998). Lehrerautorität: Aus der Sicht der Schüler [Teacher authority: The students' view]. In N. Seibert (Hrsg.), *Erziehungsschwierigkeiten im Unterricht* (pp. 127–160). Bad Heilbrunn, Germany: Klinkhardt.

Kohlberg, L. (1984). *Essays on moral development: Vol. 2. The psychology of moral development*. San Francisco: Harper & Row.

Kuechler, M. (1993). Political attitudes and behavior in Germany: The making of a democratic society. In A. S. Huelshoff, A. S. Markovits, & S. Reich (Eds.), *From Bundesrepublik to Deutschland* (pp. 33–58). Ann Arbor: University of Michigan.

Melton, G. B. (1980). Children's concepts of their rights. *Journal of Clinical Child Psychology*, 9, 186–190.

Moshman, D. (1999). *Adolescent psychological development: Rationality, morality and identity*. Mahwah, NJ: Erlbaum.

Rogoff, B. (1998). Cognition as a collaborative process. In D. Kuhn & R. S. Siegler (Eds.), *Handbook of child psychology: Vol. 2. Cognition, perception, and language* (pp. 679–744). New York: Wiley.

Ruck, M. D., Abramovitch, R., & Keating, D. P. (1998). Children's and adolescents' understanding of rights: Balancing nurturance and self-determination. *Child Development*, 64, 404–417.

Selman, R. L. (1980). *The growth of interpersonal understanding*. New York: Academic Press.

Taylor, C. (1989). *Sources of the self: The making of modern identity*. Cambridge, MA: Harvard University Press.

Triandis, H. C. (1995). *Individualism and collectivism*. Boulder, CO: Westview Press.

4

TOWARD A CULTURAL THEORY OF RIGHTS AND DUTIES IN HUMAN DEVELOPMENT

FATHALI M. MOGHADDAM AND CARA JOY RILEY

"Let the jury consider their verdict," the King said, for about the twentieth time that day.
"No, no!" said the Queen. "Sentence first—verdict afterwards."
"Stuff and nonsense!" said Alice loudly. "The idea of having the sentence first!"

—Lewis Carroll (1960, p. 161)

Trials, as even the child Alice knows, follow well-established legal guidelines, and we learn about these formal rules and laws that are "on the books" in numerous ways. Black-letter law is extensive in its scope, explicit, and widely publicized and accessible (e.g., Alvarado, 1999), particularly in modern Western societies, and growing increasingly so at the international level. However, black-letter law does not always provide an effective avenue for understanding *commonsense rights and duties* (after Finkel, 1995), those rights and duties in informal, everyday social life. Unlike the explicit and publicly acknowledged nature of formal rights and duties, commonsense rights and duties remain, for the most part, implicit. The research of symbolic interactionists, ethnomethodologists, ethnogenicists,[1] and others in microsociology and social psychology traditions (see Moghaddam & Harré, 1995) has highlighted numerous rules regulating social relationships in everyday life, and underlying such rules are informal rights and duties, such as those operating in family relations, as in "Mary, the oldest child, can drive the station wagon," and "Joe, the youngest child, must take out the trash."

Some attention has been given, albeit indirectly, to rights and duties in the lives of children as part of a much larger body of literature on moral development and the acquisition of rules by children (Bennett, 1993; Eckensberger & Zimba, 1997). Rules pertaining to a broad array of domains in the lives of children have been studied, including chores and responsibilities in everyday family life (Goodnow, 1988), disagreements with siblings and violations in the rights of the self and others (Ross, Filyer, Lollis, Perlman, & Martin, 1994), and also differences between children and parents in the types of rules emphasized in relationships (Piotrowski, 1997). However, there is need for more attention to be given specifically to the development of commonsense rights and duties among children, and particularly the learning of certain practices by children that can be interpreted through culture as involving rights and duties.

Our point of departure in this discussion is the proposition that well before children learn about formal law or about rights and duties as abstract ideas, they learn to carry out certain *primitive social relations*, or universal social behaviors such as turn taking that are essential for the survival of a child, and these are later interpreted for children as involving rights or duties, depending on cultural conditions. For example, children learn to practice turn taking in conversations, and later they learn that a person can have a right or a duty to a turn to speak. Rights and duties, we argue, are not so much complementary as they are replaceable: A right can become a duty, and a duty can become a right depending on cultural conditions. However, there are a few exceptions to this general "law."

The relationship between children and adults, and particularly parents, is characterized by change. Children grow older, and the rules and norms for correct behavior appropriate to them continually change. The rules and norms that apply to a 5-year-old do not necessarily apply to a 9-year-old. This ambiguity is associated with tension, as well as potential or actual conflict about rules and norms for correct behavior for children. In such situations of flux, we argue, the child gives priority to rights that push the envelope in the hope of increasing freedom ("I want to play with my friends and stay up until 10 tonight"); parents, however, give priority to duties that restrict behavior ("No, tomorrow is a school day and you have to finish your home work and go to bed by 9").

We argue that the relationship between children and parents reflects a much broader trend, whereby in relationships characterized by potential or

---

[1]Symbolic interactionists study mediating processes in everyday social interaction; ethnomethodologists study the creation of moment-by-moment interpersonal order; ethnogenicists study the dynamic structure of interpersonal episodes.

actual conflict, those with less or equal power give priority to their personal rights and those who enjoy greater power give priority to the duties of those underneath. Thus, shared constructions or *interobjectivity* (Moghaddam, 2003) is limited by different power positions. This is particularly so in times of change, when rules and norms become ambiguous. For example, a variety of minority movements, including those involving African Americans and women, highlighted demands for equal rights during the 1960s, a time of social, economic, and political change. Majority group representatives and central authorities gave priority to the duties of the less powerful, such as the duty of everyone to obey existing laws, which of course supported the status quo.

This chapter is divided into two major sections. In the first section, we outline a cultural theory of the development of rights and duties. Our goal is to explore the development of children with reference to some particular types of rights and duties arising from particular primitive social relations. Thus, in the present discussion we are not concerned with all the possible varieties of rights and duties. In the second section, we discuss three empirical studies as examples of research on central aspects of our theory. Studies 1 and 2 explore attitudes among samples of American and Iranian adults toward the rights and duties of adults and children. We postulate that adults will give priority to the duties of children but will give priority to the rights of adults. These two studies highlight certain fundamental differences in the way rights and duties are applied to adults and children, thus focusing on discontinuity rather than continuity in the world of adults and children. Study 3 involves American, Chinese, and Russian adult samples and highlights cross-cultural similarities in certain features of rights and duties, in contrast to the traditional bias toward highlighting cross-cultural differences (Moghaddam, Taylor, & Wright, 1993). In this study, we test the proposition that in relationships that are potentially or actually adversarial, rights will be given greater priority, whereas in less adversarial relationships duties are emphasized more.

THEORETICAL BACKGROUND

We begin by noting there are as yet few universals in the domain of formal law and rights and duties of the child. Despite some efforts to establish universal formal law standards, there continue to be major differences across cultures on basic questions, such as the chronological age definition of a child. Second, where there are attempts to establish universals, commonsense law intrudes in major ways. For example, Section C of Article 29 of the United Nations Convention on the Rights of the Child (accepted by the United Nations General Assembly on November 20, 1989) states that the education of the child shall be directed to, among other things, the develop-

Nature of constraints	Universal consequences	Behavior of individual
Biological condition	Innate capacity	Imitating
Functional condition	Primitive social relation	Turn taking
Cultural condition	Interpretation of actions	Practicing rights or duties

Figure 4.1. Schematic representation of the development of rights and duties.

ment of respect for his or her own cultural identity and the national values of the country in which the child is living. Clearly, this gives high priority to local practices, which in some cases directly conflict with democratic values and supports rather than challenges cultural variation. Our move toward a cultural theory of rights and duties of children acknowledges the powerful impact of the same cultural practices.

Toward a Cultural Theory

Our goal in this section is to move toward a cultural theory of the development of rights and duties by outlining the basic elements of a theory that depicts behavior as constrained by three different types of conditions with each type of condition leading to a different type of universal consequence and individual act (see Figure 4.1).

Clearly, not all cultural and functional conditions arise out of biological constraints, but given the necessity to be selective in our discussion, we focused on a major example that clearly is linked to biological constraints. The individual acts we have selected as a focus for our discussion are *imitation*, an innate capacity arising out of biological condition; *turn taking*, a socially learned primitive social relation arising out of functional condition; and *practicing rights and duties*, a cultural activity arising from the interpretation of actions circumscribed by cultural conditions (Figure 4.1). Using these specific examples, we formulate arguments for the following propositions:

1. Common to the human experience are a number of biological and functional conditions that give rise to primitive social practices, social behaviors that are universal and essential for the survival of individuals.
2. The development of language in children is associated with the learning of cultural interpretations of primitive social relations, such as turn taking, as involving rights and duties.

3. In relationships that are (a) changing, so that the norms and rules of behavior are uncertain or (b) adversarial, so that conflict is actual or very possible, those with equal or less power will give priority to rights and those who enjoy greater power will give priority to duties.

Proposition 1

Human beings everywhere have been confronted by a number of basic common challenges arising out of the interaction between their biological makeup and their physical environment. One of the most important of such challenges has been to develop means through which useful knowledge and skills can be effectively communicated to others, particularly from parents to children. In this regard, language has served a unique function. However, other means have been developed that are available even before the development of language, imitation being chief among these. Imitation shares with language the feature of turn taking: Turn taking arises from imitation and leads to the development of language.

In the last two decades of the 20th century a fundamental shift took place in how researchers conceptualized the role of imitation in human development (Nadel & Butterworth, 1999). Although earlier research hinted at this new direction (Zazzo, 1957), the impetus for the more recent change was a series of pioneering studies demonstrating that newborns only a few minutes old can imitate certain adult facial and gestural behaviors (Meltzoff & Moore, 1977, 1983). Imitation was shown to be an innate human capacity, not dependent on mechanisms envisaged in Piagetian, Skinnerian, Freudian, or other major models. Given the recent dominance of Piaget's stage model, it is particularly important that deferred imitation, in which infants reenact behavior on the basis of their representation of the past, has been shown in 6-week-olds (Meltzoff & Moore, 1994) and 6-month-olds (Barr, Dowden, & Hayne, 1996), posing a very strong challenge to the Piagetian idea of a shift from sensorimotor to representational functioning at 18 months of age.

A major implication of the "new look" research on imitation in infancy is that the demarcation between sensorimotor, cognitive, and social development, as well as the notion of developmental stages, is in major ways flawed (see also Moghaddam, 2002). Such traditional classifications may help researchers categorize and label behavior in a way that seems "neat," but actual behavior does not fit into such convenient boxes. With this viewpoint, we turn to consider the development of turn taking.

We argue that turn taking is not itself innate but builds on imitation, an innate capacity. Second, turn taking appears very soon after imitation, and certainly within the first six months of life. Imitation involves alternation (see reports in Nadel & Butterworth, 1999). At the simplest level, only one turn takes place: For example, a mother makes a facial gesture and the infant imitates. When additional steps are added, turn taking takes place: For example, a mother makes a facial gesture, the infant imitates, then the mother repeats the same gesture, the infant imitates again, and so on. We have known for some time that such turn-taking sequences play an important role in the development of communications skills, even before verbal communications (Brazelton & Tronick, 1980). Next, we consider in greater detail what seems to happen when infants take turns and the cultural interpretation of such turn taking.

Proposition 2

Children learn to participate in certain primitive social relations before they can truly conceptualize the idea of rights and duties. These social relations are essential for the successful functioning of children and in the course of development become understood by children within the format of rights and duties. One such primitive social relation is turn taking. Turn taking appears early in a child's development and is vital to acquiring language, which is itself an absolute necessity to functional competency. Learning to communicate involves first mastering such alternation, with the later addition to that basic construction of language structure, rules, and appropriate social use. The knowledge of these factors depends largely on the child's progressive procurement of the cultural interpretations of the rights and duties involved, for example, understanding that a person may or may not have a right to speak. This process evolves as an integral part of the learning of communications skills in both informal (e.g., family) and formal (e.g., day-care and school) settings.

The Centrality of Turn Taking in Adult Life. Turn taking is central to human behavior, as evidenced by the literature on social linguistics, at both the adult level and the developmental level. Research in the adult realm primarily concerns the characteristics of successful communication, and turn taking is considered essential to the process. Research suggests that to manage the taking of speaking turns and thereby to communicate effectively, there exists a routine communication mechanism (e.g., Duncan, 1972). This mechanism is arbitrated through behavioral cues, which, in turn, are governed by rules. The rules vary by culture, but the act of turn taking is universal. Two of the most common rules for successful dialogue are first not to interrupt the speaker (alternation or turn taking) and second to maintain continuity in the subject matter of the conversation (coherence) (Collis, 1985). Adult communication is thus characterized by smooth coordination, as there is an orderly alternation of speaking with little overlapping speech or hesitation. Nonverbal signals such as making eye contact may aid in this process. Usually, speakers look away when they begin speaking, and then at the end of their utterance, they tend to look at the auditor, showing that they are finished and the listener may now have a turn. In between, brief glances at the auditor are made looking for feedback, and the auditor signals his or her attention with long, steady gazes (Rutter & Durkin, 1987). Such actions as gesticulation, changes in pitch and loudness, head movement, pausing, and audible inhalation have also been implicated as signals to coordinate alternation (Duncan, 1974). In this manner, the ability to communicate effectively in adult conversations requires the mastery of turn taking.

The Development of Turn-Taking Skills. Linguistics research also suggests that the learning of alternation begins early in life during mother–infant interaction (Barrett, 1985). The ability to cooperate in such a way is crucial to social development as a whole, and interacting with one's parents is fundamental in building this skill. The rudiments of turn taking can be established as early as six weeks of age as infants interact with adults. These exchanges, or *protoconversations* (Collis, 1985), tend to include brief vocalizations, gazing, and head and postural movement. From such interactions single-word speech and then full-blown verbal exchanges may develop. The fact that parents and their babies commonly exhibit coordinated sequences of vocalizations and gazes, even from the earliest weeks of life, is generally attributed to the skill of the parent in molding his or her own behavior to that of the infant rather than to a genuine reciprocity between the two. That is, mothers tend to structure the interactions with their children through their own vocalizations, which also serve as reinforcement and motivation for the infants to partake more actively in the exchanges. Moreover, mothers who respond contingently to their children, paying attention to what the infant is focused on or involved with, have children with a greater range of referential and symbolic language skills (Reissland & Stephenson, 1999). Similar trends have been found with parent–infant gazes, and generally, during the early stages of the infant's life the behavior depends on the action of the mother. In the child's second year, a pattern of development similar to the action of adults emerges wherein infants use the *terminal gaze* to signal the end of their turn as well as begin to interrupt less often (Rutter & Durkin, 1987). By the third year, children are quite active in controlling their exchanges with parents, having mastered the art of alternation.

The Cultural Interpretation of Turn Taking and Language Practices. Clearly, turn taking is essential to parent–child interactions as well as adult conversations. Simultaneous speaking is highly detrimental to communication, for it obscures the meaning of what each player is saying. Alternation is thus a fundamental and universal rule of communication on which other not necessarily universal rules of communication build. Conversation gains meaning from these rules with the qualification that they must be consensually held. The rules applied in communication are used to encode and decode the input of the conversation, and culturally created symbols and symbol systems aid this process. Symbols carry the information to be communicated as well as manage the use of the rules to be applied with the goal of evoking the correct interpretation by the receiver of the message. In this way, to successfully communicate, there must be an agreement between parties about what symbols signify in a particular context. The meaning varies between cultures and groups and must be taught to children through imitation and experience. The effective use of symbols depends on turn taking, for when one conversationalist uses a symbol, she or he expects a certain rule-governed response from the other, which she or he will respond to in turn (Cushman & Whiting, 1972). Using communication rules effectively therefore depends on internalizing the cultural interpretation of those rules, such as turn taking, and involves grasping the idea that such rules involve rights and duties. For example, one conversationalist has a duty to defer a speaking turn to the other, who has a right to speak next.

A working knowledge of alternation, among other linguistic rules, is a rudimentary part of communication (Schegloff, 2000). In acquiring language, however, a child must learn more than such constructions. She or he must ascertain when and where certain communication routines are appropriate, which varies by culture. The cultural difference in attitudes toward speaking freely is an example. In some cultures, certain members of the population are denied the right to speak their mind, whereas in others, the right to voice one's opinion is considered a basic privilege.

To take an extreme example, in India untouchables would not have a right to speak unless spoken to in the presence of individuals from higher castes. To take a more widespread example, consider the practice of free speech. Although the right to speak freely on political matters is accepted as normative in most Western societies, this right is in practice denied to several billion people around the world, including those in communist states such as China and Islamic states such as Iran. Individuals are socialized from an early age to function according to such local normative systems, so that a child is taught what to say and when in private and public domains. Part of this socialization involves learning rights and duties involved in such practices as turn taking and the application of communication rules. This socialization therefore includes the development of specific language routines, which, once learned, lend to socially appropriate behavior.

Another example of language routines is saying "thank you" at the closing of conversations. Thanking is a politeness convention, and caregivers give special attention to teaching children the appropriate use of thanking. How and when to initiate or accept a thank you, that is, the rights and duties of thanking, varies cross-culturally (Aston, 1995), although the need for such politeness is universal. The differences in thanking style stem, in part, from cultural differences in the perception of relative power, social distance, and degree of indebtedness. However, thanking also plays a role in directing conversation, which relates to turn taking. That is, saying "thank you" appropriately can serve to bring to a close the current topic, to make possible the (re)introduction of additional topics, and to temporarily bring turn taking to a close. Thus, thanking is motivated not only by situational factors but also by the need to manage the conversation. The preference for certain procedures over others inherent in such management also varies by culture, for example, preferences regarding the use of turn taking. Children learn these skills through observation and experience and then later understand them to involve rights and duties as they internalize the social appropriateness of the acts. That is to say, in thanking someone, the speaker has a duty to thank and the auditor a right to be thanked, and that understanding develops after the practice of thanking does itself, as influenced by the child's culture.

A study by Margaret Wilhite about end-of-meal routines further supports our proposition. The study involves the development of a language routine seen in Cakchiquel-speaking Indians in Guatemala (Wilhite, 1983). At the end of a meal when a person wishes to depart, he or she is expected to cross the arms in front of the chest, engage in eye contact with the person of highest status in the room, and say "thank you." The person addressed is then expected to respond, stating "God gave it to you." Eye contact is broken, and the person to depart repeats the routine with everyone else, in hierarchical order, according to Wilhite's study. The involvement of rights and duties in this procedure is clear, for the person departing has a duty to thank everyone in the correct manner and order, and the people to be thanked have a right to be acknowledged appropriately. Wilhite's research also showed that the routine as such develops progressively in young children, with the setting and nonverbal elements appearing first (crossing the arms and gazing), followed by the verbal elements (receptive response, then productive thanks, then productive response), and finally the socially appropriate use of the language routine (status hierarchy). These elements are governed largely by turn taking as they involve an action–response–counterresponse format. Children learn their duty to perform this specialized turn taking gradually, coming to a complete comprehension of the rights and duties inherent in the routine by the time they master the social rules of appropriate use. Wilhite also noted that parents concentrate mostly on coaching the more complex verbal-response and status-hierarchy elements, that is, the appropriate form of response and the appropriate order of turns, thus emphasizing the finer details of the child's duty to ensure that she or he will acquire the language routine correctly.

When a child acquires such rules and routines as delineated in the preceding paragraph, the child is socialized into the expectations of the culture and comes to grasp what is his or her duty to do in certain social situations. That is to say, using language appropriately in a wide variety of circumstances entails adhering to communication rules and routines and comprehending the rights and duties among the players involved. Children first seize upon the basic building blocks of language use, most important turn taking, and upon mastery of that structure. Next they develop the linguistic rules and routines that they have a further duty to perform before they can communicate successfully. Culture influences this comprehension, for what is a right or a duty in one place may not hold in another.

However, the significance of alternation extends well beyond the boundaries of linguistics; learning to take turns is a fundamental part of social development in general and typifies much of human behavior. It can be categorized as a primitive social relation necessary to successful existence in society as a whole, from mediating communication to regulating traffic. Indeed, turn taking is a universal of human behavior, although its practice is influenced by cultural interpretations. Once alternation has been elicited, it undergoes interpretation on the cultural level, being judged to involve rights or duties depending on the norms of the society. That process is certainly essential to the development of language but functions in other social contexts as well: Depending on the cultural ethos, people have a right to a turn, whether it be a turn to speak or a turn at the bank, and a duty to let others have theirs as well.

Proposition 3

Proposition 3 states that priority will be given to rights by those who have less or equal power in relationships that are changing or adversarial.

Child–Parent Relations as Characterized by Conflict and Change

Contemporary developmental science underscores the view that the world of the child is characterized by physical, social, cognitive, and other changes in the behavior of the child as well as by the relationships the child has with others (National Research Council, 2000). During the initial phase of this development, the child is completely dependent on adult caretakers; but very soon the child begins to assert some measure of independence and to embark on a struggle central to which are negotiations about resources, fairness, feelings of deprivation, and rights and duties.

From the perspective of a number of major theories, the developing child is in some ways in an adversarial relationship with parents and other authority figures. From a psychoanalytic perspective, the infant at least initially acts according to the pleasure principle, driven by instant gratification and maximum pleasure. In the language of rights and duties, infants give exclusive priority to their own rights, and directly or indirectly, to the duties of caretakers to serve them. But caretakers gradually place restrictions on infants, limiting and redirecting the ways in which they can attain pleasure. The process of education, then, involves harnessing the child's energies and directing the child toward duties rather than rights, which inevitably implies diminishing personal pleasure, "Unpleasure remains the only means of education" (Freud, 1886–1899/1966, p. 370). In this process, adults can be viewed as superiors and oppressors, "There is little that gives children greater pleasure than when a grown-up lets himself down to their level, renounces his oppressive superiority and plays with them as an equal" (Freud, 1905/1960, p. 227). Thus, from a psychoanalytic viewpoint, relationships between children and parents are in important ways antagonistic with the child as the less powerful of the combatants.

From a number of other theoretical perspectives, also, the parent–child relationship involves potential conflict. For example, parent–child conflict can be interpreted on the basis of realistic conflict theory (Sherif, 1966) regarding resources (Child: "I have to have that toy, buy me that toy." Parent: "We can't afford to buy you that, we need money for other things."); social identity theory (Tajfel & Turner, 1979) regarding the nature of social identity (Child: "I don't want to wear that shirt; it's not for me." Parent: "As long as you live in this house, you have to make yourself presentable in front of family."); relative deprivation theory (Crosby, 1982) regarding feelings of deprivation (Child: "How come I have to go to bed now and Sara can stay up?" Parent: "Don't compare yourself with her, she's older."); and equity theory (Messick & Cook, 1983) regarding judgments of fairness (Child: "It's not fair that I have to share my toys with John." Parent: "Yes it is fair, either you share or I take all your toys away.").

An important influence on the adversarial relationship between parents and children is that the relationship is continually changing because parents and, in particular, children are changing, growing more capable of independent thought and action. More specifically, the norms and rules regulating parent–child relations are continually shifting, and with each passing month, the child is pushing toward greater independence and revised rules and norms. In many ways the norms and rules that children have to follow are special to the world of the child.

The Margin of Generational Development

Most children are influenced by socialization processes to eventually become integrated into the normative system of the adult world, but this does not mean that the normative system guiding children is a simplified version of the normative system guiding adult behavior. There are fundamental rifts between the worlds of children and adults, and the size of this rift reflects the *margin of generational development* (Moghaddam, 2002; after Fine, 1987; Opie & Opie, 1972).

The margin of generational development is sometimes planned and made explicit. For example, in the domain of knowledge and experience about sexual behavior, adults often go to great lengths to maintain discontinuity between the experiences of children and those of adults. Children are explicitly kept ignorant about sex, particularly in middle-class Western families. In cases in which adults expect children to conform to norms that are fundamentally different from those applied to adults, the margin of generational development is wide, but not necessarily explicit. That is, the discontinuity between the normative system of adults and children may still not be acknowledged. Consider, for example, the norm that "children have to share."

David and George are 4-year-olds playing in George's house. David is playing with a toy car, and George tries to grab it from him, crying, "That's my blue car! Mom, David won't give me my blue car!" George's mother responds by saying, "It's David's turn to play with the blue car." "But it's my blue car," complains George. "You have to share your toys with friends," his mother tells him, "David will give it to you when it's your turn."

Now consider the relationship between George and David when they become 24-year-olds and are driving real cars. Will George's mother insist that George share his car with his friends? Not at all. Private ownership, personal responsibility, and personal property are now given the highest priority. George will be seen to have every right in the world if he now refuses to let David or any other friend drive his car. Clearly then, the margin of generational development is very large in one of the most fundamentally important domains of modern Western societies, that of ownership of property.

One of the most important areas in which the margin of generational difference is significant is that of rights and duties. In parent–child relations specifically and adult–child relations generally, parents and adults focus on the duties of the child, whereas children give priority to the rights of the child. The socialization of children in the informal social world, as well as the formal context of education, involves emphasizing duties more than rights. The vast part of training children has traditionally involved setting constraints on what they are not allowed to do and on what they are duty bound to do, and less on what they have a right to do. Often, caretakers make explicit the boundaries of duties ("You have to be back by 9 p.m.; you have to do your homework; you have to clean your room."), and rights are implied as anything outside the forbidden boundaries.

A number of studies provide empirical support for the view that children give priority to their rights and parents give priority to their children's duties. In studies of dual-parent families with two young children, Lollis and her associates found that whereas parents tried to solve sibling conflicts more through a "care" orientation that emphasized responsibilities, younger children in particular gave priority to a "justice" orientation that emphasized rights (Lollis, Ross, & Leroux, 1996; Lollis, Van Engen, Burns, Nowack, & Ross, 1999). A series of other studies have found that mothers in particular act as guardians of the social order by giving priority to the duties of children to follow rules (Piotrowski, 1997; Smetana, Schlagman, & Adams, 1993). These studies underscore the idea that there is a continual negotiation between children and parents about rights and duties with children constantly pulling toward personal rights and liberties in their tug-of-war.

The Primacy of Duties in Education and Traditional Conceptions of Human Nature

This priority to the duties of children on the part of parents, educators, and adults generally can be traced to the negative view of human nature dominant in many cultures. That view dictates how society conceptualizes basic human tendencies, and therefore, influences how society trains children to manage those tendencies. Because humans are commonly assumed to be self-centered, personal rights seem more in keeping with their natural inclinations than do duties, and it appears easier to stray toward selfish behavior. To keep children on the right path, society must therefore stress their duties.

This view of humans as largely selfish beings has carried over from religion into other realms, including economics, politics, and the sciences. The major religions depict humankind as inclined to lean toward the evil side of their dual nature, although the good and evil parts are constantly battling for dominance. The social sciences adopt a similar negative perspective on human nature. Psychological domains are no exception, as illustrated by the work of such thinkers as Freud (1886–1899/1966) and Piaget (1952) as well as the literature on altruism. We have already mentioned Freud's depiction of infants as dangerously pleasure seeking, striving for instant gratification without thought of consequences. Civilization's role is to tame this savage and self-satisfying human tendency. Piaget carried similar ideas into the domain of cognitive development, particularly by highlighting the child's assumed egocentrism. Kohlberg (1963) made the same assumption in the domain of moral development, postulating that only a minority of people grow beyond moral thinking based on selfishness and arrive at principled moral thinking.

The vast majority of the contemporary literature on altruism adopts a similar negative view of human nature (Moghaddam, 1998). Almost all of the major theories of helping behavior assume that people are essentially guided by self-serving motives; these include social exchange theory (Piliavin, Dovidio, Gaertner, & Clark, 1981), the negative state relief hypothesis (Cialdini, Schaller, Houlihan, Arps, Fultz, & Beaman, 1987), the image-repair hypothesis (Cunningham, Steinberg, & Grev, 1980), the empathy–joy hypothesis (Smith, Keating, & Stotland, 1989), the just-world hypothesis (Lerner, 1977, 1991), equity theory (Walster, Walster, & Berscheid, 1978), and various sociobiological explanations (e.g., Rushton, 1988, 1991). Among these pessimistic theories of altruism exists only one major hypothesis, the empathy–altruism hypothesis (Batson, 1995), that posits that humans have a genuine desire to help others. Thus, most major models of altruism assume that all motivation arises with the egoistic goal of increasing one's own well-being. Human nature is presented as fundamentally self-serving.

This assumption implies that individual rights are more in harmony with natural tendencies than are duties. Humans more "naturally" understand what they have a right to almost by default, whereas the concept of having a duty to perform is less "natural" and harder to accept. Thus, teaching children their responsibilities in regard to personal rights ("I have a right to play with my toy") will be easier than teaching them their responsibilities in regard to personal duties ("I have a duty to share my toy"), and the latter must be emphasized in education. Indeed, society appears to do just that as it sets up prohibitions on human action. Consider, for example, the Ten Commandments and many of our basic laws. All restrict humans ("Thou shalt not. . ."), rather than delineating what we are allowed to do. The implication is that humankind's largely self-centered inclinations must be controlled and its duties to others stressed to create a moral world. Thus, at a young and impressionable age, humans are taught to disregard their self-serving proclivity for rights and to embrace the idea of duties.

Implications of the Cultural Theory to the Development of Rights and Duties

The cultural theory outlined in the preceding discussion has two implications: first, the replaceability of rights and duties, and second, universals in the priority given to rights and duties.

Replaceability or Renaming a Behavior as a Right or a Duty

We have proposed that primitive social relations, such as turn taking, are common to all human social life, and after they arise, are culturally interpreted as a right or a duty (see also Moghaddam, 2000). Most, and perhaps all, rights can be reconceived as duties, and most, if not all, duties can be reconceived as rights. That is to say, a right can be renamed as duty and a duty as a right. There are no objective criteria by which an act such as giving or taking a turn to speak is a priori a right or a duty for an interlocutor. It could be either or it could be both, depending on cultural conditions.

Priorities Given to Rights and Duties

In practice, however, we find that some acts are more likely to be interpreted as rights, whereas others are more likely to be interpreted as duties. These trends are strongly related to the situation of the person doing the interpreting. We have argued that in parent–child relations, children emphasize their own personal rights, but parents emphasize their children's duties. More generally, in situations involving conflict or change, those with less power emphasize their own rights and those who enjoy more power emphasize the duties of the less powerful. This is almost a universal trend. However, we can also find exceptions to this trend.

Consider, for example, the duty to serve one's country at times of war. Both authorities and citizens tend to emphasize "the duty to serve." But even in this situation, the label *rights* is not far away. For example, during World War II thousands of Japanese Americans were interned and lost their right to serve in the United States military. More recently, gays have complained of being excluded from the U.S. military, which has been denying them their right to serve. This hearkens back to the replaceability issue, although the situation of the person doing the interpreting influences whether rights or duties are prioritized.

EXPLORATORY STUDIES

In the first section, our first proposition is that biological and functional constraints of the human condition necessarily lead to certain social behaviors termed primitive social relations and that these are universal across cultures, arising early in life through the interactions of infant and caretaker. Our second proposition is that these primitive social relations are later interpreted for the child as being either rights or duties, depending on cultural conditions. In this second section, we empirically bolster these propositions through several exploratory studies. The first two studies delve into the rift between the normative world of the child versus that of the adult and support the idea that there exists a wide margin of generational development between the priority given to rights or duties, depending on one's age and power alignment in relation to others. The third study highlights cross-cultural similarities and universals in the domain of rights and duties and reflects the existence of primitive social relations common to all human societies. In particular, this study examines the idea that priority will be given to rights by those who are in potentially adversarial relationships, thus testing an aspect of Proposition 3.

Studies 1 and 2

Priority Given to Rights and Duties in Changing Relationships: Property Rights and Duties of Children and Adults

We have argued that in parent–child relations, characterized as they are by change and power inequalities, adults give priority to the duties of children. In this respect, we have highlighted differences and discontinuities in the worlds of adults and children. In certain domains, the normative system regulating the behavior of youngsters functions only in childhood and therefore cannot strictly be considered "an early form of" the normative system that regulates adult life. As evidenced by the studies briefly reported in the following paragraphs, there is not a consistent trend in the relative weight given to rights and duties from 3-year-olds to 23-year-olds; rather, the scheme used by adults when comparing "the right to use one's belonging versus the duty to share it" deviates from that used in childhood.

The first experiment involved 49 native Iranian parents (41 women, 8 men), between the ages of 19 and 44 years old. Each had at least one child below the age of 7, the majority of their children being 3 to 4 years old. The research instrument was a questionnaire involving four short story lines. In each story, there were two characters whose gender was matched to the gen-

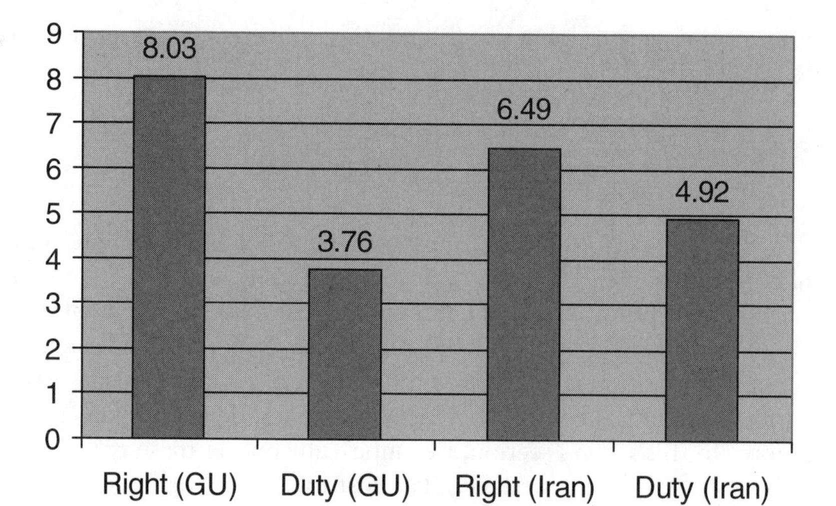

Figure 4.2. Adult means for both the Georgetown University (GU) data and the Iran data.

der of the participant's child. The scenarios varied in the age of the characters, either both 3-year-olds or both 23-year-olds. In each story, one character wished to borrow something from the other character. When they were 3, it was a toy, and when they were 23, it was a car, and the two began to fight over that object. The participants, on being presented with the four stories, were asked to rate, on a scale of 1 to 9 (1 = *lowest priority*; 9 = *highest priority*), the priority they believed the parents of the toy or car owner would give to (a) the character's right to play with the toy or use the car and (b) the character's duty to share the toy or car with the other character.

The second study involved 37 Georgetown University undergraduate students. Again, participants completed questionnaires. This time, however, each student analyzed only two of four possible story lines. All of the scenarios included one character, G, who wanted to borrow something from another character, M, leading the two characters to fight over that object. Again, both characters were either 3-year-olds or 23-year-olds. When M and G were 3, the object of their desire was a toy, whereas at 23 it was a car. After reading the stories, each participant was asked to rate the level of priority they believed the parents of M would give to (a) M's right to play with the toy or use the car and (b) M's duty to share the toy or car with G.

Rights were consistently given higher priority than duties in the scenario involving the 23-year-olds, especially by the Georgetown students. Looking at individual cases, 42 out of 49 Iranians gave higher or equal priority to rights in the scenario involving two adults, and 34 out of 37 Georgetown students did the same. However, a different pattern emerges for the scenario involving 3-year-olds: Rights and duties were rated at similar levels of priority, with duties edging out rights by a small margin. In terms of individual cases, 26 (out of 49) Iranians gave higher or equal priority to rights in the

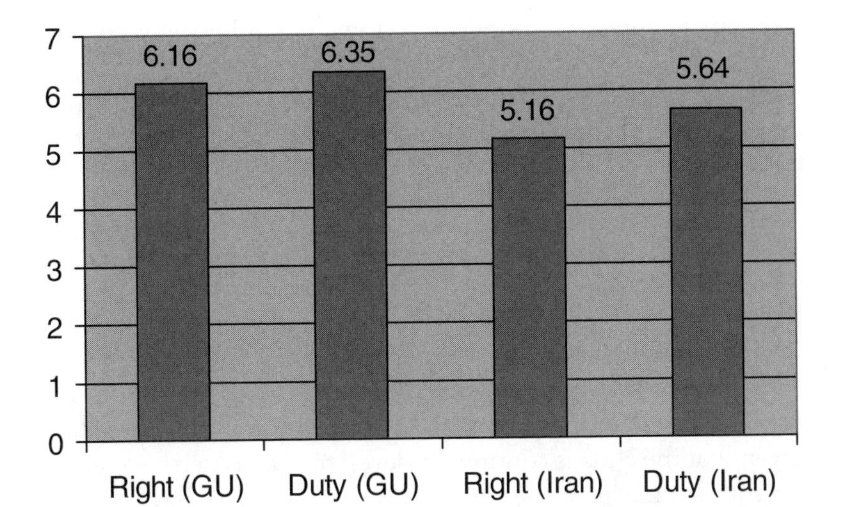

Figure 4.3. Child means for both the Georgetown University (GU) data and the Iran study data.

scenario involving two children, and 23 (out of 37) Georgetown students did the same. See Figures 4.2 and 4.3 for a comparison of means in both studies.

Clearly, these results support our notion of a rift between the respective normative systems that guide the behavior of children and adults, and that rift exists, we believe, almost universally across cultures. Our explanation for the disparity is the different functional conditions experienced by children and adults, for such conditions ultimately direct the practice of rights and duties. That is, the primitive social relations arising out of the different age-dependent constraints differ accordingly between the two age groups, each being interpreted in its own way as practicing rights or duties. Thus, the domain of rights and duties is differentiated according to age. Furthermore, although most children are socialized to eventually incorporate the normative system of adults, the normative system guiding children is not simply a reduced version of that guiding adult behavior. We have argued for and our exploratory studies have supported this fundamental incongruity between the world of children and adults, terming the extent of the dissimilarity the margin of generational development. The rights and duties determined by the different normative systems can be considered complementary, but they also replace one another as the relationship between parents and children changes.

We have already argued for the evolution of the relationship between children and adults. As children grow, the normative rules from which they mold their behavior continually change, and children are constantly pushing toward the more liberal and liberating of these rule systems. Parents, conversely, give priority to duties that restrict the behavior of their children. Thus, parents are in a continual state of flux vis-à-vis their power alignment, which is often associated with tension and discord. To further explain the rift in normative system, we consider how the relationship between children and parents reflects a much broader trend: In any relationship characterized by potential or actual conflict, those with less or equal power (e.g., children) give priority to their personal rights, whereas those who enjoy greater power in the relationship (e.g., parents) give priority to the duties of those with less power. Study 3 further explores this general pattern.

Study 3

Priority Given to Rights and Duties in Less and More Adversarial Relationships: Attitudes Toward Family, Friends, and Neighbors

We have described the parent–child relationship as adversarial in some ways, given that the child is continually developing and exerting pressure for greater rights and independence. In such relationships, we have argued that adults place more emphasis on children's duties. But what about other relationships that are potentially adversarial? How general is this tendency to emphasize one's own rights in adversarial relations? Is there any consistency across cultures? As an exploratory foray toward addressing these questions, we conducted a study of the importance given to rights and duties in relations with family, friends, and neighbors among samples of American, Chinese, and Russian participants.

Despite the priority given to finding cross-cultural differences in traditional cross-cultural psychology (Brislin, 2000; Matsumoto, 2000), research has unearthed surprising consistency in attitudes toward human rights. For example, the research of Doise and his associates (Doise & Spini, chap. 2, this volume) suggests that the fundamental tenets of the Universal Declaration of Human Rights (see Appendix for full text) are similarly evaluated by young people in approximately 40 different Western and non-Western societies around the world. In examining possible cross-cultural consistencies, we look back to the concept of primitive social relations, particularly those involving groups of people present in most societies, such as family, friends, and neighbors.

Although family structure varies considerably around the world, the concept of family relations is present in all societies. Similarly, although friendship patterns and even the nature of friendship varies from culture to culture, most human cultures do have relationships that we understand as friendship. The same holds for neighbors; that is, although neighbors are different for different cultures, even nomadic tribes do have experiences of interacting with others who might resemble "mobile neighbors." In all societies, individuals have relationships with other individuals in these three categories. Even in the case of the Tiwi of Northern Australia (Hart, Pilling, & Goodale, 1988) and other groups who lived for long periods of their history in isolation, people still created neighbors through imaginary out-groups, that is, groups of people and humanlike creatures imagined to exist in the unexplored regions beyond the known world. Thus, in all human societies relations seem to exist between people we would recognize as family, friends, and neighbors.

The nature of relations within these three groups seems to involve some cross-cultural consistency. Family and friends are involved in less formal and nonlegalistic relations with one another compared with neighbors (of course, in some cases a neighbor might also be a family member or a friend). Neighbors typically have rights in relation to scarce resources such as land. In most modern societies, the property rights of neighbors are formally regulated through deeds and other documents, but this does not prevent conflicts between neighbors over property and privacy issues. The study we report was conducted to explore possible *etics*, behaviors common to most or all societies, and *emics*, behaviors common to one or a few societies, in human rights and duties in relationships involving family, friends, and neighbors (the data reported are from Moghaddam, Slocum, Shand, & Ward, 2000). The study involved comparable samples of young adult Americans (n = 182), Chinese (n = 122), and Russians (n = 355). Participants were presented with three scenarios, the first concerning family, the second friends, and the third neighbors. The scenarios involved social situations that could be interpreted as a matter of rights or duties for the self or others. Participants were asked to indicate the extent to which in this situation they would give importance to their own rights and duties as well as the rights and duties of the others (family, friends, or neighbors) involved.

The scenario involving neighbors was as follows:

> A very large tree on your neighbor's property has grown to partially block your ocean view. In order to expose your scenic view, the entire treetop would need to be removed, which would decrease the beauty of your neighbor's garden.

The scenario involving friends was as follows:

> Your best friend has just been hospitalized and is close to dying. You would like to visit your friend, but you have to give a job presentation that requires much preparation and offers you the chance for a new and much better position. If you visit your friend you will most likely do poorly on your presentation, but your friend's condition is dire.

The scenario involving family was as follows:

> This weekend is your mother's birthday. Your father and mother have a big party planned, and they expect you to come home from school for the weekend. However, you are in the middle of doing a project that is due on Monday. You need to stay on campus to have access to the library and so must choose between going home and having sufficient time to do an excellent job on the project.

Each of the above three scenarios was followed by six questions: In this situation, I give (on a rating scale of 1–9, where 1 represents "*very little importance*" and 9 represents "*a lot of importance*")

____importance to my duty to my neighbor
____importance to my duty to myself
____importance to my neighbor's rights
____importance to my rights

Overall, in this situation, I give ____ importance to rights and ____ importance to duties.

The results show remarkable consistency across cultures (see Table 4.1). Looking first at ratings on the question "Overall, in this situation, I give ____ importance to rights and ____ importance to duties," the consistent pattern is that all groups give higher importance to duties in relations with close family and close friends but higher importance to rights in relations with neighbors. The only nonsignificant finding is in the case of the Chinese in relations with close family, but the trend of the results in this case also is in line with higher importance being given to duty.

Regarding the first four more specific questions, in the case of relationships with close family members and close friends, the Chinese, Russian, and American participants all gave higher priority to duty to the self and duty to others than they did to rights of the self and rights of others. Even in the four cases in which the difference between priority given to duty and that given to rights was nonsignificant (Table 4.1), the trend of the differences was in the direction of higher priority being given to duty.

Exactly the opposite pattern emerges on the first four specific questions with respect to relationships with neighbors: The Chinese, Russian, and American participants gave higher priority to rights of the self (vs. rights of others) and rights of others (vs. duty to others). The only exception to this trend is for the Russian participants, for whom there is a nonsignificant difference between rights of self and duty to self. The consistency across Chinese, Russian, and American groups in the priorities given to rights and duties, and the shift in priorities across neighbors versus friends and family is all the more remarkable when we consider that the study was conducted using different groups of interviewers and different languages in very different parts of the world.

The results of Study 3 indicate that in relationships that are potentially adversarial, such as those involving neighbors, individuals generally give priority to rights rather than duties. More specifically, particular importance is given to one's personal rights. In relationships not characterized by conflict, such as with family and friends, it is one's duties, and particularly one's duties to others, that come to the foreground, whereas one's rights are allowed to fade into the background. One interpretation of the difference between ratings for neighbors versus family and friends is that the scenario we used for neighbors relates to property, whereas the scenarios for family and friends involved personal careers and studies. It may be that personal property issues are more likely to bring to mind rights rather than duties. However, it may also be that relationships with neighbors are more formal and legalistic in the minds of members of all three samples.

CONCLUDING DISCUSSION

In this final section we turn directly to apply our theoretical perspective to address a number of questions raised in the introductory chapter.

Question 4. How do children come to acquire notions relating to duties and rights?

Children acquire notions relating to duties and rights first through the training they receive from adults, particularly parents, other caretakers, and teachers, and second through being taught by other children, particularly those just ahead of them developmentally. The research of Opie and Opie (1972) and Fine (1987) suggests that each generation of children passes on certain knowledge and skills in the domain of rights and duties to the next generation of children without adults necessarily being involved in this process. Both this information passed from child to child within the self-regulated world of children and the teaching of children by adults about notions of duties and rights serve to continue the rift between the normative system of the child and that of adults.

A common feature of the different ways in which children learn about rights and duties is that already encountered segments of the social world are culturally interpreted for the child as a right or a duty. Among the earliest of such experiences is the labeling of primitive social relations, such as turn taking, as a right or a duty. This kind of labeling is intimately related to the characteristics of the larger society, such as the nature of the economic system.

Children learn about rights and duties in the context of the larger social and economic system. On the surface, it may appear that Iranians and Americans have very different social and economic systems as well as different views regarding rights and duties relating to ownership. After all, the political rhetoric of the Iranian and American governments is often fundamentally different. However, underlying this rhetoric is a deeper similarity: Both are capitalist societies organized around free enterprise and respect for private property. Consequently, perhaps it is not surprising that both Iranian and American samples showed the same rift in applying rights and duties to children and adults: Children should share, but when they become adults, the rights of the property owner trump duties to others. In answering our question, then, we argue that children adopt ideas about rights and duties

TABLE 4.1
Rights and Duties to Self and Others Across Ethnic Groups and Relationships

Ethnicity of participant	Relationship	Reference	*M*	Direction of difference	*p*
Chinese	Close family	Right of self	6.14		
		Duty to self	6.57	–0.43	0.001
		Right of others	6.61		
		Duty to others	7.25	–0.64	0.000
		Rights	6.60		
		Duties	7.15	–0.55	*ns*
Russian		Right of self	6.86		
		Duty to self	6.81	0.05	*ns*
		Right of others	6.85		
		Duty to others	7.35	–0.51	0.000
		Rights	6.78		
		Duties	7.34	-0.55	0.000
American		Right of self	6.39		
		Duty to self	7.14	–0.75	0.000
		Right of others	6.01		
		Duty to others	6.83	–0.82	0.000
		Rights	6.15		
		Duties	7.15	–1.00	0.000
Chinese	Close friend	Right of self	5.23		
		Duty to self	5.88	–0.65	0.000
		Right of others	7.44		
		Duty to others	8.05	–0.61	0.000
		Rights	6.39		
		Duties	8.22	–1.84	0.029
Russian		Right of self	6.54		
		Duty to self	6.25	0.29	*ns*
		Right of others	6.63		
		Duty to others	8.06	–1.43	0.000
		Rights	6.51		
		Duties	8.01	–1.50	0.000
American		Right of self	4.71		
		Duty to self	5.00	–0.29	*ns*
		Right of others	7.08		
		Duty to others	8.54	–1.46	0.000
		Rights	5.40		
		Duties	8.02	–2.62	0.000
Chinese	Neighbor	Right of self	6.88		
		Duty to self	6.52	0.36	0.000
		Right of others	6.09		
		Duty to others	5.82	0.27	0.035
		Rights	6.89		
		Duties	6.07	0.83	0.000
Russian		Right of self	6.26		
		Duty to self	6.34	–0.08	*ns*
		Right of others	6.02		

TABLE 4.1 (Continued)

	Duty to others	5.41	0.61	0.000
	Rights	6.51		
	Duties	5.95	0.56	0.000
American	Right of self	6.99		
	Duty to self	6.32	0.66	0.000
	Right of others	5.91		
	Duty to others	5.33	0.58	0.000
	Rights	6.69		
	Duties	5.84	0.85	0.000

through interactions with both adults and peers, but that rights and duties applied to children are in some important domains, such as ownership, fundamentally different from rights and duties applied to adults.

Question 5. Are there universals regarding rights and duties, and if there are universals, what is the source?

The tentative move we have taken toward a cultural theory of the development of rights and duties has, on the one hand, postulated rights and duties as replaceable, and on the other hand, claimed that there are a number of very basic universals in rights and duties. It may appear that we endorse a relativistic view of rights and duties, and at the same time, we claim there to be universals. In this section we provide further clarification of this position and argue that our position is not relativistic but supports a small number of basic universals.

Rights and duties, we claim, are cultural interpretations of actions. As such, in theory any action can be interpreted as a right or a duty. However, in practice, commonalities in functional and biological conditions of human life lead to similarities in interpretations across cultures. For example, during the course of their development, children tend to give priority to the rights of children, whereas parents give priority to the duties of children. We have argued that this relationship is common to other situations characterized by change and potential or actual conflict within a relationship, such as between ethnic minorities and Whites in North America.

The priority given to rights or duties depends on the power alignments of the relationship. In relationships marked by change and adversity, such as the caregiver–child dyad, the normative world of the more powerful player differs from that of the less powerful player. The less powerful child constantly attempts to push his or her way into the adult normative realm in the hopes of garnering more rights and independence. When such rearrangement occurs so that the players' positions in relation to one another have changed, the priority given to rights and duties will change as well. That is to say, the child who gives priority to rights of the child will later give priority to duties of the child when he or she becomes a parent and has a child to train.

Similarly, rebels and revolutionaries give priority to rights before they gain power, but after they gain power themselves and become the central authority, they shift emphasis and give priority to the duties of citizens to obey the laws of the land (Moghaddam, in press). This cycle of change in priority to rights and duties has been discussed by Pareto (1935) among others and is well documented in discussions of revolutions starting with the French revolution (Schama, 1990). This trend toward legitimization of the existing order and the reemergence of inequalities led some revolutionaries, most notably Mao Zedong (1893–1976), to call for a "perpetual revolution" so that new elites do not become established in a way that the duties rather than the rights of the masses become emphasized. However, in practice Mao himself has been shown to behave more in line with the ancient emperors and to be less of a revolutionary (Mao was dubbed one of the "New Emperors," see Moghaddam, Hanley, & Harré, 2003). Thus, the cycle of new elites coming to power and emphasizing the duties of citizens rather than the rights of citizens has so far remained the rule rather than the exception (e.g., Moghaddam, 2002, chap. 2; Moghaddam & Crystal, 2000).

Such common trends in the human condition give rise, we argue, to a few basic but important similarities in the ways in which acts are interpreted as rights or duties. In this discussion of rights and duties in development, we have focused particularly on conditions characterized by change and potential conflict and have found that priority given to rights or duties depends on the relative power of the players involved. We have also discussed the need for communication as a universal human condition, and how imitation begets turn taking, which is essential to language and the successful exchange of ideas. Rights and duties, we argue, are deeply ingrained in language processes and routines because turn taking is interpreted to involve rights and duties. That is, when conversing with another person, one has a right to take turns speaking and a duty to defer turns to the other interlocutor. This is a universal feature of human communication, although local cultures influence who has a right to a turn and when. In this way, we support the idea of universals in some aspects of rights and duties arising from universalities in biological and functional conditions across cultures.

Question 17. What are we to make of the affective distinction between rights that are generally happily embraced by individuals who have them and duties that seem imposed and even burdensome?

It is useful to address this question at two levels, a general level relating to all humans and a more specific level relating to majorities (who enjoy greater power) and minorities (who have less power). At the general level, we discussed the tendency in social science research, in major psychological models, and more specifically the literature on altruism, to assume that humans are selfish and self-serving in both cognition and overt behavior. From this perspective, humans embrace rights because rights most directly fulfill their "naturally" selfish motives. In cases in which priority is given to duties rather than rights, such as in relationships with family and friends, this may also be self-serving because of the expectations individuals have that family and friends will help them in times of need.

With respect to a second more specific level of assessing the embracing of rights and duties by groups with different levels of power, we have argued that personal rights are in general emphasized by children and others who have less power, whereas the duties of children and others with less power are emphasized by those who enjoy greater power. The child who at the age of 10 has to be in bed by 8:30 p.m. happily embraces the right to stay awake until 9:00 p.m. when she is given such an opportunity. Similarly, minorities generally seek to add to their rights, including increased rights in education and employment domains. Minorities happily embrace rights; for example, women and African Americans embraced the right to vote in national elections in the United States when offered this right in the 20th century. Rights empower children and others in similarly powerless positions.

Duties, however, are generally used by those in power to control the less powerful. Parents, teachers, and others involved in the training of children emphasize the duties of children, as in "You have to hand in your homework tomorrow"; "Make sure your room is clean"; and the like. Duties seem imposed and even burdensome because children, and others who are less powerful, view duties as primarily targeted at them and designed to limit their freedoms. Duties serve to uphold the status quo, and because the status quo maintains the disadvantaged position of those with less power, duties seem to them to be an imposition and burden. However, those in power typically see duties as fundamentally important, even imperative, because when people fulfill their duties, as duties are normatively defined, the position of the more powerful is safeguarded (Moghaddam, in press).

Thus, the observation that *rights are generally happily embraced by individuals who have them, whereas duties seem imposed and even burdensome* reflects a tendency for rights to be the focus of children and others with less power and duties to be the focus of parents and others with more power. The explanation for this trend relates to the perceived interests of the parties involved. When the perceived interests change, so does the relative priority given to rights and duties. We clarify this issue in discussion regarding the next question.

> *Question 18. How is it that rights need not be exercised or can be waived, whereas waiving duties is not so easily done?*

Again, the answer to this question becomes clear when we consider that in practice rights and duties are associated to different degrees with different groups. Typically, rights are demanded by children and others who are less powerful from parents and others who enjoy greater power. A child who has the right to stay up until 8:30 p.m. may choose not to exercise this right.

If the child decides to go to bed at 8:00 p.m. instead of 8:30 p.m., parents typically do not object. However, if a child wants to stay awake until 9:00 p.m. instead of the customary bedtime of 8:30 p.m., then parents typically do object and remind the child of a duty to be in bed by 8:30 p.m. Similarly, when ethnic minorities do not exercise their right to vote, the authorities typically do not object; but minorities face opposition when they seek to extend their rights.

But this relationship changes when the interests of minority and majority groups demand a change. For example, when minorities already enjoy a right but are denied the opportunity to exercise that right, then they typically resort to raising issues of duties rather than rights. For example, when a child "has a right" to $2 a week pocket money, and her parents have forgotten to provide the money for several weeks, the child will most likely remind them of their parental duty to pay up. Similarly, when African Americans faced challenges in officially registering their vote in parts of Florida during the 2000 presidential elections, they demanded that the authorities do their duty and create conditions that would allow African American voters to exercise their democratic voting rights. But those in power may choose to waive their duties in such circumstances.

Thus, we agree that in general rights need not be exercised or can be waived, whereas waiving duties is not so easily done, because in most cases it is minorities, children, and the less powerful generally who need to enforce rights, whereas it is the majority group, parents, and the more powerful who enforce duties. Rights can be waived, because the less powerful have fewer resources to uphold their own rights. It is not easy to waive duties because those with power have the resources to enforce the duties of those with less power.

CONCLUDING COMMENT

We have taken tentative steps toward a cultural theory of the development of rights and duties. We have implicated both biological and social factors to this end, claiming that certain practices that later are interpreted as a right or a duty according to local normative systems are rooted in biological constraints. We have also articulated that normative worlds are in some ways distinct for adults and children and that children are socialized to their normative world by both adults and peers, progressively changing the framework of their ideas regarding rights and duties as they develop. We used this relationship between adults and children to exemplify a broader trend in the priorities given by more and less powerful groups on duties and rights. That is to say, in relationships that are changing or conflicted, those who enjoy greater power emphasize duties and those with less power emphasize rights. In our experimental examination of this (Study 3), we found that interlocutors with equal power but in relationships involving potential conflict emphasized rights. This represents one of a small number of possible universals in the realm of rights and duties, although the possibility of exceptions was noted. Finally, we argued that rights and duties are replaceable, although in practice the interests of the more powerful groups dictate under which conditions a behavior will be interpreted as a right or a duty. Because of the tendency for such interests to remain fairly stable, the labeling of behaviors as rights or duties also remains fairly stable.

REFERENCES

Alvarado, R. (1999). *A common law: The law of nations and western civilization*. Aalten, the Netherlands: Pietas Press.

Aston, G. (1995). Say 'thank you': Some pragmatic constraints in conversational closings. *Applied Linguistics, 16*, 57–86.

Barr, R., Dowden, A., & Hayne, H. (1996). Developmental changes in deferred imitation by 6- to 24-month-old infants. *Infant Behavior and Development, 19*, 159–170.

Barrett, M. D. (Ed.). (1985). *Children's single-word speech*. Chichester, England: Wiley.

Batson, C. D. (1995). Prosocial motivation: Why do we help others? In A. Tesser (Ed.), *Advanced social psychology* (pp. 333–381). Boston: McGraw-Hill.

Bennett, M. (Ed.). (1993). *The development of social cognition: The child as psychologist*. New York: Guilford Press.

Brazelton, T. B., & Tronick, E. (1980). Preverbal communication between mothers and infants. In D. R. Olson (Ed.), *The social foundations of language and thought* (pp. 299–315). New York: Norton.

Brislin, R. (2000). *Understanding culture's influence on behavior* (2nd ed.). New York: Harcourt.

Carroll, L. (1960). *The annotated Alice: Alice's adventures in wonderland and through the looking glass*. New York: Wings Books.

Cialdini, R. B., Schaller, M., Houlihan, D., Arps, K., Fultz, J., & Beaman, A. L. (1987). Empathy-based helping: Is it selflessly or selfishly motivated? *Journal of Personality and Social Psychology, 52*, 749–758.

Collis, G. M. (1985). On the origins of turn-taking: Alternation and meaning. In M. D. Barrett (Ed.), *Children's single-words speech* (pp. 217–230). Chichester, England: Wiley.

Crosby, F. (1982). *Relative deprivation and working women*. New York: Oxford University Press.

Cunningham, M. R., Steinberg, J., & Grev, R. (1980). Wanting to and having to help: Separate motivations for positive mood and guilt-inducing helping. *Journal of Personality and Social Psychology, 38*, 181–192.

Cushman, D., & Whiting, G. C. (1972). An approach to communication theory: Toward consensus on rules. *Journal of Communication, 22*, 217–238.

Duncan, S. (1972). Some signs and rules for taking speaking turns in conversation. *Journal of Personality and Social Psychology*, *23*, 283–292.

Duncan, S. (1974). On the structure of speaker–auditor interaction during speaking turns. *Language and Society*, *2*, 161–180.

Eckensberger, L. H., & Zimba, R. F. (1997). The development of moral judgment. In J. W. Berry, P. R. Dasen, & T. S. Saraswathi (Eds.), *Handbook of cross-cultural psychology* (Vol. 2., pp. 299–340). Boston: Allyn & Bacon.

Fine, G. A. (1987). *With the boys: Little league baseball and preadolescent culture*. Chicago: University of Chicago Press.

Finkel, N. J. (1995). *Commensense justice: Jurors' notions of the law*. Cambridge, MA: Harvard University Press.

Freud, S. (1960). Jokes and their relation to the unconscious. In J. Strachey (Ed. & Trans.), *The standard edition of the complete psychological works of Sigmund Freud* (Vol. 8, pp. 1–258). London: Hogarth Press. (Original work published 1905)

Freud, S. (1966). Extracts from the Fliess Papers. In J. Strachey (Ed. & Trans.), *The standard edition of the complete psychological works of Sigmund Freud* (Vol.1, pp. 175–280). London: Hogarth Press. (Original work published 1886–1899)

Goodnow, J. J. (1988). Children's household work: Its nature and functions. *Psychological Bulletin*, *103*, 5–26.

Hart, C. W. M., Pilling, A. R., & Goodale, J. C. (1988). *The Tiwi of north Australia* (3rd ed.). New York: Holt, Rinehart & Winston.

Kohlberg, L. (1963). Development of children's orientations toward a moral order. *Vita Humana*, *6*, 11–36.

Lerner, M. J. (1977). The justice motive: Some hypotheses as to its origins and forms. *Journal of Personality*, *45*, 1–52.

Lerner, M. J. (1991). Interpreting societal and psychological rules of entitlement. In R. Vermunt & H. Steensma (Eds.), *Social justice in human relations* (Vol. 1, pp. 13–32). New York: Plenum Press.

Lollis, S., Ross, H., & Leroux, L. (1996). An observational study of parents' socialization of moral orientation during sibling conflicts. *Merrill-Palmer Quarterly*, *42*, 475–494.

Lollis, S., Van Engen, G., Burns, L., Nowack, K., & Ross, H. (1999). Sibling socialization of moral orientation: "Share with me!" "No, it's mine!" *Journal of Moral Education*, *28*, 339–357.

Matsumoto, D. (2000). *Culture and psychology: People around the world* (2nd ed.). Belmont, CA: Wadsworth.

Meltzoff, A. N., & Moore, M. K. (1977, October). Imitation of facial and manual gestures by human neonates. *Science*, *198*, 75–78.

Meltzoff, A. N., & Moore, M. K. (1983). Newborn infants imitate adult facial gestures. *Child Development*, *54*, 702–709.

Meltzoff, A. N., & Moore, M. K. (1994). Imitation, memory, and the representation of persons. *Infant Behavior and Development*, *17*, 83–99.

Messick, D. M., & Cook, K. S. (1983). *Equity theory: Psychological and sociological perspectives*. New York: Praeger.

Moghaddam, F. M. (1998). *Social psychology: Exploring universals in social behavior*. NewYork: Freeman.

Moghaddam, F. M. (2000). Toward a cultural theory of human rights. *Theory & Psychology, 10*, 291–312.

Moghaddam, F. M. (2002). *The individual and society: A cultural integration*. New York: Worth Publishers.

Moghaddam, F. M. (2003). Interobjectivity and culture. *Culture & Psychology, 9*, 221–232.

Moghaddam, F. M. (in press). The cycle of rights and duties in intergroup relations: Interobjectivity and perceived justice re-assessed. *New Review of Social Psychology*.

Moghaddam, F. M., & Crystal, D. (2000). Change, continuity, and culture: The case of power relations in Iran and Japan. In S. A. Renshon & J. Duckitt (Eds.), *Political psychology: Cultural and crosscultural foundations* (pp. 201–216). London: Macmillan.

Moghaddam, F. M., Hanley, E., & Harré, R. (2003). Sustaining intergroup harmony: An analysis of the Kissinger papers through positioning theory. In R. Harré & F. M. Moghaddam (Eds.), *The self and others: Positioning individuals and groups in personal, political, and cultural contexts* (pp. 137–155). Westport, CT: Praeger.

Moghaddam, F. M., & Harré, R. (1995). But is it science? Traditional and alternative approaches to the study of social behavior. *World Psychology, 1*, 47–78.

Moghaddam, F. M., Slocum, N., Shand, G., & Ward, C. (2000, March). *The end of community?* Paper presented at the annual convention of the Eastern Psychological Association, Baltimore, MD.

Moghaddam, F. M., Taylor, D. M., & Wright, S. C. (1993). *Social psychology in cross-cultural perspective*. New York: Freeman.

Nadel, J., & Butterworth, G. (Eds.). (1999). *Imitation in infancy*. Cambridge, England: Cambridge University Press.

National Research Council. (2000). *From neurons to neighborhoods: The science of early childhood development*. Washington, DC: National Academy Press.

Opie, P., & Opie, I. (1972). *The lore and language of schoolchildren*. Oxford, England: Oxford University Press.

Pareto, V. (1935). *The mind and society: A treatise in general sociology* (Vols. 1–4). New York: Dover.

Piaget, J. (1952). *The origins of intelligence in children*. New York: International University Press.

Piliavin, J. A., Dovidio, J. F., Gaertner, S. L., & Clark, R. D., III. (1981). *Emergency intervention*. New York: Academic Press.

Piotrowski, C. (1997). Rules of everyday family life: The development of social rules in mother–child and sibling relationships. *International Journal of Behavioral Development, 21*, 571–598.

Reissland, N., & Stephenson, T. (1999). Turn-taking in early vocal interaction: A comparison of premature and term infants' vocal interaction with their mothers. *Child: Care, Health and Development, 2*, 447–456.

Ross, H. S., Filyer, R. E., Lollis, S. P., Perlman, M., & Martin, J. L. (1994). Administering justice in the family. *Journal of Family Psychology, 8*, 254–273.

Rushton, J. P. (1988). Epigenic rules in moral development: Distal–proximal approaches to altruism and aggression. *Aggressive Behavior, 14*, 35–50.

Rushton, J. P. (1991). Is altruism innate? *Psychological Inquiry, 2*, 141–143.

Rutter, D., & Durkin, K. (1987). Turn taking in mother–infant interaction: An examination of vocalizations and gaze. *Developmental Psychology, 23*, 54–61.

Schama, S. (1990). *Citizens: A chronicle of the French revolution*. New York: Vintage Books.

Schegloff, E. A. (2000). Overlapping talk and the organization of turn-taking for conversation. *Language in Society, 29*, 1–63.

Sherif, M. (1966). *Group conflict and cooperation: Their social psychology*. London: Routledge & Kegan Paul.

Smetana, J. G., Schlagman, N., & Adams, P. W. (1993). Preschool children's judgements about hypothetical and actual transgressions. *Child Development, 64*, 202–214.

Smith, K. D., Keating, J. P., & Stotland, E. (1989). Altruism reconsidered: The effect of denying feedback on a victim's status to empathic witnesses. *Journal of Personality and Social Psychology, 57*, 641–650.

Tajfel, H., & Turner, J. C. (1979). An integrative theory of intergroup conflict. In W. G. Austin & S. Worchel (Eds.), *The social psychology of intergroup relations* (pp. 33–47). Monterey, CA: Brooks/Cole.

Walster, E., Walster, G. W., & Berscheid, E. (1978). *Equity: Theory and research*. Boston: Allyn & Bacon.

Wilhite, M. (1983). Children's acquisition of language routines: The end-of-meal routine in Cakchiquel. *Language in Society, 12*, 47–64.

Zazzo, R. (1957). Le problème de l'imitation chez le nouveau né [The problem of imitation in the newborn]. *Enfance, 10*, 135–142.

5

RIGHTS AND DUTIES AS GROUP NORMS: IMPLICATIONS OF INTERGROUP RESEARCH FOR THE STUDY OF RIGHTS AND RESPONSIBILITIES

WINNIFRED R. LOUIS AND DONALD M. TAYLOR

Rights? Duties? Just in the last 10 years the world has witnessed two genocides in Rwanda and Bosnia; the war in the Congo characterized by the terrorization of civilians and the enlistment of child soldiers; traffic in slavery in southern Sudan; the mutilation of civilian populations by rebel armies in Sierra Leone; civilian deaths perpetrated by both sides in the Middle East; kidnapping, murders, and extortion by government forces in Columbia and Chechnya; the use of torture in Turkey and China; the terrorist attacks on the World Trade Center in New York and the Pentagon in Washington, DC; and the death penalty in the United States and elsewhere. These events might lead us to wonder whether noble concepts such as rights and duties have any meaningful place in today's world. At the very least, they seem to document empirically that across societies there are no rules of human conduct that are universally endorsed: There is apparently no universally honored conception of human rights and duties.

In the present chapter, we present a strongly relativist account of rights and duties. We criticize universalism on both empirical and theoretical grounds. Although some social psychologists attempt to discover universals in social behavior generally, and rights and duties in particular, our approach is quite different. We suggest that social behaviors change fundamentally across contexts and across time. We believe that universal motivational and cognitive aspects of human psychology are behaviorally expressed in interaction with social norms that vary importantly by group membership within and across societies.

The claim that there are important universals in social behavior is a testable, empirical hypothesis that is certainly within the mandate of social psychological research. However, at present the behavioral evidence for such universal principles may rely on operationalizations that are allowed to vary across national or cultural contexts in either content or level of analysis. So, for example, it might be argued that turn taking in social interaction is universal even though low-power groups are routinely silenced and excluded from social discourse. Similarly, how do we reconcile a possible universal such as "the innocent shall not be harmed" with holocausts, infanticide, and genocide? Faced with such arguments, we feel methodologically alienated as well as politically skeptical. Indeed, we argue that psychology's (context-specific, socially defined) norms specify that theoretical models must be evaluated empirically on the basis of their predictive power. Although we seek universals at the level of process, universals at the level of specific content by definition predict no variance in human behavior! In the context of cross-disciplinary dialogue, we set out to articulate some of the ways in which we believe rights and duties may usefully be understood in terms of intergroup conflict and group-based normative variations.

Within North American history, an emphasis on individual rights appears to have given way to radical changes in the conception of rights and duties with respect to the treatment of many groups (Ishay, 1997). Government policies in the early 1900s included forced sterilization of the disabled, the exclusion of Black Americans and women from political and economic power, the criminalization of homosexuals, and assimilationist government policies for aboriginal groups. Yet government and society largely rejected these policies in the year 2001. Clearly, over the last century much has changed in terms of rights and duties.

Which structure of rights and duties will prevail in the year 2501? We do not believe that there is any linear dimension of progress or that there are any consensually defined criteria that will allow us to predict the world social structure in 500 years; even 50 seems overly ambitious. Across societies, the United Nations (UN) Universal Declaration of Human Rights (see Appendix for full text) attempts to formulate a definition of rights that is universally endorsed (Office of the UN High Commissioner on Human Rights, 2001a). Yet as of November 2001, only 48 of 189 member states of the UN are parties to the five component treaties of the UN International Bill of Human Rights; more than 40 member states are not party to the International Covenant on Civil and Political Rights, which might be seen as the most basic component of the set (Office of the UN High Commissioner on Human Rights, 2001b).[1] Across time, unexpected changes in the publicly tolerated standards for civil rights and duties in the United States appear to have occurred even in the last several years as a function of the September 11, 2001, terrorist bombings (e.g., Rutenberg, 2001; "U.S. Charges," 2001).

The type of discourse concerning rights and duties has also changed over the 20th century: *Human rights talk* has emerged as an organizing principle of modern political interactions (Ishay, 1997). That is, whereas changes in the social hierarchy might formerly have been discussed in the context of religious duties, changes are now sought on the grounds of a secular ideology that centers on the rights of disadvantaged groups: women's rights, Black American's civil rights, gay rights, and aboriginal rights, to name a few. This change in the function of rights talk, however, does not capture its essence fully because there is not always a correspondence between rights talk and actual social change. The status of disadvantaged groups may be dramatically altered even in the absence of a formal recognition of rights, as when women were drawn into the workforce during World War II. Moreover, a dialogue on rights and duties is not limited to situations in which the privileged position of advantaged groups is challenged by those who are less advantaged. The language of politics, of the empowered, may be used to assert the rights of advantaged groups and the duties of disadvantaged groups, as in the internment of Japanese Americans during World War II.

If there is no universal conceptualization of the content of human rights and duties across societies or within societies over time and no universal conceptualization of the social function of rights and duties talk, how can we understand the ongoing debates in modern society in these areas? Three arguments structure the present chapter. First, we propose that an understanding of rights and duties may usefully be framed in terms of socially defined norms and normative influence. The foundation for this proposition is the argument that there are no objective criteria by which rights and duties may be established independent of social influence. Thus, people's perceptions of their rights and duties are learned in a social context, and this learning process may be studied through the lens of normative influence. Second, we argue that the very emergence of a debate of particular rights and duties implies the existence of conflicting rather than universal norms: Otherwise the rights and duties would be taken for granted. The death penalty, abortion, contraception, and stem cell research motivate debates concerning the

[1]The UN International Bill of Human Rights comprises the Universal Declaration of Human Rights; the International Covenant on Economic, Social, and Cultural Rights; and the International Covenant on Civil and Political Rights and its two Optional Protocols (Office of the UN High Commissioner for Human Rights, 2001).

right to life; declining electoral participation motivates discussion of civic duties. If there were societal consensus on these issues, there would be no evocation of rights and duties. Thus, the salience of debates over rights and duties in society points to normative conflict. Third, a focus on conflicting norms for social interaction directs attention to the question of whose norms influence individuals' behavior, that is, to theories and research regarding intergroup relations and normative influence. Evoking intergroup relations points to the potential role of not only in-group norms but also those of the out-group and indeed broader societal norms. Individuals' resolutions of these conflicting norms need to be understood in terms of psychological mechanisms, especially identity management strategies. Studies of group members' reactions to rights violations are reviewed to illustrate the manner in which societal, in-group, and out-group norms differentially influence behavior.

The present chapter, then, delineates an intergroup approach to rights and duties, conceptualizing rights and duties as socially defined norms. Norms are defined as group-based standards or rules for behavior. Norms are characterized by within-group social consensus, and as such, are policed by social groups. The principle distinction between current models of rights and duties and our intergroup approach is our de-emphasis of the importance of societal or universal norms for behavior. Whereas rights and duties are often conceptualized as applicable across whole societies or even universally across humanity, our intergroup approach presupposes group differences in the perceptions of rights and duties. Moreover, our intergroup perspective emphasizes conflict between groups and attempts to understand the process by which individuals resolve competing normative claims.

WHAT ARE RIGHTS AND DUTIES? A NORMATIVE FRAMEWORK

The present chapter focuses on the common grounding of rights and duties in group-based social norms. Formally, "a right is a demand placed on others by the person who possesses it, while a duty is a demand placed by others on the person who owes it" (Moghaddam, Slocum, Finkel, Mor, & Harré, 2000, p. 275). As we define them, then, both rights and duties are behavioral demands that are rooted in the individual's social relationships. As such, they are prototypic group norms: They vary across groups rather than characterizing humans universally.

Historically, a dominant theme in research on human rights and duties has been the attempt to model top-down processes of influence. Societal authorities such as national governments or international organizations pass laws that restrict pleasurable activities or mandate onerous activities and create contingencies of external reinforcement that reward compliance, or more usually, punish deviance. Researchers then seek to understand what governs individuals' willingness to obey these laws (e.g., Smith & Tyler, 1996; Tyler, 1994).

Many important social changes have been driven by these top-down changes in social duties and rights, such as desegregation in the United States, the recognition of aboriginal treaty rights in Canada, and the implementation of language legislation in the province of Québec to render French the normative language of commerce. However, many of the duties that we perform in day-to-day life, and perhaps many of the rights that we exercise, are not covered by these black-letter norms and are not motivated by external contingencies of formal reward and punishment (Finkel, 2001; Moghaddam, 2000). Instead, day-to-day behavior is largely governed by social rewards and punishments and by internalized contingencies of self-worth. Throughout this chapter, our own discussion of rights and duties as norms considers processes that affect both commonsense and black-letter formulations. When we expand our attention from legal definitions of rights and duties to include commonsense formulations, we may study the socially and theoretically important questions, "Why are some rights and duties formalized and others not?" and "How do people respond to informal conceptualizations of rights and duties?" A complete understanding of rights and duties, therefore, requires an understanding of social influence processes that link groups and individuals in addition to the relationship between formal authorities and individuals.

The Power of Norms

Rights and duties as socially defined standards for behavior are examples of norms as defined by social psychological research. The influence of social norms on individuals' behavior has been dramatically illustrated by classic experiments in social psychology. First, norms guide individuals' perceptions, and thus their behavior, when the environment is difficult to interpret. For example, in an early experiment, Sherif (1936) analyzed groups of participants observing a light source in a dark room. Although the light was stationary, the absence of reference points led to the illusion of movement: the "autokinetic effect." Participants were asked to judge the distance that the light "moved." An individual participant's judgment was influenced dramatically by the estimates of other group members. With the help of confederates posing as participants and in a very short sequence of trials, the group converged with increasing certainty on a high- or low-magnitude norm (several feet vs. several inches) for the illusory movement.

Social norms may also be so influential that they cause individuals to override their evaluation of objective reference points. For example, in Asch's (1956) classic experiment, participants were asked to judge which of three target lines was most similar to a reference line. When participants were faced with a unanimous group of confederates of the experimenter who chose the wrong line, nearly 40% conformed by choosing the same objectively wrong answer. Such a process underscores how dependent individuals are on others as a source of social reality. When faced with a social consensus that contradicts their personal experience, many individuals rely on learned social information rather than their personal perceptions. Another line of research with respect to the perception of colors has shown that even social information that is not the product of a unanimous majority may bias individuals' perceptions: Even minorities of confederates who wrongly identified blue as green systematically influenced the perceptions of other members of the group (Moscovici, 1985; Moscovici & Faucheux, 1972). If the views of others can influence an individual's perception of a stimulus as concrete as the length of a line, social influence must be even more powerful with less concrete stimuli such as rights and duties.

Finally, norms may actually cause individuals to override their own moral values. For example, Milgram (1965, 1974; see also chap. 4, this volume) asked individuals to participate in a study of the effects of punishment on learning. Participants were assigned a "teacher" role and instructed to administer shocks of increasing intensity to a confederate "learner" whenever an error was made. The confederate provided signs of mounting discomfort as the shock intensity allegedly increased ranging from complaints to demands to stop the experiment to screams of agony and reported heart pains, and finally, an ominous silence. Only 15% of participants refused to administer shocks after the "learner" complained of heart pain, and nearly 65% of participants continued to administer shocks up to the highest, apparently life-threatening, level.

Thus, classic experiments in conformity confirm the enormous impact of norms on individuals' behavior not only in cases of high judgmental uncertainty (Sherif, 1936) but also in cases in which conformity means ignoring objective reality (Asch, 1956) or performing apparently life-threatening actions (Milgram, 1965, 1974). The Sherif and Asch experiments demonstrate norm-based resolution of ambiguity with natural phenomena. But the process is even more widely apparent with social phenomena. Effective social interaction requires that individuals constantly make accurate judgments about the intentions of others and what behavior they might expect from others. Unfortunately, judging the intentions and future behavior of others is an especially ambiguous process and therefore vulnerable to social influence. In the face of attributional ambiguity in the context of social interaction, individuals have been found to ignore or distort "objective feedback" that they receive for socially important outcomes.

Research concerning disadvantaged group members' reactions to rights violations in the form of group-based discrimination illustrates the dramatic influence of norms on social behavior. Discrimination on the basis of membership in ascribed social groups violates Western ideologies of individualism and meritocracy. For example, the 1948 UN Universal Declaration of Human Rights affirms that "Everyone is entitled to all of the rights and freedoms set forth in this Declaration, without distinction of any kind, such as race, color, sex, language, religion, political or other opinion, national or social origin, birth or other status" (cited in Ishay, 1997, Appendix 1). Accordingly, one might expect that people who perceive that they are negatively affected by group-based discrimination would unite to claim redress and restitution. Yet a recurrent finding of research on reactions to discrimination has been that, surprisingly, disadvantaged group members typically react with passivity in the face of blatant violations of their rights.

In one early instance of this phenomenon, Anglophone Québecers were asked to describe their coping strategies for dealing with group-based threats in the context of the debate over language rights in Québec (Taylor, Wong-Rieger, McKirnan, & Bercusson, 1982). The strategies listed by Anglophone Québecers were classified according to whether participants' intentions were to increase the status of themselves as individuals or of their group. Taylor et al. found that although threats perceived as collective in nature did elicit some collectively oriented strategies, a marked tendency for individualistic behavioral responses was observed even when participants attributed the threat to group membership.[2] Members of disadvantaged groups are silent when merit is used to justify group-based negative outcomes, and they do little to challenge the advantaged group's status. The social implications of this finding are clear: Passive responses to discrimination by its victims may perpetuate the existing social system to the continued advantage of privileged groups.

There are many reasons why disadvantaged group members might be reluctant to collectively challenge violations of their rights. First, as Crocker and Major have theorized (1989), instances of discrimination typically create attributional ambiguity for disadvantaged group members. When disadvantaged group members experience negative feedback, for example, not getting hired for a job or being refused housing by out-group members, the extent to which the feedback is caused by discrimination is unclear. The uncertainty created by the negative social feedback may be resolved with reference to societal norms shaped by the advantaged group. Theorists such as Markus and Kitayama (1991) and Sampson (1977) have proposed that disadvantaged group members, like their advantaged counterparts, internalize the dominant, individualist ideology of the North American meritocratic ideal. This focus on individual attributes then directs attention away from cues indicating the presence of group-based discrimination and leads victims of discrimination to gravitate toward individual-level solutions. Moreover, disadvantaged group members may be motivated to downplay actively their perceptions of rights violations rather than to perceive accurately the nega-

[2]Given that Anglophone Québecers have historically enjoyed economic and political advantages in Québec at the expense of Francophone Québecers, it may be misleading to classify them as victims of discrimination. However, their responses to intergroup threats are consistent with those found in other disadvantaged groups, and indeed, with those found in Francophone Québecers (Guimond & Dubé-Simard, 1983).

tive contingencies in their social environment. Ruggiero and Taylor (1995, 1997) demonstrated that minimization of discrimination on the part of disadvantaged groups is linked to attempts to maintain social self-esteem: When disadvantaged group members blame themselves for failure, the negative repercussions in terms of performance are offset by individuals' sustained sense of control over the social environment. What these experiments underscore is that social norms for individualism may play a role in shaping how disadvantaged-group individuals respond to rights violations in the form of group-based discrimination.

Even when the existence of discrimination is clear, disadvantaged-group members typically conform to advantaged group norms in reactions to discrimination: Normative individual action is the predominant response. In a laboratory context, Wright, Taylor, and Moghaddam (1990) found that individualistic responses persisted even when joining a high-status group on the basis of individual merit was described as virtually impossible and rights violations in the form of group-based discriminatory standards were made explicit. Given a choice between inaction, individual conformity to advantaged-group norms, individual violation of advantaged-group norms, collective conformity to advantaged-group norms, or collective violation of advantaged-group norms, a large majority of participants who were exposed to blatant group-based discrimination responded with inaction or normative individual action. Similarly, Lalonde and his colleagues (Lalonde & Cameron, 1993; Lalonde, Majumder, & Parris, 1995; Lalonde & Silverman, 1994) have observed a persistent preference across many minority groups for individualistic responses to scenarios involving discrimination even when the negative outcomes were explicitly linked to discrimination on the basis of group membership. In the socially important domain of behavioral reactions to human rights violations, then, research suggests that individuals are influenced by the norms of the advantaged out-group even when they perceive the advantaged group as actively discriminating against them.

Processes of Normative Influence

In discrimination research, participants are observed to conform to the norms of an out-group of higher status. The conformity may arise because their perceptions of the inequality are distorted (Ruggiero & Taylor, 1995, 1997) or because of internalized norms that shape reactions to discrimination (Wright et al., 1990), or because of fears of advantaged-group reprisals (Lalonde et al., 1995; Louis & Taylor, 1999). How can we understand these different processes of conformity?

A central organizing principle of research concerning the influence of norms on decision making has been the contrast between rational or mindful processes of normative influence on the one hand and irrational or mindless processes on the other. *Mindful* is used for the present discussion of normative influence to categorize cognitive influence processes variously labeled as comparative (Kelley, 1952; Festinger, 1954), informational (Deutsch & Gerard, 1955), integrative (Kelman, 1958), systematic (Chaiken, 1980), and central (Petty & Cacioppo, 1986), whereas *mindless* is used to refer to motivational processes labeled normative (Kelley, 1952; Deutsch & Gerard, 1955), compliance or identification (Kelman, 1958), group locomotion (Festinger, 1954), heuristic (Chaiken, 1980), or peripheral (Petty & Cacioppo, 1979).

Whereas mindful normative influence drives behavior by changing the manner in which individuals evaluate and process information cognitively, mindless normative influence drives behavior by establishing motivational contingencies of social rewards and punishments, such as eschewing rational behavior for behavior designed to gain the approval or disapproval of one's peers (cf. van Knippenberg, 2000). For example, norms such as "red means danger" and "green means go" might be thought to influence behavior mindfully by providing the context in which information is evaluated. Integrating such mindful influence requires cognitive resources as well as motivation, but the effects are strong, and because the underlying cognitions have been changed, the effects are long lasting. By contrast, norms such as "boys don't cry" and "children should be seen and not heard" may be thought to influence behavior mindlessly through direct social control and esteem concerns. Such an influence process is less draining of cognitive resources, but the effects may be transient and superficial. Over time, the original beliefs and attitudes may reassert themselves to overwhelm the temporary change. Norms may also operate via both processes simultaneously. For example, departmental norms concerning the publication record expected of a tenure-track junior professor both set a standard against which the budding academic evaluates her progress and overtly establishes a contingency of behavior and in-group approval.

The distinction between the two categories of process by which norms might take effect is important for the purposes of the present argument because it allows us to distinguish between internalized and extrinsic normative influence: between compliance and conformity. One process operates from the cognitive level outward: In mindful social influence, individuals use norms to evaluate themselves and their world, with corresponding implications for cognitive evaluations of the costs and benefits of behaviors, attitudes toward behaviors, and behavior itself. A second process operates from the behavioral level inward. That is, individuals change behavior or attitudes in a situation in which the norm is in force without necessarily integrating the changes into existing beliefs. Accordingly, mindless normative influence may produce incongruency among expectancy-value processes, attitudes, and behavior as people behave in a way that contradicts their private attitudes or their evaluations of the costs and benefits of the action.

In accordance with the philosophy of natural law, many Westerners have asserted the existence of universal rights. However, empirical data suggest that rights and duties are not universal in time and space: Perceptions of social entitlements as well as obligations may change across groups and over time (e.g., Thibault & Walker, 1975). Moreover, there is no a priori level at which rights and duties are observed to operate: Far from being universal, rights and duties may be specific to small groups such as families or dyads, linked to social roles within communities, or characteristic of membership in communities or nation states. Accordingly, researchers who are interested in studying human rights and duties may usefully study the impact of social norms on daily action and thinking. Individuals may use norms to identify the salient obligations and entitlements of the social environment, to categorize the social environment and identify their place in it, and to interpret the meaning of abstract principles in particular social contexts. These norms arise from social relationships; as intergroup researchers, we are particularly interested in the group level of analysis. Rights and duties are special and important types of norms: They are signals of the valued or threatened behavioral goals of the group.

A universalist conception of human rights—a laudable political agenda, many would argue, even if it is not justified as natural—signals a goal of establishing worldwide norms of human conduct. However, all societies and social groups within societies are likely to have existing conceptualizations of duties and rights in important social domains such as gender roles and reproduction, social roles, labor, status, religious and political roles, and morality (Moghaddam, 2000). Thus, establishing universal norms in these areas involves normative conflict. As all social groups come to adhere to a common code of rights and duties, particular groups' moral, political, and social codes may be assimilated or marginalized.

In summary, we contend that reactions to rights and duties claims are governed by processes of normative influence and that the contrast between mindful processes of normative influence and mindless processes are important in understanding individuals' attitudes and behaviors. When perceived rights and duties influence the manner in which individuals evaluate and process information cognitively, both attitudes and behavior are congruent with the perceived norm. However, when perceived rights and duties influence individuals through motivational contingencies of social rewards and punishments, interesting attitude–behavior discrepancies arise. Individuals may privately reject the rights and duties claim but publicly conform under the influence of rational cost–benefit analyses. As we argue, group dynamics are central in determining which of these two processes takes effect. However, an intervening proposition must be discussed: that rights and duties claims themselves are evidence of social conflict.

SOCIETAL RIGHTS AND DUTIES AS EVIDENCE OF CONFLICT

We have suggested that rights specify a protected behavioral repertoire open to particular groups and that duties specify the behaviors in which group members are expected to engage. In the present section, we present two arguments: first, that public discourse about rights and duties is associated with the perception of social normative conflict; second, that the predominance of rights versus duties rhetoric may provide cues as to whether advantaged or disadvantaged groups are taking the initiative.

When certain rights are publicly promoted, it may be taken to imply that the righteous behaviors are expected to generate opposition or reprisal: If this were not the case, the right would be taken for granted. For example, although the right to academic freedom is nominally the right to publish research on any topic, it is interpreted to mean the right to publish research that is unpopular and controversial. The right to publish socially acceptable research is taken for granted. Thus, the social significance of claiming a right is twofold: an explicit assertion of desire and an implicit expectation of challenge. When groups make public assertions of their rights, individual group members are assured that the in-group will support their righteous action and are mobilized against the expectation of challenge from out-groups. Claiming rights implicitly suggests the existence of normative conflict: Others do not recognize our rights, otherwise we would take them for granted.

Moreover, to the extent that hegemonic in-group power would reduce the expectation of challenge, claiming a right must be associated with perceived weakness vis-à-vis the out-group. Thus, we argue that a predominance of rights talk compared with duties talk suggests a state of social conflict in which a disadvantaged-group member is challenging an established and more powerful advantaged group. Rights talk may be the normative focus of public discourse for disadvantaged groups, whereas it should only arise from powerful advantaged groups if there is a perceived threat to advantaged-group superiority. To the extent that rights talk reflects disadvantaged-group initiative, then the prevalence of rights talk may be a sign of relative empowerment.

When duties are publicly promoted, it may be taken to imply that there are individuals who would not engage in the duty if it were not backed by social pressure; if this were not the case, the duty would be taken for granted. Thus, a public assertion of duties establishes that members' sense of self-worth as group members may be established through conformity to the norm. Again, the social significance of claiming a duty is twofold: an explicit assertion of the desired behavior and an implicit expectation of challenge.

Under most conditions, duties suggest the self-regulation of groups. For example, Christians may perceive a duty to attend church on Sunday; they do not perceive that other groups share this obligation. Academic psychologists conform to the American Psychological Association's standards for ethics, research, and writing; they do not perceive that academic lawyers must also conform. Failure to perform the duty may result in expulsion from a group, sanctions from group members, or a loss of status among group members, which are all extrinsic contingencies that arise from mindless normative influence or personal feelings of inadequacy as an unworthy or incompetent being to the extent that the norms have been mindfully internalized.

Duties as most people understand them arise from shared social relationships such as group membership. Thus, when conflicts arise over duties, we are led to predict an underlying phenomenon of conflict between subgroups over the definition of the superordinate social category. That is, when societal conflict over duties arises, it is frequently associated with conflict among subgroups over the definition of the society. For example, English-speaking Americans or Canadians may assert that theirs is an English-speaking country, denying the national identity of linguistic minorities and therefore justifying the imposition of a duty to conform to Anglophone language norms. Alternatively, religious majorities may assert that theirs is a Christian, Islamic, or Jewish country, denying the national identity of religious or secular minorities and therefore justifying the imposition of a duty to conform to particular religious norms.

If duties talk implies, as we have argued, an attempt to delegitimize dissident groups by asserting a superordinate societal norm, then duties talk may be characteristic of advantaged-group discourse. Advantaged groups are much more likely to straight-facedly claim that they represent society at large; disadvantaged groups may be too aware of their own minority status to make such claims. Thus, a predominance of duties talk compared with rights talk may characterize a state of social conflict in which advantaged groups are actively resisting a challenge or potential challenge to their superiority.

The argument presented here that duties talk may characterize advantaged-group members' resistance seems to contradict the phenomenon that disadvantaged groups in modern Western conflicts often accuse advantaged groups of being derelict in duties. For example, disadvantaged group members may attempt to activate advantaged-group members' sense of duty to implement existing equal rights legislation or to afford low-status-group members equal opportunities for success. We make two points in respect to disadvantaged-group members' use of this strategy. Most generally, it is consistent with the argument that rights and duties discourse is a function of intergroup conflict and with the argument that duties talk arises from conflict over superordinate social norms. More specifically, disadvantaged-group members are restricted in their use of this strategy to contexts with egalitarian or meritocratic advantaged-group norms, and the application of those norms may be strongly resisted by the advantaged group. For example, arguments by gay rights groups that employment discrimination in the military violates heterosexual soldiers' duties to be egalitarian are controversial. We return to this discussion of disadvantaged-group members' strategic use of duty talk in the paragraphs that follow.

In general, our argument that rights and duties talk implies the existence of social conflict and that the prevalence of rights talk versus duties talk may reflect relative disadvantaged- or advantaged-group initiative lacks an empirical foundation. Moreover, there is no theoretical consensus concerning the relationship between rights and duties claims and social conflict versus harmony. A contrasting theoretical perspective for the hypothesis that rights talk reflects disadvantaged groups' initiative is presented by Moghaddam in his cultural theory of human rights (Moghaddam, 2000). According to the cultural theory of rights, increasing attention on rights relative to duties may be understood as a historical phenomenon that arose with industrialization as a function of

> new means by which the rights of very large numbers of people could be systematically violated by relatively small numbers of elites. This became possible particularly because of the more sophisticated and effective apparatus for centralizing power in modern societies. . . . Legislated rights represent a reaction to this trend. (p. 308)

Thus, rights talk is seen in the cultural theory of rights as a reflection of increasing exploitation of disadvantaged groups in the modern era relative to a historically defined set of baseline rights. By contrast, we have argued that rights talk may be an index of relative empowerment for disadvantaged groups because it characterizes social debate in which disadvantaged groups are taking the initiative.

These hypotheses might be tested empirically by correlating perceptions of conflict with explicit discussion of rights and duties and correlating perceptions of perceived advantaged-group or disadvantaged-group initiative with the prevalence of rights versus duties. Although it was not the focus of the research program, a study of perceptions of human rights across 35 countries by Doise and his colleagues is suggestive in this context (Doise, Spini, & Clémence, 1999). The study observed that the perception of social conflict and injustice was linked to both differences among individuals in the perception of human rights and differences among national groups. National groups that experienced collective injustice were more involved with human rights issues. In addition, when the national differences were independently controlled, individuals who experienced collective injustice and had greater awareness of social tensions felt more personally involved in human rights issues. Thus, both at the individual and group level of analysis, people who were disadvantaged through their shared experience with collective injustice were more involved in human rights issues. We argue that these data support the hypothesis that perceived disadvantaged-group status and personal experience of disadvantage is linked to rights talk.

Future research must be conducted to replicate the link explicitly and to test whether greater power differentials increase rights talk by increasing the perception of rights violations or reduce rights talk by reducing the likelihood of disadvantaged-group initiative. Such studies might also be used to test the corollary that advantaged-group members are more involved in duties talk, either as a function of their perceived need to take the initiative, as in the threat model proposed here, or as a function of their secure ability to exploit their status, as in the Moghaddam (2000) cultural model.

UNDERSTANDING REACTIONS TO CONFLICTING NORMS

In the present chapter, we have argued that rights and duties talk is normative and that norms guide social behavior in important ways. We have suggested that rights and duties talk reflects the existence of social conflict. Such an approach implies that rights and duties must be studied in terms of norms that differ among social groups of unequal power. We turn now to the question, "If rights and duties talk reflects social normative conflict, what factors determine which rights and duties will prevail?"

In-Group Norms

If rights and duties are defined as social norms and rights and duties talk is linked to social conflict, the first questions are "Whose rights?" and "Whose duties?" An important distinction in the study of normative influence is between in-group norms, which are associated with groups of which the individual is a member, and out-group norms, which are associated with groups to which the individual does not belong. In-group norms are usually observed to be substantially more influential than any out-group norms (Terry, Hogg, & McKimmie, 2000; Terry, Hogg, & White, 2000). The primacy of in-group norms is rooted in *self-categorization theory* (Turner, Hogg, Oakes, Reicher, & Wetherell, 1987; Turner, Oakes, Haslam, & McGarty, 1994) that serves as the basis for a multistep model of in-group normative influence and the *referent informational influence* model (Terry & Hogg, 1996; Turner, Wetherell, & Hogg, 1989).

Referent informational influence theory proposes that at the perceptual level, individuals perceive themselves as members of social groups through the process of self-categorization. Individuals are members of many groups at different levels of inclusion, for example, academic, female, White, Canadian, and so forth. The interaction of personal history with the social context cues the activation of particular identities (e.g., Oakes, Turner, & Haslam, 1991). For example, for one woman, an occupational identity at work may be salient, but in response to a sexist comment from a colleague, the individual may suddenly feel aware of her gender. This personal experience might then cause her gender identity to be salient in interactions with the colleague in the future as she is vigilantly attentive to other cues of sexism.

The second step in social influence processes, social comparison, occurs at a cognitive level. Knowledge of group membership leads to an evaluation of one's group compared with other groups along dimensions of comparison defined by norms for the intergroup context. For example, in the context of modern North America, women may compare themselves with men on the dimension of pay equity and perceive themselves as worse off than men; 300 years ago, the dimension would not necessarily have been seen as relevant to gender differences. Dimensions of comparison may include traits, attitudes, and behaviors.

Third, the comparison of one's own group to an out-group is thought to result in a positive or negative emotional reaction to the position of one's group. At the individual level, self-evaluation is in terms of personal identity as a unique individual different from other in-group members. However, when individuals self-categorize as group members, self-evaluation is in terms of social identity as group members, similar to other in-group members and different from members of out-groups. Positive social identities are created when one's own group is distinct from other groups and superior according to the normatively defined dimension of comparison. Negative social identities are created by inferiority along normatively defined dimensions of comparison. For example, a woman might feel good about herself as a researcher within psychology (successful on dimensions important to the field) but unhappy about the status of women in academia compared with that of men (e.g., inferior on the salient dimensions of salary and office size).

For the purposes of the present discussion, it is important to stress that activated social identities include prescriptive norms for behavior. The result is that across different situations, when individuals perceive themselves differently, they behave differently. In the absence of intergroup conflict, self-categorization as a group member produces conformity to in-group norms. If in a given context one sees oneself as an academic, one unthinkingly conforms to professional norms; in another context, self-categorization and behavior may change. As we have already noted, group membership serves socially as a cue to relevant rights and duties: For example, professors have the right to pontificate in class and the duty to attend class without fail; students have neither this right nor this duty. According to the referent informational influence model, we do not conform to the norms of out-groups; out-groups' norms are seen as irrelevant to our decision making. In one empirical example, when students were presented with information about the norm for littering at their own university, their littering behavior changed, whereas when students were presented with information about the littering norms at another university, no change was observed (Wellen, Hogg, & Terry, 1998).

Influence of Intergroup Status on Reactions to Out-Group Norms

We argue that despite the important role played by in-group norms as identified by the referent informational influence model (Terry & Hogg, 1996), out-group norms are by no means irrelevant to decision making. Instead, we argue that it is the nature of the relationship between groups that affects individuals' susceptibility to both in-group and out-group norms (Louis, 2001; Louis & Taylor, 2001). In social psychological research, positively distinct social identities have been associated with the desire to maintain and extend comparative superiority. Thus, advantaged groups not only follow their own in-group norms but also are vigilant in their rejection of out-group norms. What advantaged group member wants to be associated with the visible norms of a disadvantaged group?

The reactions of disadvantaged-group members to their negative social identity are more differentiated. Social identity research suggests that negative social identities result in one of three classes of actions (Tajfel & Turner, 1979). Disidentification and social mobility are characterized by individuals' attempts to exit the disadvantaged group and enter the advantaged group: "I would willingly abandon my working-class identity and seek to enter the middle class." Psychological strategies of identity enhancement are characterized by either a focus on alternative dimensions of comparison, "We may be less wealthy, but we're more insightful and creative," or by a redefinition of the value of the in-group position, "We're not broke, we're nonmaterialists." Finally, social competition is characterized by attempts to compete with out-groups on established dimensions of comparison: "We want to be rich."

For the purposes of the present chapter, we stress that disidentification and social mobility create conformity to out-group norms, whereas social creativity and social competition create normative conflict (Louis, 2001; Louis & Taylor, 2001). We have argued earlier that public discourses about rights and duties arise when groups and individuals perceive the existence of normative conflict. Under conditions of normative conflict, then, which factors determine whether individuals will conform to in-group versus out-group norms?

Coercive, Unequal Power Relations

First, out-groups may coerce members of other groups against their will using extrinsic reinforcement as has been documented by research on majority influence processes (Moscovici, 1980, 1985). Moscovici demonstrated that powerful advantaged out-groups may force minorities to change their public behavior in compliance with out-group norms, but that the minorities' private views are not affected. Compliance is produced without conformity. In a study demonstrating this process regarding English–French conflict in Québec, out-group Francophone norms for intergroup behaviors influenced Anglophones' perceptions of the costs and benefits of intergroup behavior for the individual Anglophone actor (Louis & Taylor, 2001). Even controlling for perceived Anglophone norms, violating Francophone norms was associated with higher costs and fewer benefits to the individual Anglophone actor than conformity to out-group norms. Powerful out-groups may thus produce behavioral compliance with out-group conceptions of duties and impose recognition of out-group conceptions of rights by linking behavior to individual-level rewards and costs. For example, even individuals who do not privately subscribe to academic norms regarding the relative importance of work versus family may conform to powerful academic norms and so spend countless hours in the laboratory to attain a relevant individual-level benefit such as tenure.

This form of coercive normative influence, however, would not be expected to produce changes in disadvantaged groups' attitudes. As long as disadvantaged groups remain conscious of the coercive relationship, behavior change may be produced without attitude change because individuals attribute their behaviors to the external contingencies. Thus, given the opportunity, disadvantaged-group members would be expected to rebel against out-group norms and reassert the norms of the in-group. A great deal of research arising from dissonance theory demonstrates that participants who are given high justification for engaging in counterattitudinal behavior experience little attitude change and thus do not repeat the counterattitudinal behavior (e.g., Festinger & Carlsmith, 1959). Within intergroup research, moreover, Reicher and Levine (1994) have demonstrated that individuals conform to the norms of a higher status out-group publicly but not if the out-group's surveillance is relaxed.

Internalized Unequal Power Relations

However, in some recent research in intergroup psychology, it has been argued that norms for intergroup behaviors may be known and shared across both groups within a given conflict (Wright et al., 1990). For example, Anglophone and Francophone Québecers in conflict over political separation or language rights in Québec may both reject violence and endorse democratic participation. As a result, it has been argued that one may speak of "normative" and "antinormative" behaviors for a given intergroup conflict without attaching a particular group source (Taylor, Moghaddam, Gamble, & Zellerer, 1987; Wright et al., 1990). An emphasis on societal normative consensus is consistent with functionalist accounts of social norms, such as Parsons (1949) in which the societywide internalization of shared norms is seen as important in the maintenance of social order.

Shared societal norms have often been understood in terms of subgroups conforming to consensually shared norms representative of all groups. However, a contrasting view has been presented by Wright and his colleagues, who argue that the norms of importance in an intergroup context are those of the advantaged group, which disadvantaged-group members internalize (Wright et al., 1990). For example, Whites would be expected to define the norms for racial conflict, men to define the norms for gender conflict, and heterosexuals to define the norms for conflict over sexual orientation. Although disadvantaged-group norms may also regulate the behavior of members of disadvantaged groups, Wright et al. (1990) argued that advantaged-group norms, backed by social and institutional coercion, define the intergroup context more powerfully. On an empirical level, many studies adopting the Wright et al. (1990) view have supported the importance of the normative–antinormative distinction conceived in terms of a consensus driven by the norms of the advantaged group (Boen & Vanbeselaere, 1998, 2000; Ellemers, Wilke, & van Knippenberg, 1993; Kawakami & Dion, 1995; Lalonde & Cameron, 1993; Lalonde & Silverman, 1994; Louis & Taylor, 1999; Wright & Taylor, 1998; Wright et al., 1990).

To the extent that disadvantaged-group members internalize out-group norms, both behavioral conformity and attitudinal conformity will be produced so that external contingencies of reward and punishment are no longer needed. One process that may produce this internalization is the perception of in-group inferiority, as discussed previously. When individuals are trying to move into attractive high-status out-groups, they may consciously embrace out-group norms as they learn to see themselves subjectively as members of the advantaged out-group. For example, students may readily learn professional norms concerning writing and research processes; converts may embrace new religious norms for social behavior; and immigrants may readily learn native norms for language, education, or politics.

A second process that might produce this internalization of out-group norms, however, is reduced perception of the intergroup conflict. Individuals are often susceptible to social influences without being aware of the influence processes that are shaping their behavior. If individuals are led to conform behaviorally to out-group norms while perceiving personal control over their choices, their attitudes may shift toward out-group norms without any conscious attitudinal conformity. Instead of attributing the conformity to social influence, individuals may infer their attitudes from their actions, effectively creating lasting attitude change motivated by dissonance (e.g., Festinger & Carlsmith, 1959) or self-perception (Bem, 1967). For example, women may not attribute departmental norms concerning work habits to any historical gender bias, and thus, may not perceive an underlying conflict between gender norms, "I must do all the housework and raise the children," and work norms, "I must make work my first priority." If they do not make this attribution, they may conform to departmental norms without consciously making a decision to abandon their original internalized gender norms.

Strategic Conformity to, or Violation of, Out-Group Norms

In contrast to the subtle influence of out-group norms described previously, however, there are many examples of bitter intergroup conflict in the real world characterized by the salience of normative conflict and conscious, deliberate violation of out-group norms: proindependence agitation in East Timor, partisan violence in Ireland, and political and military conflict in the Middle East, to name a few. In each of these instances, the dynamic relationship of each group's behaviors is apparent in its actions and reactions to cycles of contact with the other group. During intergroup conflicts, groups may accurately perceive that norms differ and be able to identify conflicting group norms (Louis, Neil, & Taylor, 2001). For example, women may become explicitly aware of the conflict between professional norms and gender norms or minority language groups may become explicitly aware of the conflict between majority and heritage language norms.

When individuals are conscious of conflicting group norms, individuals may be led to consider explicitly the costs and benefits of conforming to the out-group norm and the costs and benefits of violating these norms (Louis, 2001). When social identities are activated, these costs and benefits may be considered at the group level of analysis. Specifically, groups may come to associate violations of out-group norms with increased benefits and reduced costs to the in-group and with a greater likelihood of motivating in-group members to reject the status quo, creating exploitable instability (Louis & Taylor, 2001). For example, the choice between peaceful protest and throwing rocks at police officers may be influenced by individuals' perceptions that violating out-group norms for protest action is more likely to prod advantaged groups to change their ways, whereas conformity will be ineffective in changing the status quo. In such a case, advantaged out-group norms need not produce either behavioral or attitudinal conformity. Deliberate violations of out-group norms may be endorsed in strategic attempts to produce instability in the social hierarchy. For example, advantaged groups' duty norms may cue deliberate violations of these norms.

Processes of Normative Influence in Rights and Duties Conflict

To return to rights and duties, then, we propose that several processes may be more or less likely to operate as a function of the relative power and status of the in-group and out-group. When group members make rights claims or reject the duty claims of out-groups, it reflects a process of identification with the in-group rather than disidentification.[3] Group members who disidentify will attempt social mobility and thus accept the norms of the relevant out-group. By contrast, rights and duties claims are assertions of an in-group norm founded on self-categorization and identification.

Rights and duties rhetoric by disadvantaged groups characterizes social conflict that seeks to motivate advantaged-group members to change their behavior by moral suasion rather than, or in addition to, coercive external contingencies. Specifically, rights and duties talk attempts to generate the perception that advantaged-group moral norms are inconsistent with out-

[3]This is not the place to review literature on changes in social identity in depth, but disidentification and attempts to exit low-status groups have been linked to the perceived permeability of group boundaries, the perceived stability of the status quo, and the perceived legitimacy of the intergroup structure (see Ellemers, 1993, for a review). Identification versus disidentification has also been demonstrated to influence duty perceptions: For example, Whites who identify as White in contrast to American were found to feel less obligation to support national laws concerning Black Americans' rights (see Tyler, Lind, Ohbuchi, Sugawara, & Huo, 1998; Tyler & Smith, 1999).

group behavioral norms. Groups win a rights and duties conflict when they have changed the perceptions of out-group members concerning the societal norm. For example, aboriginal groups must convince mainstream Canadians that the Canadian norm is for aboriginal treaty rights to be respected.

Because the desired goal of rights and duties conflict is consensual out-group change, an interesting aspect of rights and duties conflict is the tendency to produce alliances between groups of broadly disparate vested interests, for example, feminists and Christian groups united in campaigns against pornography motivated by women's right not to be exploited and religious duties to protect the sanctity of marriage. Yet feminists and Christian groups are simultaneously in conflict over the abortion debate: women's right to choose versus fetal rights to life. It is because rights and duties talk is normative that groups may bring multiple sources of normative influence to bear. Clearly, it is the nature of the intergroup relationship that affects the rights and duties norms that are salient.

Two types of rights claims may be distinguished: rights claims involving a novel dimension of comparison and rights talk involving an existing dimension of comparison. Rights claims involving a novel dimension of comparison constitute social creativity attempts in that group members are attempting to establish positive social identities by persuading advantaged out-group members to invest behaviors, attitudes, or traits with new social meaning. Although high-status group members have been observed to be unlikely to accept low-status out-group norms, as a general rule, social creativity may be less threatening to the intergroup hierarchy. Some accommodation of high-status groups to low-status requests may be observed when low-status groups attempt to establish new norms in areas that the advantaged out-group perceives as irrelevant to the intergroup relationship. For example, a general norm that police officers must wear the traditional flat cap may be challenged by Sikh police officers seeking the right to wear a turban. The majority out-group may have little vested interest in opposing the new dimension of comparison: hat wearing is not especially important as a duty or a right to non-Sikhs. Thus, the behavior is an important norm of group membership to the minority but largely irrelevant to the majority.

High-status group members' reactions to socially creative rights talk may be a function of security of status. Advantaged groups may accommodate on irrelevant dimensions of comparison to encourage disadvantaged groups to accept the legitimacy of the overall intergroup structure, preserving high-status superiority on the dimensions of comparison important to the advantaged group. For example, advantaged groups may allow low-status groups to establish unique cultural norms as long as low-status group members assimilate to majority norms for political and economic interaction. However, insecure advantaged groups may seize on new dimensions of comparison as a means of asserting control over the intergroup structure such that denying a minority group a newly asserted right serves as a message of rejection from the advantaged group. In intergroup research, social creativity has been observed to be a favored strategy of disadvantaged groups in stable, impermeable intergroup structures (e.g., Mummendey, Klink, Mielke, Wenzel, & Blanz, 1999). In the empirical study of rights and duties, we predict that disadvantaged groups are most likely to make rights claims involving novel dimensions of comparison when the intergroup structure is perceived as legitimate, stable, and impermeable.

By contrast, when the intergroup structure is impermeable and unstable or illegitimate, disadvantaged groups may attempt to compete with advantaged groups on established dimensions of comparison. In the case of rights claims involving an established dimension of comparison, disadvantaged groups are directly challenging an advantaged out-group behavioral norm that out-groups have a vested interest in maintaining. For example, the norm that Christian holidays are state holidays may be challenged by groups seeking to add recognition of major Jewish or Muslim holidays. Because there are a finite number of days on which the state is willing to give employees a paid vacation, conformity to such a rights claim would occur at the expense of advantaged out-groups' interests.

Decision-making research suggests that individuals may be motivated to act by the desire to acquire benefits and avoid costs or that individuals may be induced to act against their own immediate interests by the perception of countervailing norms (e.g., Ajzen, 1987; Fishbein & Ajzen, 1975). A disadvantaged group trying to change the behavior of a powerful out-group may strive to establish contingencies of external rewards and punishments, for example, by increasing the costs of the status quo (Louis & Taylor, 2001). However, the disadvantaged group by definition has less coercive power to establish the contingencies of reward and punishment than the advantaged out-group does. Accordingly, when attempting to challenge advantaged out-groups on established dimensions of comparison, attempts to manipulate out-group perception of norms rather than out-group perception of costs and benefits may be a favored strategy of low-status groups.

A rights or duties claim involving established dimensions of comparison is founded in the attempt to assert that an out-group norm is inconsistent with out-group behavior. Psychological research suggests that in the absence of external coercion, individuals find it psychologically unpleasant to behave in ways that are inconsistent with important attitudes. Typically attitudes change to match the behavior, rather than vice versa (e.g., Festinger & Carlsmith, 1959). However, if there is some moral stigma attached to abandoning the norm, it may be plausible to suggest that advantaged out-group members will respond to the rights or duties claim by changing their behavior. Thus, rights talk may be used by disadvantaged-group members for strategic reasons because it is the best tool with which they can induce advantaged out-group members to change. It is in this context, also, that disadvantaged-group members may attempt to exploit the existence of egalitarian advantaged-group norms. Duties talk concerning advantaged-group members' duties to implement existing egalitarian norms, particularly if these are formalized as black-letter antidiscrimination laws, may be a powerful tool for some disadvantaged groups, particularly those in 20th and 21st century Western contexts.

We have argued, however, that duties claims may often rest on a different foundation. To plausibly assert a duty claim, groups must be in a position to argue that their norm represents the "true" societal norm. We have argued that majority, advantaged groups are more likely to be able to claim to represent societal norms, and thus, more likely to assert duty claims. Disadvantaged-group members internalize such claims under two conditions, we hypothesize. First, if disadvantaged-group members fail to attribute the influence attempt to group status, they may conform behaviorally and thus internalize the norm without conscious processes of influence. Second, if they perceive the advantaged group as superior on established dimensions of comparison, disadvantaged-group members may disidentify from their own group and actively seek to embrace advantaged-group norms.

If disadvantaged-group members do not disidentify and perceive the existence of intergroup conflict, then behavioral conformity may be produced by individual-level contingencies of reward and punishment (e.g., Moscovici, 1985; Reicher & Levine, 1994). However, a fourth outcome is also possible: deliberate violation of advantaged out-group norms motivated by group-level cost–benefit analyses (Louis, 2001; Louis & Taylor, 2001). In this instance, the advantaged out-group norm provides a guide on how to express a rejection of out-group influence. For example, the duty to respect the flag as a national symbol is the motivation for flag burning: The only meaning of flag burning is a deliberate violation of out-group norms.

IMPLICATIONS OF AN INTERGROUP MODEL ON THE STUDY OF RIGHTS AND DUTIES

In their opening chapter, Finkel and Moghaddam (chap. 1, this volume) propose seven questions that we might address relevant to the discussion of rights and duties. Although we have not addressed these questions empirically, our normative intergroup analysis creates a framework for hypotheses concerning the social analysis of rights and duties.

Question 13. Are duties an independent discourse from rights?

We would support those (e.g., Harré & Robinson, 1995) who argue that they are. From an intergroup perspective, both duties and rights are related to identity or group membership, and group membership probably entails both duties and rights. But there need be no psychologically or socially important relationship of complementary duties and rights. Such an argument would mean that salient rights and duties are always defined on the same dimension of behavior, which seems an inaccurate characterization of rights and duties discourse. For example, one current debate concerns the legitimacy of trading the duty not to commit a felony with the right of prisoners to vote (e.g., Zeilbauer, 2001). Thus, the social argument centers on the link between noncontingent rights and duties.

In addition, rights and duties may have quite different social ontologies (Harré & Robinson, 1995): We frame the difference in terms of group differences in power. We have argued that rights claims may characterize low-power groups' political rhetoric and that duties claims characterize the rhetoric of high-power groups. Little research has been performed in this area, but some cross-national research in involvement in human rights (Doise et al., 1999) is consistent with our framework.

Question 15. Is there an origins distinction between rights and duties because rights are often linked to our very being, as in inalienable rights, whereas duties seem to stem from relationships—person to God, person to society, person to person, or person in role?

No, we do not believe so. As we have argued throughout the present chapter, rights are awarded to classes of individuals, and rights are articulated when individuals and groups perceive conflict within an existing relationship. Thus, both rights and duties arise in the context of social relationships.

Question 16. Are there social duties and supererogatory duties?

It seems highly likely to us that supererogatory duties may usefully be framed in terms of group membership. Empirically, social definitions of duties to the environment or to God are characterized by salient differences among social groups. Within North American history, changing perceptions of the duty to conquer and mold nature versus the duty to save and protect the earth seem closely linked to changing resource needs of social groups. To the extent that supererogatory duties are bounded by history and social group membership, they are normative social duties.

Question 14. Is there a greater normative weight on a duty in that the duty conveys an "ought" that the right does not have?
Question 17. What are we to make of the affective distinction between rights that are happily embraced by individuals who have them and duties that seem imposed and even burdensome?
Question 18. How is it that rights need not be exercised or can be waived, whereas waiving duties is not so easily done?

For us, these questions rest in the definition that is applied to socially defined duty and right. Debate, therefore, should not be conducted in terms of an essentialist argument regarding the true nature of rights and duties but rather should seek to describe and interpret rights and duties as prevalent theoretically defined, empirically observed phenomena.

In the present chapter, we have defined duties as mandated behaviors and rights as protected behavioral repertoires: As such, duty norms constrain behavior, whereas rights norms enable behavior. Moreover, we have argued that duty talk characterizes advantaged-group discourse and thus that duty norms are often backed by more coercive power than rights talk, which characterizes disadvantaged-group discourse. For both of these reasons, we might argue that duties have more normative weight than rights.

However, we would caution that the concept of normative weight may involve several processes of normative influence: changed perception of the status quo, perceived moral obligation derived from internalization, social pressure derived from group membership, and black-letter contingencies of punishment and reward derived from formalization of the discourse. In our view, the most weighty norms are those that are taken for granted because they guide group members' perceptions of the status quo. Thus, norms are most influential not when they feel like imperatives to the individual ("I ought to send my parents money every month") nor when they feel like guides to self-esteem ("I am worthy because I send my parents money every month") but rather when they are devoid of affective or moral tone because they are taken for granted ("I send my parents money every month . . . that's how it is").

In terms of the phenomenology of duties and rights, we have argued that duty claims are asserted when groups expect that in the absence of sanctions the desired goal would not be achieved. Thus, by definition, duty claims may signal an onerous behavior. By contrast, rights claims are attempts to establish protected behavioral repertoires of desirable actions. By definition, then, rights are more desirable than duties.

However, personal feelings regarding socially important rights may not be characterized by blithe positive affect because we have argued that socially important rights claims are made when groups expect that the righteous behavior will generate interference and sanction from out-groups. Rights may be happily embraced when they are won; a more usual situation, we have argued, is that obtained rights are devoid of affect because they are taken for granted. How much positive affect have you personally experienced in the last week over academic freedom of expression or the right to political liberty? We would expect that only those suffering from repression have actually considered their rights at all. Thus, rights become socially salient in conditions of conflict. Rights may be fearfully asserted more often than they are happily embraced.

Similarly, duties that are salient to individuals may indeed be characterized by the perception of burden, because we have argued that duties become socially salient when groups expect that members will refrain from the action in the absence of sanctions. However, to the extent that duties are internalized, duties should be taken for granted rather than affectively loaded. Thus, it may not feel burdensome for undergraduates to refrain from pontificating during large lecture classes; most take the role for granted. Similarly, we have already noted that acceptance and inaction are characteristic reactions to human rights violations for most disadvantaged groups when the intergroup context is stable.

Question 19. When rights and duties appear to clash, how do ordinary citizens reconcile such clashes, and are these reconciliations different from the solutions and reasons offered by judges and justices?

We have discussed at some length our model of how ordinary citizens reconcile rights and duties clashes. Application of an intergroup model to the question of how judges reconcile rights and duties at once raises the question of judges' group membership. Because the judiciary is a seat of social power, judges are disproportionately likely to be members of advantaged groups. We have argued that advantaged-group norms are often framed in terms of duties rather than rights, and therefore as a general rule, we would expect judges to endorse duties over rights when the two clash. In so doing, judges' views would be disproportionately likely to be congruent with the views of citizens who were members of advantaged groups and disproportionately incongruent with the views of disadvantaged citizens.

However, as Moghaddam (2000) has argued in his cultural theory of rights, in present-day Western society, rights may be more likely to be formalized in law than duties. Because judges have a normatively imposed duty to uphold black-letter legal codes rather than implicit advantaged-group norms per se, the prevalence of legal rights over duties may be reflected in judges' decision making. In fact, many important changes in societal rights have been won in the courts despite opposition from the majority of the population: Earlier we cited the example of aboriginal treaty rights in Canada. It would be an interesting empirical exercise to code existing laws for rights-versus-duties focus and then to predict judicial decisions on the basis of social group membership and legal rights and duty norms. The most socially desirable outcome would clearly be that gender, race, and other social category markers of advantaged-group status would contribute nothing to the prediction of judicial decisions and would be unrelated to tendencies to uphold, extend, or curtail rights and duties laws.

CONCLUSIONS

The study of rights and duties is an area of great social and theoretical interest. In applying an intergroup model to the present research area, we have argued that rights and duties may usefully be framed in terms of socially defined norms and normative influence. Norms are defined as group-based standards or rules for behavior and are characterized by within-group social consensus. However, universalist approaches to rights and duties are rejected in the present model. Social discussion of particular rights and duties is argued to imply the existence of conflicting norms because otherwise the rights and duties would be taken for granted. Thus, the salience of debates over rights and duties in political life points to normative conflict between social groups. Finally, we have argued that individuals' resolutions of conflicting norms may be predicted importantly by their group membership and by relative in-group power and status.

REFERENCES

Ajzen, I. (1987). Attitudes, traits, and actions: Dispositional prediction of behavior in personality and social psychology. In L. Berkowitz (Ed.), *Advances in experimental social psychology* (Vol. 20, pp. 1–63). San Diego, CA: Academic Press.

Asch, S. E. (1956). Studies of independence and conformity: A minority of one against a unanimous majority. *Psychological Monographs, 70*, 1–70.

Bem, D. J. (1967). Self-perception: An alternative interpretation of cognitive dissonance. *Psychological Review, 74*, 183–200.

Boen, F., & Vanbeselaere, N. (1998). Reactions upon a failed attempt to enter a high-status group: An experimental test of the five-stage model. *European Journal of Social Psychology, 21*, 689–696.

Boen, F., & Vanbeselaere, N. (2000). Responding to membership of a low-status group: The effects of stability, permeability and individual ability. *Group Processes & Intergroup Relations, 3*(1), 41–62.

Chaiken, S. (1980). Heuristic versus systematic information processing and the use of source versus message cues in persuasion. *Journal of Personality and Social Psychology, 39*, 752–756.

Crocker, J., & Major, B. (1989). Social stigma and self-esteem: The self-productive properties of stigma. *Psychological Review, 96*, 608–630.

Deutsch, M., & Gerard, H. B. (1955). A study of normative and informational influences upon individual judgement. *Journal of Abnormal and Social Psychology, 51*, 629–636.

Doise, W., Spini, D., & Clémence, A. (1999). Human rights studied as social representations in a cross-national context. *European Journal of Social Psychology, 29*, 1–29.

Ellemers, N. (1993). The influence of socio-structural variables on identity management strategies. In W. Stroebe & M. Hewstone (Eds.), *European review of social psychology* (Vol. 4, pp. 27–57). New York: Wiley.

Ellemers, N., Wilke, H., & van Knippenberg, A. (1993). Effects of the legitimacy of low group or individual status on individual and collective status-enhancement strategies. *Journal of Personality and Social Psychology, 64*, 766–778.

Festinger, L. (1954). A theory of social comparison processes. *Human Relations, 7*, 117–140.

Festinger, L., & Carlsmith, J. M. (1959). Cognitive consequences of forced compliance. *Journal of Abnormal and Social Psychology, 58*, 203–210.

Finkel, N. J. (2001). *Not fair! The typology of commonsense unfairness*. Washington, DC: American Psychological Association.

Fishbein, M., & Ajzen, I. (1975). *Belief, attitude, intention and behavior: An introduction to theory and research*. Reading, MA: Addison-Wesley.

Guimond, S., & Dubé-Simard, L. (1983). Relative deprivation theory and the Quebec nationalist movement: The cognition–emotion distinction and the personal group deprivation issue. *Journal of Personality and Social Psychology, 44*, 526–535.

Harré, R., & Robinson, D. N. (1995). On the primacy of duties. *Philosophy, 70*, 513–532.

Ishay, M. R. (Ed.). (1997). *The human rights reader: Major political essays, speeches, and documents from the bible to the present*. New York: Routledge.

Kawakami, K., & Dion, K. L. (1995). Social identity and affect as determinants of collective action. *Theory and Psychology, 5*, 551–577.

Kelley, H. H. (1952). Two functions of reference groups. In G. E. Swanson, T. M. Newcomb, & E. L. Hartley (Eds.), *Readings in social psychology* (2nd ed., pp. 410–414). New York: Holt.

Kelman, H. C. (1958). Compliance, identification, and internalization: Three processes of attitude change. *Journal of Conflict Resolution, 2*, 51–60.

Lalonde, R. N., & Cameron, J. E. (1993). Behavioral responses to discrimination: A focus on action. In M. P. Zanna & J. M. Olson (Eds.), *The psychology of prejudice: The Ontario symposium* (Vol. 7, pp. 257–288). Hillsdale, NJ: Erlbaum.

Lalonde, R. N., Majumder, S., & Parris, R. D. (1995). Preferred responses to situations of housing and employment discrimination. *Journal of Applied Social Psychology, 25*, 1105–1119.

Lalonde, R. N., & Silverman, R. A. (1994). Behavioral preferences in response to social injustice: The effects of group permeability and social identity salience. *Journal of Personality and Social Psychology*, 66, 78–85.

Louis, W. R. (2001). *Grumbling, voting, demonstrating, and rioting: Social identity and decision-making in intergroup contexts*. Unpublished doctoral thesis, McGill University, Montréal, Canada.

Louis, W. R., Neil, T., & Taylor, D. M. (2001, June). *The construction and influence of in-group versus out-group norms in an intergroup context.* Poster session presented at the annual meeting of the Canadian Psychological Association, Ste-Foy, Québec.

Louis, W. R., & Taylor, D. M. (1999). From passive acceptance to social disruption: Towards an understanding of behavioural responses to discrimination. *Canadian Journal of Behavioural Science, 31*(1), 19–28.

Louis, W. R., & Taylor, D. M. (2001, June). *Law-abiding protests, calibrated riots: Social identity and in-group versus out-group norms in intergroup conflict.* Paper presented at the annual meeting of the Canadian Psychological Association, Ste-Foy, Québec.

Markus, H. R., & Kitayama, S. (1991). Culture and the self: Implications for cognition, emotion, and motivation. *Psychological Review, 98*, 224–253.

Milgram, S. (1965). Some conditions of obedience and disobedience to authority. *Human Relations, 18*, 57–76.

Milgram, S. (1974). *Obedience to authority: An experimental view.* New York: Harper & Row.

Moghaddam, F. M. (2000). Toward a cultural theory of human rights. *Theory & Psychology, 10*, 291–312.

Moghaddam, F. M., Slocum, N. R., Finkel, N., Mor, T., & Harré, R. (2000). Toward a cultural theory of duties. *Culture & Psychology, 6*, 275–302.

Moscovici, S. (1980). Towards a theory of conversion behavior. In L. Berkowitz (Ed.), *Advances in experimental social psychology* (Vol. 13, pp. 209–239). San Diego, CA: Academic Press.

Moscovici, S. (1985). Social influence and conformity. In G. Lindzey & E. Aronson (Eds.), *The handbook of social psychology* (3rd ed., pp. 347–412). Hillsdale, NJ: Erlbaum.

Moscovici, S., & Faucheux, C. (1972). Social influence, conforming bias, and the study of active minorities. In L. Berkowitz (Ed.), *Advances in experimental social psychology* (Vol. 6, pp. 149–202). New York: Academic Press.

Mummendey, A., Klink, A., Mielke, R., Wenzel, M., & Blanz, M. (1999). Socio-structural characteristics of intergroup relations and identity management strategies: Results from a field study in East Germany. *European Journal of Social Psychology, 29*, 259–285.

Oakes, P. J., Turner, J. C., & Haslam, S. A. (1991). Perceiving people as group members: The role of fit in the salience of social categorizations. *British Journal of Social Psychology, 30*, 125–144.

Office of the UN High Commissioner on Human Rights. (2001a). *Fact sheet No. 2 (Rev. 1), The International Bill of Human Rights.* Retrieved November 28, 2001, from http://www.unhcr.ch/html/menu6/2/fs2.htm

Office of the UN High Commissioner on Human Rights. (2001b). *Status of ratifications of the principal international human rights treaties.* Retrieved November 29, 2001, from http://www.unhchr.ch/html/menu3/b/a_cescr.htm

Parsons, T. (1949). *The structure of social action.* New York: Free Press.

Petty, R. E., & Cacioppo, J. (1979). Issue involvement can increase or decrease persuasion by enhancing message-relevant cognitive responses. *Journal of Personality and Social Psychology, 37*, 1915–1926.

Reicher, S., & Levine, M. (1994). Deindividuation, power relations between groups and the expression of social identity: The effects of visibility to the out-group. *British Journal of Social Psychology, 33*, 145–163.

Ruggiero, K. M., & Taylor, D. M. (1995). Coping with discrimination: How disadvantaged group members perceive the discrimination that confronts them. *Journal of Personality and Social Psychology, 68*, 826–838.

Ruggiero, K. M., & Taylor, D. M. (1997). Why minority group members perceive or do not perceive the discrimination that confronts them: The role of self-esteem and perceived control. *Journal of Personality and Social Psychology, 72*, 373–389.

Rutenberg, J. (2001, November 5). Torture seeps into discussion by news media. *New York Times*. Retrieved November 28, 2001, from http://www.nytimes.com

Sampson, E. E. (1977). Psychology and the American ideal. *Journal of Personality and Social Psychology, 35*, 767–782.

Sherif, M. (1936). *The psychology of social norms*. New York: Harper & Brothers.

Smith, H. J., & Tyler, T. R. (1996). Justice and power: When will justice concerns encourage the advantaged to support policies which redistribute economic resources and the disadvantaged to willingly obey the law? *European Journal of Social Psychology, 26*, 171–200.

Tajfel, H., & Turner, J. C. (1979). An integrative theory of intergroup conflict. In W. G. Austin & S. Worchel (Eds.), *The social psychology of intergroup relations* (pp. 33–47). Monterey, CA: Brooks/Cole.

Taylor, D. M., Moghaddam, F. M., Gamble, I., & Zellerer, E. (1987). Disadvantaged group responses to perceived inequality: From passive acceptance to collective action. *Journal of Social Psychology, 127*, 259–272.

Taylor, D. M., Wong-Rieger, D., McKirnan, D. J., & Bercusson, J. (1982). Interpreting and coping with threat in the context of intergroup relations. *Journal of Social Psychology, 117*, 257–269.

Terry, D. J., & Hogg, M. A. (1996). Group norms and the attitude–behavior relationship: A role for group identification. *Personality and Social Psychology Bulletin, 22*, 776–793.

Terry, D. J., Hogg, M. A., & McKimmie, B. M. (2000). Attitude–behaviour relations: The role of in-group norms and mode of behavioural decision-making. *British Journal of Social Psychology, 39*, 337–361.

Terry, D. J., Hogg, M. A., & White, K. M. (2000). Attitude–behavior relations: Social identity and group membership. In D. J. Terry & M. A. Hogg (Eds.), *Attitudes, behavior, and social context* (pp. 67–93). London: Erlbaum.

Thibault, J., & Walker, L. (1975). *Procedural justice: A psychological analysis*. Hillsdale, NJ: Erlbaum.

Turner, J. C., Hogg, M. A., Oakes, P. J., Reicher, S. D., & Wetherell, M. S. (1987). *Rediscovering the social group: A self-categorization theory*. Oxford, England: Blackwell.

Turner, J. C., Oakes, P. J., Haslam, S. A., & McGarty, C. (1994). Self and collective: Cognition and social context. *Personality and Social Psychology Bulletin, 20*, 454–463.

Turner, J. C., Wetherell, M. S., & Hogg, M. A. (1989). Referent informational influence and group polarization. *British Journal of Social Psychology, 28*, 135–147.

Tyler, T. R. (1994). Governing amid diversity: The effect of fair decision-making procedures on the legitimacy of government. *Law & Society Review, 28*, 809–831.

Tyler, T. R., Lind, E. A., Ohbuchi, K.-I., Sugawara, I., & Huo, Y. J. (1998). Conflict with outsiders: Disputing within and across cultural boundaries. *Personality and Social Psychology Bulletin, 24*, 137–148.

Tyler, T. R., & Smith, H. J. (1999). Justice, social identity, and group processes. In T. R. Tyler, R. M. Kramer, & O. P. John (Eds.), *The psychology of the social self* (pp. 223–264). London: Erlbaum.

U.S. charges brought against 650 since Sept. 11. (2001, November 27). *New York Times*. Retrieved November 28, 2001, from http://www.nytimes.com

van Knippenberg, D. (2000). Group norms, prototypicality, and persuasion. In D. J. Terry & M. A. Hogg (Eds.), *Attitudes, behavior, and social context* (pp. 157–170). London: Erlbaum.

Wellen, J., Hogg, M., & Terry, D. (1998). Group norms and attitude–behavior consistency: The role of group salience and mood. *Group Dynamics, 2*(1), 48–56.

Wright, S. C., & Taylor, D. M. (1998). Responding to tokenism: Individual action in the face of collective injustice. *European Journal of Social Psychology, 28*, 647–667.

Wright, S. C., Taylor, D. M., & Moghaddam, F. M. (1990). Responding to membership in a disadvantaged group: From acceptance to collective protest. *Journal of Personality and Social Psychology, 58*, 994–1003.

Zeilbauer, P. (2001, May 15). Felons gain voting rights in Connecticut. *New York Times*. Retrieved November 29, 2001, from http://www.nytimes.com

II

EMPIRICAL CONTRIBUTIONS ON THE RELATIONSHIP BETWEEN RIGHTS AND DUTIES

6

A DEFERENCE-BASED PERSPECTIVE ON DUTY: EMPOWERING GOVERNMENT TO DEFINE DUTIES TO ONESELF AND TO OTHERS

TOM R. TYLER

Recent discussions of Americans and of American culture have presented our national character as being dominated by feelings of entitlement, as a *rights culture* in which people focus on what they feel society owes to them (see Etzioni, 1993; Glendon, 1991; Lasch, 1979; Mitchell, 1998; Putnam, 1995; Spragens, 1999; Taylor, 1989). Further, people are viewed as motivated to protect the freedom and liberty that allow them to act on their own desires, being suspicious of and resisting government and other forms of authority that might tie them to obligations and responsibilities to others. In short, people are depicted as being focused on their own desires and needs, which they want to be free to fulfill, and resistant to responsibilities and obligations to others in society.

This chapter addresses the issue of how Americans construe, understand, and interpret their duties (see chap. 1, Question 2, this volume). In particular, I seek to examine the nature of people's commonsense notions of duty (chap. 1, Question 3, this volume), and to connect those views of duty to the formal types of duty articulated in law. My basic thesis is that the relationship between duties and rights (chap. 1, Question 2, this volume) has been posed in a way that portrays people's views of personal duty as declining. However, if we think about people's commonsense model of duty, we find that people continue to feel a strong sense of duty, responsibility, and obligation toward others when duty is framed in a way that is consistent with people's views about justice (chap. 1, Questions 11 and 12, this volume). In other words, I suggest that people feel strong responsibilities toward others and are not simply self-interested or rights focused. But, to be effective, calls to duty need to be presented to people in ways that they judge to be consistent with their norms of fairness.

There are certainly examples of people's unwillingness to act on behalf of others easily available from any examination of current events. The Kitty Genovese incident in which a large number of people failed to act to help a woman in distress provides a dramatic example of this failure to act on behalf of others. That incident highlights in graphic fashion people's willingness to ignore harm that is occurring to others and their unwillingness to feel a sense of duty and responsibility for others, at least in some settings.

The current intellectual climate in the United States is one within which social critics and commentators are increasingly focusing on the need to balance feelings of personal entitlement, *rights talk*, with greater feelings of responsibility and obligation to society and to others in society. It is believed that people's feelings about their duties and responsibilities to others are in decline (see chap. 1, this volume).[1] For example, people are viewed as lacking feelings of responsibility to others and as resisting feeling that they have a duty to intervene in emergencies, to proactively take actions on behalf of those around them.

Beginning with an examination of everyday life, I argue that Americans do have strong feelings of duty and responsibility of at least one particular type. The duty that I suggest that people feel is the sense of responsibility and obligation to defer to and to accept the decisions of government authorities. I argue that people generally feel that government agents, such as the police, the courts, and other regulatory agents, are entitled to be obeyed and that it is their personal responsibility to defer to and follow their decisions and the rules they enact. I show that this feeling of obligation leads people to bring their behavior into line with the law.

Further, contrary to the image of Americans as resisting government and wanting smaller and less powerful government to be better able to pursue their individual rights unfettered from restraint, I argue that studies sug-

[1]Because all of the studies I examine focus on Americans, my discussion of these issues focuses on questions of rights and duties as those concepts are understood within the United States. I do not address the larger question of the universality of these conceptions. Recent examinations of social psychological processes make clear that basic processes differ markedly across cultures (see Moghaddam, 1998).

gest that people express the desire to empower government and to allow it to restrict their personal freedoms when they feel that they need to do so to solve social problems and resolve social issues. My impression is that Americans look to government to act as a rule maker and a referee in a wide variety of situations, including managing shortages, protecting the integrity of markets, and interpreting the meaning of the Constitution.

This desire to empower government combines with the already noted feeling of responsibility to obey government authorities. Hence, once empowered, authorities enjoy a widespread presumption that they ought to be obeyed. This combination of the desire to have government take on the power to resolve problems, combined with the feeling that government ought to be obeyed, portrays a different image of Americans. It suggests that Americans believe that government authorities should be deferred to once they have used the authority people give them to make rules and decisions about rules for resolving controversial issues. Of course, this power is not absolute. People recognize that there are circumstances under which they might disobey government rules and decisions.[2] Although not absolute, such power is considerable. People seem to generally feel that they should defer to government rules and decisions, although such feelings are qualified.

These findings suggest that Americans are not simply self-focused and self-absorbed. They have a particular conception of how responsibility to others should be manifested. It should be handled, under certain circumstances, through compliance with the decisions of government after government has formulated appropriate rules and procedures for public conduct. So, when there are controversial issues to be resolved, people want to empower authorities to resolve those issues by coming up with a decision or a rule. People then feel responsible for conforming to that rule.

One important reason for this desire to empower government is the view that voluntarism produces unfair outcomes. For example, those who volunteer to help the disadvantaged provide their hard work without reward, whereas others can "ride free" on their efforts by lowering the amount of money that they give the government or charities to deal with the problems of disadvantage. The efforts of volunteers to work to solve social problems are examples of feelings of duty and responsibility to help others. But, they may also lead those volunteers to feel, over time, that their effort has allowed others to reap unfair advantages by keeping their resources and promoting their personal goals, counting on volunteers to manage society's problems.

[2]Because the law limits people's ability to do what they choose, it would seem strange to talk about a right to obey. Instead, we view obedience as a duty to put obligations and responsibilities ahead of personal desires. However, disobedience can be either a right or a duty. We think of people as having the right to disobey unjust laws. Hence, much of the discussion of legitimacy is focused on whether legal authorities are entitled to be obeyed. If they are not, then people have a right to ignore their orders. We might also say that people have a duty to disobey unjust laws. For example, when officers order soldiers to murder civilians, we might say that those soldiers have not only the right to disobey but also the duty to disobey.

When people feel that their good efforts resulted in the unfair allocation of responsibilities across the members of society, they want to have a fair referee who allocates responsibilities, rather than relying on volunteers (Finkel, 2001).

Consider an example of this idea for managing social problems. Society might, for example, stop imposing taxes on citizens and simply ask the members of society to voluntarily donate money to help society. If we did so, we would probably find wide differences in the amount of money that people gave to society. Over time, those who were willing to contribute to help society in general might grow angry with those who made no contribution, but who drove on collective roads, vacationed in collective parks, and so forth. They might well feel that it was unfair for those "deadbeats" to profit from the voluntary contributions of others. So, they might advocate rules dictating how much each person had to contribute to society. Such a social dynamic is, in fact, why we have a tax code. Now, with such rules, we have an authority that dictates the "fair" solution to the problem of responsibility and obligation in society. People are, of course, free to contribute more to society than is required by law, but they can also feel that if they pay their taxes, society feels they have met some level of reasonable responsibility and obligation toward government and society. If they follow the law, people are entitled to feel that they have "done their duty" and they are free to use their resources to pursue their own self-interest (although, of course, they can give even more to others).

This sense of responsibility to defer to government authorities and rules does not fit the needs of all situations. The situation of Kitty Genovese, the innocent victim attacked by a stranger in an alley at night, is a good example. In that case, what was needed from neighbors was a feeling of responsibility to act individually in a unique and unstructured way, to help the person or call the police for help. There was no formal rule requiring a response, so an assumption of individual responsibility to take some action was needed. In people's experiences with the police, for example, the legal system has two concerns. First, it views obeying the law as an obligation; people should do it. Obeying the law is a duty, and those who fail to observe that duty can be and are formally and informally sanctioned. Second, the legal system views it as desirable and valuable for people to help the police by reporting crimes, patrolling neighborhoods, and the like. But this latter issue is not a duty, and people are generally not held to account if they do not do it, just as it is not a crime not to vote, even though society encourages people to participate in government.

The type of responsibility I am outlining does not involve the need to invent appropriate actions as an individual. Instead, people are faced with a rule or decision, and they need to take the responsibility to self-regulate by obeying that rule or decision. So, for example, those faced with someone being attacked on the street need to think about what their duty is and, if

TABLE 6.1
Perceived Obligation to Obey the Chicago Police Courts

Survey statement	Percentage agreeing
People should obey the law even if it goes against what they think is right.	82
I always try to follow the law even if I think it is wrong.	82
Disobeying the law is seldom justified.	79
It is difficult to break the law and keep one's self-respect.	69
If a person is doing something and a police officer tells them to stop, they should stop even if they feel that what they are doing is legal.	84
If a person goes to court because of a dispute with another person, and the judge orders them to pay the other person money, they should pay that person money, even if they think that the judge is wrong.	74

Note. The number of respondents was 1,575, and the alpha level on the six items was .57.

they think it is appropriate, implement some voluntary plan of appropriate actions. If a policeman is present, however, they need only be willing to follow that authority's directives about what they should do. The authority determines what their duty is and communicates it to them.

DUTY IN EVERYDAY LIFE: DO PEOPLE FEEL A DUTY TO OBEY THE LAW?

My first argument is that people do feel a sense of duty in the arena of obedience to legal authorities. This suggests that we should find considerable feelings of obligation to obey laws expressed in samples of the American public. Research findings confirm that we do. For example, I explored people's feelings about their perceived obligation to obey laws during their everyday lives in a survey based on a random sample of 1,575 of the residents of Chicago (Tyler, 1990).

The percentages found are shown in Table 6.1. They indicate widespread support for the argument that people feel that they should obey the law. For instance, in the interviews, 82% of those interviewed indicated that "People should obey the law, even if it goes against what they think is right." Similarly, 82% indicated that "I always try to follow the law, even if I think it is wrong."[3]

These findings suggest a considerable reservoir of feelings of duty and responsibility to obey the law among those studied in this sample, a represen-

[3]As in any study that relies on self-reports, we should have some sensitivity to issues of social desirability as a possible motivation for responses. In this case, it is important to recognize that people may feel it is important to present an image of themselves as having values that they may not hold. One piece of evidence that these self-reports are not mere artifacts is the suggestion that they shape people's behavior (Tyler, 1990). For a detailed discussion of the validity of self-report data in this context, see Tyler (1990).

TABLE 6.2
Percentage of Agreement in Perceived Obligation to Obey the Chicago Police and Courts

Survey statement	Group	
	White	Nonwhite
People should obey the law even if it goes against what they think is right.	80	84
I always try to follow the law even if I think it is wrong.	81	83
Disobeying the law is seldom justified.	80	79
It is difficult to break the law and keep one's self-respect.	65	73
Average	77	80

tative sample of the people living in Chicago. This is true both for people's personal feelings ("I should obey") and for their general feelings about what is right ("People should obey").

It is also interesting that these feelings of obligation to obey the law were high among disadvantaged subgroups (in this study, African Americans) within the population. For example, a separate analysis of White versus Nonwhite respondents indicated similarly high levels of obligation to obey the law within both groups as shown in Table 6.2. (For a more detailed discussion of subgroup feelings, see Tyler, Boeckmann, Smith, & Huo, 1997.) So, the feeling of obligation to obey the law is widespread within this diverse urban population.

In Tyler (1990), the behavioral impact of such feelings of obligation was examined.[4] It was found that those who felt obligated to obey the law did so frequently during their everyday lives.

In these analyses, it is striking that the impact of obligation was greater than the influence of deterrence judgments. In other words, personal feelings of responsibility and obligation (i.e., duty) were more influential than were fears about being caught and punished for wrongdoing. Expressions of responsibility had clear behavioral impact: They influenced what people did in their everyday lives.

These findings suggest that people feel a considerable sense of personal responsibility to curb personal freedoms when those freedoms conflict with social rules. In this sense, Americans seem like a group of people who are generally willing to restrict their personal freedom to act as they wish when required to do so by social rules. In such a situation, of course, the nature of the required behavioral changes is clear-cut, and people can also feel confident that general norms are being applied uniformly such that the fairness

[4]In the analysis conducted, obligation is combined with institutional trust to form an index of legitimacy. This index is used in the analysis reported here.

principle of equal justice is likely to result. In other words, Americans generally expect people to conform to rules.

It is also possible to view the conflict that people feel as a conflict between the strength of duties-versus-rights feelings, something addressed elsewhere in this volume (chap. 1, this volume). People were asked what they would do if the law conflicted with their personal sense of what is right. We might expect that people would disobey or at least say that they are entitled to disobey, supported by their personal beliefs that the truth is on their side. Yet, we do not find that people indicate that they would disobey. Over 80% of respondents in the Chicago study favored the duty to obey and comply, even in a situation in which they might be viewed as feeling that they have the right to disobey and follow their personal moral values.

The California Study

The general feelings of responsibility and obligation outlined in the study of the residents of Chicago were found to shape people's everyday behavior toward the law. Tyler and Huo (2002) ask whether those same general feelings about the duty to obey authorities influenced whether people followed directives during their personal encounters with police officers and judges. For example, when a police officer tells someone to "move along" on the sidewalk, do they do so? When a judge issues an order to pay child support, does the person who receives the order follow it?

The Tyler and Huo (2002) study is based on interviews with 1,656 citizens of Oakland and Los Angeles, California, each of whom had a recent personal experience with the police or courts. The question addressed whether people voluntarily deferred to the authorities when given a specific directive. Such voluntary deference is distinguished from simple compliance by self-reports about whether people deferred when they could have avoided detection for noncompliance, could have appealed, or could have continued to contend with the authorities.

One factor that might shape deference in a particular situation is the outcome of the experience. One would expect people to defer more readily to favorable and fair decisions, that is, when the outcome is desirable. Another reason that people might defer is that they think that they have a duty to defer to legal authorities. In this study obligation to defer was measured using three items: "I feel that I should accept the decisions made by legal authorities" (72% agree); "People should obey the law even if it goes against what they think is right" (77% agree); and "It is difficult to break the law and keep one's self-respect" (62% agree). People generally endorsed the duty to defer, as shown by the percentage agreeing with each statement.

Tyler and Huo (2002; also discussed in Tyler, 2001b) compared the influence of the nature of the outcome a person received during an experience and their broader feelings about their obligation to defer[5] on their willingness to defer in particular personal experiences (see Tyler, 2001b, p. 393). The analysis found that, considered together, these two factors explained 38% of the variance in voluntary decision acceptance.

Both factors mattered in the analysis, with people being more willing to accept a favorable outcome ($\beta = 0.40$, $p < .001$) and people being more willing to accept an outcome when they thought that legal authority was legitimate ($\beta = 0.36$, $p < .001$). So, people were more likely to accept decisions voluntarily if those decisions were favorable and if they viewed legal authorities as entitled to be obeyed. Further, these two factors were of approximately equal magnitude. This is striking because the judgment about the outcome is linked to the particular situation in which acceptance occurs, whereas feelings of obligation are general in nature. Psychologists recognize that specific, situational judgments are better predictors of situational behaviors than are general attitudes, yet in this case both influences were of about the same magnitude.

Taken together, these two studies suggest that people feel a considerable sense of obligation to defer to the law and to the decisions of legal authorities, an obligation that is distinct from assessments of the likelihood of being caught and punished if one breaks rules. Viewed from this perspective, the feeling of duty is high among the Americans studied, in this case a group of Californians.

The people in this California sample also recognized that this duty to obey legal authorities was not unlimited. For example, 61% of those interviewed said that there were situations in which they would consider disobeying the law. So, the feeling of obligation is limited to situations in which people believe that the authority is entitled to direct their behavior. However, within the range of such situations, responsibility to accept decisions, favorable or unfavorable, was found to be strong.

EMPOWERING LOCAL GOVERNMENT AUTHORITIES DURING A PERIOD OF SHORTAGE: DO PEOPLE FEEL THAT THEY SHOULD DEFER TO GOVERNMENT?

We can also ask about obligation in the context of local level regulatory authorities, such as a community regulatory committee that makes water use rules for California cities. This type of obligation was examined in a sample of 401 residents of San Francisco (see Tyler & Degoey, 1995). In this study, people were asked during telephone interviews about the degree to

[5]In the analysis, obligation to defer was combined with institutional trust, cynicism about the law, and feelings about legal authorities to create an index of legitimacy. That combined index was used in the analyses reported here.

TABLE 6.3
Obligation to Obey Local Government

Survey statement	Percentage	Response
If the government urged people to voluntarily use less water, how likely would you be to do so (very or somewhat)?	96	Likely
If there were rules telling people how much water they could use, how likely is it that you would voluntarily follow them (very or somewhat)?	95	Likely
Respect for government authority is an important value for people to have.	86	Agree
Disobeying the law is seldom justified.	68	Agree
People should obey laws even when they go against what they think is right.	60	Agree
It is important for people to learn when to question authority.	97	Agree
There are times when it is perfectly all right for people to disobey water-use decisions.	47	Disagree
There are times when it is perfectly all right for people to disobey government water-use rules.	51	Disagree

which they felt responsible for following guidelines and rules enacted by this government agency to regulate their water use. This shortage is a classic example of the *commons dilemma*, that is, a situation in which there is a scarcity of a shared resource.

The results are shown in Table 6.3. They indicate that people almost universally say that they feel responsible for following the rules government regulatory groups put forward to deal with a resource allocation problem, in this case a water shortage. For example, 96% indicated that they would voluntarily use less water if asked to do so by government and 95% that they would follow rules that were enacted by government regulating their water use.

In addition to indicating widespread feelings of obligation to obey specific rules in the case of water use restrictions, many of those interviewed expressed a broader feeling of duty to accept the decisions of government authorities. Of those interviewed, 86% indicated that they felt that respect for government is an important value for people to have; 68% that disobeying the law is seldom justified; and 60% that people should obey the law even when they think it is wrong. These levels of obligation are lower than those found in Chicago but generally similar to those found in Oakland and Los Angeles. They suggest widespread but not universal feelings of responsibility to obey the law and the decisions of government authorities. These findings support the prior studies by finding that, both in general and in the case of specific rules and decisions, people feel that they should accept the decisions made by government authorities.

However, it was clear that the people in this sample recognized the possibility that it would be appropriate to disobey government, as did those people interviewed in the earlier study conducted in Oakland and Los Angeles. Of those interviewed in this San Francisco sample, 97% indicated that it was important for people to learn when to question authority; 53% that there were times when it was acceptable to disobey water-use decisions; and 49% that there are times when it was acceptable to disobey water-use rules. Hence, both in general and in the context of specific rules and decisions, people recognized that their responsibility to obey was not absolute: There were situations in which they could and should disobey. However, they generally felt a responsibility to follow rules and policies put forward by government.

This study supports the argument that people feel considerable duty or responsibility to defer to authorities associated with government. It also makes clear that people recognize that there are limits to government power, and that under some conditions, it is reasonable to disobey government.

Further, the results of this study also make clear that people felt more than just a duty to obey government. The results shown in Table 6.4 indicate that there was support for the idea that people wanted to empower government to make rules and decisions about how to handle community problems like the water shortage that were the focus of this survey. In this case, 73% of those interviewed indicated that the government should make water-use decisions and 74% that government should make water-use rules. When asked to agree or disagree, 92% agreed that the government should make voluntary guidelines; 70% that it should make water-use rules; and 80% that it should impose water-use fines. Even more strongly, 61% agreed that government should have the authority to make whatever decisions it needed to make to manage water use effectively; 62% that government should have the authority to do whatever it thought was best; and 60% that we need governmental authority to solve the water shortage problem.

When we asked questions in which individual decision making and volunteerism (i.e., rights) could be endorsed, the contrast to the government empowerment and duty compliance questions was striking. Only 28% thought that households should be left free to make their own water-use decisions. Further, only 28% regarded it as desirable to let households make their own decisions, whereas 73% thought it was desirable for government to make water-use decisions, and 74% thought it was desirable for government to make water-use rules.

The people in this sample did not resist government regulation. They wanted to empower government to manage water use. This included both support for specific decisions, rules, and policies, and a considerable degree of support for authorizing government to do whatever was needed to solve the problem. Hence, the image of people resisting government control over their access to personally desired resources does not fit the findings in this setting. People wanted government to structure the situation. Further, they then felt responsible for following the structure created by government.

TABLE 6.4
Solutions to the Water Problem

Survey statement	Percentage	Response
Some type of governmental authority should determine how much water each household uses.	73	Yes
There should be mandatory rules telling each household how much water they can use.	74	Yes
How much authority should government have to determine the amount of water each household can use?	85	A great deal, some
The government should have the authority to make voluntary guidelines.	92	Agree
The government should have the authority to make rules.	70	Agree
The government should have the authority to impose fines.	80	Agree
The government should have the authority to make whatever decisions necessary to conserve water.	61	Yes
The government should have the authority to do whatever it thinks is best.	62	Yes
We need a governmental authority to tell us how to solve our water problems.	60	Yes
It should be up to each household to decide how much water they use.	28	Yes
How desirable are the following solutions?		
Letting households make their own decisions	28	
Having some type of government authority decide how much water people can use	73	
Making mandatory, government enforced, rules	74	
Selling water	25	
Giving out equal amounts to each person	45	
Giving water out by need	75	

Why did people want to empower government? Table 6.5 makes clear that it is not simply because they thought that government would be effective. People rated voluntary conservation and government rule making as equally likely to be effective. So, the strong feelings indicating a preference for government decisions and rules expressed in the study do not reflect the belief that it was necessary to have government intervention in the problem. Instead, they reflect the view that it is desirable to have that intervention, even in a situation in which people indicate that the problem could be solved without it.

The results shown in Table 6.4 suggest an answer to the question of why people wanted government intervention. People did not think that it was desirable to allocate water by the use of markets (25% desirable) or by giving equal water to everyone (45% desirable). Instead, most people wanted to allocate water by giving people the amount of water that they needed (75% desirable). To allocate water by need, people need some group to be involved because need requires that estimates of need be made. It would, of

TABLE 6.5
Effectiveness of Different Solutions to the Water Shortage

Possible solution	Percentage of effectiveness
Urging people to voluntarily conserve	75
Giving government the power to make and enforce policies	71
Making mandatory, government enforced, rules	76
Raising the price of water	64

course, be possible to allow everyone to take as much water as they felt that they needed, but this was probably not what people had in mind. Instead, they were thinking of some expert authority, in this case government, that might determine need and make rules for use that are based on that determination of need. This is suggested by the existence of a correlation between the desirability of having water allocated by need, and the view that "we need government" to deal with the energy problem ($r = 0.25$, $p < .05$). In contrast, support for using market-pricing solutions to solve the water problem and for the view that empowering government is the way to solve the water problem is lower ($r = 0.14$, *ns*).

The desire to allocate water by need also makes clear why people did not want voluntary solutions to the water allocation problem. If they conserved water and urged others to do the same, that approach would not lead water to be allocated by need. Rather, it would lead good citizens to use less water and bad citizens to use more. Hence, people did not like the idea of allocating water by voluntary choice; they wanted rules and policies that limited the possibility that others would ride free on the sacrifices of good citizens. This is consistent with the image of government authorities as referees, ensuring the fairness of allocations in society.

This study of water shortages adds a second element to the story. Not only did people support the responsibility and obligation to obey rules but they also wanted to empower government to make rules that would govern the solution to a problem of resource scarcity. Although this problem could have been handled by voluntary conservation or by selling water, people wanted another type of solution. They wanted government rules because such rules could handle the problem of those in need more fairly and also handle unfairness that would arise with voluntary conservation.

It is striking that people rejected two types of solution to the water shortage that one might expect people who are focused on personal rights to strongly endorse. The first is voluntarism, which gives people the freedom to do as they wish. The second is market pricing, which also provides people considerable freedom of choice. Instead of accepting these high-freedom solutions in which people could determine for themselves how and in what way they would help others, people endorsed government regulation. Such regulation potentially imposes duties toward others in the form of rules about water use. Hence, people seemed quite willing to support obligations to others if those obligations were framed in a particular way.

WILL PEOPLE EMPOWER CONGRESS TO REGULATE AGAINST DISCRIMINATION IN ECONOMIC MARKETS?

The study of the local water board suggests that people are comfortable empowering a government agency to make rules in a crisis. A similar question can be asked in the case of a national policy-setting agency, Congress. One of the classic issues in policy setting is the degree to which Congress actively regulates the functioning of economic markets. American society is based on the belief that economic markets are generally fair, with those who work hard or have better skills having greater opportunities and the result and outcome of allocations being generally fair. Consequently, most Americans support the justice of the market system and its outcomes (Kluegel & Smith, 1986).

The question of whether people support government control over the market procedure of social allocation was explored in a study based on interviews with a random sample of 397 people who live in northern California (the San Francisco Bay area). These people were interviewed about their views on Congress in the context of a study on public support for laws regulating the economic marketplace.

People were asked about their support for laws made by Congress that regulate the marketplace with the goal of preventing discrimination against the members of ethnic minority groups. Although the marketplace is generally viewed by Americans to be a fair mechanism of social allocation, the study found substantial support for intervening in the market. For example, 70% to 80% of those interviewed supported empowering Congress to make laws regulating markets (Table 6.6). As an example, 82% indicated that "Congress should make whatever laws are necessary to protect all people from discrimination in hiring and promotion." These findings suggested that people wanted to empower Congress to intervene in markets to correct failures of neutrality in hiring and promotion. When the question is asked more generally, 77% favor passing laws that prevent discrimination.

In this case, it is not clear how people would be expected to comply personally with a rule of this type if it were enacted by Congress. So, the focus of this study was on political support for those authorities who enacted rules regulating the market. Tyler, Lea, and Smith (1999; also see Tyler, 2004) looked at support for congressional policies in the workplace and found that those who felt that Congress should enact such policies indicated that they would support politically those who did so. They would also feel obligated to obey those policies once they were enacted. Hence, support for a

TABLE 6.6
Obligation to Defer to Congress

Survey statement	Response	Percentage
Congress should make whatever laws are necessary to protect all people from discrimination in hiring and promotion.	Strongly agree	64
	Agree	18
	Disagree	10
	Strongly disagree	8
Do you favor or oppose having Congress make laws to prevent discrimination?	Favor	77
If politicians support such laws, would you be . . .	More willing to vote for them	52
	No influence on vote	33
	Less willing to vote for them	16
When it comes to preventing job discrimination, do you think that the federal government is doing . . .	Less than it should	41
	As much as it should	41
	More than it should	19

policy-making role for Congress led to a greater willingness to defer to the policies created by Congress.

Of course, there were limits to support for congressional empowerment. In the same study, people were asked about policies in which Congress sought to change market rules to meet ethnic group goals (quotas). Here people indicated widespread disagreement with the idea that Congress should be empowered to make laws to achieve this goal. So, as with the water board, people could clearly imagine a set of policies that would not have their support. Nonetheless, there was widespread support for congressional actions that involve intervention into markets and private industry to achieve social objectives, in this case to guarantee the neutrality of economic markets.

These findings on the national level suggest that people are willing to have government act to regulate their freedom when they view those actions as consistent with desirable social goals. In this case, the goal was having a fair market system in which discrimination was not allowed to dictate people's opportunity for success or failure in economic life.

DUTY IN EVERYDAY LIFE: THE CASE OF EMPOWERING THE SUPREME COURT

A key function of the American Supreme Court is to interpret the meaning of the Constitution. Studies suggest that the public generally willingly empowers the Court to take on this role. Tyler and Mitchell (1994) explored that source of empowerment among a sample of the citizens of northern California (the San Francisco Bay area). People are asked to indicate the degree to which they want to have the Supreme Court making Constitutional interpretations.

TABLE 6.7
Obligation to Accept Decisions by the Supreme Court

Survey statement	Response	Percentage
In general, how much respect do you have for the Supreme Court as an institution of government?	A great deal	48
	Some	38
	A little	10
	Not much at all	4
Some people feel that we should get rid of the Supreme Court.	Strongly oppose	64
	Oppose	33
	Support	1
	Strongly support	3
The Supreme Court can usually be trusted to make decisions that are right for the country as a whole.	Strongly agree	31
	Somewhat agree	53
	Somewhat disagree	19
	Strongly disagree	7
Do you favor giving the Supreme Court the power to declare acts of Congress unconstitutional?	Strongly favor	30
	Somewhat favor	41
	Somewhat oppose	23
	Strongly oppose	7
Should we keep the Supreme Court as a part of government even if it makes decisions that people disagree with?	Yes	77

The percentages shown in Table 6.7 indicate substantial support for the idea that the Court is entitled to interpret the Constitution. Between 70% and 80% of those interviewed deferred to the Court and indicated that the Court should keep this power even if it makes decisions that people disagree with. For example, 71% said that the Court should have the power to declare acts of Congress unconstitutional, and 77% said that the Court should be supported even if it makes decisions that people disagree with. Hence, as with the local water board, people empowered the Court to make the decisions that it feels are right.

There is no simple measure of compliance with the Supreme Court any more than with Congress because members of the public are not asked to comply with Court-mandated policies in any direct way. However, the results of the study suggest that those who feel that the Court should be empowered to interpret the Constitution indicated that in the case of one contentious issue, abortion, they readily deferred to the decision made by the Court in *Roe v. Wade*. So, general feelings that the Court ought to be empowered to interpret the Constitution were found to lead to decision acceptance in this one controversial case. Those who generally empowered the Court to interpret the Constitution accepted its right to interpret the Constitution in this particular case. That impact extended above and beyond people's own moral feelings about abortion.

Of course, as with other institutions, this power was not found to be unlimited. The study by Tyler and Mitchell (1994) focused on abortion. It found that the public was mixed in its feelings about whether the Court could reasonably evaluate the constitutionality of allowing abortion. This suggests that there are conditions, and abortion is actually on the border of those conditions, under which people might feel that the Court had exceeded its mandate and made decisions that were not appropriate within the general framework of interpreting the Constitution. Under those circumstances, acceptance would be lower.

IMPLICATIONS

Two implications are drawn from the previous discussion. The first implication is that people seem to feel a considerable duty to defer to the laws and rules promulgated by government authorities. Both in general and in response to particular authorities and particular decisions, people feel that the rules made by government agencies and authorities ought to be obeyed. Further, studies suggest that this feeling of obligation has behavioral implications. It leads both to everyday obedience to the law and to the acceptance of particular decisions by legal authorities.

The second implication is that when there are crises requiring some common social policy or rules governing rights or entitlements, people react by empowering government to take an active role in solving those problems. In the case of local regulatory authorities, people indicated the desire to have government make decisions and create rules about water use. On a national level, people want Congress to make rules to regulate markets in certain ways. With regard to the judiciary, people want the Supreme Court to interpret the Constitution. In each case, people are supporting giving authority to a government agency to make rules or policies resolving difficult or unclear issues, with the goal of achieving greater fairness and justice.

These findings provide us with a different image of the "American" than is suggested by the recent discussion of entitlements and rights. Under certain circumstances people will give away their freedom and autonomy. The circumstance is one in which they feel that there is a need to have some type of agreement about the rules and policies that frame the operation of society and social institutions. In the case of shortages, for example, people feel that it is unrealistic to shape water use by voluntary means. In particular, this will not lead to the desired social objective of giving the water available to the people who need it. How can this desirable goal be achieved? It can be achieved by creating a governmental entity to make rules and policies and to enforce those rules by a combination of exhortation, fines, and other means. Consistent with their feeling that such an agency ought to be created to deal with allocating scarce resources, people say that they would personally follow the directives of that agency.

WHAT SUSTAINS GOVERNMENT AUTHORITY?

People empower government to resolve problems and issues in contention, and having empowered government, feel responsible for following the policies created. However, the studies clearly suggest that such willingness to defer to government is not unlimited. People recognize that there are "circumstances under which" they would not feel responsible to government, and they express unwillingness to give government too much power. For example, quotas enacted by Congress and the abortion decisions of the Supreme Court are pushing the limits of public acceptance. Those limits are broad but not infinite. Hence, we have to be concerned about what gives the mantle of legitimacy to the government's policies and decisions.

Although it is not the focus of this chapter, studies in the social psychology of justice suggest strongly that the factor that is the key antecedent to legitimacy is procedural justice. Studies consistently find that the primary factor shaping feelings of obligation to obey government authorities and their decisions is an assessment of the fairness of their decision-making procedures (Tyler et al., 1999). When psychologists examine feelings of obligation to obey laws, judgments about procedural fairness are the dominant factor shaping reactions to decisions made by government authorities and institutions (Tyler, 1990, 2001b; Tyler & Huo, 2002). They also dominate the influence of institutional evaluations of the police and the courts (Tyler, 1990, 2001a) as well as evaluations of local government regulatory agencies (Tyler & Degoey, 1995), Congress (Tyler, 1994), and the Supreme Court (Tyler & Mitchell, 1994).

These strong and consistent findings suggest the nature of the social contract under which Americans are operating. They are willing to empower authorities to make rules, and they feel obligated to obey those rules within reasonable limits. But, they evaluate government authorities against criteria of fair decision-making processes. If the authorities involved are not seen as making their decisions through fair procedures, people feel much less inclined to accept responsibility for following those decisions. Obligation is linked to the assessment that policy decisions are fairly made.

Where does this leave the influence of issues of morality and policy fairness on deference? It suggests that people regard the decision about whether to defer as linked to the fairness with which authorities make decisions, that is, to procedural justice, rather than to evaluations of the fairness or morality of those decisions themselves. This suggests that the key to maintaining deference lies in how decisions are made. Government authorities need to exercise their authority fairly to develop and maintain public acceptance and support for their institutional roles.

Of course, one aspect of a fair decision is that all parties are allowed to participate in the process, making arguments and suggesting desired policies and rules. However, having had an opportunity to participate, people are willing to defer even if their own desired policy position is not accepted. It is participation in a fair policy-making process that people regard as central to their allegiance to government and their feeling of personal responsibility to defer to government decisions and rules.

Participation is not the only element of procedures that shape their fairness. The neutrality of decision makers, the trustworthiness of their intentions, and their recognition of citizen rights are all-important elements of procedural justice. Strikingly, each of these procedural elements is distinct from the fairness or favorability of the decisions or policies enacted, suggesting that government agencies can make rules that people disagree with, or even view as unfair, and still gain considerable deference if they make those rules in fair ways.

How do we reconcile this image of the American with the image of the irresponsible and self-centered American depicted by many discussions of a rights-based society? The way to do so is to think about what is gained by government intervention. When the government intervenes and creates laws and policies or when authorities make decisions, there is, first and foremost, an element of fairness in the distribution of responsibilities and duties that is often missing from the voluntary actions of helpful citizens. If a particular person steps forward to help, others may ride free, and the burdens of group membership are not fairly allocated. By creating authorities to enforce fairness, people can be confident that their good impulses are not being taken advantage of by others. They then need only focus on whether government is itself fair, something that people judged by focusing on issues of how government makes decisions, that is, procedural fairness.

A second gain concerns the removal of ambiguity because government intervention also helps to legitimize requests for help. In situations of individual action, it is often unclear whether requests for help are appropriate and reasonable. When we see someone begging on the street, we do not know if that person genuinely needs our help or might want money to buy drugs or alcohol. Hence, we lack knowledge of others that would tell us who is riding free and who is genuinely in need. So, it is difficult to know when action will lead to a good result, that is, will truly aid those in need.

A third gain from government intervention concerns the removal of vagueness given that norms are oftentimes unclear when we hear sounds of trouble on the street or see people in distress. We have trouble knowing if help is needed and if it is appropriate for us to provide it. A man who opens a door for a woman may be accused of sexism; a person who intervenes in a dispute on the street or calls the police when neighbors are fighting may be accused of meddling in a domestic dispute; and someone who tries to help a child may be confronted by angry parents sensitive to issues of child abuse and kidnapping. Even when need is less ambiguous, it is sometimes hard to know if help is appropriate. When we see someone begging for food on the street we have trouble knowing if that person will spend money received on food or on drugs. When and where action on behalf of others is appropriate has become more difficult to gauge in a modern and multicultural world lacking in common norms and values.

When governments step in and make decisions that rules and policies are needed, acting in accord with those rules and policies is legitimized. Our criterion for judging such legitimacy is our understanding of whether a fair process has been used to make those rules and policies. If it has, we trust that the rules are reasonable, and we are willing to assume the duties they specify.[6]

If we view Americans from this perspective, the nature of the problem presented by modern society is different than that of selfishness and indifference. It does not seem that people are so much indifferent to their duties to others as they are unsure when and how to activate them. In a situation in which people do not know others in their community and are uncertain about the norms of appropriate conduct, it is hard to know when and how to help others. Our well-intentioned actions may be misunderstood or taken advantage of by others.

Of course, we should not present this deference to government as an unambiguous good. In recent years we have seen the enactment of the USA Patriot Act as well as a wide variety of informal and formal efforts by government to increase its power over citizens. These actions are benevolently motivated by a government concerned about terrorism, but they raise the issue of when members of the public do, in fact, resist their obligations to and duties under the law and the government. There are circumstances in which legitimate authorities can seek to impose duties on people that can be seen as leading to "crimes of obedience" (Kelman & Hamilton, 1989). For example, when soldiers are ordered to kill civilians, we hope that they will refuse to carry out these orders and not defer to authority. In other words, people's willingness to defer to government authorities is in some situations viewed as problematic. Although citizens are not being asked to accept orders to harm others proactively, they may be asked to defer to laws that limit their freedoms or the freedoms of others.

My conclusion, based on these studies, is that Americans are willing to give away certain freedoms under certain conditions and act in ways that restrain their own self-interest. In fact, Americans seem strikingly willing to do so under circumstances that help to ensure people that their actions work to good purposes. The intervention of government, although hardly a guarantee that a policy or rule is effective and reasonable, is certainly suggestive of some collective effort to judge the reality of a problem and to create a socially appropriate response to that problem. When people know that a law

[6]Of course, this is not a function that can only be provided by government. One reason that people give money to organized charities is that those groups typically conduct an investigation of people's needs before they give them money. If we want to know that our money is being used to meet legitimate needs, we can also turn to private groups. A key distinction between private and public groups is that private groups typically have no power to compel "free riders" to contribute. What they can do is ensure that the contributions voluntarily made are distributed in legitimate ways.

or a policy exists, they can believe that some true issue is being addressed and that there is a good reason to restrain their conduct. Further, they can have some assurance that their actions will be normatively appropriate if those actions involve conformity to rules and policies defined by government.

In addition, government makes some effort to ensure that policies make sense from a normative perspective. Consider the water shortage. One approach to conservation is to urge people to exercise self-restraint. In that circumstance, we might wonder why more people do not voluntarily step forward to help the group. One reason is that individual actions to use less water, although certainly responsive to the need to lower water use, are not necessarily a desirable public policy goal. Who uses less water? Often, it is the people whose social values have already led them to conserve water. So, we see one group of light water users working to use less water. But, what about people who do not have such social values? They can and do continue to use large amounts of water. This is not necessarily a desirable way to resolve the problem, and it certainly is inconsistent with public feelings that water should be allocated by need. To have a desirable public policy, we need government rules and "teeth" to enforce the rules.

If we think of responsibility in this way, we recognize that voluntary and individual acts on behalf of others are only one approach to social issues and problems. Why, for example, should we not complain that Americans do not contribute money to the government to help it run its programs? Most Americans only pay their taxes and do not contribute more. Does this mean that people are lacking in civic spirit? Not necessarily. It may suggest that people look to government to define a reasonable level of contribution to society, and having made that contribution, people do not feel that they need to do more. So, following rules may be viewed by many people as being socially responsible.

Do the rules define the universe of desirable actions to help others? No. Emergencies, such as the Kitty Genovese case, make that clear. Under some conditions people need to be willing to act in unstructured situations out of responsibility to others. It may well be true that such motivations are lacking among Americans. However, we should not over generalize and suggest that Americans lack a feeling of responsibility to others. Under other circumstances people seem willing to act in ways that are very responsive to others, as that responsibility is defined by social rules and policies. People are clearly willing to act out of social responsibility when responsibility is defined in particular ways. One way is in terms of an obligation to follow social rules and the directives of social authorities.

REFERENCES

Etzioni, A. (1993). *The spirit of community: Rights, responsibilities, and the communitarian agenda.* New York: Crown House Publishing.

Finkel, N. J. (2001). *Not fair! The typology of commonsense unfairness*. Washington, DC: American Psychological Association.

Glendon, M. A. (1991). *Rights talk: The impoverishment of political discourse*. New York: Free Press.

Kelman, H. C., & Hamilton, V. L. (1989). *Crimes of obedience*. New Haven, CT: Yale University Press.

Kluegel, J. R., & Smith, E. R. (1986). *Beliefs about inequality: Americans' views of what is and what ought to be*. New York: Aldine de Gruyter.

Lasch, C. (1979). *The culture of narcissism*. New York: Norton.

Mitchell, L. E. (1998). *Stacked deck: A study of selfishness in America*. Philadelphia, PA: Temple University Press.

Moghaddam, F. M. (1998). *Social psychology: Exploring universals across cultures*. New York: Freeman.

Putnam, R. D. (1995). Bowling alone: America's declining social capital. *Journal of Democracy, 6*, 65–78.

Spragens, T. A., Jr. (1999). *Civil liberalism: Reflections on our democratic ideals*. Lanham, MD: Rowman & Littlefield.

Taylor, C. (1989). *Sources of the self: The making of the modern identity*. Cambridge, MA: Harvard University Press.

Tyler, T. R. (1990). *Why people obey the law*. New Haven, CT: Yale University Press.

Tyler, T. R. (1994). Governing amid diversity: Can fair decision-making procedures bridge competing public interests and values? *Law and Society Review, 28*, 701–722.

Tyler, T. R. (2001a). Public trust and confidence in legal authorities. *Behavioral Sciences and the Law, 19*, 215–235.

Tyler, T. R. (2001b). Trust and law abidingness: A proactive model of social regulation. *Boston University Law Review, 81*, 361–406.

Tyler, T. R. (2004). Affirmative action in an institutional context. *Social Justice Research, 17*, 5–24.

Tyler, T. R., Boeckmann, R. J., Smith, H. J., & Huo, Y. J. (1997). *Social justice in a diverse society*. Boulder, CO: Westview Press.

Tyler, T. R., & Degoey, P. (1995). Collective restraint in a social dilemma situation: The influence of procedural justice and community identification on the empowerment and legitimacy of authority. *Journal of Personality and Social Psychology, 69*, 482–497.

Tyler, T. R., & Huo, Y. J. (2002). *Trust in the law*. New York: Russell Sage Foundation.

Tyler, T. R., Lea, J., & Smith, H. (1999). *Predicting support for compensatory public policies*. Unpublished manuscript, New York University.

Tyler, T. R., & Mitchell, G. (1994). Legitimacy and the empowerment of discretionary legal authority: The United States Supreme Court and abortion rights. *Duke Law Journal, 43*, 703–815.

7

ON THE COMMONSENSE JUSTICE AND BLACK-LETTER LAW RELATIONSHIP: AT THE EMPIRICAL–NORMATIVE DIVIDE

NORMAN J. FINKEL

Justice Oliver Wendell Holmes, whom Pollock and Maitland (1968) called the greatest jurist in Anglo-American jurisprudence, wrote not only *The Common Law* (1881/1963) but also memorable aphorisms such as "great cases, like hard cases, make bad law," which he penned in his dissent in *Northern Securities Company v. United States* (1904, p. 197). That case, as it turned out, involved a clash of a right and a duty: the right of individuals (e.g., J. Pierpont Morgan and associates) to buy majority stock in two competing railroads to form a corporation that might suppress competition and the duty of the government to prevent monopolies. In Holmes's explication of his aphorism, he relied on a series of empirical assertions (e.g., about how great cases arouse the community's passions, which affect judicial decision making, and thereby create psychological headaches for justices and make bad law for the nation) because they generate an "immediate overwhelming interest which appeals to the feelings and distorts the judgment

. . . a kind of hydraulic pressure which makes what previously was clear seem doubtful, and before which even well-settled principles of law will bend" (p. 197).

Holmes indubitably was speaking of one kind of law, *black-letter law* (BLL). But in *Commonsense Justice: Jurors' Notions of the Law* (Finkel, 1995a, p. 2), I put forth the view that there is another type of law, *commonsense justice* (CSJ), which "reflects what ordinary citizens think is just and fair," what they "think the law ought to be." Given these two types of law, the first major question I take up is, "What is the relationship between BLL and CSJ?" This is clearly an empirical question. Although there is considerable anecdotal evidence and speculation on this topic, "hard evidence," the type that is substantively grounded and could pass the *Daubert* test (*Daubert v. Merrell Dow Pharmaceuticals, Inc.*, 1993) for admissibility into court as scientific evidence, is scarce. However, the empirical slate is not completely blank.

In a previous study (Finkel, 2001b), I assessed how ordinary citizens adjudicated 45 "hard cases," the sort of cases that generate headaches for judges and justices, and then compared their verdicts and reasons for their decisions with Supreme Court decisions on some of the same cases. In that work, the central questions (Question 19 from chap. 1, this volume) were about how ordinary citizens decide such clashes, and how CSJ adjudications compare with those of BLL. Regarding the major outcome results, I found, contrary to what a rights-dominated view (e.g., Dworkin, 1978; Glendon, 1991) would predict, that duties more than held their own in these clashes, and in a few cases, there was evidence for a supererogatory duty (where there was no corresponding right). And when CSJ and Supreme Court's decisions were compared, disparate verdicts and different reasons for verdicts were the more frequent result.

In addition to outcome differences, there were also differences in the process of adjudicating. Although these rights and duties were presented as abstract principles, participants did not stay at the abstract level. Participants began their analyses by de-abstracting the claims of the plaintiff and defendant; then they attached these claims to the concrete unfairnesses in the case; next they contextualized, nuanced, and weighted these unfairnesses with certain mitigating factors (e.g., whether the claims were limited or were overreaching, whether the motives propelling the claims were legitimate or impure, and whether distributive justice or injustice would result); and finally they used both instrumental and constitutive fairness solutions. What did not enter their decision making as a determinative factor was stare decisis, which is quite different from the law's decision making, but surprisingly, on constitutive grounds, CSJ seemed to hold the high ground, with participants citing these reasons more frequently than they were cited in Supreme Court decision making. Looked at broadly, citizens exercised moral decision making rather than legal decision making. Finally, there was evidence that participants embraced an ethical duty to be fair in their adjudicating much as judges and justices do.

But that work asked and answered a simpler question regarding differences between BLL and CSJ in the verdict outcomes and in the decision-making process; in this chapter, through an in-depth qualitative analysis of cases involving selective rights versus duties, the question focuses on the nature of the relationship between CSJ and BLL, which is a more difficult matter. That matter is made more difficult and complex by my second major question: "What ought to be the relationship between BLL and CSJ?" This second question is clearly a normative question, and as such, it is one that can be answered independently of any empirical considerations. Posing this normative *ought* question triggers two questions that the empirical *is* question never raises. First, why, in a chapter in Part I of this volume, Empirical Contributions on Rights, Duties, and Culture, is this "empirical author" crossing the *is–ought* divide into normative ground in the first place, rather than staying on his side of the divide? And second, even if the empirical author proffers his empirical evidence to the law on the first question, why should those strict normativists in the law even bother to consider that evidence when they can choose to answer the second question independently of empirical considerations?

This chapter provides the long answer to those two questions, but the short answer is as follows. Beginning with my analysis of a current and contentious jurisprudential debate on the place and weight of CSJ in legal decision making and continuing through the empirical evidence I present, and with some cautious inferences that go beyond the data, I advance two interrelated arguments: first, an empirical argument that there is a connection between the empirical *is* and the so-called normative *ought*, and second, a normative argument that severing this nexus (if such a psychological dissociation can be done) poses grave perils for the law and the society, for that connection is vital and vitalizing for both.

This work derives from my CSJ perspective (Finkel, 1995a), and it is predicated on the belief that empirical evidence can inform normative questions, although I make no claim that such evidence can fully answer normative questions. Still, I believe that illuminating the evidence from my first question may offer BLL substantive answers to some of the law's knottiest questions, for these so-called *ought* questions, on close examination, are oftentimes predicated on psychological ground, like the judicial decision making that is brought to bear on them, which is not syllogistic, but psychological in nature. Moreover, in a concrete case with a plaintiff, a defendant, and specific facts, the governing laws' lofty normative principles must come to ground, as Rawls (1999) and Rousseau (1950) understood, for these principles must pay homage to and make connection with the psychological reality by taking "men as they are."

AN EMPIRICAL–NORMATIVE CONNECTION? A CONTENTIOUS DEBATE

When the Pragmatics of Holmes is Confronted by the Objectivity of Scalia

The connection between CSJ and BLL was drawn most clearly by none other than Oliver Wendell Holmes. In *The Common Law* (1881/1963, p. 1), Holmes noted that community sentiment, be it "avowed or unconscious," exerts a powerful influence on judges' decision making and thus strongly affects the law. This was one of his many psychological insights, which he turned into a generalization in the language of science, one grounded, no doubt, not only in his own experiences but also in his observations of fellow judges. However, Holmes went beyond his empirical facts to take a normative position on the relationship of community sentiment and law, which turned out to be an extreme position, for he claimed that the law "should correspond with the actual feelings and demands of the community, whether right or wrong" (p. 35).

But what, we may ask, is the justification for that claim? Just because something is so does not mean that it ought to be so. In *The Common Law* (1881/1963, p. 35), Holmes held that this community sentiment generally exerts a "sound" force on judges and the law. Although this is an empirical claim, in his quote from *Northern Securities*, he seemed to hold to the contrary, stating how this hydraulic force can cloud what was formerly clear, which is another empirical claim. If the two quotes leave the soundness of community sentiment in doubt, there is little doubt about the community sentiment's "strength," for Roscoe Pound (1907, p. 615) predicted that in "all cases of divergence between the standard of the common law and the standard of the public, it goes without saying that the latter will prevail in the end." Put in my terms, Pound is saying that BLL will ultimately end up aligning with CSJ. If Pound's sociological jurisprudence and predictive point is also Holmes's thesis, then Holmes's argument appears to collapse the empirical–normative (*is–ought*) divide merely because judges live and decide cases within community sentiment's powerful gravitational field and thus cannot resist its force (i.e., resistance is futile). Is his argument a pragmatic giving in to the inevitable power of CSJ, or does Holmes believe that there is a deeper soundness, a wisdom perhaps to CSJ, which lies beneath the din of sentiment? This is not clear.

But what is clear is that not everyone is either in favor of CSJ's sway over BLL or resigned to the fact of its inevitability, and very few scholars, even those most sympathetic with the "life" in Holmes's law, are persuaded by his "logic." Anchoring the other extreme of this debate on the place of CSJ within the law is Justice Antonin Scalia, who has been the most vociferous critic of both his fellow brethren on the Supreme Court and the citizenry regarding the intrusion of community sentiment into legal decision making. In his concurring and dissenting opinion in *Planned Parenthood of Southeastern Pennsylvania v. Casey* (1992), Scalia wrote the following:

> How upsetting it is, that so many of our citizens . . . think that we Justices should properly take into account their views, as though we were engaged not in ascertaining an objective law but in determining some kind of social consensus. (pp. 999–1000)

Yet Scalia (*Planned Parenthood of Southeastern Pennsylvania v. Casey*, 1992, p. 981) reserved his sharpest criticisms for "a few of the more outrageous arguments in today's opinion, which is beyond human nature to leave unanswered." Scalia focused his ire on the majority's concern for community sentiment, the justices' attempt, by not overturning *Roe v. Wade*, to call "the contending sides of a national controversy to end their national division by accepting a common mandate rooted in the Constitution" (pp. 866–867), and the Court's concern that its legitimacy would be subverted if the decision did not rest on community sentiment. Scalia argued that it was the Court's attention to community sentiment that inflamed the controversy to begin with and that the

> Court's description of the place of *Roe* in the social history of the United States is unrecognizable . . . [and] to portray *Roe* as the statesmanlike 'settlement' of a divisive issue, a jurisprudential Peace of Westphalia that is worth preserving, is nothing less than Orwellian. (p. 995)

For Justice Scalia (*Planned Parenthood of Southeastern Pennsylvania v. Casey*, 1992, p. 984), the way out of this mess was clear, and he cited Justice Curtis's warning approvingly, saying it was "as timely today as it was 135 years ago" when Curtis dissented in *Dred Scott v. Sandford* (1857):

> [W]hen a strict interpretation of the Constitution, according to the fixed rules which govern the interpretation of laws, is abandoned, and the theoretical opinions of individuals are allowed to control its meaning, we have no longer a Constitution; we are under the government of individual men, who for the time being have power to declare what the Constitution is, according to their own views of what it ought to mean. (p. 984)

Yet scholars of jurisprudence from the left and right of the political spectrum (e.g., Dworkin, 1986; Posner, 1990) seem in accord that this objective law that Justice Scalia yearns for cannot be ascertained by hermetically sealed legal reasoning, for there are no fixed rules of interpretation. Justices can neither agree on the major nor the minor premise, so the syllogism fails from the start, and the notion that there is some distinct specie of reasoning called legal reasoning is but a legal fiction. Thus, the textualist's holy grail of a strict interpretation appears to give way to the sort of pragmatism Holmes

(1881/1963, p. 1) argued for more than a century ago when he said that "the life of the law has not been logic."

Still, Scalia wants sentiment removed, and he clearly chafed at Justice Kennedy's majority opinion in *Lawrence & Garner v. Texas* (2003), particularly over Kennedy's reference to "an emerging awareness." In his dissent, Scalia noted that "an 'emerging awareness' is by definition not 'deeply rooted in this Nation's history and tradition[s],' as we have said 'fundamental right' status requires," and he believed that the Court's opinion resulted from "a law-profession culture signing on to the so-called homosexual agenda," seeking to eliminate the "moral opprobrium that has traditionally attached to homosexual conduct," and seeking to expand fundamental rights, while it overturns its duty to "the 'societal reliance' on the principles confirmed in *Bowers* and discarded today" (slip op. at pp. 14, 18).

But closing the door on an emerging awareness is difficult, particularly when the high Court opens that door and lets community sentiment enter its Eighth Amendment cases. The Court has hinged the very meaning of cruel and unusual punishment to the community's "evolving standards of decency that mark the progress of a maturing society" (*Trop v. Dulles*, 1958, p. 102). That door is also opened in certain right-to-privacy cases, which hinge on the reasonable expectations of citizens to privacy (e.g., Finkel, 1995a), which may change with time, circumstance, and sentiment. Thus, despite Justice Scalia's wish that it wasn't so, community sentiment continues to enter and affect the uppermost reaches of BLL. And that sentiment certainly affects the bottommost reaches, where law and citizens meet at the very beginning of a case, for here, citizens-turned-jurors, "the conscience of the community," bring their CSJ notions to the courtroom, judging both fact and law as they have for centuries.

While a normativist may wish this phenomenon away, the empiricist chooses to study it, for empirical research on CSJ (e.g., Finkel, 1995a, 2001a; Robinson & Darley, 1995) can inform the law in at least two ways. First, it may reveal disparities between BLL and the community's views, identifying those topics on which the law is most likely to be nullified, disrespected, or disregarded and on which the institutional legitimacy of the Court is likely to be called into question. And second, it offers the law answers to those hard cases in which empirical and normative issues likely mix. Such answers, in the words of Law Professor George Fletcher (1988, p. 154), seek "not to defeat the law, but to perfect the law, to realize the law's inherent values."

WHEN RIGHTS AND DUTIES COLLIDE, IMPLICIT DUTIES EMERGE

In this in-depth qualitative analysis of a variety of rights-versus-duties clashes, my aim is to uncover what is implicit, for I seek to show that beneath many apparent clashes of rights versus duties, there are often deeper dilemmas between different types of duties, and these duty dilemmas can most clearly illuminate the relationship between CSJ and BLL. But to do this, I must first bring greater visibility to duties in this alleged rights-dominated culture in which "rights march down the middle of main street to the clash of cymbals and the beat of drums . . . while duties, no matter how powerfully they may shape conduct, generally trudge along in the shade, unaccompanied and unnoticed" (Haskell, this volume, p. 247). I begin with three cases (*Bennis v. Michigan*, *Hendricks v. Kansas* [see *Kansas v. Hendricks*], and *Hardwick v. Georgia* [see *Bowers v. Hardwick*]) in which at the surface level, a state presses a statutory duty claim against an individual, and the individual counters with a related rights claim.

Bennis (P) v. Michigan (D)

Tina Bennis, a Michigan woman, worked and saved along with her husband to buy a car that was supposed to be used to provide transportation to his job. They paid $600 for an 11-year-old Pontiac. Mr. Bennis, however, didn't always come right home from work, and he didn't explain those detours to his wife. Shortly after the car was purchased, Mr. Bennis used it to entertain a prostitute and commit what the law describes as a "gross indecency" with her in the front seat. After successfully prosecuting him for that offense, the state moved to declare the car a public nuisance and to confiscate it. Michigan law, like the law in other states, permits the state to take property without compensation if the state, for example, seeks to deter illegal activity that contributes to neighborhood deterioration and unsafe streets. Tina Bennis brought suit to retrieve her property (the car), as she had committed no crime and knew of no crime. She argued that the state was punishing the victim, herself, that punishment must be based on culpability, and that she was not culpable for what had happened.

The U.S. Supreme Court ruled for Michigan in its 5 to 4 decision (56%); however, the participants were nearly unanimous (98%) in deciding for Bennis, as her right's claim trumped the state's duty claim. Participants stated as their reason for their decision that CSJ rejects punishment (i.e., the taking of a woman's car) when a woman was neither aware of nor culpable for the criminal activity of her husband (although it took place in her car). Furthermore, although participants acknowledge Michigan's position as the law, they reject the law in its application as an impermissible and blatantly unfair overreaching. Her due process rights, they believe, should trump the state's duty under law unless the state could show that she was either aware of or culpable in some way for the criminal activity. In sum, participants explicitly cite constitutive reasons and CSJ and fairness principles (Finkel, 1995a, 2001a) in support of their decisions.

But implicitly, through some of the participants' comments, a second duty, or more precisely a failure of a duty, emerges. To make this explicit, a few participants angrily asked, "Why didn't the state uphold its duty to one of its citizens and protect the innocent Mrs. Bennis?" From this view, the state had a choice between upholding two duties, to protect a citizen's right or to misapply a law aimed at drug and racketeering enterprises in order to confiscate a car, and it chose the latter. From this construal, this is no longer a right-versus-duty case, but a duty-versus-duty case, with the state backing the wrong duty, the one that sacrifices a sacred principle of justice and fairness.

Hendricks (P) v. Kansas (D)

When a criminal serves the sentence imposed by the criminal law (i.e., he "does the time") and is released, that criminal is considered to have paid the penalty society imposed. Hendricks was a convicted sex offender who did his time and expected to be released, but the state of Kansas created a sex offender statute that allowed the state to involuntarily commit him after he had served his time. The state argued that under its police powers authority it could commit those who pose a danger to the community. Hendricks, the state claimed, was "volitionally impaired," making it likely that he would commit new sex crimes. Hendricks argued that he had committed no new crime, that he had served his time for the old crime, that the state was punishing him a second time for what he had done, and that this was unconstitutional. When the U.S. Supreme Court decided *Hendricks*, the Court split 5 to 4 (56%) in favor of Kansas, whereas 71% of the participants favored Hendricks.

To understand the CSJ reasoning of the majority, I created a hypothetical case (Finkel, 2001b) called *Sex Offender (P) v. State (D)*, which provides context, for in that case the law allowed for community notice (i.e., a Megan's Law situation), which included circulating flyers and putting signs on the person's lawn, and in that case the majority of participants (65%) favored the state. One factor that discriminates between the two cases is the greater deprivation of liberty in *Hendricks* compared with *Sex Offender*, and supporting this is the fact that participants frequently cited right trumping duty in *Hendricks* but not in *Sex Offender*. A second discriminator combines the qualifying factors of overreaching versus limited duty and impure versus legitimate motives, both of which cut differently in the two cases: In *Hendricks*, there is the appearance of double jeopardy because the state seems to be overreaching and acting on impure motives, punishing Hendricks a second time for the same offense; in *Sex Offender*, the state's actions appear legitimate and limited to setting the conditions of release.

Although many participants in both *Hendricks* and *Sex Offender* explicitly expressed disgust for pedophiles and clearly understood the community's fears, there was nonetheless a limit on how far the state's crime control duty could go in infringing on privacy and liberty, and in *Hendricks* the majority believed that the state had crossed not only the Constitution's double jeopardy line but also a line that fundamental fairness marks.

Implicitly, though, through some of the participants' comments, we see something similar to *Bennis*. A few participants recognized that the state of Kansas also had a duty to a citizen, even a repugnant citizen who had served his time. These participants felt that this citizen deserved a second chance, for he had paid his penalty to society, despite the fearful sentiments of the community that the legislators were no doubt responding to. Even more than for the case of the innocent Mrs. Bennis, here the true test of liberty, as some participants implied, was whether the government would uphold its duty to protect the rights of an individual whom most citizens find repugnant and frightening and want put away. Implicitly, then, these participants cite deep constitutive, normative principles and ask the state's elected representatives not to yield to the current sentiment, for by doing so, baser passions and fears will wipe away fundamental duties and rights and what we truly aspire to.

Hardwick (P) v. Georgia (D)

The Supreme Court has spoken of the "sanctity of the bedroom" and the "sacred precincts of marital bedrooms," phrases that denote that if there is any place where privacy should be supreme and protected from state intrusion, it is there, where consensual acts between adults ought to be beyond the reach of the state. But the state of Georgia passed a law making consensual sodomy a crime, and under this law, the police searched the bedroom of Hardwick, a homosexual, and charged him with a crime. Georgia maintained that the state has a legitimate interest in promoting welfare and the moral fiber of the community and in suppressing acts that weaken the morals of the community. Hardwick contended that his privacy was violated and that the law discriminates against one class of citizens, homosexuals, because it does not make consensual sodomy between heterosexuals a crime. When the U.S. Supreme Court decided *Bowers v. Hardwick* (1986), the Court split 5 to 4 (56%) in favor of Georgia (Bowers), but in our version of the case, participants decided in favor of Hardwick 93% of the time.

In all cases examined, privacy was the right most strongly endorsed by participants overall. Still, strong endorsement does not mean that the right to privacy will always prevail, for some privacy claims lose to broader duties. For example, in a case in which individuals assert a privacy right not to have their children vaccinated but a state asserts its duty to vaccinate to protect the safety of children and citizens, the state wins 100% of the time. In a second example (which has implications for the recent outbreak of severe acute respiratory syndrome [SARS]), when citizens assert a right not to have themselves quarantined when a contagious disease is diagnosed but a state asserts its duty to protect its citizens by having them quarantined, the state's duty trumps the citizens' rights 90% of the time.

Government intrusion into privacy is judged by participants' own version of strict scrutiny, and in *Hardwick*, participants were not only deeply offended about the state being in anyone's bedroom but their ire was compounded by the state's discriminating against one group (homosexuals). They were further offended by the state's use of what they saw as a nonsense pretext of crime control. Participants explicitly cited equal rather than discriminatory treatment as the constitutive reasons for supporting *Hardwick*.

Many participants recognized that beyond discriminatory treatment lay the deeper issues of privacy and autonomy and that the Georgia law had taken leave of its moral base, which left it standing on an anachronism. The proper moral base, they believed, had shifted significantly because community sentiment had changed. The Supreme Court's decision in *Bowers* was close and contentious, and years later, after his retirement, Justice Powell, who voted with the majority, said in a speech that he had changed his mind and thought the decision was wrong (Dworkin, 1996). Seventeen years after *Bowers*, Justice Kennedy, writing the 6 to 3 majority opinion in *Lawrence & Garner v. Texas* (2003), acknowledged that the *Bowers* Court did not "appreciate the extent of the liberty at stake," for it framed the case in a way that demeaned Hardwick's claim, and he further acknowledged that the community's sentiment had changed, concluding that the Court's former decision "was not correct when it was decided, and it is not correct today. It ought not to remain binding precedent. *Bowers v. Hardwick* should be and now is overruled."

In *Hardwick*, as in *Bennis* and *Hendricks*, CSJ uses a moral rather than a legal analysis. And in *Hardwick*, the CSJ analysis of where community sentiment stood on the moral issue and on the meaning of privacy seemed ahead of the BLL analysis. But we cannot generalize from this, for *Hendricks* reveals that the community's wider sentiment was punitive, which the Kansas legislators were surely responding to when they passed the statute. Yet some of our participants were implicitly asking states like Kansas not to respond to that "take them out of society" sentiment but rather to uphold a duty to a normative principle (i.e., not to trample on the protection from double jeopardy) and not be swayed by current sentiment. In *Bennis*, the implicit message was similar: The state should uphold a duty to an innocent citizen and honor the deeper principles of justice and fairness. In *Hardwick*, by contrast, CSJ also reached for the deeper constitutive principles (e.g., privacy and autonomy), but participants found those principles grounded in the community's moral sentiment, which had shifted from times long past.

DUTIES INDEPENDENT OF RIGHTS AND THE INTERACTION BETWEEN MORAL AND LEGAL DUTIES

In this part of the chapter, I highlight two cases in which the initial right-versus-duty clash ultimately leads to a clash between two different types of duties. In the first case (*Stayton v. Cincinnati*), the explicit analysis finds a right trumping a duty handily. But the implicit analysis finds a supererogatory duty motivating this Good Samaritan's act for which a duty exists independent of any right. In this case the duty cannot be replaced by a right (see Moghaddam and Riley's replaceability notion, chap. 4, this volume) and the principle of logical correlativity (Feinberg, 1969) does not hold for there is no corresponding right anywhere in sight. This case leads to a discussion of how supererogatory duties may become mandatory duties (see also, chap. 10 by Harré, this volume).

The second case (*Student Group v. Cash*) takes place not in a courtroom but on a college campus, as a grievance brought by students against Cash before the student honor council to have him expelled from Berkeley, and this turns out to be the most difficult of our cases, dividing citizens' verdicts down the middle. In this case, citizens want a civic and moral duty made into a mandatory legal duty. Here is an example of the interaction between moral and legal duties in which a two-way interaction occurs between CSJ and BLL: On one hand, CSJ pulls on the law to codify the moral sentiment; on the other hand, there is a countervailing pressure as the law exerts a restraining influence on the community's passions to punish and as the law's duty to uphold Cash's legal right acts as a stop, preventing passions from both overriding an individual's right and overturning the rule of law.

Stayton (P) v. Cincinnati (D)

In 1996 in Cincinnati, 62-year-old Sylvia Stayton was grabbed, handcuffed by a police officer, hauled into jail, and charged with obstruction of official business. The crime involved feeding two parking meters so strangers' cars would not be ticketed. Acting as a Good Samaritan, Mrs. Stayton did this to spare fellow citizens the grief and cost of parking fines, but the city held that her act interfered with a legitimate government interest, deterring and punishing offenders who park but do not pay.

This was an easy case, as the participants' verdicts were one sided (88% for Stayton), and in their reasons for their decisions, Stayton's right to put coins in parking meters for strangers to spare them fines easily trumped the duty of the police to charge Stayton with obstruction of official business. Some participants wrote that the world needs more Good Samaritans like Stayton; others wrote critically of the officer's lack of discretion and of Cincinnati's motives and overreaching of this duty.

But implicitly, when we ask what motivated Stayton to act, the answer is not her right, but her supererogatory duty. In the full story from *The Washington Post* (Seigle, 1996), Sylvia Stayton was on her way to photocopy some urgently needed materials to avoid a bank foreclosure on her home! Yet, at this stressful time in her life, she noticed the police officer about to ticket the cars, and then stopped, reached into her purse, grabbed some coins, and inserted them in the two meters, taking the time to spare these unknown strangers hardship. Speaking of her act as her right explains nothing and discriminates her from no one. Every person on the street had such a right, but only Stayton acted. Thus, rights talk fails to explain the motivation for the act, as a good dramatist would demand; only duty works in this story (e.g., Bennett & Feldman, 1981; Bruner, 1986; Pennington & Hastie, 1992) to explain coherently why she did what she did.

The independence of this duty from any right can be shown in two other ways. First, by making use of the notion of replaceability developed by Moghaddam and Riley (see chap. 4, this volume) in which a right can be construed as a duty (and vice versa) depending on perspective and vantage point, we find that this interchangeability works for the police officer's act, for that can be seen as a duty to uphold the law or as an exercise of an officer's right (Orren, 2000). But replaceability fails to work for Stayton's altruistic act, for her supererogatory duty cannot be replaced by a rights locution without radically altering the focus from her motivation for what she did to some after-the-fact justification of her act when it came under legal attack. The second way of illustrating the independence of Stayton's duty is that we can find no correlative right (Feinberg, 1969) for it. For example, when we park our cars by meters, we have a duty to put money in the meters; but we have no corresponding rights claim that others should (i.e., have a duty to) fill our parking meters for us.

Supererogatory duties seem to represent a distinct class of duties separate from rights, and they appear to exist outside the law, stemming from individuals' moral convictions of what they ought to do. But during this past century, particularly with the appearance of environmental laws, we see that supererogatory duties can become legal duties. For example, there have always been people, even groups of people, who have embraced duties to the land, water, and air and to the flora and fauna that live in those habitats, duties not to foul nature or overuse its resources. When these minorities reach some political critical mass, they may convince the majority of the wisdom of their position and convince politicians of the need for environmental legislation in order to make supererogatory duties into mandatory legal duties.

In the next case, we begin not with a supererogatory duty but with a civic and moral duty, the duty to intervene, which seems to take us back to the tragedy of Kitty Genovese, except now we are in a shifting legal climate in which a few states had turned that civic duty into a legal duty. In the aftermath of this case, we see the interaction between civic and moral duties and legal duties.

Student Group (P) v. Cash (D)

David Cash, a 19-year-old Berkeley engineering student, walked into a women's restroom of the Primadonna Casino, 43 miles from Las Vegas. He walked into the women's restroom because he saw his best friend Jeremy Strohmeyer following a 7-year-old girl, Sherrice Iverson, into the restroom. David Cash saw his friend carrying the struggling girl into a toilet stall saying, "Shut up, or I'll kill you." Cash observed his friend sexually assaulting the girl, but he walked out of the bathroom without intervening. Strohmeyer assaulted her, squeezed her throat, and snapped her neck, killing her. Strohmeyer pleaded guilty to first-degree murder charges in an agreement to save himself from the death penalty. Cash was never charged with a crime because in Nevada, as in most states, there is no law requiring a person to stop a crime in progress. When the story broke, a group of students at Berkeley tried to have Cash expelled. They brought a grievance against him before the student honor council. Cash argued that he should not be expelled because he broke no law.

This case produced the closest verdict decision (52% for Cash) of all the cases and a close battle of whether rights trump duties or the reverse. Whichever side participants came down on, there was moral condemnation for what Cash failed to do. For the narrow majority, the law (i.e., that there was no law in the state of Nevada requiring that Cash intervene and thus he broke no law) worked as a restraint, reining in punitive moral sentiments, which were harsh. But as the rewritten participants' vignettes make clear, had Cash's action taken place in a state that made this a crime or on campus where the honor code was applicable or had Cash been a lookout or participant in the crime, then Cash would have lost under these circumstances.

Switching to those participants who felt that culpability was evident and that punishment was due, they held that a moral crime had been committed even if failure to act was not illegal, and with a proverbial moral red pen in hand, they were willing to overwrite BLL. Yet the differences between majority and minority were narrower still: The majority cited the law as their reason for not punishing Cash in a legal way, and many preferred to administer punishment in a social and moral way, by shunning him. This punishment, they felt, would send a strong moral message that his act was wrong in the eyes of his peers, despite what the law says, such that his place among his peers within the university community would now be forfeit. Thus, despite the deep division inferred from the close verdict, both majority and minority participants, if they had their way, ended up inflicting punishment, albeit of a different type.

But the aftermath of the case illustrates the interaction between moral and legal duties. Many participants who came down on either side of the case wanted this moral and civic duty to be made a legal duty: They wanted fellow citizens to be obligated to do something to prevent serious injury and death, like shouting for help or calling the police. If citizens' moral consciences did not summon them to do that on their own, then they wanted BLL to fortify those consciences with a legal onus. But until such time as legislatures enact those laws and impose that duty, the legal system is duty bound to uphold the law on the books, and more broadly, the rule of law. It also means that the legal system is duty bound to protect an individual's right under the existing law from the community's moral sentiments, which may be inflamed, for not all sentiments are lofty and noble (Finkel, 1995a). The legal system, committed to due process under law and the rule of law, puts the brakes on runaway passions, and within this legally created pause, a more considered political process can occur with its checks and balances.

AN ETHICAL AND MORAL DUTY VERSUS A LEGAL DUTY

The discussion to this point has involved hard cases in which rights and duties explicitly collide and the implicit analysis revealed even greater complexity. In three cases (see the section titled When Rights and Duties Collide, Implicit Duties Emerge, this chapter) in which the counterclaims of rights and duties seemed closely connected, the implicit analysis revealed a second duty or the failure of the state to uphold a duty to a citizen. In two rights-versus-duties cases (see the section titled Duties Independent of Rights and the Interaction Between Moral and Legal Duties) the implicit analysis revealed a clash of a supererogatory duty with a legal duty and a clash of a civic and moral duty with a legal duty. Thus, a variety of duties (e.g., the government's duty not to punish an innocent person and not to punish a person twice for the same offense, the government's duty to protect a person's right to privacy and autonomy, a supererogatory duty, and a civic and moral duty) emerge, coming out of the shade in this alleged rights-dominant culture as Haskell (see chap. 11, this volume) predicted they would. But contrary to Haskell's other claim, some duties did not emerge in tandem with rights; rather they emerged independent of rights, and the deeper conflict was between one duty and another duty. In this section, we begin with one more duty, an ethical duty to be fair, which turns into an ethical and moral duty in conflict with a legal duty.

Participants went about their adjudicative task by embracing an ethical duty, trying to judge these cases and their plaintiffs and defendants fairly and accurately, much as judges and justices commit to doing. Part of this ethical duty to treat all claimants "with equal concern and respect" (Dworkin, 1996, p. 17) manifests itself most clearly in the two cases (e.g., *Hendricks* and *Cash*) in which sentiments of disgust and revulsion were expressed for those claimants. Still, the CSJ process of adjudicating appears different from that of judges and justices, for these participants were performing a moral rather than a legal analysis and were seldom citing stare decisis as a determinative factor for their decisions. They were frequently willing to set aside statutory laws when they believed that fundamental fairness, normative values, and constitutive principles needed to be reached. But at a metalevel, there may be a greater similarity than we first see if Ronald Dworkin's (1996, p. 2) "moral reading of the Constitution" has validity. According to Dworkin, the "moral reading proposes that we all—judges, lawyers, citizens—interpret and apply these abstract clauses [of the Constitution, and particularly the Bill of Rights] on the understanding that they invoke moral principles about political decency and justice." Our citizen participants seem consistently to reach for a moral reading of these cases in which perceived unfairnesses are weighed against the ought of what should be—that is, the fair process, the fair outcome, and the morally decent course of action. Finding a fair resolution, however, becomes exceedingly difficult when law and morality do not align, and the majority found a misalignment in these cases.

It is not a far stretch to go from these participants to ordinary citizens who serve as jurors, the "conscience of the community," as they have been called. Jurors, it is said, decide the facts, whereas the judge decides the law, and the jurors formally commit to this distinction as they swear an oath to obey the law as the judge gives them the law. Yet much has been made of cases in which jurors apparently decide the law for themselves, and the most frequent and hyperbolic explanation for this has been "jury nullification" (e.g., Finkel, 1995a). But the more likely explanation, I suggest (Finkel, 2000), is that jurors are simply exercising their discretion, given the vagueness of laws and the meanings of words.

Jurors must interpret the very words of the law that the judge gives them, and as James Madison (Hamilton, Madison, & Jay, 1788/1961, p. 229) recognized with some embarrassment, "no language is so copious as to supply words and phrases for every complex idea, or so correct as not to include many equivocally denoting different ideas." How, then, given their ethical duty to be fair, do they solve these dilemmatic (Lemmon, 1978) conflicts between different duties, explicit and implicit, when obligations and moral principles conflict?

Given that stare decisis is not a significant factor, it might be said that CSJ is freer than legal decision making from the historical chain of past constitutional or common-law cases and current statutes that bind judges. Judges must attempt to square current decisions with prior cases and current law, for they have appellate courts looking over their shoulders. But this does not imply that CSJ's context lacks either weight or historical gravity, for participants invoke a history that is no less long and deep than legal history and that may be even more so (e.g., Finkel, 1995a). Participants seek those animating roots that give rights, duties, fairness, and justice their broadest reading. Those root sources may include notions extracted from the Declaration of Independence, the Constitution, the Bible, and natural law, though more likely they reach into participants' deepest notions of justice and fairness. These sources, taken together, may be seen as the LAW (in capital letters) to which they have the higher duty, and this can be contrasted to their duty derived from the oath, which they may see as to the law (in lowercase letters). Consequently, this lesser duty is what may yield when the two are in conflict. These root sources, then, give participants' moral reasons an integrity (Dworkin, 1986) as they try to achieve resolutions that square with their deepest understandings of what right, duty, fairness, and justice require.

THE CASE FOR THE LONG-RUNNING CASE: THE COMMUNITY VERSUS THE LAW

Charles Dickens (1868), a noted court watcher himself, gave the world the interminable case of Jarndyce and Jarndyce in *Bleak House*:

> This scarecrow of a suit has, in the course of time, become so complicated, that no man alive knows what it means. The parties to it understand it least; but it has been observed that no two Chancery lawyers can talk about it for five minutes, without coming to a total disagreement as to all the premises. Innumerable children have been born into the cause; innumerable young people have married into it; innumerable old people have died out of it. Scores of persons have deliriously found themselves made parties in Jarndyce and Jarndyce, without knowing how or why; whole families have inherited legendary hatreds with the suit. (p. 4)

In either its longevity or, more important, its import, Jarndyce and Jarndyce pales beside the case of the community's moral analysis versus the law's legal analysis, yet, there are some literary-to-real-world similarities. The case I am addressing, falsely cast as CSJ versus BLL, in my opinion, has grown more complicated and contentious in part because some learned hands seem to be in such sharp disagreement about its ontogeny, its very nature, and what it portends. A few final thoughts on the topic are in order, and these go beyond the data.

If the framers of the Constitution created a "living organism," then law grows and develops as do the meanings of rights and duties. That development, I submit, is stimulated and prodded by the ongoing discourse between the community's moral sentiment and BLL, as each has notions about what "the law ought to be" (Finkel, 1995a, p. 2). That discourse, I believe, contributed substantially, though belatedly, to the *Lawrence* Court's "emerging awareness" of what CSJ already understood, that the moral ground had shifted and that the meaning of privacy and autonomy in an intimate relationship was deeper and wider than what the *Bower* Court had understood, as the *Lawrence* Court apologetically acknowledged. The discourse was also enhanced, in my opinion, when the law said *stop* to the sizable minority in *Cash* who wanted to formally punish without the legal grounds to do so, for the rule of law, due process, and an individual's right were too important to sacrifice to inflamed moral sentiments. The development of that living organism, I submit, is also stimulated by the chides, challenges, prods, and stops that BLL and CSJ each puts before the other, but most of all by the defensible reasons each offers for its views.

This has been the way it has been since formal law became codified. The very fact that laws become codified, whether by constitutional ratification, statutory enactment, or the finality of Supreme Court decisions, neither silences citizens nor stops their thinking. When statutory laws are enacted after legislators receive input from representative elements of the community, those laws are more likely to sit well with the community for they are likely to best reflect the broad sentiment. When the Supreme Court takes up an Eighth Amendment case in which the community's evolving sense of cruel and unusual punishment is at issue, for example, it is judicious for the Court to gauge that sentiment as accurately as it can (e.g., Finkel, 1990, 1993, 1995b; Finkel & Duff, 1991). When it does, such decisions stand a better chance of according with the broad sentiment and being respected and obeyed by that citizenry.

But when a Supreme Court opinion conflicts with current sentiment, because the justices judge a sacred principle too important to yield to current sentiment, then the law has the opportunity to enlighten and elevate citizens' sentiments. Although the Court's decision represents finality for the case, the long discourse between BLL and CSJ merely resumes. The evolution of BLL cannot still the parallel evolution of CSJ nor vice versa, though they can and should interact. In this chapter, I have shown that CSJ, at its best, can inform the law, and I have argued that CSJ may help perfect the law. Still, for these potentially positive outcomes to occur, there must be a process, a relationship.

In considering this rough-and-tumble relationship, I judge these perspectival clashes to be generally healthy for the society. Just consider, for an instant, the alternative, those societies, past and present, in which there is only one perspective and no dialogue. Thus, in light of my argument, the Holmes extreme of community sentiment whether right or wrong has to be rejected. Wrong sentiments, base sentiments, and prejudicial sentiments are not what we want the law to rest on, as this position relegates BLL to the lemming in the relationship, merely following, when at times it ought to be leading and enlightening. But in light of my argument, the Scalia extreme must be rejected as well. If the intrusions of community sentiment ever cease, if the legal decision making is ever hermetically sealed, or if the dialogue ever stops, then the society will truly have major headaches the likes of which neither Holmes or those who favor the ongoing interplay of perspectives want to experience.

REFERENCES

Bennett, W. L., & Feldman, M. S. (1981). *Reconstructing reality in the courtroom: Justice and judgment in American culture*. New Brunswick, NJ: Rutgers University Press.

Bennis v. Michigan, 517 U.S. 1163 (1996).

Bowers v. Hardwick, 478 U.S. 186 (1986).

Bruner, J. (1986). *Actual minds, possible worlds*. Cambridge, MA: Harvard University Press.

Daubert v. Merrell Dow Pharmaceuticals, Inc., 509 U.S. 579 (1993).

Dickens, C. (1868). *Bleak house*. New York: Books.

Dred Scott v. Sandford, 60 U.S. 393 (1857).

Dworkin, R. (1978). *Taking rights seriously*. Cambridge, MA: Harvard University Press.

Dworkin, R. (1986). *Law's empire*. Cambridge, MA: Harvard University Press.

Dworkin, R. (1996). *Freedom's law: The moral reading of the American Constitution*. Cambridge, MA: Harvard University Press.

Feinberg, J. (1969). The nature and value of rights. *Journal of Value Inquiry, 4*, 243–257.

Finkel, N. J. (1990). Capital felony-murder, objective indicia, and community sentiment. *Arizona Law Review, 32*, 819–913.

Finkel, N. J. (1993). Socioscientific evidence and Supreme Court numerology: When justices attempt social science. *Behavioral Sciences and the Law, 11*, 67–77.

Finkel, N. J. (1995a). *Commonsense justice: Jurors' notions of the law*. Cambridge, MA: Harvard University Press.

Finkel, N. J. (1995b). Prestidigitation, statistical magic, and Supreme Court numerology in juvenile death penalty cases. *Psychology, Public Policy, and Law, 3*, 1–31.

Finkel, N. J. (2000). Commonsense justice and jury instructions: Instructive and reciprocating connections. *Psychology, Public Policy, and Law*, 6, 591–628.

Finkel, N. J. (2001a). *Not fair! The typology of commonsense unfairness*. Washington, DC: American Psychological Association.

Finkel, N. J. (2001b). When principles collide in hard cases: A commonsense moral analysis. *Psychology, Public Policy, and Law, 7*, 1–46.

Finkel, N. J., & Duff, K. B. (1991). Felony-murder and community sentiment: Testing the Supreme Court's assertions. *Law and Human Behavior, 15*, 405–429.

Fletcher, G. P. (1988). *A crime of self-defense: Bernhard Goetz and the law on trial*. Chicago: University of Chicago Press.

Glendon, M. A. (1991). *Rights talk: The impoverishment of political discourse*. New York: Free Press.

Hamilton, A., Madison, J., & Jay, J. (1961). *The federalist papers*. New York: A Mentor Book. (Originally published circa 1788)

Holmes, O. W., Jr. (1963). *The common law* (M. D. Howe, Ed.). Cambridge, MA: Belknap Press. (Original work published 1881)

Kansas v. Hendricks, 521 U.S. 346 (1997).

Lawrence & Garner v. Texas, No. 02-102 (U.S. June 26, 2003).

Lemmon, J. (1978). Moral dilemmas. In T. L. Beauchamp & L. Walters (Eds.), *Contemporary issues in bioethics* (pp. 6–11). Belmont, CA: Wadsworth.

Northern Securities Company v. U.S., 193 U.S. 197 (1904).

Orren, K. (2000). Officers' rights: Toward a unified field theory of American constitutional development. *Law & Society Review, 34*, 873–909.

Pennington, N., & Hastie, R. (1992). Explaining the evidence: Tests of the story model for juror decision making. *Journal of Personality and Social Psychology, 62*, 189–206.

Planned Parenthood of Southeastern Pennsylvania v. Casey, 505 U.S. 833 (1992).

Pollock, F., & Maitland, F. W. (1968). *The history of English law before the time of Edward I.* Boston: Little, Brown.

Posner, R. A. (1990). *The problems of jurisprudence*. Cambridge, MA: Harvard University Press.

Pound, R. (1907). The need of a sociological jurisprudence. *Green Bag, 19*, 615.

Rawls, J. (1999). *The law of peoples*. Cambridge, MA: Harvard University Press.

Robinson, P. H., & Darley, J. M. (1995). *Justice, liability & blame: Community views and the criminal law*. Boulder, CO: Westview Press.

Roe v. Wade, 410 U.S. 113 (1973).

Rousseau, J. J. (1950). *The social contract and discourses* (G. D. N. Cole, Trans.). New York: Dutton.

Seigle, G. (1996, November 9). The day they nabbed my Aunt Sib. *The Washington Post*, p. A27.

Trop v. Dulles, 356 U.S. 86 (1958).

8

PATIENTS' RIGHTS AND PHYSICIANS' DUTIES: IMPLICATIONS FOR THE DOCTOR–PATIENT RELATIONSHIP AND THE QUALITY OF HEALTH CARE

PHILIP J. MOORE, STEPHANIE SPERNAK, AND ENID CHUNG

"All human beings are born free and equal in dignity and rights."
—Universal Declaration of Human Rights, 1948
(see Appendix, Art. 1)

Rights and duties are central to many fundamental human activities, from the birth of nations and the nature of citizenship to interpersonal relationships and the roles within them. Although they take many forms and affect most every aspect of social interaction, rights and duties have rarely been subject to empirical, social psychological investigation. However, given the complexities, contradictions, and sheer number of rights and duties, such analyses face a variety of important questions.

First, what is the nature of rights and duties? Research on black-letter law and commonsense law indicates not only that these two types of rules have different origins but also that they can come into conflict. When such conflicts occur, do black-letter or commonsense notions of rights or duties carry more weight and under what circumstances?

A second set of questions concerns the relationship between rights and duties. For example, for each right, is there a corresponding duty? If so, are they merely correlated, or is there a causal relationship between them such that rights originate from duties or vice versa? Some propose that rights are correlative, and others point out that the successful exercise of an individual's rights requires that others accept a duty to respect them. However, Moghaddam, Slocum, Finkel, More, and Harré (2000) argued against complete symmetry between rights and duties, stating that the existence of a duty does not imply a right on the part of the recipient. Which is the more plausible proposition? Also, there are a number of behaviors (e.g., voting), that reflect both an individual's right and an individual's duty. What does this suggest about the behavioral overlap between rights and duties? For example, can one actually have a "duty to oneself?"

Finally, how do rights and duties change over time? Although fundamental, human rights and duties are by no means static. And although their general definitions may remain relatively constant, specific rights (i.e., privileges to which one has a legitimate claim) and duties (i.e., morally based obligations to behave in a particular way) invariably change in accordance with societal views of what constitutes appropriate, or at least acceptable, behavior. As stated by Thomas Jefferson in describing the U.S. Declaration of Independence, "All its authority rests then on the harmonizing sentiments of the day" (Plattner, 1984, p. 149).

This chapter examines these questions in the context of the rights of medical patients and the duties of the doctors who treat them. Few, if any, aspects of society are more important than the health of its population. In the United States, for example, health care is among the largest single expenditure, representing over 14% of the gross domestic product. And no relationship is more central to the delivery of this health care than that between doctors and patients, including their respective rights and duties.

As with health care more generally, the doctor–patient relationship has undergone profound changes over a relatively short period of time. In conjunction with these and other social changes, there has been a dramatic shift in emphasis away from physicians' duties and toward the rights of patients. Reflected in court decisions, societal views, and public policy, the results of this shift can also be seen in people's everyday lives, including any visit to a doctor, clinic, or hospital. In addition to being given detailed information about their various rights, patients are told how to proceed if they feel any of these rights have been violated. Commonplace today, this was almost unheard of only 20 years ago.

These changes also have significant implications in the context of intergroup relations, for as the emphasis on patients' rights increases, so too does their power as a group increase relative to that of physicians. As a result, patients are not only afforded more rights but also are increasingly in a position, as a group, to determine how these rights and physicians' duties are defined.

We begin by tracing the development of the doctor–patient relationship, including its emphasis on various medical rights and duties as well as the fundamental principles from which they are derived. We then review empirical research, examining how these principles, rights, and duties are interpreted, how these perceptions relate to patients' and physicians' actual experience, and what happens when they do not. Finally, we discuss the implications of this research for our understanding of the doctor–patient relationship as well as human rights and duties more generally.

THE DOCTOR–PATIENT RELATIONSHIP

Although efforts to treat illness and disease are presumably as old as the maladies themselves, the practice of modern medicine can be traced to the 5th century B.C. when a fundamental change occurred in the assumptions about the causes of illness. Attributed largely to Hippocrates (c. 460 B.C. to c. 370 B.C.), previous beliefs that sickness was caused by capricious gods were eventually replaced by an observation-based view that illness and disease were the result of natural, and therefore treatable, conditions.

With maladies increasingly viewed as subject to human intervention, physicians were expected to bear more responsibility for the management of these conditions. Accordingly, principles that prescribed various rights and duties among doctors and their patients were established. The 20th century witnessed dramatic changes in the structure and practice of medicine, especially in the last half of the century. And although many of the fundamental principles of medicine have endured, their attendant rights and duties have continued to evolve.

To examine this evolution, in this chapter we investigate different models of the doctor–patient relationship. Research on doctor–patient models is not new, with previous frameworks including patient-centered models as well as paternalistic, political, and conversational models of doctor–patient relations. Although they have provided important insights about the doctor–patient relationship, these models share three significant limitations for a broader understanding of rights and duties.

First, because these models are typically defined in terms of one dimension, often representing a specific medical principle (e.g., autonomy or fidelity), they are unable to provide a comprehensive description of the various rights and duties that make up the doctor–patient relationship. Second, even when multiple models are examined simultaneously, they are generally presented as mutually exclusive entities with little or no overlap. Third, with a few limited exceptions, previous doctor–patient models do not generally include a chronological component, which is important to show the development of patients' rights and physicians' duties over time.

In this chapter we describe four models of the doctor–patient relationship: the *paternalistic* model, the *expert* model, the *consumer* model, and the *partnership* model. These models combine multiple elements of previous models, and each includes a variety of medical principles. However, these principles, rights, and duties are not model-specific. Rather than being defined by the presence or absence of certain rights, duties, or principles, these models differ in terms of their relative emphasis on these elements. Finally, although presented in chronological order, transitions between models are not associated with specific dates.

The Paternalistic Model

Also referred to as the parental or priestly model, the paternalistic model is dominated by the physician as the primary decision maker. Prominent until the early decades of the 20th century, this is considered the traditional model for the doctor–patient relationship. This model is essentially duty based, with the physician's role emphasizing four fundamental principles: *beneficence*, *fidelity*, *nonmaleficence*, and *confidentiality*.

Beneficence refers to physicians' duty to work in the best interest of their patients, though defined solely by the physician. A second principle, fidelity, directs physicians to protect patients' welfare from the competing interests of others. This fiduciary responsibility typically contrasts the health-related interests of the patient with the personal interests of the physician, compelling the physician to render care when necessary, even at the expense of his or her own sleep, convenience, personal time, or financial gain.

The third principle of modern medicine is nonmaleficence, or a physicians' duty to do no harm to those they treat. As a practical matter, this principle directs physicians to avoid unnecessary harm to patients, for many treatments cause at least temporary harm (e.g., chemotherapy), whereas others carry a risk of more permanent harm or even death (e.g., surgery). Finally, in accordance with the principle of confidentiality, physicians in the paternalistic model are duty-bound to refrain from discussing sensitive details about a patient's case with anyone not directly involved in the patient's care.

The patient's role in the paternalistic doctor–patient relationship is more limited than that of the physician. In general, patients are expected to answer physicians' questions honestly and accurately, and to comply with physicians' treatment recommendations, even if they disagree with them. Finally, the rights of patients are neither emphasized nor made explicit. Instead, patients' rights in this traditional doctor–patient relationship correspond to and are derived from physicians' duties. In sum, the paternalistic model operates on the principle of *guardianship* in which the physician acts in what he or she judges to be the patient's best interest largely independent of others' input.

The Expert Model

By the 1920s, a number of social and technological developments led to the professionalism of medicine and the emergence of a new expert model of doctor–patient relations. Encompassing elements of the scientific, informative, and engineering models, this model also emphasizes the original four physicians' duties. However, within the principle of fidelity, there is a decreased emphasis on physicians' duty to make financial sacrifices for the sake of their patients. In addition, there is an emergent emphasis on physicians' education, technical knowledge, and professional certification. Although physicians in the paternalistic model were not necessarily incompetent, they were often trained to focus more on the public perception of their abilities.

Although the expert model did not engender any fundamental changes in either physicians' duties or the corresponding rights of their patients, it sparked a tremendous increase in the power, wealth, and prestige of physicians. Combined with subsequent social, cultural, and economic changes, these developments also set the stage for some of the most dramatic shifts in patients' rights and physicians' duties in the history of medicine.

The Consumer Model

In the wake of various civil rights movements that began in the 1950s, a number of social, legal, and economic changes took place that altered the nature of health care in the United States. Increasingly, health came to be viewed as a service commodity, casting physicians as service providers and patients as consumers of that service. The development of this consumer model is associated with two fundamental changes in medicine, both with profound implications for the doctor–patient relationship.

First, medical principles were increasingly expressed in terms of patients' rights. This, in turn, has led to the development of a new set of principles as well as a reinterpretation of those already established. The second major change involved the emergence of *managed care* in which third parties (e.g., insurance companies and health maintenance organizations) assumed a primary role in the payment for and delivery of health care. Also referred to as the business model, this doctor–patient relationship has become the dominant model in the current American health care system, and it is likely to remain dominant for the foreseeable future.

Although physicians retain the duty to practice for the benefit of patients, under a consumer model, patient beneficence is defined primarily by patients themselves. Accordingly, patients' satisfaction has become increasingly prominent, both in research and as part of physician performance evaluations.

In the consumer model, fidelity is commonly discussed in terms of a conflict of interest. In addition to the earlier mentioned conflict between patients' interests and the personal interests of physicians, there is a new potential conflict between the patients' interests and those of third-party payers. With over 200 million people enrolled in some form of health plan in the United States, physicians are increasingly called on to act as "double agents," responsible for the interest of their patients yet increasingly pressured to minimize the expenditure of medical resources.

Another development related to fidelity involves the conflict between a patient's right to confidentiality and a physician's responsibility to those whom patients may threaten to harm. In the case of *Tarasoff v. Regents of the University of California* (1976), the California Supreme Court imposed a duty on physicians to warn potential victims of threats made by their patients when (a) the danger to the intended victim is foreseeable and (b) the victim is readily identifiable. This ruling illustrates a third potential conflict of interest in the doctor–patient relationship, pitting the physicians' duty to their patients against the welfare of society as a whole.

Perhaps the most significant change in doctor–patient s relations under the consumer model involves patients' *autonomy*, or their right to be involved in decisions concerning their medical care. This is the first of two definitions of patient-centered medical care. Medical patients' autonomy encompasses many different issues, including a patient's right to be informed about the nature of his or her condition as well as the risks, benefits, and potential alternatives to the recommended treatment. The second aspect of patients' autonomy is their right to make certain decisions about their medical care. The most fundamental of these rights prohibits physicians (or anyone else) from proceeding with any treatment or procedure without the expressed consent of the patient.

This issue of informed consent was first addressed legally in the case of *Salgo v. Leland Stanford Jr. University* (1957) in which the court ruled that competent adult patients must give their voluntary consent before any medical procedures are performed. Although overturned on appeal, this ruling was followed by other legal decisions (e.g., *Canterbury v. Spence*, 1972) that firmly established a patient's right to information about his or her condition and treatment, as well as the right to have this information presented in a readily understandable way.

Patients also have the right to refuse medical intervention, even treatment necessary to save or maintain their lives. This "right to die" requires that physicians defer to a competent adult patient's desire not to be treated, even when lack of such treatment is likely to result in their death. Although not absolute (courts may also consider society's interest in preserving life and protecting innocent third parties), a patient's right to refuse treatment has consistently been upheld by the courts.

In general, the decisions concerning the right to die have also been extended to the surrogates of incompetent patients (e.g., those in a permanent coma or other vegetative state) whose prospects for recovery are poor. Beginning with the case of Karen Ann Quinlan (1976), the court has ruled relatively consistently over the last three decades that surrogates, rather than doctors, should decide what kind of care incompetent patients should receive at the end of life.

The contract-based nature of the consumer model has also fostered patients' rights to hold physicians accountable for the quality of treatment they provide. This right of *accountability* is manifested in at least two ways in the doctor–patient relationship. The first is an emerging emphasis on patient satisfaction, which is increasingly used to inform both administrative policy and physicians' compensation. A related change, discussed later, is an increased demand for redress among patients who feel they have suffered as a result of medical malpractice.

Finally, although the information examined in this chapter comes from the United States, recent research indicates that managed care is becoming increasingly prominent in many other parts of the world. And given the increasing pace of globalization, there is every reason to anticipate that this trend will continue.

The Partnership Model

Citing problems associated with the consumer model of doctor–patient relations, many researchers have proposed an alternative partnership model in which patients and physicians interact in a more personal, cooperative way. This model includes elements of the other three models and combines them with additional rights, duties, and a new operating principle. In essence, it includes the interpersonal commitment associated with the paternalistic and expert models, while retaining the rights and duties established under the consumer model. In the partnership model, the initial four physicians' duties are identical to those in the previous models. However, with respect to competence, the partnership model also emphasizes the physician's interpersonal skills, including empathy and patient education.

THE PSYCHOLOGY OF MEDICAL RIGHTS AND DUTIES

A wide variety of laws, principles, and policies have been established to formally delineate what medical rights and duties are, as well as how they are to be implemented. However, merely establishing formal rights and duties is insufficient for a better understanding of the beliefs and behaviors these rights and duties are designed to represent. There are a number of reasons for this: First, official rules and regulations typically set a minimum standard for behavior and as such are not applicable to the majority of interpersonal relations, including the doctor–patient relationship. A second reason is that rules, however firmly established, are often interpreted quite differently depending on an individual's background interests and agenda. Finally, even if recognized as a matter of policy or law, certain rights and duties may simply not be followed in practice.

There is little empirical psychological research on rights and duties. However, there is substantial research literature on the doctor–patient relationship that can provide insight into doctors' and patients' conceptualizations of their respective rights and duties, the extent to which these expectations are realized, and the consequences when they are not. To better understand how patients' rights and physicians' duties are actually experienced in the doctor–patient relationship, we examine empirical results from four related research areas: information seeking, medical decision making, patient satisfaction, and medical malpractice.

Information Seeking

In a survey of 84 breast cancer patients, 64 oncologists, and 140 oncology nurses, Girgis, Sanson-Fisher, and Schofield (1999) asked participants to indicate their agreement with a variety of medical principle statements. The first of these statements was "The patient has a legal and moral right to accurate, reliable information," with which 97% of patients, 93% of physicians, and 94% of nurses agreed. Although future research may determine the generalizability of these findings, they suggest that patients have internalized their right to full and accurate disclosure and that this right is recognized by doctors and nurses.

The results of research on patients' desire for information are similarly consistent. Although some differences have been found between patients of different socioeconomic status, the vast majority of medical patients—typically between 90% and 100%—report a desire to be completely informed about their condition and treatment options.

A final question regarding information dissemination is whether patients are actually getting the information they appear to want and to which they have a right. Unfortunately, there is substantial evidence that suggests they are not. Specifically, studies examining this question have found that patients consistently report not getting all of the information they desire from their physicians. A potential explanation for these results is suggested by Waitzkin (1985), who found that doctors tend to spend little time informing patients, to overestimate the time they do spend informing patients, and to underestimate patients' desire for the information. In other words, these results suggest that physicians continue to apply a traditional, paternalistic model with respect to informing patients about their conditions.

This lack of information may also be attributable to patients' reluctance to ask questions or otherwise request information. Although such diffidence may not be as prevalent today as in decades past, research suggests that patients continue to leave many questions and desires unspoken, and that physician confirmation of patient understanding is extremely rare.

In sum, although there may be broad recognition of patients' right to be fully informed about their medical conditions and treatment alternatives, for many patients, the right to this information—or conversely, physicians' duty to provide it—has yet to be realized.

Medical Decision Making

Although changes in the doctor–patient relationship over the last century have been varied and dramatic, the most fundamental shift appears to be in terms of patients' autonomy, that is, their authority to make decisions about one's medical care. This perspective is summarized by Brock and Wartman (1990), who stated that "the paternalistic approach has generally been replaced by the concept of shared decision making, in which both physicians and patients make active and essential contributions" (p. 1596). Although this is certainly true as a matter of black-letter policy, the question remains as to whether patients actually desire principal autonomy in terms of their medical treatment.

As with information seeking, most research on medical patients' autonomy desires has been conducted on cancer patients, although it has also included patients without cancer as well as nonpatients. However, unlike information seeking, patients' desire to be involved in their medical treatment varies widely, ranging from about 20% to 100%.

As pointed out by Johnson et al. (1996), many patients may wish to be informed but have no desire to participate in any medical decision making. Finding no correlation between patients' information-seeking and decision-making preferences, Ende, Kazis, Ash, and Moskowitz (1989) concluded that information seeking and decision making are qualitatively distinct dimensions of autonomy. Of course, such a nonsignificant relationship may also result from a ceiling effect in information seeking, reflecting patients' consistently strong desire for information.

In general, nonpatients are most likely to desire a decision-making role, with approximately 9 out of 10 reporting a preference for at least some decision-making involvement. Cancer patients are the next most likely, with an average of about 60% indicating a desire for some autonomy. Noncancer medical patients are the least likely to desire participation, with only 2 out of 5 wanting to be involved in decisions about their treatment.

Patients' medical decision-making preferences are often assessed on three possible levels of participation: (a) passive, (b) collaborative, or (c) active. Of the three levels of involvement, most participants in the previous studies, about 60%, preferred a collaborative relationship with their physician, while about 15% desired an active decision-making role.

Patients' desire for medical autonomy has also been associated with a variety of personal characteristics. In general, younger patients appear to prefer more active roles, as do females, patients with more education, and those with less severe diseases.

These results indicate the importance of considering patients' decision-making preferences in medical treatment plans, and to the extent possible, of matching physicians' practice styles to these preferences. Results from Harvey, Kazis, and Lee (1999) suggest that this matching is particularly important for patients with a high preference for decision-making involvement. In a recent study by Gattellari, Butow, and Tattersall (2001), only about one third of patients reported experiencing a good match between their preferred and perceived decision-making roles, with 29% more active and 37% less involved than they preferred.

This apparent lack of matching may be due in part to the tendency of physicians to dominate doctor–patient communications. For example, many researchers have found that the shared-decision model is not descriptive of most doctor–patient relations and that physicians rarely ask their patients open-ended questions. Although physicians need a certain amount of specific information (for which closed-ended questions are best suited), this evidence suggests that the opportunity for patients to offer their opinions or perspectives is extremely limited. Thus, it appears that patients' right of autonomy has yet to be realized, for many patients who desire to play a decision-making role are not given the opportunity to do so.

Patients' Satisfaction

In the context of patients' rights and physicians' duties, patients' satisfaction can be viewed as a patient's perception that his or her beneficence has been adequately addressed. As with autonomy, patients' satisfaction is influenced by a wide variety of factors. Not surprisingly, medical patients' satisfaction is strongly associated with symptomatic improvement, lower levels of pain, and greater request fulfillment.

Greater satisfaction is also reported by patients who experience fewer unmet expectations as well as by those whose decision-making preferences are matched by their opportunity for autonomy. Although not providing patients with desired information has been found to reduce their satisfaction, this relationship has not always been found, nor are personal characteristics necessarily a strong determinant of patient satisfaction.

Among the most powerful and consistent predictors of patients' satisfaction in the doctor–patient relationship are physicians' psychosocial behaviors. These include nonverbal communication and a positive and supportive approach as well as expressions of attention, reassurance, and personal interest. This is the second definition of *patient-centered* care, namely, a focus on the interpersonal aspects of the doctor–patient relationship.

Medical Malpractice

The issue of medical malpractice may provide the most direct psychological examination of patients' rights and physicians' duties, albeit in the negative sense. That is, a medical malpractice claim represents, by definition, a patient's belief that one or more of his or her rights—and physicians' duties—were violated. Although the relative emphasis on particular rights and duties differs across cases, each malpractice claim is inherently relevant to the principles of beneficence, nonmaleficence, competence, and accountability, and it may also involve any combination of the remaining principles.

Over the last 30 years, medical malpractice has become one of the most difficult health care issues in the United States. In addition to billions of dollars in legal fees and court costs, medical malpractice premiums in the United States total more than $5 billion annually (Hiatt, 1992), and *defensive medicine* (i.e., procedures performed to protect against potential liability) is estimated to cost more than $14 billion a year (Rubin & Mendelson, 1994). However, studies have repeatedly shown that the quality of medical care alone is a poor predictor of a medical malpractice claim.

As psychosocial factors are increasingly recognized as an important element of health care, many researchers have posited that the doctor–patient relationship may be a principal determinant of medical malpractice claims. Although early examinations of this question were largely anecdotal, more recent research has found that physicians who exhibit more negative communication behaviors are more likely to have been sued in the past for malpractice than those with more positive doctor–patient relations.

Although these studies demonstrate empirical associations between doctor–patient relations and malpractice claims, they cannot establish a causal link between them. For it is possible, indeed probable, that past experiences with malpractice claims have influenced physicians' subsequent interactions with their patients. In the first experimental examination of this *doctor–patient hypothesis*, Lester and Smith (1993) showed students a videotape of a hypothetical dermatology office visit that resulted in damage to the patient. This study found that negative physician communication behaviors decreased perceptions of physician competence and raised expressed intentions to file a malpractice claim.

Extending the experimental approach to medical patients, Moore, Adler, and Robertson (2000) presented obstetric patients with scenarios depicting the interactions between an obstetric patient and her physician throughout the hypothetical patient's pregnancy, labor, and delivery. Consistent with the results of Lester and Smith (1993), this study found that increased perceptions of physician competence decreased patients' malpractice claim intentions. In addition, these results were independent of medical outcome severity.

In addition to what Falk (1999) referred to as the "accountability revolution" in medicine, these research results suggest the potential emergence of a new perceived patient right: the right to empathy. More specifically, medical patients appear to view interpersonal behavior as an integral component of physicians' competence. Combined with the increasing importance of patients' satisfaction, good bedside manner is something that patients have apparently come to expect and may eventually demand as a right.

Emerging Issues

As the doctor–patient relationship continues to evolve, a number of issues have begun to emerge with significant implications for physicians, patients, and society at large.

Physicians' Income

This concerns whether physicians' incomes, although lower than in the recent past, are still too high. On the basis of this belief, Brody (1992) proposed reducing the salary of specialists and using the surplus to fund health programs. Although its political viability is uncertain, we believe that the Resource-Based Relative Value Scale (RBRVS; Hsiao et al., 1988) is an appropriate model for this purpose. Developed for the federal government to pay physicians under Medicare, the RBRVS more closely ties physicians' compensation to the amount (rather than the type) of work they perform.

Patients' Right to Treatment

Whether patients have a right to treatment regardless of their personal, social, or financial resources—in short, the right to be a patient—is also an important issue related to the doctor–patient relationship. It is also an issue about which there is little consensus in the United States. However, there does appear to be a strong consensus that the current U.S. health care system is seriously deficient. For example, American health care costs currently take up a significantly greater percentage of the country's gross national product than in any other industrialized nation, and yet almost 16% of the population is without health care coverage.

Virtually everyone becomes ill or injured at some point, and such maladies often require medical attention. In 1999 alone, over 35 million people—more than one in eight Americans—were hospitalized in the United States. And because the doctor–patient relationship is the nexus at which patients typically come in contact with the health care system, it can have a profound impact on the use and effectiveness of health care. The rights of patients and the duties of their physicians are a cornerstone of this relationship, shaping many of the expectations and behaviors of those involved. As such, patients' rights and physicians' duties are not only useful for a better understanding of rights and duties more generally but also for the development of more effective health care policy.

RIGHTS AND DUTIES REVISITED

The preceding discussion of patients' rights, physicians' duties, and the doctor–patient relationship suggests some potential answers to the questions posed earlier concerning human rights and duties more generally.

The Nature of Rights and Duties

As determinants of behavior, rights and duties obviously come in many forms. It is equally clear that such rights and duties are not always concordant. Black-letter versus commonsense law illustrates one such distinction. For example, patients' black-letter right to ask questions regarding their condition or treatment may not, in practice, be recognized by patients or respected by physicians. However, what is much less clear is whether black-letter or commonsense rights and duties predominate when they come into conflict. For example, physicians do not (as yet) have a legal obligation to treat patients in a respectful, empathic manner, for when "push comes to shove"—or rather, when "ire goes to court"—the majority of such cases are dismissed. On the other hand, research suggests that neglecting such commonsense duties may leave patients disgruntled, ill-informed, and more inclined to seek satisfaction through costly and often traumatic black-letter proceedings.

It may be useful for future research to expand on this dichotomous distinction between formal and informal rights and duties, for although not all rights and duties are formal, neither are all formal rights and duties legally binding. Moreover, the implications of these rights and duties, whether formal or informal, depend largely on the relationship(s) between the parties involved. This suggests that people's respective rights and duties may also depend on their *affiliation*, or the context in which the relationship is set.

The broadest level of affiliation would be the *sociopolitical* level, referring to members of a society or other incorporated community. At this level, rights and duties are usually enforced by the passage of laws, sanctions, or other proscriptions established by recognized authorities. Examples range from local town ordinances to universal crimes against humanity established by an international court.

A second level of affiliation is *organizational*, at which rules, guidelines, and other codes of conduct apply specifically to members of a particular organization or group. This would include organizations whose rules and regulations, even if enacted for the benefit of society, are only enforceable among its members. For example, the principles of medical ethics of the American Medical Association are not laws but rather standards of conduct that define acceptable behavior for physicians. Like political entities, organizations vary widely in size from neighborhood groups to multinational corporations, and there are often punishments for failure to perform one's duties or respect the rights of others. However, sanctions in the organizational setting are typically limited to a maximum of dismissal from the organization or forfeiture of other resources derived from membership.

The final level of affiliation is *interpersonal*, namely personal relationships between two or more individuals. Violations of rights or duties at this level are generally addressed by informal means, and typically only by those personally affected by the transgression. Although informal, such violations can have significant effects, including the dissolution of important relationships, such as those between doctors and patients. It is on this level, for example, that any informal right to empathy would presumably operate.

The Relationship Between Rights and Duties

Do rights derive from duties or vice versa? The evolution of the doctor–patient relationship indicates that the answer to this question depends on the model being considered. First, it is clear that rights certainly can derive from duties, as is the case in both the paternalistic and expert doctor–patient models. Similarly, the converse is equally true, as in the consumer-based health care model. For example, in the paternalistic model, the emphasis on the physician duty of nonmaleficence implies that the patient has a reasonable expectation (or right) not to be unduly harmed. Likewise, a physician's duty to obtain informed consent is required as a result of a patient's right to informed consent, as in the consumer and partnership models.

The issue of symmetry between rights and duties is rather more complex than that of relative dominance. It has been argued by Starr (1982) and others and assumed throughout this chapter that rights and duties are inherently symmetrical; in other words, for every right, there is a corresponding duty. However, Moghaddam et al. (2000) disputed this, stating that the existence of a duty does not imply a right on the part of its recipient. This point is illustrated by an individual who takes it upon himself or herself to assist someone else out of a personal duty to help others, for clearly the recipient of this assistance has no actual right to it.

However, rights and duties are social constructions, and as such, require some degree of consensus. And because consensus requires agreement between at least two people, an individual conviction to help others, although laudable, does not represent a duty. Similarly, although an individual may be convinced that he has a right to something (e.g., money) that he does not currently possess, to the extent that this perspective is not shared by anyone else, the individual cannot be said to have a right to that item. For given that a right is a privilege (e.g., ownership) to which people have a legitimate claim, and given that this legitimacy is determined by consensus, a right cannot exist in the absence of such agreement. Even if this individual is entirely sincere in his belief and may even have the capacity to obtain what he wants (e.g., through force), this does not give him a right to it.

This same logic applies to the so-called duty to oneself. If one has a duty to oneself, then the corresponding right to this duty is the individual's own right to the action specified by that duty. Such a privilege is therefore also self-contained and thus lacks the consensus necessary to be a right. Put another way, given that duties are morally based obligations, the moral behind a duty to oneself amounts to self-interest (i.e., beneficence), which may exist as a right, but not as a duty. Thus, a duty to oneself is akin to owing oneself money, which, although perhaps useful for describing one's personal accounting strategy, is meaningless in the context of rights and duties.

The Evolution of Rights and Duties

Patients' rights and physicians' duties have changed in many ways over time. These changes appear to have been particularly notable in the last hundred years, with the most dramatic changes occurring during the last three decades. Consistent with the hypothesis of Moghaddam et al. (2000) and others, there has been a profound shift in focus from an early emphasis on the duties of physicians (to their patients and their profession) to a current focus on patients' rights in the medical context. One may consider this a good thing or a bad thing, depending on whether one is a patient or a physician (or a malpractice attorney), but we view it as an imbalance between patients' rights and physicians' duties, possibly in response to a previous disparity in the other direction.

However, this does not appear to be a self-correcting or even a self-limiting process, and given its apparent adverse effects (e.g., patient and physician dissatisfaction and malpractice claims), prudence would seem to dictate efforts to address this imbalance. To that end, we suggest an emphasis on the partnership model described earlier, without a focus on either rights or duties, or on patients as mere consumers. Rather, we would argue for an alternative emphasis on the collaborative, educational, and empathic nature of this approach. In addition, given the progressively smaller amounts of time physicians are able to spend with patients, it may also be important to conduct future research to determine the relative importance of office visit duration versus the quality of the doctor–patient interaction. In sum, although it may not be possible to turn back the clock on managed care, we may be able to strike a better balance between patients' rights and physicians' duties while simultaneously promoting more constructive and effective doctor–patient relations.

The purpose of this chapter was to address certain fundamental questions about human rights and duties by examining them in the context of the doctor–patient relationship. In so doing, we hope to promote a more complete understanding (and consensus) of what rights and duties actually are, and in concert with the other sections of this volume, to facilitate a healthy balance between these two important social tools. Or, as expressed in Virgil's *Aeneid* (as translated by Humphries, 1951, p. 227): "Surely as the divine powers take note of the dutiful, surely as there is any justice anywhere and a mind recognizing in itself what is right, may the gods bring your earned rewards."

REFERENCES

Brock, D. W., & Wartman, S. A. (1990). When competent patients make irrational choices. *New England Journal of Medicine, 322,* 1595–1599.

Brody, D. S. (1992). *The healer's power.* New Haven, CT: Yale University Press.

Canterbury v. Spence, 464 F.2d 722 (DC Cir. 1972).

Ende, J., Kazis, L., Ash, A., & Moskowitz, M. A. (1989). Measuring patients' desire for autonomy: Decision making and information-seeking preferences among medical patients. *Journal of General Internal Medicine, 4*(1), 23–30.

Falk, G. (1999). *Hippocrates assailed: The American health delivery system.* Lanham, MD: University Press of America.

Gattellari, M., Butow, P. N., & Tattersall, M. H. (2001). Sharing decisions in cancer care. *Social Science & Medicine, 52,* 1865–1878.

Girgis, A., Sanson-Fisher, R. W., & Schofield, M. J. (1999). Is there consensus between breast cancer patients and providers on guidelines for breaking bad news? *Behavioral Medicine, 25*(2), 69–77.

Harvey, R. M., Kazis, L., & Lee, A. F. (1999). Decision-making preference and opportunity in VA ambulatory care patients: Association with patient satisfaction. *Research in Nursing & Health, 22*(1), 39–48.

Hiatt, H. (1992). Medical malpractice. *Bulletin of the New York Academy of Medicine,* 68(2), 254–260.

Hsiao, W. C., Braun, P., Dunn, D., Becker, E. R., DeNicola, M., & Ketcham, T. R. (1988). Results and policy implications of the resource-based relative-value study. *New England Journal of Medicine, 319,* 881–888.

Humphries, R. (1951). *The Aeneid of Virgil.* New York: Scribner.

Johnson, J. D., Roberts, C. S., Cox, C. E., Reintgen, D. S., Levine, J. S., & Parsons, M. (1996). Breast cancer patients' personality style, age, and treatment decision making. *Journal of Surgical Oncology, 63*(3), 183–186.

Lester, G. W., & Smith, S. G. (1993). Listening and talking to patients. A remedy for malpractice suits? *Western Journal of Medicine, 158*(3), 268–272.

Moghaddam, F. M., Slocum, N. R., Finkel, N. J., More, T., & Harré, R. (2000). Toward a cultural theory of duties. *Culture and Psychology,* 6, 275–302.

Moore, P. J., Adler, N. E., & Robertson, P. A. (2000). Medical malpractice: The effect of doctor–patient relations on medical patient perceptions and malpractice intentions. *Western Journal of Medicine, 173*(4), 244–250.

Plattner, M. F. (Ed.). (1984). *Human rights in our time: Essays in memory of Victor Baras.* Boulder, CO: Westview Press.

In re Quinlan. 355 A.2d 647 (N.J. 1976).

Rubin, R. J., & Mendelson, D. N. (1994). How much does defensive medicine cost? *Journal of American Health Policy, 4*(4), 7–15.

Salgo v. Leland Stanford Jr. University, 317 P.2d 170 (Cal. Ct. App. 1957).

Starr, P. (1982). *The social transformation of American medicine: The rise of a sovereign profession and the making of a vast industry*. Boulder, CO: Perseus Publishing.

Tarasoff v. Regents of the University of California, 551 P.2d 334, 342 (Cal. 1976).

Waitzkin, H. (1985). Information giving in medical care. *Journal of Health and Social Behavior*, *26*(2), 81–101.

9

THE RIGHTFUL PLACE OF HUMAN RIGHTS: INCORPORATING INDIVIDUAL, GROUP, AND CULTURAL PERSPECTIVES

STEPHEN WORCHEL

The high drama and excitement of securing a mate is one of the most interesting of all human rituals, but it is often concluded rather quickly and its outcome is rarely in doubt. At the risk of offending both poets and evolutionary psychologists, I suggest that the most fascinating and universal human endeavor is the delicate negotiation that occurs between individuals and their groups over the rights and duties of each. Unlike most if not all other behaviors, the intricate sparring that occurs between individuals and their groups never reaches a final climax; rather the participants are doomed to a lifetime of bobbing and weaving, like shadow boxers attempting to reach that which is always outside their grasp. Indeed, the individual may tire of the game and forsake one group only to become entwined in a tug of war with another group or groups.

Work on this chapter was supported by a National Science Foundation Grant BCS-0078867 and a National Institute for Occupational Safety and Health grant. I thank Dawna Coutant for her insightful comments on early versions of this chapter.

The fatal attraction that binds individuals and groups together is the fact that each is dependent on the other for establishing an identity. Eric Erickson (1959) observed that the individual's search for identity begins at birth and continues unabated till death. To this observation, Worchel, Coutant-Sassic, and Grossman (1992) suggested that groups, too, struggle to define their identity and secure their right to exist from the time of inception until the group ceases to exist. The ground rules that ultimately define the relationship between individual and group are the rights and obligations (duties) of each. Using this framework as a beginning, I chart a journey designed to establish several guideposts. First, rights and duties represent the two sides of the same coin (in considering the relationship between individual and group), and therefore, any meaningful examination must consider both rights and duties. Second, both individuals and groups are endowed with rights and duties, and the positions of both parties must be included to truly comprehend the system of rights and duties. Third, and possibly most controversial, because of the dynamic and contextual nature of the relation between individuals and groups, there are few, if any, absolutes or universals (rights and duties). The rights and duties of groups and individuals are largely defined by the needs of each, the relationship that exists between the two, and contextual factors such as the cultural framework. Although these positions place me at apparent odds with scholars such as Doise (see chap. 2, this volume) and esteemed bodies such as the United Nations (Universal Declaration of Human Rights, see Appendix for full text) and the World Court, I attempt to explicate these points and demonstrate their value in developing a utilitarian approach to understanding the relationship between individuals and groups.

LONELY PLANET: THE INDIVIDUAL'S STRUGGLE FOR IDENTITY

Several investigators (Brewer, 1991; Worchel, 1998) have argued that individuals face the maddening dilemma between the desire for uniqueness and the longing to be one of the group: the quest for independence versus the hunger for interdependence. Brewer has described this Zen riddle as achieving a state of being "the same and different at the same time" (p. 475). Maslach, Stapp, and Santee (1985) anticipated this struggle in their presentation of the delight and fright of being deindividuated. According to their analysis, there is security and freedom in being an undistinguishable member of a group. This state frees the individual from feeling responsible for his or her actions, and normative inhibitions can be shed without fear of exposure or censor. However, there is a flip side to this perfect picture of unbridled freedom. A gnawing discomfort at being a group clone grips the individual, motivating him or her to fight for uniqueness and identity apart from others. Standing apart from the group and being distinguished from others allows the individual to develop a sense of personal importance and unique purpose. The individual becomes locked into an agitated dance between deindividuation and individuation, attempting to find a comfortable balance between the two states of being.

Social identity theory (Tajfel & Turner, 1979) offers yet another perspective on the development of individual identity and the individual's relationship with the group. This theory argues that the identity of the individual is built on two pillars, one involving unique personal attributes and the other resulting from the embrace of the group (social identity). A challenge for the individual is to find a satisfying accommodation between the personal and social identities. Too much emphasis on the personal can result in the individual feeling alienated and alone. Yet being identified only by one's group memberships obliterates the unique features of one's identity. The tension between conflicting desires for independence and interdependence locks individuals into an eternal love–hate relationship with their groups. John Donne reminded us, "no man is an island, entire of itself." Yet men and women are attracted like a moth to the flame to the image of being an island unto themselves. But being an island adrift in a vast sea of emptiness is terribly frightening, so individuals attach themselves to the continent, only to long for the independence of the island.

I have suggested that this eternal conflict between the simultaneous desires for independence and interdependence contributes to the dynamic quality of groups (Worchel, 1999). Individual members both embrace and resist the lure of groups. One result is that the group is placed in a constant state of flux as individuals' commitment waxes and wanes to meet their personal comfort levels. Although this vacillation may satisfy the individuals' desires for identity, it creates havoc for the group's goal to function and survive. Group members cannot predict the behavior of their comrades.

Brehm (1966) captured a somewhat different nuance of this dilemma in his theory of psychological reactance. He argued that individuals have a set of behavioral freedoms, acts that they could engage in should they so desire. Threats to or elimination of these freedoms create psychological tension (reactance) that initiates efforts to restore these freedoms. According to Brehm, behavioral freedoms are necessary for the security of the person; they aid in the quest for survival. Having behavioral alternatives allows the individual to deal effectively with changing situations and personal needs. I would argue that these behavioral freedoms have another function. Like unique personal attributes, they define the identity of the individual. One's sense of identity and self-esteem are etched by the behaviors in which one can engage. My view of myself is shaped by the fact that I am free to buy a house in any neighborhood in my town or that I can take a trip to Bali. These freedoms may also define the uniqueness of the individual because the freedoms of one person are different from those of another person. Further contributing to the personal identity is the fact that importance of various freedoms differs between individuals. Hence, one person's identity may be defined by the fact that the freedom to travel is ranked high, whereas the freedom to play golf may be of high importance to another person. Threats to these freedoms instigate immediate reactions to restore the freedom and to feel anger against those who threatened the freedom, not because the freedoms themselves are so important but because the loss of freedom inflicts damage to the individual's identity.

With this first stroke of the brush, I paint the picture of a social landscape composed of individuals striving to establish their personal identity. This identity is based on both the uniqueness that separates the individual from all others and the sameness that protects the individual from appearing as a freak of nature. Uniqueness is achieved by establishing independence, whereas interdependence and acceptance are gained by emphasizing the similarities one has with other members of his or her group(s). Identity is important because it guides individual's behavior, creates a sense of continuity of being, and leads to positive self-esteem.

INDEPENDENCE AND INTERDEPENDENCE FROM THE GROUP'S PERSPECTIVE

As a psychologist, there is an ingrained tendency to view the world from the perspective of the individual, an egocentric bias, if you will. However, there is another actor on the stage of identity. That player is the group. My colleagues and I have argued that groups, like individuals, constantly strive to establish their identity (Worchel & Coutant, 2001; Worchel, Iuzzini, Coutant, & Ivaldi, 2000). The group's identity, indeed the group's survival, is dependent on its ability to capture members and to ensure that these members march in unison to the group's drummer, its norms. Groups expend significant amounts of energy and capital to invite, pressure, and force members to follow group rules. Like the consummate farmer, groups plow their fields by educating members about group rules and expectations. Those members who display their loyalty to the group are rewarded and martyred. Those who deviate are punished and eventually weeded out if they fail to fall in line.

The psychological literature is filled with examples of the effectiveness of group pressures on individual's behaviors. Milgram (1974) shocked the academic community by his demonstrations of obedience. His research showed that individuals felt obliged to follow commands, even commands that resulted in harm to others. An equally revealing demonstration of the power of groups is found in Asch's (1956) research on conformity. These studies demonstrated individual's reluctance to violate informal group norms, even when these norms were clearly incorrect. People who had low status or whose membership was not secure were most likely to conform (Hancock & Sorrentino, 1980; Raven & French, 1958). Although the threat of punishment and banishment was unspoken, Schachter (1951) demonstrated that fear of rejection for deviation is well founded. Schachter's studies showed that individuals who persisted in deviating from the group were eventually rejected. The group's concern with deviates is well placed. Studies of conformity have shown that the existence of a single dissenting member who is left unpunished significantly decreases the conformity of other members (Asch, 1956). A rotten apple that is not discarded from the barrel of the group can destroy the integrity of the group.

At first glance, ensuring obedience and conformity appears easily achievable. To function smoothly, groups need only to perfect their ability to force members to follow the orders of leaders and the group norms. However, there are several flies in this seemingly simple ointment. Most groups are faced with the constant need to attract new members and retain old ones. Few individuals willingly join the ranks of a group that wields a bloody hatchet on members who exercise personal latitude in their behavior. Groups can best entice new members by demonstrating that they offer broad opportunities for individuals to flourish while still preserving the group's integrity. Indeed, creating an atmosphere of individual freedom can serve other group goals in addition to attracting new members. The abilities and skills of the group members may vary widely. In order for the group to thrive, it must encourage its members to exercise and develop their unique skills so long as these skills service the group (Tuckman, 1965). The inventions of these members who create and discover as they exercise their unique talents allow the group to change and adapt to an ever-changing environment. Without the mutations spawned by these individual efforts, the group would soon decay and become a relic.

The group, like the individual, must solve a Zen riddle of its own. The group must secure and protect its collective identity while allowing each individual to develop a personal identity that is unique. The whole of the group is greater than the sum of its parts. Most groups have a history that predates any individual member, and the future of the group will likely extend far longer than the life of any single member. These points embolden the group to focus on its own identity and satisfy its own needs at the expense of any individual's identity or need. Yet lurking in the background is the recognition that it is ultimately the individual who is the building block of the group. And defection or dissatisfaction on the part of individuals can destroy or weaken the entire group.

ANSWERING THE RIDDLE: RIGHTS AND DUTIES

The challenge facing both individuals and groups seems unsolvable. A slight of hand worthy of Houdini seems the only route to enable individuals to be independent and interdependent at the same time and to ensure that the identities of the group and the individual member are secure. Indeed, the challenge to both individual and group is enormous. The difficulty is seen in the fact that groups are often unstable and attention is constantly focused on trying to maintain membership; the task is often similar to that of a person trying to fill a sieve with water. Even the most attractive groups lose and gain members at a rapid rate (Moreland & Levine, 1982), and leaders seldom seem confident of the loyalty of their followers. Likewise, individuals are rarely satisfied with their group memberships, often moving from one group to another like agitated bees seeking the most fragrant flower. But the picture is not completely bleak. Groups are able to survive and both attract and retain members. And individuals do settle into relationships that feed their incompatible hungers for independence and interdependence.

The glue that ultimately binds individuals and groups in a state of accommodation, even an uneasy accommodation, is the combination of rights and duties. The system of rights and duties defines the relationship between group and individual. Indeed, I would argue, that both groups and individuals have rights and duties, and the lives of both individuals and groups are continually dedicated to negotiating these rights and duties.

Through the Eyes of the Individual

In an earlier section, I discussed Brehm's concept of *free behaviors*. Brehm (1966) argued that behavioral freedoms are important because they ensure the individual's survival. Although a large arsenal of freedoms may enhance coping, I suggest an additional function for freedoms. Free behaviors, I argue, define the individual's domain in which he or she can make personal decisions. Viewed in this manner, individual freedoms form part of the self-concept, and a threat to one's freedom ignites both awareness of one's self-concept and efforts to protect one's identity. Stealing one's rights is tantamount to chipping away part of one's being.

Although the range of behavioral freedom may be limitless, there is a category of personal freedoms that stands apart from others in terms of both importance and impact on individual identity. These freedoms constitute the domain of individual rights. Individual rights can be conceived as those free behaviors that involve the individual's relationship to others (and the group) and define those areas in which the individual can act independently from the social group. For example, the right of privacy implies that others cannot intrude into the individual's personal (private) domain. Rights are vitally important because they denote the individual's social independence, the individual's unique being.

Although this perspective of individual rights is based on a concern with the individual's personal identity, it is decidedly social, dealing with the relationship of the individual to the group. Because of this, individual rights are neither absolute nor universal. Rather they result from negotiations between the individual and group(s). Individual rights (and the conditions under which they exist) are ultimately bestowed by a group, not simply claimed by an individual. Because individuals belong to different groups and have different histories, positions, and relationships with the groups, the rights of any single individual may be different from the rights of any other individual. For example, the rights (within the family) of my 20-year-old daughter are different from those given to my twin 14-year-olds. The constellation of an individual's rights not only defines self-identity but also makes that individual unique from all other individuals. Rights are critical because they define the individual's independence and separate the individual from others.

It is interesting to consider the importance of rights within the context of group membership and identity. According to social identity theory (Brewer & Gardner, 1996; Hogg & Abrams, 1990; Tajfel & Turner, 1979), one's social identity is formed by the groups to which one claims membership. The shared social identity prepares individuals to act in support of their common group. In fact, Tajfel (1970) has shown that individuals will act to advantage their group even when there is no direct benefit to them. Social identity (along with duties, see the discussion that follows) helps define the interdependence (or the sameness) between people. However, although individuals may share a common group identity, it is the rights and the exercise of these rights that give individuals a sense of personal uniqueness within the common group. Rights define independence, and independence is the guardian of uniqueness.

Although the argument that individual rights are the result of negotiations between individuals and groups suggests that no right can be assumed as necessarily applying to all individuals, it does not preclude the possibility that some rights will be common to all or most people. The fact that all humans have basic (and common) needs suggests that individuals will negotiate certain common rights with their groups or seek to leave groups not granting these rights. The juncture at which the present approach differs from that of Doise, Dell'Ambrogio, and Spini (1991), and others is whether there are specific predetermined rights that are bestowed on individuals because of their humanity and separate from any group or social relationship. My position is that individual rights are inherently relational and must be developed within specific social and group contexts. This position suggests that attention should be focused on explicating the process by which individual rights are developed rather than attempting to identify specific rights that should be absolute or universal.

The emphasis on process leads to another domain that places individual rights within a larger context on human behavior. Because individual rights are ultimately the result of a bargain between individual and group, there is a price to be paid for these rights. The group exacts its payments in the form of duties. Duties are obligations (e.g., required behaviors) that one has for the group or group members. Duties comprise the actions (and some would argue, the sacrifices) one must perform to ensure the identity and health of the group. Some duties are explicitly spelled out in the form of laws or commandments, whereas other duties may be implicit and unspoken but equally stringent. Duties may be cloaked in the mantel of prohibitions that deny certain rights (you do not have the right to steal from your neighbor), or they may define actions that one must take (e.g., honor the leader or parent or elder, attend group meetings, pay dues, or wear group uniform). Overall, duties define the behaviors that are necessary if one desires to remain a member of the group and enjoy personal rights.

Although duties, like rights, may vary as the conditions of a group change and the individual assumes different roles, there is generally a commonality of duties that homogenize all members of a group. The web of duties has specific and necessary functions for individuals and groups. From the individual's perspective, whereas rights allow a certain amount of unpredictability in individual behavior, duties are designed to instill predictability in individual behavior. If helping (or not helping) in times of emergency, as discussed in chapter 1 of this volume, is a right, a victim cannot count on others to provide aid. However, if helping one's fellow group members is a duty, one can expect to receive help so long as common group membership is determined.

A second function of duties for individuals is to define the nature of interdependence in groups. The adequate performance of duties is the passport for group membership, just as neglect of duties invites punishment or rejection. Although duties may appear confining and limiting, they offer the individual a sense of security by detailing the relationship between group members. From the group standpoint, duties are designed to ensure the identity and survival of the group. Duties bind individuals to the group and dictate that needs of the group will be met. It is the duty of the member to serve the group: All for one so long as one is for all.

Just as individuals have common and important needs that often lead them to negotiate common individual rights, groups, whether large or small and regardless of purpose, have common needs to function and survive. Therefore, the duties that individuals have across groups may have similar components. For example, in my own research, I have found that one of the most prized behaviors demanded by groups is loyalty. Indeed, loyalty is generally more valued than being correct, and hence, a common duty across groups is loyalty. However, it would be unwise to identify loyalty as a "universal" duty because the group demands for loyalty may differ depending on the conditions faced by the group (e.g., threat vs. security).

Rights, then, grant independence, freedom, and uniqueness. Duties define interdependence and ensure predictability in human relationships. An obligation to perform duties is the price of group membership, and rights are purchased from the group through the satisfactory performance of duties. Neither rights nor duties can be separated from group membership. Both rights and duties are developed through the interaction between individuals and their groups.

Groups, Too, Have Rights and Duties

For the most part, rights and duties are viewed as the domain of individuals. However, my colleagues and I (Worchel & Coutant, 2001; Worchel et al., 2000) have argued that groups, too, function within a web of rights and duties. Groups, as Asch (1952) pointed out, are more than the mere sum of the members. Groups enter into agreements (treaties) with other groups. These agreements obligate existing and future members. Similarly groups take on financial debts to other groups and accept other groups as debtors. Groups have a longevity that often extends beyond that of any single member and a history that predates any member. Groups, like individuals, grapple with issues of identity, recognition, and value, and this struggle has a profound effect on the interpersonal relations that take place within the group and between members of different groups.

Unfortunately, psychologists sometimes ignore the pervasive influence of groups on social behavior. However, this is an unwise oversight. I served for several years as a group facilitator at the Seeds of Peace International Camp. The camp brings together individuals from ethnic groups involved in violent and protracted conflicts (e.g., Israeli/Palestinian/other Arab, Bosnian/Croat/Serb, Greek/Turkish Cypriot, and Indian/Pakistani). Each summer, the programs include adolescent youth (14–17 years old) and their adult delegation leaders in each camp session (2–3 per summer). This unlikely collection of individuals gathers in a remote location in the Maine woods. The participants find themselves face-to-face with people whom they have considered their enemy. The tension increases when they find themselves sharing a common cabin. During the 3-week sessions, the campers (and delegation leaders) live and play together, participate on common teams, and attend each other's religious services. Former enemies often develop close friendships and respect for each other.

However, this atmosphere of harmony is interrupted by frequent coexistence group sessions. These sessions bring together 15 to 20 participants from the different regions. The group sessions transport the campers' minds away from the bucolic setting to their home countries where conflict and hatred rule. Participants discuss their feelings, fears, hopes, and anger about their conflict. The increasing salience of old group boundaries that occurs during these discussions ignites impassioned emotions, conflict, and hurt. Although the coexistence groups focus on the present strife in the various homelands, discussion invariably turns to history. History is used to justify the group's right of existence, social and political positions, and claim to territory. Group history is presented and debated. Each side justifies its position in the present conflict with the veil of interpretations of group history.

Indeed, the most contentious arguments often revolve around these interpretations. One gets the impression that if agreement about group history could be achieved, a major step in resolving the present conflict could be taken. Without this agreement, even small steps are difficult. History is not only used to explain the existing conflict but also becomes the basis for justifying the rights of groups (for survival and recognition). Also tightly interwoven in this discussion is a focus on the duties of groups to protect and ensure the future of present and future members. These discussions are wonderfully illuminating because they demonstrate the strong perceptions that groups, in addition to individuals, have rights and duties, and these group rights and duties are deeply rooted in the history of the group and intergroup conflict.

A similar scenario is played out in many locations throughout the world. My own university sits at the base of a dormant volcano. Mauna Kea rises nearly 35,000 feet from the ocean floor, punching a hole through the clouds as it reaches for the heavens. The bald summit of Mauna Kea is sometimes blanketed with snow, but if one looks closely, several seemingly surreal structures shimmer in the sun across the summit. These structures are the observatories manned by international scientific teams. Although the telescopes are turned skyward, much of the action takes place at ground level. This activity does not involve the stars, but rather its focus is on the rights of various groups to be on the mountain and the duties of these groups to protect the mountain and the rights of their constituents. Mauna Kea is sacred ground for Hawai'ian culture, and some native Hawai'ian groups argue that outsiders have no rights to occupy the summit. These groups feel that it is their duty to protect and preserve Mauna Kea for the present and future generations. Intrusion by others on this sacred land threatens the identity of Native Hawai'ians. The scientific community, however, feels that it has a duty to collect data on the stars that can advance the science of astronomy and may impact the future of humankind. This duty gives the scientists certain rights to establish their observatories in the optimal locations for their research. This seemingly intractable conflict, like that addressed in the Seeds of Peace Camp, swirls around issues of rights and duties of groups.

A fascinating commonality of the conflicts at the Seeds of Peace Camp and on Mauna Kea involves the control of land. Each situation involves ethnic groups with long histories of occupying territory, homelands. There is a (nearly) general acceptance of the principle that each ethnic group has a right to its homeland and a duty to protect and preserve this land. The caveat to this perspective is often supplied by participants from the United States who interject that individuals have the right to own (and sell) land. In other words, the right to own land is endowed in the individual not the group. This position is supported by Article 17 of the UN Universal Declaration of Human Rights that states "Everyone has the right to own property alone as well as in association with others" (see Appendix, Art. 17). The question of property ownership is worthy of discussion on its own, but for present purposes it illustrates the position that both individuals and groups are endowed with rights (and duties), and the interests of both parties can meet on "common ground" with conflicting views.

The point of this discussion is to suggest that groups, like individuals, are clothed in a garment consisting of group rights and duties. The most important group rights center on the right of the group to exist, be recognized, and exercise control over their members (and their resources). From the group's position, no individual member has license to threaten the group's right to survive and thrive. The right of group survival is particularly critical when groups feel threatened, either by internal events (e.g., economic strife, group fragmentation, or rebellion) or outside conditions (e.g., invasion by another group or natural disaster). During these periods, the punishments meted out to individuals who threaten the group's survival are especially swift and excessive. Hence, an individual who sells state secrets during peacetime may be jailed, whereas the same offense merits execution during wartime. Likewise, looting is viewed as a crime against an individual victim (punishable by jail) during most normal situations. However, looting during a natural disaster may be portrayed as threatening the existence of the group (community), and looters risk being shot on the spot. The threat to the group's right to exist may be direct (e.g., selling secrets or questioning the group's doctrines) or it may be indirect and symbolic (e.g., burning group symbols or desecrating group shrines).

Protecting group rights generally involves limiting the rights of the individual member. This situation presents an intriguing human conundrum, pitting group rights against individual rights. Unfortunately, with some exceptions, notably research on social dilemmas (Hardin, 1968; Orbell, van de Kragt, & Dawes, 1988), this area of human drama has largely escaped careful study by psychologists. Several factors influence the course of negotiations to reach an accommodation between group and individual rights. One of the major factors, culture, is discussed later in this chapter. Hollander (1958) anticipated another factor in his discussion of *idiosyncratic credits*. He argued that individuals "earn" the freedom to deviate from group norms by building a history of conformity. Hollander's work suggests that individuals earn individual rights by prior acts in support of the group's rights.

The struggle to balance group and individual rights continues through eternity, like two children bound to an endless life on a seesaw. Given the egocentric nature of humans, the group seems bound to lose this struggle, except for one fact. In addition to rights, groups also have duties. Group duties include protecting the individual members, enabling them to achieve personal goals, and satisfying their needs for interdependence and the formation of a positive social identity (Tajfel & Turner, 1979). In many groups, such as families and nations, the group's duty extends beyond the individuals in the present time. The group is responsible for preserving relics and symbols from the past, guarding the homeland, and maintaining the language, myths, and customs. The group may be expected to ensure the well-being of the individual member's offspring. In some cases, the individual may take steps to ensure that the group shoulders prescribed duties well into the future. For example, the individual who endowed the Jungian professorship in my previous psychology department stipulated that the funds could only be used for this purpose; in accepting the gift, the university obligated itself (accepted the duty) to maintaining the professorship and library well into the future.

The burden of group duties often constitutes a heavy load that can only be carried to the extent that groups are allowed rights. Groups "purchase" their rights by fulfilling their duties to group members. And individuals capture their rights by meeting their obligations to groups. From this perspective, neither entity is endowed with inalienable rights. Rather, individual rights and duties and group rights and duties create a tightly bound system of complementarity. No part can be truly understood without considering all of the other parts and the dynamic relationship that exists between them.

Magnets of the Social Experience

Individual rights and duties and group rights and duties form the web that binds individuals and groups into an often uneasy relationship that is the fabric of all human behavior. On the one hand, individuals buy their rights by offering to accept individual duties to the social group that may ultimately limit these rights. On the other hand, groups ensure their rights through ransom in the form of group duties. Perfect harmony could be achieved if individual and group rights were completely compatible. But perfection occurs only in fairy tales not in individual–group relationships. Indeed, there may be times when this harmony seems within the grasp.

But because the life and needs of both individuals and groups are dynamic and ever changing and because there is inherent conflict between individual and group rights (see discussion of homeland and territory on p. 206), tension and incompatibility constantly stalk individual–group relations. As a result, the individual's desire for independence and interdependence is constantly in flux, just as the balance between the group's concern for its survival versus support for its members vacillates. Added to this social stew is the fact that groups resemble active ant colonies in which new members enter and old members leave or die (Moreland & Levine, 1982). There is seldom long-term stability in the composition of group membership, thereby, challenging the continuity of group rights and duties.

THE STEADYING HAND OF CULTURE

Up to this point, I have painted a disturbing picture of social life as being plagued by constant chaos and consumed by uneasy negotiations between individuals and groups over rights and duties. I have certainly offended the humanist in suggesting that there are no absolute and inalienable individual rights. This portrayal has some validity, but the situation is not as hopeless as implied. There is a dynamic quality between individual–group relations that frustrates psychologists' efforts to develop a still-life snapshot of human relations and present these photos as ultimate outcomes or effects. In fact, several investigators have argued that the psychological study of human behavior should take the form of a motion picture, incorporating time as a factor and focusing on change and process rather than static outcomes (Lacoursiere, 1980; McGrath, 1988; Worchel et al., 1992). These investigators suggest that there are no simple cause-and-effect relationships. Rather, effects are essentially causes for other actions or reactions. Gottman (1981), for example, captured this concept in his time-series analysis in which he demonstrated that a specific utterance might be the result of all communication that preceded it. However, that utterance then becomes part of the cause that leads to future utterances or behaviors. However, even within this time-series approach, there are influences that give both structure and predictability to the bargaining between individuals and groups over the rights and duties of each.

One influence is external events. My colleagues and I (Worchel, 1999; Worchel & Coutant, 1997; Worchel, Coutant-Sassic, & Wong, 1993) have shown that threats to the group's identity create conditions in which group rights become paramount and individual duties are stressed. This research showed that during times when the existence or independence of a group is in jeopardy, punishment for deviance is most severe. Our research (Worchel et al., 1992) also demonstrated that the greatest emphasis on group rights and individual duties occurs during the formative stages of groups. When groups are attempting to establish their identity, attention is focused on group rights, and individual members are treated as a homogenized collection rather than as individuals with separate rights and duties. Conformity is highest during this time, and deviants are punished and rejected quickly and severely.

For the most part, these situational influences on rights and duties are transitory. There is, however, a more pervasive and constant hand that writes the social contracts between individuals and groups; this is culture. Culture is generally defined as a set of attitudes, values, beliefs, and behaviors shared by a group of people and communicated from one generation to the next. Culture includes the philosophical ideals, values, ideologies, religious beliefs, and passions that give meaning to people's lives, producing differences in beliefs, goals, planning, and action (Berry, Conkling, & Ray, 1997). Culture represents the group's effort to adapt to its environment throughout its history (Matsumoto, 1996; Triandis, 1994). According to Hofstede (1991), culture is like a computer program that controls behavior and thinking; it is the "software of the mind."

Culture is composed of a variety of factors including language, religion, and even human-made objects. From the present perspective, however, the most germane aspect of culture is that it serves as a roadmap for the relationship between individuals and groups. Hofstede (1980) and others (Bochner, 1994; Kim, Triandis, Kagitcibasi, Choi, & Yoon, 1994) have classified cultures along a dimension running from high to low individualism (or collectivism). Cultures high in individualism emphasize personal autonomy and individual independence. Individuals in these cultures are saddled with the burden of personal responsibility for actions. Rewards and punishments are meted out to individuals on the basis of the individual's achievements and failures. Causal attributions typically focus on personal intention or traits rather than situational variables. Groups are recognized, but their defined role is to serve and protect the individual.

Given these tendencies, we would expect individualistic cultures to emphasize individual rights and group duties (to individuals). Further, the greatest conflicts should revolve around individual duties and group rights, with social and legal decisions being decided in favor of individual rights. Indeed, this pattern is clearly visible in nearly all areas of life and law in the United States, a strongly individualistic culture. The clearest example of this individualistic foundation is the United States Declaration of Independence. It is interesting that this document was designed to establish the right of the new nation to exist separate from Great Britain. However, the document takes a decidedly individualistic focus beginning with the proclamation that "all men are created equal . . . endowed by their Creator with unalienable Rights, that among these are Life, Liberty, and the pursuit of Happiness." The Bill of Rights extends this individualistic focus by granting individuals specific rights such as freedom of speech, the right to bear arms, and the right to privacy. The rights of the group (government) are not clearly delineated, but the Bill of Rights emphasizes the paramount position of the individual by securing for the individual the right to overthrow the government. The duties of the group, however, are spelled out as revolving around the obligation to secure the safety and happiness of the individual. The Bill of Rights instructs the government to give individuals speedy and public trials and refrain from cruel and unusual punishments. All this seems curious for a document designed to establish the independence of the group. Yet, it clearly illustrates the primacy of the individual (and individual rights) within the cultural milieu. The ultimate challenge facing cultures that emphasize individual rights is how to entice sufficient conformity and loyalty to ensure that the group survives and is able to perform its duties. I suggest that it is precisely this challenge that makes individual rights not so "unalienable" even in the most individualistic cultures.

Indeed, some of the most persistent and controversial legal disputes in the United States concern group rights and individual duties. For example, persistent legal bickering occurs over the right of the state to execute those who violate rules that define individual duties (capital punishment). The debate over abortion centers on the right of the state to force women to protect future group members. Battles over welfare laws often concern whether the state has the right to force members to work (individual's duty to the group) to obtain welfare. Legal decisions painstakingly define the duties of the group in such areas as executing an arrest of a private citizen (Miranda decision) and the search of private property. In addition to focusing on the emphasis on individual rights in the Declaration of Independence, it is also important to recognize that these individual rights are granted only to members (citizens) of the group (United States). Indeed, when a situation involves individuals outside the group, whether in Panama, Afghanistan, or in an airport, individual and group rights take decidedly different forms.

The situation in collective cultures has a very different hue from that in individualistic cultures. In these cultures, interdependence is emphasized, and the group is supreme. Group rights and individual duties form the fabric of these societies. The individual's role is to serve the group and promote harmony within the group. Axioms such as "The nail that sticks up highest is the one that receives the first blow of the hammer" warn individuals of the price of independence and uniqueness. Personal achievement is valued when it serves the group, but it is treated with disdain if it sets the individual above peers. Groups, not individuals, often own and control land and resources. Responsiveness to group or situational demands is expected rather than personal consistency.

To illustrate these points, one can examine the constitution of the former Soviet Union. The preamble of the 1977 constitution states that "It [the Soviet Union] is a society of mature socialist social relations, in which, on the basis of the drawing together of all classes and social strata and of juridical and factual equality of all its nations and nationalities and their fraternal co-operation, a new historical community has been formed—the Soviet people." In other words, the people exist to build and serve the greater group. The articles of the constitution enunciate the rights of the group and the duties of the individuals. Article 3 states, "The Soviet state and all its bodies function on the basis of socialist law, ensure the maintenance of law and order, and safeguard the interests of society and the rights and freedoms of citizens." Article 8 emphasizes the rights of groups (rather than individual rights) in dictating that "Work collectives take part in discussing and deciding state and public affairs, in planning production and social development, in training and placing personnel." And most pointedly, Article 17 turns individual rights (granted by the state) into individual duties (to the state): "In the USSR, the law permits individual labour in handicrafts, farming, the provision of service. . . . The state makes regulations for such work to ensure that it serves the interest of society."

The difference in emphasis on group rights in collective cultures and individual rights in individualistic cultures is seen in the most basic human activities and the response to group intrusion in these areas. Several years ago, I had delivered a series of lectures at Fudan University in Shanghai, Peoples Republic of China (PRC). During one lecture a lively class discussion about the one-child policy that existed in China ensued. The students were candid in expressing their dislike for the policy, but the general feeling was that the group had the right to regulate the number of offspring to ensure the survival of the Chinese people (a collective culture). Individuals had the duty to follow the regulation. Informing about the transgressions of one's neighbors was not viewed as a betrayal of interpersonal relations, but rather it was seen as an act of loyalty to the group (a duty of the individual).

When I returned to the United States, I raised the issue of a one-child policy with my students and received a very different response. The students were repulsed by the idea that the government would dictate behaviors that were "so clearly the right of the individual." One student insisted, "Even my family doesn't have the right to tell me how many children to have." All agreed that overpopulation was a problem that should be addressed. But there was general agreement that the role of groups (government, family, and school) was to make people aware of the problem and offer means to control it, but not to make the ultimate decision about how many children an individual may have. One student stated, "If we (the individuals in the U.S.) have too many children, the government should (*has the duty to*) find ways to feed everyone and get more land." The group has the duty to serve the individual without trifling with individual rights.

As a result of these discussions, I conducted a survey about perceptions of rights and collected responses from university students in individualistic (the United States and Germany) and collective (the PRC, Mexico, and Japan) cultures. Table 9.1 presents the profound differences in cultural approaches to individual and group rights and duties. As can be seen, the differences in opinion are not simply the result of disagreement about what constitutes individual and group rights. Rather they illustrate fundamental differences over the basis of social order: group rights and individual duties versus individual rights and group duties. Regardless of the culture or the issue of concern, the common elements are the system of group and individual rights and duties and the fact that these must be spelled out (albeit differently) within the context of the individual–group relationship. The different cultures face the common issue of ensuring both individual and group identity. The approaches to this common goal, however, are different and strongly affected by the cultural milieu.

THE BOTTOM LINE: WHAT DOES IT ALL MEAN?

At one level the examination of culture's influences on rights and duties can be viewed as the cognitive gymnastics of fuzzy-headed academics, an

TABLE 9.1
The Impact of Culture on the Perception of Individual and Group Rights

Survey statement	Individualistic cultures	Collective cultures
The rights of the individual should be respected at all costs.	2.21	4.63
The rights of a group are more important than the rights of individual members.	5.06	2.62
Some individuals deserve more rights and opportunities than others.	6.02	1.79
Some groups deserve more rights and opportunities than others.	2.06	1.92
The most important conflicts are the ones that occur between individuals.	2.77	4.02
The most important conflicts are the ones that occur between groups.	3.92	1.66
Individuals need to be protected from the tyranny of groups.	1.30	5.97

Note. Responses were provided on a scale of 1 (*agree*) to 7 (*disagree*).

interesting piece of social trivia that might be useful in a quiz show. But on further reflection, the study of rights and duties and the influence of culture has profound implications for a whole range of social issues.

The Question of Universal Rights

On 10 December 1948, the United Nations (UN) took the bold step of adopting the Universal Declaration of Human Rights. The document enunciated specific rights of all humans. In many ways, the document looks suspiciously like the United States Declaration of Independence and the Bill of Rights. Article 3 of the UN document, for example, states, "Everyone has the right to life, liberty and security of person" (See Appendix, Art. 3). Other specific universal human rights include privacy, freedom of movement within the boundaries of one's state, the right to marry and have a family, the right to own property, freedom of thought, conscience, and religion, and the right to work and exercise free choice of employment.

The UN Declaration is intriguing on a number of grounds. Most important, it advances the position that there are universal human rights that are bestowed on individuals because they are human. These rights are not determined by the groups (countries) to which individuals belong. Further the Declaration is largely silent on the topic of individual duties. Rights apparently exist in isolation of duties. This is an especially striking position in light of the fact that many of the specific rights are interpersonal in nature and have significant implications for social, economic, and political groups. These rights involve areas such as work, the family, social services, security, and political process. The underlying implication, made explicit in the last article, is that it is the group's duty to protect these individual rights: No state, group, or person may "perform any act aimed at the destruction of any of the rights and freedoms set forth herein (Article 30)." As was pointed out earlier in this chapter, this combination of individual rights and group duties is the foundation of individualistic cultures.

According to the present analysis, the attempt to delineate individual rights in isolation of individual duties and group rights and duties is inherently flawed and will prove of limited practical utility. I suggest that individual rights exist only within a system that includes individual rights and duties and group rights and duties. Indeed, a list of ideal individual rights may be developed on moral, ethical, or other bases, but to be truly influential and functional, such a list must be constructed within a context that includes individual duties and group rights and duties. As if by divine intervention, the day that I began writing this chapter, the television news broadcast a story that the United States was resisting UN efforts to define the "right to shelter" as a universal human right. Apparently, U.S. officials were concerned that this action would initiate a spate of legal suits by the homeless against the government claiming that it was not fulfilling its duty to provide housing. This is an example of the relational link between the individual and the group as applied to the domain of rights and duties.

The complexity of the relationship between individual and group rights is exquisitely demonstrated in the issue of property rights, especially those related to issues of homeland (see p. 206). Article 17 of the UN Universal Declaration of Human Rights states that "(1) Everyone has the right to own property alone as well as in association with others. (2) No one shall be arbitrarily deprived of his property" (see Appendix, Art. 17). At the turn of the millennium, the geopolitical climate was tilted toward the formation of increasingly small nation-states with homogeneous ethnic populations. Some of these surgical divisions occurred with little or no violence, such as the birth of the Czech Republic and Slovakia. Others, however, such as the division of Yugoslavia, the Basque Country, and the Israeli and Palestinian situation saw new or escalated violence. Even in areas where separation was not an issue (New Zealand and Maori; Hawai'i), the question of homeland was at the center of conflict. The renewal of ethnic awareness and identity raises several fascinating questions for a world order concerned with human rights (Worchel, 1999). One issue is the determination of the grounds on which one can claim membership in an ethnic group. Does being one-quarter Basque "qualify" one as a Basque? Another issue is who controls property that is deemed the homeland of an ethnic group: the individual or the group? In many cultures (including Maori and Native American), individuals are viewed as guardians, not owners, of the land. As such, individuals do not have the right to sell tribal property. Even the group, as it is presently constituted, does not have the right to barter away property. Given this situation, how can one accommodate a declaration that prescribes a basic and universal human right as including the ownership of property?

But it is not only the entwined nature of group and individual rights and duties that is being questioned. At the risk of being branded an amoral heretic, my analysis raises the basic question of whether any individual right can be proclaimed as universal. Those who study culture have demonstrated that the role of the individual (vis-à-vis the group) is different in collective and individualistic societies. Therefore, it is reasonable to expect that the rights and duties of individuals will be different in the various types of cultures. Further, given that the condition of both the group and the individual is dynamic, it seems prudent to conclude that the rights and duties of each will be adjusted by social and cultural fluctuation. For example, the individual right to free speech has decidedly different meanings in the United States during wartime as opposed to times of peace and on some topics (sexuality and ethnic issues) compared to others (food preferences and environmental practices). Hence, there are no truly universal rights and duties for groups or individuals, but rather these are subject to negotiation between groups and individuals.

Although I suggest that it is futile to develop lists of rights and duties that are (should be) universal to individuals or groups, the examination of human rights and duties is both socially and theoretically vital. I propose that the most constructive approach is to direct attention toward identifying the processes by which groups and individuals negotiate these rights and duties, the relationship that exists between group and individual rights and duties, and the procedures by which rights and duties are changed and limited. This approach should draw heavily on existing research in the areas of group dynamics and social influence. The examination should adopt a longitudinal and historical perspective, and it must include the larger social contextual factors such as culture. It is important to recognize that this discussion does not address such important philosophical questions as the value of human life or the need to enhance the condition of human existence. Rather, the aim is to develop a functional analysis of human rights and duties and to find a workable framework in which to develop these. In addition, this discussion does not address the issue of who should define universal human rights and duties.

The Importance of Rights and Duties in Social Relationships

According to the present analysis, rights and duties define the relationship between individuals and groups. This position has profound implications in several domains. With respect to culture, it has been argued that in collective cultures, groups hold the dominant position, whereas in individualistic cultures, individuals reign supreme. Therefore, one would suspect that group rights and individual duties are more carefully defined in collective cultures than in individualistic cultures. This difference should be evident in all types of groups within these cultures.

I have found support for this position in a variety of questionnaires that my students and I have given to individuals in a variety of countries. Although the aim of the questionnaires was to examine self-identity, many questions allowed individuals to define their relationship to a variety of groups such as country and family. Several features of the results were of interest. First, individuals from collective cultures listed significantly more rights for groups and significantly fewer individual rights than did respondents from individualistic cultures. Indeed, in one survey (conducted with William Webb and Michael Hills) nearly half the respondents from individualistic cultures failed to identify any group right, whereas no respondent from a collective culture ignored this category. The most common group rights identified by this sample involved controlling territory, expecting obedience from group members, and controlling individuals (especially in times of crisis). Likewise, respondents from collective cultures tended to identify numerous obligations they had to their group and the conditions under which these duties must be performed. It is interesting that they were equally clear about group duties: the "what, when, and how" of the way in which the group was expected to aid them. Participants from individualistic cultures were generally vague about the specific duties they had to perform for their group and the expectations they had for the group. For example, 70% of the respondents in collective cultures stated that one's family or government was responsible "to feed you if you were starving." The most common responses to this item in individualistic cultures were "no one" or "myself." Overall, the results painted a conditional and changing relationship between the individual and groups in individualistic cultures. Individuals were viewed as changing groups or positions in groups, and a change in rights and obligations accompanied these changes. On the other hand, collective cultures seemed to have a stable relationship between individuals and groups. Rights and duties were clearly identified with an emphasis on individual duties and group rights and duties.

At first glance, these data seem only to suggest that groups are more important in collective than in individualistic cultures. This position, however, was not supported in studies conducted by my students (Steve Whalquist and Maria Sanchez-Ku). Exchange students from numerous countries were questioned about their relationship with groups both in their home countries and at the university since arriving. All students stated that membership in groups was very important to them, and group membership figured prominently in their identities. In fact, individuals from collective cultures listed fewer groups to which they belonged ($X = 3.76$) than did individuals from individualistic cultures ($X = 5.63$). This finding seems counter to expectations, until several other data are considered. First, respondents from individualistic cultures indicated that they were *highly likely* to change groups during a one-year period; individuals from collective cultures reported that they were *highly unlikely* to change groups during that period. Second, students from individualistic cultures had joined more groups ($X = 2.34$) at the university than collective culture students ($X = .72$). Further, groups in their home countries were listed as being significantly more important (at the present time) to collective culture students than to individualistic culture students. These results indicated that although groups were important to (the identities of) all students, those from individualistic cultures tended to be group gypsies, migrating from one group to another as the situation dictated. Individuals from collective cultures had stable relationships with groups, rarely changing groups and maintaining ties and expectations with groups even when they were physically absent.

This pattern of data has profound implications for any examination of rights and duties. In collective cultures, not only is the group paramount but the system of individual and group rights and duties is also both stable and enduring. Rights and duties are clearly defined and exist whether the individual member is present or not. In individualistic cultures, the rights of the individual are of utmost importance, and group rights are often vague and implicit. The fact that individuals can leave the group relatively easily or be expelled by the group further reduces the prominence of group rights. Individuals tend to carry their personal rights as they move from group to group, whereas the group's rights and duties and the individual's duties are subject to negotiation as the individual temporarily embraces a new group.

A PARTING WORD

Any attempt to define universal human rights is similar to the search for the Holy Grail: The effort may be noble in intent, but bound to end in failure. This conclusion is based on the position that any discussion of rights cannot be separated from a consideration of duties. The two concepts are woven so tightly together that an attempt to tease them apart destroys the whole fabric. Just as skin and bones form the physical being of the human, rights and duties compose the human social skeleton. As a result, any document such as the UN Universal Declaration of Human Rights that deals with only one side of this social coin may make interesting reading, but its actual utility is limited.

In a similar fashion, any effort to describe the individual (especially in relation to rights and duties) without giving equal attention to the group will have limited impact. I fear that much of modern psychology runs the risk of being immediately obsolete if it embraces too tightly a myopic focus on the individual in isolation from the social context. Individual rights and duties gain substance and form only when considered within the framework of group rights and duties. Additional understanding of human rights and duties can be gained by examining the role they play in psychological and social behavior. Two such roles have been suggested in this chapter. One is that rights and duties not only result from interaction between individuals and their groups but they also guide this interaction. Second, rights contribute to defining the identities of individuals. Because of this important function, individuals are willing to accept obligations to the group to secure personal rights.

A fundamental goal for research and theory is to explicate the process by which rights and goals are established in a social system. How does each social organization (family, social or work group, and society) manage the negotiation between groups and members to identify the rights and duties of each? Indeed, the meaning of any single right is defined by other rights. For example, the right of the individual to survive has very different interpretations depending on whether the group is endowed with the right of survival. In addition, the rights of individuals must also be considered within the framework of whether the individuals have the freedom to leave one group and join another. And given the premise that rights and duties are dynamic (rather than universal and fixed), what are the processes that have been developed to deal with this change? Durkheim (1898) recognized the critical role of this process when he suggested that human and group behavior becomes dysfunctional (a state of *anomie*) when the process for negotiating the rights and duties of individuals and groups becomes undefined.

Although my initial hypothesis was that culture plays its hand by defining the rights and duties of groups and individuals, the veiled message is that the handprint of culture is most cunningly seen in setting the rules (the process) through which this negotiation is undertaken. Culture defines the relationship between individuals and groups, and it describes the basic architecture of groups (hierarchical or egalitarian). Culture skillfully manipulates the ground rules of human cognition and attribution. Within this framework individuals and groups are left to bargain and barter rights and duties. Efforts to dictate rights and duties without specific consideration of the cultural context will ignite conflict and confusion. Although this problem is most clearly seen when the group involves a nation or ethnic group, it will also be evident in smaller groups, such as family or community, which are also influenced by the culture in which they exist.

The aim of this chapter has been to redirect and expand the consideration of rights and duties. I suggest that the identification of specific rights and duties will have a hollow ring without first understanding and explicating the process through which individuals and groups bestow rights and duties on each other. The implied message is that the human condition can best be advanced by shining the light of understanding on the process rather than on specific rights. With clear recognition that the process of negotiation is strongly influenced by culture, I maintain that efforts to improve the process will have greater impact than attempts to identify rights and duties outside the social context.

REFERENCES

Asch, S. (1952). *Social psychology*. New York: Prentice-Hall.

Asch, S. (1956). Studies of independence and conformity: I. A minority of one against a unanimous majority. *Psychological Monographs, 70*(9).

Berry, B., Conkling, E., & Ray, D. (1997). *The global economy in transition*. Englewood Cliffs, NJ: Prentice Hall.

Bochner, S. (1994). Cross-cultural differences in self-concept: A test of Hofstede's individualism/collectivism distinction. *Journal of Cross-Cultural Psychology, 25*, 273–283.

Brehm, J. (1966). *A theory of psychological reactance*. New York: Academic Press.

Brewer, M. (1991). The social self: On being the same and different at the same time. *Personality and Social Psychology Bulletin, 17*, 475–482.

Brewer, M., & Gardner, W. (1996). Who is this "We"? Levels of collective identity and self-representations. *Journal of Personality and Social Psychology, 71*, 83–93.

Doise, W., Dell'Ambrogio, P., & Spini, D. (1991). Psychologie sociale et droits de l'homme [Social psychology and human rights]. *Revue Internationale de Psychologie Sociale, 4*, 87–107.

Durkheim, E. (1898). *The rules of sociological method*. New York: Free Press.

Erickson, E. (1959). Identity and the life cycle: Selected papers. *Psychological Issues, 1*, 50–100.

Gottman, J. (1981). *Time-series analysis: A comprehensive introduction for social scientists*. New York: Cambridge University Press.

Hancock, R., & Sorrentino, R. (1980). The effects of expected future interaction and prior group support on the conformity process. *Journal of Experimental Social Psychology, 16*, 261–270.

Hardin, G. (1968, December 13). The tragedy of the commons. *Science, 162*, 1243–1248.

Hofstede, G. (1980). *Culture's consequences: International differences in work-related values*. Beverly Hills, CA: Sage.

Hofstede, G. (1991). *Cultures and organizations: Software of the mind*. London: McGraw-Hill.

Hogg, M., & Abrams, D. (1990). Social motivation, self-esteem, and social identity. In D. Abrams & M. Hogg (Eds.), *Social identity theory: Constructive and critical advances* (pp. 28–47). New York: Springer-Verlag.

Hollander, E. (1958). Conformity, status, and idiosyncrasy credit. *Psychological Review, 65*, 117–127.

Kim, U., Triandis, H., Kagitcibasi, C., Choi, S.-C., & Yoon, G. (1994). Introduction. In U. Kim, H. Triandis, C. Kagitcibasi, S.-C. Choi, & G. Yoon (Eds.), *Individualism and collectivism: Theory, method, and application* (pp. 1–16). Thousand Oaks, CA: Sage.

Lacoursiere, R. (1980). *The life cycle of groups*. New York: Human Sciences Library.

Maslach, C., Stapp, J., & Santee, R. (1985). Individuation: Conceptual analysis and assessment. *Journal of Personality and Social Psychology*, *49*, 729–738.

Matsumoto, D. (1996). *Culture and psychology*. Pacific Grove, CA: Brooks/Cole.

McGrath, J. (Ed.). (1988). *The social psychology of time*. Newbury Park, CA: Sage.

Milgram, S. (1974). *Obedience to authority*. New York: Harper & Row.

Moreland, R., & Levine, J. (1982). Socialization in small groups: Temporal changes in individual group relations. In L. Berkowitz (Ed.), *Advances in experimental social psychology* (Vol. 15, pp. 137–192). New York: Academic Press.

Orbell, J., van de Kragt, A., & Dawes, R. (1988). Explaining decision-induced comparison. *Journal of Personality and Social Psychology*, *54*, 811–819.

Raven, B., & French, J. (1958). Legitimate power, coercive power, and observability in social influence. *Sociometry*, *21*, 83–97.

Schachter, S. (1951). Deviation, rejection, and communication. *Journal of Abnormal and Social Psychology*, *46*, 190–207.

Tajfel, H. (1970). Experiments in intergroup discrimination. *Scientific American*, *223*(2), 96–102.

Tajfel, H., & Turner, J. (1979). An integrative theory of intergroup conflict. In W. Austin & S. Worchel (Eds.), *The social psychology of intergroup relations* (pp. 33–47). Monterey, CA: Brooks/Cole.

Triandis, H. (1994). *Culture and social behavior*. New York: McGraw-Hill.

Tuckman, B. (1965). Developmental sequences in small groups. *Psychological Bulletin*, *63*, 384–399.

Worchel, S. (1998). A developmental view of the search for group identity. In S. Worchel, J. Morales, D. Paez, & J.-C. Deschamps (Eds.), *Social identity: International perspectives* (pp. 53–74). London: Sage.

Worchel, S. (1999). *Written in blood: Ethnic identity and the struggle for human harmony*. New York: Worth Publishers.

Worchel, S., & Coutant, D. (1997). The tangled web of loyalty: Nationalism, patriotism, and ethnocentrism. In D. Bar-Tal & E. Staub (Eds.), *Patriotism in the life of individuals and nations* (pp. 190–210). Chicago: Nelson-Hall.

Worchel, S., & Coutant, D. (2001). It takes two to tango: Relating group identity to individual identity within the framework of group development. In M. Hogg & S. Tinsdale (Eds.), *Blackwell handbook of social psychology: Group process* (pp. 461–481). Oxford, England: Blackwell.

Worchel, S., Coutant-Sassic, D., & Grossman, M. (1992). A developmental approach to group dynamics: A model and illustrative research. In S. Worchel, W. Wood, & J. Simpson (Eds.), *Group process and productivity* (pp. 181–202). Newbury Park, CA: Sage.

Worchel, S., Coutant-Sassic, D., & Wong, F. (1993). Toward a more balanced view of conflict: There is a positive side. In S. Worchel & J. Simpson (Eds.), *Conflict between people and groups* (pp. 118–139). Chicago: Nelson-Hall.

Worchel, S., Iuzzini, J., Coutant, D., & Ivaldi, M. (2000). A multidimensional model of identity: Relating individual and group identity to intergroup behavior. In R. Brown & D. Capozza (Eds.), *Social identity process: Trends in theory and research* (pp. 15–32). London: Sage.

III

NORMATIVE COMMENTARIES

10

AN ONTOLOGY FOR DUTIES AND RIGHTS

ROM HARRÉ

The chapters in this volume notably lack explicit discussions of the ontology of rights and duties. There is no clear view as to what sort of beings they are and in what mode or domain they exist. The deep question to be addressed in my commentary is simply this: "To what type of beings do the words *right* and *duty* refer?" What is the ontological status of a duty and a right? This question springs to mind in discussing almost any of the issues raised in the contributions to this volume. For example, the ontological question lurks in every paragraph of the text in which Spini and Doise (see chap. 2, this volume) present their research. It is made more pressing by the lack of any explicit and plausible interpretation for the statistical presentation of the results of their surveys. Because these are analyses of the answers to questionnaires, they can only be expressions of semantic rules for talking about duties and rights.

Are the topics addressed in these essays best seen as discussions of issues that pertain to discourse, narratives, and so on? It seems to me that on close examination it becomes clear that the ways in which people talk about their obligations and the demands they can make on others are what these studies are really about, rather than investigations of the attributes of a realm of abstract entities, rights and duties. Admittedly, Spini and Doise draw on the concept of *social representation* to suggest an ontology. However, it is a notoriously cloudy concept. Does it mean a representation that exists in the discursive resources of each member of a social group such that each representation is like every other? Or does it mean a representation that exists only in the joint actions of members as an emergent property of various genres of discourses in play in a culture? This is the kind of deep question that a deliberate turn to ontological reflection brings to light. The way we answer it affects much of the import of our discussions for practical living. Despite the reified language in which my coauthors write about rights and duties, there seems to be one way in which we can assign these beings to an appropriate category. In every case described in these chapters, the words *right* and *duty* seem to be used to refer to a resource that can be drawn on in a certain genre of discourse.

When do these words surface? In the case of the word *right*, it seems to be in the talk that expresses someone's belief that he or she has been denied something to which the speaker believes himself or herself to be entitled from someone else. Duty talk is often used as a reminder of obligations the speaker believes ought to be acknowledged and acted on. Both words are used to refer to something that someone should do, indeed even must do. Colloquially we can say that duties and rights involve obligations. We must see this kind of involvement as deriving from the fact that people use the vocabulary of duties and of rights to make demands on others as to what they should do for the speaker and to issue reminders to themselves and others as to what someone or some category of persons ought to do for someone else.

The people who make these demands and issue these reminders must have beliefs about their entitlements and beliefs about their own and other's obligations. Various words, such as *fairness* (Finkel, 2001), may be in play to express the relevant beliefs. Where do such beliefs come from?

The ontological issue is complex and to an extent depends on using work devoted to more superficial questions for its thrust. It is advisable to tackle some of the more superficial questions before we plunge into matters of ontology.

FOUR QUESTIONS FOR THE STUDENT OF RIGHTS AND DUTIES

The root idea, from which the more elaborated concepts of rights and duties that we encounter in contemporary forms of life germinate, can be expressed as two simple rules for the distribution and assignment of obligations between persons in duty talk and rights talk.

> A has a duty to B, if A has an obligation to do something for B.
> A has a right from B, if B has an obligation to do something for A.

These can be expressed psychologically in terms of beliefs.

However, these schemata leave much unresolved. For example, What are the sources of these obligations? In what circumstances and for what reasons are they mandatory? Are there any categories of persons among whom duties and rights are more prolific than among others? What sanctions are there to enforce the fulfillment of the obligations on which duties and rights depend? Can one have duties to oneself? Does the existence of a dutiful obligation entail the existence of a corresponding right? Does the existence of a rightful obligation entail the existence of a corresponding duty? Are there universal duties and rights recognized in every human society? Are duties and rights confined to the moral world of human beings?

Looking to anthropology and history, we find that further questions surface: Could there be just and orderly societies in which the moral order is based on duties alone, that is in which social action is regulated by a discourse in which only the concept of duty figures? Could there be societies in which the only obligations are related to the exercise of rights? A brief historical survey of some important social formations throws some light on these questions. We can show that the duties-only case is possible because there have been what appear to be just such societies.

What is the relation between the concepts of duties and rights as set down in legislative acts and edicts and those duties and rights as recognized in the talk by which the lives of ordinary people are regulated? We recollect that George Mason refused to sign the Declaration of Independence because, unlike the Constitution of Virginia, it did not incorporate an explicit Bill of Rights. This defect was largely remedied in the amendments instigated by Hamilton. For example, Amendment IV established a right of privacy. Unfortunately these developments did not suffice to bring Mason back to public life. It seems he did not think that everyday ways of managing social life would have the necessary power to maintain the basic rights of people as citizens. He does not seem to have reflected that the same could have been said of duties. Sunday reminders from the pulpit are notoriously seed thrown on stony ground.

These and other issues are addressed in the essays in this volume. I will confine myself to looking for answers to four specific questions, before returning to the problem of ontology on which any studies such as ours must ultimately rest.

1. What is the source of the obligations that the talk of duties and rights seem to create?
2. Is there a discourse rule that requires that the assertion of the existence of a right entails the assertion of the existence of a corresponding duty and the assertion of the existence of a duty, the assertion of the existence of a corresponding right? In other words, is there a universal, context-independent correspondence between duties and rights?

3. Are there any concepts of rights and duties found in the discourse of all human societies in which social order is discursively managed? Are there universal duties and rights? Are they applicable only to human beings?
4. Does informal duties and rights talk dominate or give way to formal discourse concerning rights enacted by legislative bodies? How is the transition from informal to formal managed? Formally or informally?

These four questions concerning source, correspondence, universality, and the informal-to-formal transition are very general. Each has many specific cases and applications, and each can be elaborated in various ways, such as in the discussions of major topics that follow.

1. Is there a common natural source from which the context-specific demands and obligations that constitute the content of assertions of rights and reminders of duties spring? Is the moral force of the use of these concepts derivable from aspects of human life that are premoral or perhaps not moral at all? Could it even be that biology plays a part in the genesis of these social moral imperatives?

Human beings differ along many morally relevant dimensions. The most important of these, looked at from the point of view of the topic of this survey, is the relative capacities and powers on the one hand and relative vulnerabilities on the other that one finds among the members of some population. We must beware of generalizing the powers and vulnerabilities of one group too hastily, as we find them defined by that group, to all human beings. For example, some people are tall and others short, some strong and others weak, some robust and others sickly. Now consider how these people are involved in carrying out certain tasks. Suppose the short person wants to get something that has been put on a very high shelf. The tall person, presuming he or she is a decent and friendly person, has a duty to get the object for the short person, who has a right to ask for help from the tall person. It is easy to imagine circumstances in which the attribution is reversed. Suppose the task is to get something that has rolled under the table. The short person is much better suited for crawling into a confined space, so he or she has the duty to get the missing object, and the tall person has a right to ask the short person to do it.

In this simple case we can see how strengths and weaknesses, capacities and vulnerabilities, are the bases for attributing duties to some and rights to others, relative to the task that is being undertaken. If someone is sick, and so incapacitated and in need of care, the healthy person in the family has a duty, so we all believe, to take care of him or her. Adults should take care of children and children have a right to be taken care of by adults, all else being equal.

This qualification is important. Sometimes we have to look more closely at the rough categories we are using to assign duties and rights. Suppose that a child is with his or her grandmother who is going blind. The fact that the child can see very well means that the duty of guidance in crossing the road falls on the child, and the grandmother has a right to ask for that help. However, in general, grandmothers have a duty to care for their grandchildren, especially when crossing the highway.

We must be careful not to generalize even within a certain social group, such as the family, as to the tie between this or that individual and his or her duties and rights. From time to time our capacities and powers wax and wane. Sickness, even if temporary, is a kind of loss of power and at the same time the acquisition of a vulnerability through the loss of the capacity to function in one's normal way. The healthy are capable in ways that the sick are not. The calm and well organized are better able to cope in most circumstances than are the excitable and disorganized, and so they should take charge in an emergency. They may be thought to have a duty to do so. However, for entertaining the children at a birthday party, the opposite may happen. The silly and disorganized person may be the one who amuses the children best. Adults have powers children lack. Witches have powers that ordinary folk do not. If I were to consult a witch for a love potion for some affair of the heart that was a bit shaky, the old woman would have a duty to help me. I do not know any recipes or spells for love philters myself.

Many of these differences are natural. They rest on matters of bodily endowment and temperament that in many cases seem to have a genetic origin. Others are acquired.

What about duties to take on duties? Are there rights to acquire rights? Once again when thinking in terms of strengths and weaknesses, powers and vulnerabilities can help us to think this problem through. In modern states, there are some powers that a person is required to acquire, for instance literacy. However, some people may be unfortunate and never learn to read and write. Therefore, I have a duty to help such a person fill in a form or interpret a street sign.

The thesis of this section is that the moral concepts of duties and rights are derived from and distinguished by reference to the distinctive powers and vulnerabilities that people have, both natural and acquired. This is where rights and duties have their deep origin.

The issues of what constitutes a power and what constitutes a vulnerability are surely context dependent and historically variable. If that is the case, though, then there is a universal natural basis for the possibility of duties and rights, and how these are seen and how the balance between them is drawn will also vary widely.

How do we get from practical duties and rights, such as those that arise in the kitchen when we are getting things from the shelves, to moral duties and rights? Alternatively, are these categories of duties and rights, in fact, practical and moral, incommensurable, and based on different origins?

It is clear that the step from natural to acquired differences in powers and vulnerabilities will not be transposable into the moral distinction between duties and rights unless something like a system of virtues or values, the source of an ought, can be added to the basic naturalistic distinction. Given that I have a certain power and that you are vulnerable in ways that my exercise of power can remedy, why should I exercise it? The possession of the reciprocal powers and vulnerabilities is not enough to require their exercise. And that is what the conceptual dyad, duties and rights, involves. To borrow an old formula: If I have a power and I can exercise it, and you need my help, I should exercise it. If I am much taller than you are, could I not use my possession of the relevant capacity to tantalize and tease you, enjoying a sadistic satisfaction in your frantic efforts to reach the cookie jar on the top shelf? If I know French and you are in trouble at immigration at Charles De Gaulle Aerogare, I should not quietly enjoy a sense of superiority but offer my help. People do both of these things. They tease and they smugly watch someone struggle! Why do we condemn them?

A popular move at this point in the development of the understanding of how a psychological phenomenon can become morally relevant is to look at the matter in terms of the sustaining or the undermining of personhood. In so far as ridicule and humiliation may come to you from my failure to help out, your personhood is diminished. Of course when I do come to your rescue, thanks to my having the power to which, all else being equal, you have a right, I am not thereby permitted to display an air of insufferable superiority. That would be just as bad as not fulfilling my general duty to use my capacities, perhaps even worse. Again it would diminish you as a person.

2. Is there a systematic and perhaps even a necessary symmetry or correspondence between duties and rights? If so, is this a conceptual truth or an empirical observation?

It is certainly psychologically false in real life. There are plenty of people for whom the very idea of having a right to something never comes to mind. The lives of such people are all duty. In particular, it does not occur to such people that those to whom they owe duties are subject to correlative demands that the rights of petitioners be conceded. To demand something of someone because you have a right to it is psychologically quite a different act from performing the dutiful acts one believes are required of one. We can address the correspondence question not only by displaying historical cases of societies that are based on duty alone but also by reflecting on the psychology of particularly dutiful individual persons. How does this widespread fact about how actual people manage their lives touch on the conceptual relation between duties and rights?

We can explore the second topic, the logical status of the correspondence that is often found between assertions of rights and concessions of duties, by considering the question of whether it makes sense to claim that we, human beings, have duties to nonhumans. If we do, does it make sense to conclude that by virtue of the alleged symmetry between duties and rights, these very nonhumans have a right to the treatment by which we would fulfill our duties to them? In discursive terms, is it a valid rule of reasoning to assert that one can formulate an order or command the target of which is a nonhuman entity?

Environmentalism is based on two distinct foundations. One is the recognition that it is imprudent to destroy the natural environment in a short-term search for profits, jobs, and so on. If for every job created in the logging of the Brazilian rain forest a multitude of useful products for ameliorating human health are lost, the balance may, even in the medium run, tip toward the folly of logging. The other foundation is the conviction that it is immoral to destroy the natural environment. Sometimes this is based on a further spin of the prudential argument, balancing the harm and the good for people. In such a spin, the notion of harm or good to trees, wetlands, manatees, and so on is merely instrumental.

Who are the people to whom we owe a duty to preserve the environment? Prominent among them must surely be those who are yet to be born, future people. However, these people do not now exist. Compare the case with the duty to maintain the bodily life of a person in a coma. In this case, I think all depends on how likely we believe it to be that the person will regain consciousness and begin to live some version of a fully human life again. Thus, the person in a coma has a right to our care insofar as he or she could *possibly* resume existence as a person. It seems that the duty of care exists even if the person never actually comes back into existence again. Turning to future people, we acquire a duty to them insofar as they are *possible* people. Futurity is just one of the ways that there can be a possible person. Perhaps the force of our duties toward them varies with the likelihood that they will exist. This gets complicated. If a certain environmental program makes it more likely that certain people will come to be, for example freeing the air of chemicals that simulate estrogen, does this strengthen my duty to support it?

In which way are possible people vulnerable with respect to present people like us? One way must surely be that future people are powerless to influence the past. We can influence that part of their past that is our present. So we have a duty to them to remedy this vulnerability.

More interesting, environmentalism can be based on the thesis that human beings have duties to the environment as such. In many contexts, it is not obvious how such duties could engender reciprocal rights. I may have a duty to preserve the redwoods of California based on their vulnerability to the chain saw of the developer or the attacks of some disease. However, it sounds very odd to say that these trees have a right to be preserved. Only persons can have rights as well as duties. A tree cannot be humiliated unless we allow a very stretched metaphor: the giant redwood humiliated by the forester's ax.

The conceptual structure of duty involves an obligation of a person toward some other vulnerable being, without specifying what the nature of the being might be. Rights, however, are based on obligations that another person or institution might have toward me. Only a being that can act in accordance with a sense of obligation can be the target of a rights demand. It seems as if the concept acknowledges duties without corresponding rights, indeed without any moral connotations at all that devolve onto the target of a duty. All that is required is that the target being has some vulnerability with respect to which a human being has some power of protection or succor.

However, it seems to me to be historically evident that in the human world, societies have been based more often on a system of formal and informal duties than on a system of formal and informal rights. It is surely important that the issue of formulating rights came to occupy a prominent position in political debates only in the 18th century.

Let me offer three examples of systems for the moral regulation of life in which only duties figure. The first is the ordinances of the Benedictines. The second is the Puritan political philosophy hammered out in the English revolution, for the regulation of a godly community replaced the corruption of the Stuart royal regime after the execution of Charles I. The third example is the feudal state formation.

THE RULE OF ST. BENEDICT

St. Benedict (535/2001) wrote down a set of rules that brought Benedictine Houses into existence and maintained their form of life. It is evident that there was no place for a rights discourse in the management of monasteries. The whole point of these institutions was order, tranquillity, and the obedience by which the two former virtues were accomplished. Monks had their duties, as set out in such discourses as the *Rule of St. Benedict*. Here are two excerpts:

> The second degree of humility is that a person love not his own will nor take pleasure in satisfying his desires, but model his actions on the sayings of the Lord. "I have come not to do My own will, but that of Him who sent Me." (p. 46)
>
> Let all keep their places in the monastery established by the time of their entrance, and merit of their lives and the decision of the Abbott. (p. 137)

No place is made for any discursive acts save the giving of orders and their humble acceptance.

THE POLITICAL PHILOSOPHY OF THE ENGLISH REVOLUTION

The Puritan victors in the civil war endeavored to transform their religious heritage and their informal rules of life into a series of explicit ordinances enacted by Parliament.

Tom Paine (1791/1992) wrote the *Rights of Man* in 1791; about 100 years before, John Milton, republican revolutionary and poet, wrote a series of works developing more or less the same political philosophy as Tom Paine, but the social psychological basis was very different. Whereas Paine builds his case for revolution on the thesis that there are certain natural rights that accrue to people just because they are human, Milton rests his case on liberty. A right is determined by what it is a right to do, to say, to possess, and so on. There cannot be a right in general. Liberty, by contrast, is unspecific. If someone tells a detainee "You are free to go," the jailer is not required to answer the question, "Where to?" There is a right to use the executive washroom, but this does not devolve from some right in general. As far as the moral system of the English Puritans went, it defined a world of duties, of service. But this service was not to the Crown but to God, and so, to one's fellow citizens. It was no business of the state to define the duties of citizens.

Even in trying to deal with the way that religious minorities once freed from state interference turned immediately to persecuting other religious groups, Cromwell does not use the word *rights*. He does not say every sect has a right to worship as it likes, but rather every sect is free to worship as its conscience demands.

Milton (1641/1953) occasionally referred to the "natural birthright" of the citizens. However, when he defined the role of the ruler, he said apropos of the choice of William the Conqueror as king:

> The English chose rather to accept of a king rather than live under a conqueror and tyrant; they swear therefore to William to be his liegemen, and he swears at the altar to carry himself towards them as a good king ought to do in all respects. (p. 411)

Here is the feudal system expressed in a single sentence. The liegemen swear a duty to the king who swears a duty to them. Rights have no place in this social formation.

MAGNA CARTA AND THE SHOGUNATE

At first glance, the feudal system that flourished in medieval Europe and during the shogunate in Japan might seem excessively authoritarian. In both cultures, the various levels of society seem to have been ordered in one vertical dimension, with the king, and occasionally a queen at the apex and the villeins at the bottom. In Europe, there were several intermediate castes, each level or layer owing fealty to the one immediately above and so, indirectly, to the king. In Japan, the daimyo (occupying a similar role to the barons in England) were given lands and owed service to the shogun. The practices of *sankin kotai* required formal and ritual attendance on the shogun once every two years. Duty, as the moral force that held the whole structure together, might seem asymmetrically owed because of fealty to those above. How would one describe the reciprocal demand on the higher of the pair? As a right? Did the king have a right to your military service? Did you have a right to his grant of lands be it in Europe or Japan?

Seeing the matter in the anachronistic light of rights would be to misunderstand the working principles with which both systems operated, and so, to distort the psychological processes that characterized it. As sketched in the previous section, just as far as the nobles owed a duty to the king, the king owed a duty to the nobles. When King John of England failed to fulfill his reciprocal duty, the nobles met him at Runnymede and extracted his agreement to the *Magna Carta*. This document set out the duties of the king to the nobles and of the nobles to the king.

In Japan, Yorimoto, the founder of Japanese feudalism, created a remarkably robust social structure based on personal loyalty and expressed in metaphors about the family and the duties family members owed to it. Later, in the Tokogawa shogunate, the metaphors were transformed in a formal code, *bushido*. The samurai lived by this code of conduct. Yamaga Soko has described bushido as follows: The samurai had "the business . . . [of] discharging loyal service to his master . . . and, with due consideration of his own position, in devoting himself to duty above all" (Tsumoda, 1958, p. 398). In these respects, the feudal systems of Europe and Japan were alike in placing the dominant emphasis on duty with no explicit attention to rights at all.

It should be plain from these descriptions that the core of the agreement at Runnymede and set out in *Magna Carta* was not the concession of rights to some category of persons by the king, who was to be bound by them. Rather it was a reminder to him of what his duties were to those who owed duty to him. The psychological conditions underwriting social cohesion that obtained amongst the members of a feudal, duty-driven society were different from those that obtained among the members of our rights-driven society. Whereas in medieval times one might feel betrayed by one's lord, there was no place for resentment, the characteristic emotion of those whose rights, real or imaginary, have been ignored, denied, or trampled on. Instead one would have felt demeaned and humiliated because the defaulted duty was owed to oneself as a person of a certain rank or estate.

In summary, the relation between duties and rights is historically contingent. How the balance is struck may even be the deepest stratum that defines a certain style of social order. Rather than seeing feudal Europe or the

Japan of the shogunate as the source of a priority of duties over rights, it is psychologically more realistic to look at the developments of postfeudal Europe as a historical moment the character of which stemmed from the emergence of such a priority. The very idea of a reciprocal right for every duty was not part of the discursive resources of medieval people in the East or the West.

Despite the force of these historical examples one might be tempted to respond, "That was then, this is now!" In our times it seems to be almost a matter of logic, a conceptual issue, that wherever there are duties, there are rights to demand their exercise and that wherever there are rights, there are duties to fulfill them. Indeed, in the current client society, it might seem as if the fundamental moral framework just consisted of rights of all kinds often assigned, claimed, and attributed by social or ethnic category. Each right engenders a duty on someone, usually that mysterious benefactor the government, to do something about it. However, who does have duties thrust on them by virtue of the rights of others, and how are those duties supposedly mandatory? Why do rich countries have a duty to give aid to the poor? Why should the strong assist the weak?

Our sketch of an answer above suggested that there is a root concept of *person* on which much of the moral force of rights and duties rests. There are some interesting questions that come to the surface when we start to reflect on the way that rights can easily turn into unreasonable demands. There are two main cases.

In the first case, the reciprocal duties devolve onto an individual person. As my student you have a right to my help during office hours. However, that right does not mean that I am obliged to devote unlimited time to your problems. I have a right to a certain degree of privacy and time to myself. Both come under threat if the exercise of rights is not tempered by good sense. In a way, what you can demand from me is effectively unlimited if we think of our relationship only in terms of your rights and my duties.

In the second case, we have something like the endlessly expanding demand that is made on the medical services in those nations in which there is some form of national health service. There is no end to what could be demanded by those who think their right to health and the treatment to achieve it is also unbounded.

Whereas the first case is an example of the exploitation of goodwill, the second case may look superficially more or less pragmatic. There are finite resources, and everyone cannot be dealt with on the basis of unlimited rights. One has a duty to limit one's demands to something reasonable. Why is this? It seems to me that there is a moral imperative close by, indeed the very one we drew attention to earlier in the discussion, namely the preservation of persons. There must be some limit set to how far the preservation of the good of one person can be bought at the diminution or humiliation or pain of another.

3. The universality question has two dimensions common to all people and common to all targets regardless of biological species. It would not be unreasonable to say that the point of the discourses of duties and rights is the moral protection of persons. Our question then splits along two axes. Are the discourses and practices of moral protection everywhere based on the same catalogue of rights and duties, for example as laid down in the United Nations Universal Declaration of Human Rights (see Appendix for full text)? Are there any other categories of beings to which moral protection is extended by means of a discourse of rights and duties? For example, Kant (1785/1969) makes it axiomatic for the moral life that persons may never be treated wholly as means to some end, however praiseworthy that end might be, that they may not be exploited. Does the concept of exploitation in this sense extend to other kinds of beings than persons, and if so, what is its source?

There is an answer to the first of these questions in Holiday's (1988) argument to the effect that there is a moral basis for the possibility of language. If a group of hominids is to qualify as a society of persons, these beings must be capable of using language. For language to be possible, Holiday argued, certain language games must be within the repertoire of the members of that group. Among these core language games there must be ways of using the concepts of right and duty. Putting the matter in this Wittgensteinian way allows us to consider the question in terms of practices. What are the necessary practices? Among them are such practices as giving others their due as contributors to a conversation. It is to allow those to whom one wishes to speak the right to have their turn. If the rights to the use of linguistic symbols are exclusively the privilege of only one person, then the others to whom he or she addresses remarks (usually orders!) will not count as persons.

We have already touched on the second question in discussing the symmetry or correspondence principle between claims to have rights and the ascription of corresponding duties. There I argued that there could be duties without corresponding rights in cases in which there are beings that are vulnerable to human harm, yet that are protected in that there are powers of other human beings to remedy such vulnerabilities. This route led outside the domain of human beings to any and all such vulnerable categories of beings.

The standard argument for the rights of animals to moral protection and the duties we have to attend to these depends on matters such as a common possibility of suffering. This is a kind of organic fellow feeling and involves a number of tendentious presuppositions such as our ability to tell whether an animal is suffering and our right to use a word from the human lexicon to describe the psychic state of the animal.

It seems to me that a much stronger case for the extension of duties to the nonhuman world can be made using the principles of vulnerabilities and the relevant powers of remedy than any invocation of fellow feelings.

4. Does the common discourse of rights and duties actually dominate the formal discourse of institutions whose role, in part, is to discuss them?

How does the passage from unspoken social convention or custom to informally cited duty to legally or quasi-legally established formal requirements set down in written ordinances take place? When such bodies as legislatures and higher courts are debating new rules for the regulation of the discourses of official bodies in the state, do they argue these matters out and draw conclusions using the concepts of everyday life? Though Finkel (see chap. 7, this volume) makes some nice comparisons between decision-making talk produced by laypeople and that produced by judges, there still remains the question of whether the discussions in the U.S. Supreme Court access a higher degree of rationality and philosophical sophistication from those of the lay folk.

This question is raised for me by the way several authors, notably Moghaddam and Riley and Louis and Taylor (see chapters 4 and 5, this volume), present their analyses. Is there something in the nature of human beings that leads inexorably to the regulation of the moral orders of life by duties and rights or by duties alone or by rights alone? It sometimes sounds as if the transition from unspoken convention to informal exhortation and demand could take care of itself. We need to address the issue of the kind of rationality in play.

Many people believe that they have duties other than those that are required of them by mandatory custom or law. These are the supererogatory duties. They often arise from some individual's conviction that there is a fault or failure or neglect somewhere and that something should be done! Environmentalism, now highly institutionalized, was first a matter of the anxieties experienced by individual people. Later groups of like-minded people may share a conception of a supererogatory duty. Such is the Nature Conservancy, the members of which feel a supererogatory duty to care for the environment. Moreover, what were once supererogatory duties may migrate to the mandatory if a social consensus should emerge that we should do by law what was once voluntary and personal, for example, recycling waste.

This brings out another feature of supererogatory duties. They are strictly voluntary because a failure to perform them will attract neither social obloquy (as a display of a lack of affection for one's children would) nor official sanction (as failing to send one's children to school would). There are no supererogatory rights.

Because supererogatory duties are taken on without the backing of social or legal sanctions, they seem at first sight to be outside the frame of social ethics, the consensual frame within which the moral judgments of everyday life make sense and get their force. It is a matter of what we could call *social ethics* that in Victorian times unmarried couples living together were disapproved of. People had a duty to marry; although the law, unlike society, did not proscribe informal unions. But we have seen that in the case of environmentalism, what was once a matter that lay outside the boundary of social ethics, for example, the driving of gas-guzzling cars, was not frowned on in the 1950s and became embedded in an extension of social ethics. For example, universities that invest some of their endowment in paper companies that clean cut primeval forests are disapproved of socially, and their investment decisions have led to student demonstrations in some places. Eventually all these informal demands may lead to formal legislation. One may be required by law to save old newspapers for recycling.

I have suggested that the shift from supererogatory to mandatory duties is a matter of the breadth of consensus on whether the obligation that underwrites the duty exists for all. Duty talk then develops as a discursive instrument for seeing to it that the relevant obligations are acknowledged and fulfilled. I offer the criterion that a duty is only supererogatory so long as the relevant obligation is accepted voluntarily by a minority of the local population, that is, neither by virtue of laws and regulations nor by virtue of social pressure.

The question of the mode of rationality by which supererogatory duties are taken up into formal law remains to be tackled. It runs parallel, I believe, to the question of how informally conceded rights are taken up. For example, in the northwest frontier of Pakistan and among Pathans in general, a nephew has certain rights to gifts and favors from his mother's brothers. Nowhere, so far as I know, are these rights formally recorded with the power of a constitutional authority behind them. In universities it used to be taken for granted that someone accused of a misdemeanor had the right to hear the evidence against him or her. Recent cases show vividly that this right is not engraved in the statues of some colleges. If an administration is eager to get rid of a teacher for some reason (which itself may not be disclosed), the accused will be refused access to the evidence. Now that this kind of decision is being challenged in the courts, it may well come about that the informal right will be formally established.

The questions I pose are empirical ones. Do legislators use the resources of ordinary language and its narrative conventions to discuss the transformation of informal customs and conventions into formal statutes, and is that transformation itself effected by ordinary means? I think we can say that the transformation itself must be performed according to set form or it will not take. There are then empirical studies to be conducted by Finkel and others. We need them to do for congresses, university committees, parliaments, and the like what they have already done for their student participants. What form do these discussions take, and do they use anything beyond the resources of the citizen?

REIFICATION AND DISCURSIVE CONVENTIONS

It is now time to return to the big question, proposed but left aside in the introduction to this chapter. What is the ontological status of that to which the words *duty* and *right* refer in the majority of their uses? Throughout the chapters on which I am commenting, I am struck by the persistence of reification, as if there were something that is a right or a duty. There are, of course, no such entities. The question one must ask is, What are these words being used for? What discursive tasks are they intended to accomplish or to facilitate?

The need to "dereify," if I may coin a phrase, is pressing in several chapters so that the force of the work therein reported can come through. In Finkel's chapter, for instance, he writes of law and distinguishes between two kinds. But what is the law that is so distinguished? It seems on close examination to be sets of conventions for the proper conduct of discussions and debates concerning certain matters that come to the attention of some group of persons. A law enacted by a legislator is, in practice, a discursive convention or rule on how certain people are to carry on a discussion, and that is all it is. It may be used for classifying human actions as acts. It may be used as principle of reasoning. The courts are where people talk! Nothing else happens there. In Finkel's research, ordinary people are invited to talk about certain issues, issues that have claimed the attention of other talkers engaged in the formal conversations that go on in courts and parliaments. His studies reveal that different, though not wholly different, conventions govern these discourses.

It is clear that duties and rights exist in the discursive domain. They are key materials to be used in fashioning a convincing discourse when one needs to obtain a concession from someone or to ensure that someone does what one believes to be required in some concrete circumstance. To concede a right is to concede an argument, just as it is to concede a duty. In the first case, the speaker is now free to act in whatever way was at issue, whereas in the second case, the one addressed in duty terms takes on an obligation in conceding a duty.

If Spini and Doise (see chap. 2, this volume) are right in locating such beliefs and discursive practices among social representations, we now face another vexing problem. Having said that duties and rights are socially represented or perhaps have (are?) social representations, we are not much further forward unless we have a clear idea of the nature of these beings. Despite an enthusiastic advocacy, one must confess that Moscovici's own seminal account (Farr & Moscovici, 1986) is notoriously unclear. Sometimes when he is talking of scientific theories as social representations, he means no more than that a social representation is a group or class of individual beliefs each of which is sufficiently similar in each of its human realizations to ensure actions with a common destiny.

Kant's (1787/1996) twelve categories have this character. We live in a common world because each individual uses similar schemata in constructing his or her own world.

There is an alternative. What if a social representation existed as a genuine collective entity, for example, as an emergent property of the joint performances of several people, though represented in its fullness in none? It is not at all clear from the text which of these possibilities Spini and Doise (see chap. 2, this volume) are presuming.

Their use of statistical analyses to extract the discursive conventions that are followed or manifested in the conversations they have had with their informants exacerbates our task of interpretation. The fact that these conversations are formally set up with questionnaires means that formal questions are to be treated as the contribution that Spini and Doise make to the conversation they are engaged in with the participants. This observation does alter the ontological category to which their methodology belongs. It is a species of conversation analysis, as is any methodology that makes use of a question-and-answer format. The results of analyses of patterns in conversations are semantic or grammatical rules or narrative conventions.

There are two kinds of generality that one needs to keep clearly distinct in any scientific enterprise. There is generality that is achieved by abstraction, in which the general level is reached by deleting attributes of the particulars at the individual level. As Vygotsky (1962) warned long ago, this more often than not has the effect of deleting the very attributes that are psychologically relevant. Then there is generality achieved by laying out a semantic field, a field of family resemblances in which the beings in question, such as the uses of words, are seen to form a kind of net linked by similarities and differences, few if any of which run across the whole net. In the uses of socially, legally, and psychologically significant words, and surely *duty* and *right* are such words, the technique of *surview*, of laying out the pattern of family resemblances, is the only legitimate methodology. It is the only methodology that preserves the right level of concreteness. Of course using the surview method is difficult and time consuming, but that should not deter anyone bent on good scientific work. It took Dorothy Hodgkin more than 20 years to solve the structure of insulin.

The result of a statistical analysis of the distribution of answers to questions cannot refer to anything psychologically real as a phenomenon because it is arrived at by abstraction. It can, of course, as I have emphasized, be an expression of a narrative convention or conversational rule.

In analyzing a concept (the use of a word) according to the surview methodology, we need to take account of the semantic structure of the concept the word expresses. Can the concept of duty be conjoined with that of responsibility? Does it make sense to say, "Ian is dutiful but irresponsible"? If not, then there must be a logical or conceptual tie between the concepts dutiful and responsible. However, in this case, it seems to me that there are people like Ian. In English, duty is logically related to the moral concept of obligation but not so related to the psychological concept of responsibility. This makes the studies of Hoppe-Graff and Kim (see chap. 3, this volume) very interesting. They offer a tantalizing gloss on the Korean word *Uimu* that, they remark, is close neither to responsibility nor to duty. Well, I ask, what is the semantic field of this word? Again, why are there chi-square calculations in a study of semantic rules? They add nothing to the data. Statistical significance makes sense only in contexts in which the phenomena are produced by causal processes in an environment where there are countervailing instances. I cannot imagine what would correspond to these requirements in a semantic study!

One has a duty to do something, usually for the benefit of someone else. If I have right to something, someone else is usually required to do something for my benefit. Duties are directed toward the good of others. Rights are directed to the good of myself. This sort of talk suggests that somewhere in the universe there is a realm of Platonic beings, Duties and Rights. It seems to suggest that the studies reported in this volume are studies of these mysterious beings, much as the studies reported in a book of paleontology might be taken to be studies of the shadowy inhabitants of the Jurassic era. Of course there are no such things and no such research project. What are our authors actually studying? The methodologies they adopt allow only one interpretation. Their research touches on the conventions by which people talk about certain matters of personal and social interest. Here are three such conventions.

It seems natural to say that if I have a right for something from you, you have a duty to provide me with it. It looks as if rights entail duties and duties entail rights. The first principle of the general theory of duties is as follows:

> Duties and rights are complementary so that, all else being equal, for every duty of A toward B, there exists a right of B toward A.

What sort of principle is this? I suggest that it is a discursive convention, adopted in recent times, as part of the argumentative repertoire by which positions are established, challenged, and enforced. In many cases, duties and rights are related to the roles people occupy. Most duties do not relate to being human in general. The mandatory character of duty sometimes derives from explicitly formulated prescriptions; the duties of a professor include teaching, research, and service. Sometimes duties derive from informal but generally known social demands, such as, a citizen has a duty to vote and a mother has a duty to feed her children. In most democracies, there is no explicitly formulated prescription of political participation. (Australia is an exception.)

The second principle of the general theory of duties is this:

> Social roles are strongly related to the way duties and rights are distributed among the people of a society.

To put this in more lucid clothing, discursive reminders of social roles are among the devices by which positions are regulated. Why do we need the resource provided by these concepts? What situation does it address? As I argued previously, people differ in their powers and capacities, skills and abilities. Someone who cannot see could not have a duty to help old people to cross the road.

The third principle of the general theory of duties is the following:

> One only has a duty to perform actions that are within one's power, and one only has a right to whatever it is possible to obtain.

This is clearly a discursive resource. One has been positioned as the one to undertake some task, presented in the form of a duty that is as mandatory. What better recourse can one have to resist the positioning and to repudiate the ascription of the duty than to refer to one's inherent or even momentary incapacity to perform? "I cannot drive," a permanent though in the long run remediable incapacity, is one way of repudiating being positioned as the one who has the duty to get everyone home after the party. Another is simply, "I am too drunk." This state will wear off sooner or later.

These three principles or discourse conventions seem to be reflected in the results of the research of Spini and Doise (see chap. 2, this volume). However, just what are they studying in their research? A moment's reflection shows that they can only be studies of the discursive conventions by which people make demands on others or accept or fend off the demands made on them.

CONCLUSIONS

We have seen how the concepts of rights and duties are related in a variety of discourse genres. We have seen how admonitions apropos of moral duties can be based on citations of natural powers and vulnerabilities, strengths, and weaknesses. We have also seen how the moral domain can grow by the generalization of supererogatory duties from individual convictions of what is right to general demands that everyone should fulfill what was once just a personal duty.

We have also made some headway in locating the ontological domain in which duties and rights actually dwell. It is domain of discourse, of ways of talking and writing in attempts to regulate the conduct of various classes and groups of persons. The use of statistical methods tends to obscure the reality of duty and rights talk, though, properly interpreted as the bringing out of local discourse conventions, it can illuminate it to some extent.

The logical disentanglement of duties from rights allowed us to see how it could be that people might have duties to nonhuman beings because the latter, by virtue of their intrinsic natures, could not attract attributions of rights.

REFERENCES

Benedict, St. (2001). *The rule of St. Benedict* (L. Doyle, Trans.). Collegeville, MN: Liturgical Press. (Original work published 535 A.D.)

Farr, R., & Moscovici, S. (Eds.). (1986). *Social representations*. Cambridge, England: Cambridge University Press.

Finkel, N. J. (2001). *Not fair! The typology of commonsense unfairness*. Washington, DC: American Psychological Association.

Holiday, A. (1988). *Moral powers*. Brighton, England: Harvester.

Kant, I. (1969). *Foundations of the metaphysics of morals*. (L. W. Beck, Trans.). Indianapolis, IN: Bobbs-Merrill. (Original work published 1785)

Kant, I. (1996). *Critique of pure reason*. (W. S. Pluhar, Trans.). Indianapolis, IN: Hackett. (Original work published 1787)

Milton, J. (1953). *Works* (Vol. 7). New York: Columbia University Press. (Original work published 1641)

Paine, T. (1992). *Rights of man*. New York: Dover. (Original work published 1791)

Tsumoda, R. (1985). *Sources of Japanese tradition*. New York: City University Press.

Vygotsky, L. (1962). *Thought and language*. (E. Hanfman & G. Vakar, Trans.). Cambridge, MA: MIT Press.

11

TAKING DUTIES SERIOUSLY: TO WHAT PROBLEMS ARE RIGHTS AND DUTIES THE SOLUTION?

THOMAS L. HASKELL

As experimental psychologists, Professors Finkel and Moghaddam aspire to high standards of scientific rigor. They want to bring psychological evidence to bear on a subject they think is too often treated in an exclusively normative manner, uninformed by empirical data about the way human beings actually allocate responsibility. Yet by beginning their book with the Kitty Genovese story, they knowingly take on a heavy burden of normative commitments, all of which point to duties as a promising solution to what ails modern America while implying that rights may well be part of the problem. Lest any reader miss the message, the volume's organizers follow up the Genovese story with another emotionally wrenching incident that teaches much the same lesson, the 1998 case of David Cash, a Berkeley undergraduate who passively stood by in the women's restroom of a Nevada casino as a friend raped, brutalized, and finally killed a 7-year-old girl. Duty to strangers, it appears, lacks traction in our culture even when the stakes rise to life or death, even when no decent person could fail to see what duty requires. Professors Finkel and Moghaddam (chap. 1, this volume) begin their introductory chapter with these stories because they are troubled by the predominance of rights over duties, which they think all too characteristic of modern American culture.

The two stories are so emotionally charged that some readers may get the impression that Finkel and Moghaddam are determined to present an indictment of rights talk, no matter where the evidence leads. In fact, the authors are not closed minded or monolithic in their approach to rights and duties. The opening pages of their text move first in one direction, then another, as they struggle to get the right handle on their subject. They acknowledge the dangers of premature generalization; they concede great variability between individuals and cultures; they worry about contributing to self-fulfilling prophecies about situationally induced indifference to suffering. Only hesitantly do they disclose their "guiding assumption," which is that the good life requires a balance between rights and duties, a balance they think existed in America at the time of the Revolution and for some decades afterward, but not today. They believe that allowing rights to prevail over duties breeds narcissism, selfishness, and disregard for one's fellow human beings. They fear, as they put it in a draft of the introductory chapter, that the "long shadow of rights" has "eclipsed duties." But reversing the priority of rights and duties is not their goal because they understand that exaggerating the force of duty would be just as harmful in other ways, discouraging individual creativity, for example, or fostering a stultifying obedience to authority. What they say they want is not simply to encourage greater respect for duty but to bring rights and duties into balance.

More questions arise than I can hope to address. What would a proper balance between rights and duties look like? How would we recognize balance if it were achieved? Is it true that American culture is now tilted toward rights? Was the balance ever tilted toward duty, and if so, when, why, and how did it change? What exactly is the relation between rights and duties? Is the relationship such that maintaining balance is, as the editors assume, vitally important? These questions point to potentially pivotal issues whose resolution lies far outside the domain of experimental psychology, so far outside that we cannot rule out a possibility that the editors themselves candidly acknowledged in their initial invitation to prospective contributors to this volume: that the psychologists' standard toolkit may simply not be adequate for the analysis of rights and duties. By the same token, of course, a psychological toolkit expanded and modified to grapple effectively with rights, duties, and other distinctively historical and cultural phenomena might pay off handsomely by enabling the discipline to bring its expertise to bear on problems now thought to lie beyond its competence.

BALANCING RIGHTS AND DUTIES

Historically speaking, it is of course true that *duties talk* was as emblematic of traditional society as *rights talk* is of our own era. Even though the Protestant Reformation challenged traditional authority and significantly expanded liberty of conscience, early Protestants shared with Catholics all over Europe the traditional assumption that hierarchy among human beings was entirely natural and comported with the will of the Creator. "Every degree of people, in their vocations, calling, and office, hath appointed to them their duty and order," read the English *Book of Homilies*, published in 1562 and routinely read in every pulpit of England. "Some are in high degree, some in low; some kings and princes, some inferiors and subjects; priests and laymen, masters and servants, fathers and children, husbands and wives, rich and poor; and every one have need of [every] other" (Rutman, 1970, p. 53). As children, the first British settlers to set up housekeeping on this side of the Atlantic had memorized a catechism that taught them to regard relationships of command and obedience as the will of God:

> My duty . . .[is] to submit myself to all my governors, teachers, spiritual pastors and masters; to order myself lowly and reverently to all my betters, . . . not to covet or desire other men's goods: but to learn and labor truly to get my own living, and do my duty in that state of life unto which it shall please God to call me. (Laslett, 1971, p. 176)

Self-abasing as these words may sound to modern ears, the lessons they taught did not prevent 17th-century Englishmen from priding themselves on their "ancient rights and privileges" as Englishmen. Nor was their pride misplaced: Among all the peoples of Europe, none lived within a wider orbit of personal liberty than the English (Macfarlane, 1987).

The vocabularies of rights and duties have never been mutually exclusive. Far from it, sometimes they are mutually reinforcing. This complicates the task of assessing balance. The complications multiply exponentially as soon as we acknowledge that rhetoric and practice can move in different directions at the same time. Finkel and Moghaddam's most convincing evidence for the existence of an imbalance of rights over duties in modern American culture is conspicuously concentrated at the level of everyday rhetoric, not practice. Although I ultimately argue that rhetoric is not the most fruitful level for analysis, let us begin by conceding the force of their claims regarding rhetoric.

There is no denying the hegemony of rights talk in modern America. The political movements of our era almost always march under the banner of rights. Human rights, minority rights, gay rights, women's rights, children's rights, animal rights, the rights of the disabled or the mentally ill, abortion rights, property rights, the right to sue one's HMO, the right to life—the list goes on and on, leaving scarcely any sector of the political spectrum unrepresented. Finkel and Moghaddam raise the question whether citizens could just as easily recite a similar list regarding duties (chap. 1, this volume). Plainly not. They rightly call attention to the fact that every citizen, including the vicious stalker who murdered Kitty Genovese, knows where to go to find authoritative documents, charters, and constitutions that define persons essentially as rights bearers, thereby putting them in certain limited dimensions of life beyond the reach either of public opinion or governmental authority. The centrality of rights in our lives is highlighted, and our reliance on them is systematically infused with passion, by "rights dramas," as Finkel and Moghaddam call them, that are played out every day not just in the courtrooms of this singularly litigious society but also on movie and television screens all over the country. Nothing remotely similar can be said to sustain or enliven our attachment to duties. Rights talk, as Ronald Dworkin (1977, p. 184) noted, "now dominates political debate in the United States." In contrast, as Finkel and Moghaddam (chap. 1, this volume, p. 4) say, the very idea of "duties talk" sounds "dissonant, quaint, or archaic."

The point is well taken. In a culture that puts rights talk on the tip of everyone's tongue, talk of duty and obligation becomes harder to articulate and less likely to find a receptive audience. If talk of duty is discouraged or even silenced, may not the substance of it atrophy as well? The danger may not be as great as Finkel and Moghaddam make it out to be, and what danger there is may be so deeply rooted in the conditions of modernity as to make it irremediable. Still, their concern about the one-sidedness of rights talk in modern America is justifiable, for practices and values that we hesitate to express, much less commend, are unlikely in the long run to retain their grip on us. Rights talk, with its endless variations on the inherently self-centered and polarizing theme of "Don't tread on me!" leaves much to be desired especially when a culture tries, as ours has, to make it virtually the only acceptable vocabulary for policy-oriented public discourse. Given the rhetorical hegemony of rights talk in America today, there is much to be said in favor of selectively rehabilitating the language of duty. That is just what A. M. Rosenthal, newly appointed chief of the city desk of *The New York Times*, was doing when he called public attention to the shocking passivity of Kitty Genovese's neighbors through follow-up stories and a small book (Rosenthal, 1999), thereby etching her story in the conscience of my generation.

CAN RIGHTS IMPLY DUTIES?

But the project of psychological research embodied in this book will get off on the wrong foot altogether if those participating in it mistake the rhetoric of rights for the whole story. In their chapter in this volume, Dario Spini and Willem Doise (chap. 2, this volume, p. 26) register a subtle but important objection when they say that it is "a paradox of liberalism" that as rights are proclaimed "this does not mean that duties disappear." I will be more direct in hopes of driving the point home. If we concentrate on what shapes people's conduct and how they actually act, rather than their rhetoric, it will become clear that rights and duties often march side by side and are functionally allied. Contrary to what much of the introductory chapter to this volume implies, it is not the case that, wherever individual rights flourish, duty must come under a shadow. Quite the contrary. More often than not, new rights for some mean new duties for others. For you to have a right to do something means that I (along with an indeterminate multitude of others) have a duty not to hinder your doing it. Insofar as the explicit right is enforceable at law, so is the tacit duty; to enforce either is to enforce both. Establishing new rights for some can be an efficient means of imposing new duties on others. Rights and duties often are so mutually supportive and tightly linked that we would do well to think of them not as separate entities but as two different aspects of a single interrelated package of rules governing human interaction. Establishing such a package changes the way people act in relation to one another, enabling the intended beneficiaries to do as they will, while preventing others from resisting them. The former experience the package of rules as a right, the latter as a duty. Thus "academic freedom" denominates a package of rules that encourages candor on the part of scholars while discouraging administrators and politicians from taking retaliatory action to enforce orthodoxy.

To be sure, the rhetorical dominance of rights talk in America means that rights march down the middle of main street to the clash of cymbals and the beat of drums, inspiring the applause of the crowd, while duties, no matter how powerfully they may shape conduct, generally trudge along in the shade, unaccompanied and unnoticed. But we know that rhetoric and appearance are often deceptive. Even the most rights oriented of cultures cannot help being chock-full of duties, for in practice rights and duties normally develop more or less in tandem, simultaneously doing away with certain constraints in the lives of rights bearers, while introducing new constraints, new duties of forbearance, for instance, into the lives of everyone else. Over the course of this nation's history, new rights have been invented; old rights like free speech have been dramatically redefined; and rights only nominally established have been given new substance or extended to segments of the population previously excluded. For most of this nation's history, for example, the First Amendment was construed as little more than a prohibition against prior restraint. Not until the 1920s did *free speech* come to mean that speakers were not to be punished even for whatever "bad tendencies" judges and juries might anticipate from their words (Rabban, 1997). Contrary to what Finkel and Moghaddam seem to believe, I see no reason to suppose that the overall result of this steady expansion of rights has been a general shrinkage of constraint. The proliferation of rights no doubt creates new winners and losers, but its effect is to reconfigure the network of legal, social, and cultural constraints within which each of us operates, not to eradicate it. Women and minorities have no doubt experienced a loosening of constraints over the past century and half, but that goal was achieved by imposing on all the rest of us constraints that did not previously exist.

Rights and duties are too closely allied to be at war with each other. Some years ago in a different context I suggested in passing that rights may be "the principal means by which duty is smuggled back into cultures dominated by the rhetoric of individualism" (Haskell, 1998, p. 380, footnote 1). One could go further and contend that in modern American culture defining oneself or one's kind as the bearer of hitherto unacknowledged rights (e.g., the right to abortion) has become the preferred fast-track means of imposing on others a duty of noninterference with whatever it is one wants to do or to become. Whether to applaud or lament this development is debatable, but either way, once we get beneath the rhetorical surface of things, there are good reasons to think that duty has much greater purchase in our lives than appears at first glance and that rights help give it that purchase. I agree with Finkel and Moghaddam that rights talk overshadows the discourse of duty in America and that the undeniable rhetorical hegemony of rights has some regrettable consequences. But it does not follow that that rights and duties typically work at cross-purposes or that duty is an endangered species.

Finkel and Moghaddam are careful to specify that the relationship between rights and duties is not a zero-sum game in which expanding one necessarily contracts the other. They know better than to treat rights and duties as if they were a case of matter and antimatter, each obliterating the other on contact. They try to acknowledge some degree of correlativity of rights and duties by referring to possibilities of "replacement" and "complementarity." But some of their assumptions about rights and duties remain puzzling. For instance, their introductory chapter to this volume treats turn taking, a practice that virtually all cultures inculcate in the young, exclusively as a duty. They even go so far as to suggest that it is a duty whose origins are likely to be much older than rights (chap. 1, this volume). As I see it, the lesson that children learn about turn taking cannot help but be as much about rights as duties. Children not only learn not only to wait patiently while the other child has his turn but also learn that by waiting patiently they acquire the right to a turn of their own. Rights and duties are not cleanly differentiated sorts of entities that could, even in principle, have come into being at different moments in time. Over a wide range of cases, rights and duties come linked together. Each implies the other; each presupposes the other. They usually are, as I have been contending, different aspects of a single package of rules governing human interaction in some specified situation.

The editors' anxiety about the subordination of duties to rights in American culture contrasts sharply with the attitude of moral philosophers, among whom it is common to give at least qualified assent to what Joel Feinberg (1970, p. 243) calls the "doctrine of the logical correlativity of rights and duties." That doctrine comes close to treating rights and duties as two sides of the same coin. It holds that (a) "all duties entail other people's rights" and (b) "all rights entail other people's duties." As a historian, I have no interest in defending the claim that correlativity is universal or that rights always come paired with duties. Some plainly do not, as Feinberg understood. But if a relationship of mutual entailment holds true in any substantial number of cases, as it obviously does, then anyone claiming that rights and duties are on a collision course shoulders a heavy burden of proof.

CONCEPTUAL SEPARATENESS

In defense of what they call the "conceptual separateness" of rights and duties, Finkel and Moghaddam quote a leading political theorist, Ronald Dworkin. The passage they quote, which is subsequently reproduced, comes from Dworkin's (1977) influential volume, *Taking Rights Seriously*, a book mainly concerned with showing that rights are indispensable for any adequate liberal theory of law and politics. If anyone as friendly to rights as Dworkin actually supported Finkel and Moghaddam's claim of the "conceptual separateness" of rights and duties, I would regard that as very strong testimony in their favor. But understood in context, I do not see how Dworkin's words can provide them with any support. Showing that this is so will permit us to situate Finkel and Moghaddam's project in the universe of political theory and help bring into focus a question I think the psychologists must ask and answer at the outset of their project if it is to succeed: To what problem are rights (or duties) the solution?

Dworkin is a liberal. He wrote *Taking Rights Seriously* to challenge what he regards as the "ruling theory" of the law in both England and the United States. His target is a rival interpretation of liberal tradition. It descends from Jeremy Bentham and consists of two linked parts, legal positivism and utilitarianism. *Legal positivism* holds that law needs no deep roots in morality or principle, that it is simply a system of rules that duly constituted bodies have in their wisdom chosen to adopt. *Utilitarianism* contends that these rules can have but one legitimate aim, which is to serve the general welfare. Although the liberal tradition has usually accorded rights a place of honor, Bentham dismissed them as "nonsense on stilts." Dworkin expressly sets out to vindicate rights from a scorn that he believes is built into the utilitarian system of law and politics that prevails today in the Anglo-American world. This he does by defining rights as "political trumps held by individuals" and by calling attention to a grave problem that he thinks rights help alleviate, if not solve. Their function, he believes, is to provide a principled check against the relentlessly majoritarian tendencies of a political and legal system that is loath to acknowledge any authority higher than the will of a governing majority. Rights carve out exceptions and qualifications to the otherwise overwhelming primacy that the "greatest good of the greatest number" must enjoy under utilitarian auspices. "Individuals have rights," says Dworkin, "when, for some reason, a collective goal is not a sufficient justification for denying them what they wish, as individuals, to have or to do, or not a sufficient justification for imposing some loss or injury upon them" (Dworkin, 1977, p. xi). Rights function as a counterweight, restraining majorities from oppressive conduct. "The bulk of the law—the part which defines and implements social, economic, and foreign policy—cannot be neutral," says Dworkin. "It must state, in its greatest part, the majority's view of the common good. The institution of rights is therefore crucial, because it represents the majority's promise to the minorities that their dignity and equality will be respected" (p. 205).

The passage of *Taking Rights Seriously* that Finkel and Moghaddam rely on to affirm the "conceptual separateness" of rights and duties reads as follows:

> There is a difference between the idea that you have a duty not to lie to me because I have a right not to be lied to, and the idea that I have a right that you not lie to me because you have a duty not to tell lies. (Dworkin, p. 171)

Finkel and Moghaddam take this passage to mean that Dworkin shares their view that the dominance of rights over duties is not necessitated by logic and could just as well be reversed, putting duty ahead of rights (chap. 1, this volume, p. 7). They are not exactly wrong, but neither are they right. They feel an urgent need to show that rights do not, in their own revealing words, "stand, somehow, closer to heaven," or "spring from more sacred soil" than duties. They see Dworkin as an influential ally in that struggle. But in this they are pushing at an open door, for it would be hard to find any serious student of history or politics who believed that the prevalence of rights over duties in America today is necessitated either by logic or divine commandment. (chap. 1, p. 7). What they are struggling to demonstrate is already taken for granted. Dworkin would of course agree that it is history rather than logic or the essential nature of human beings that accounts for the predominance of rights over duties in modern America, but that was not at all his point.

The passage in question is but a passing moment in Dworkin's larger argument, the purpose of which is to amend John Rawls's well-known conception of the "original position." What Dworkin is trying to demonstrate is that the original position cannot really do all the argumentative work Rawls assigned it and that underlying the original position and sustaining it, Rawls tacitly assumed the existence of a right so fundamental that it does not derive from the hypothetical contract made in the original position but precedes and legitimizes that contract along with all the rights derived from it. The foundational right in question will be familiar to anyone acquainted with Dworkin's work: It is the "natural right of all men and women to equality of concern and respect" (Dworkin, 1977, p. 182; also Dworkin, 2000).

In the course of developing that argument, Dworkin devotes several pages to what he calls an exercise in "ideological sociology" that compares and contrasts three different kinds of political theory: one based on goals, another based on rights, and a third based on duties. He identifies utilitarianism with the goal-based type, Kant's categorical imperative with the duty-based type, and Tom Paine's theory of revolution with the rights-based type. Dworkin takes it entirely for granted that any of the three, including duty, could in principle serve as the basis for a plausible theory of politics. But the option so alluring to Finkel and Moghaddam, that a system of politics might be based on duty instead of rights, holds no interest whatsoever for Dworkin. He compares the three types only for the sake of showing that "political theories will differ from one another . . . not simply in the particular goals, rights, and duties, each sets out, but also in the way each connects the goals, rights, and duties it employs" (Dworkin, 1977, p. 171). His distinction between "the idea that you have a duty not to lie to me because I have a right not to be lied to, and the idea that I have a right that you not lie to me because you have a duty not to tell lies" was meant merely as an illustration of the interconnectedness of goals, rights, and duties. Once Dworkin has used that minor point to advance his claims about Rawls's tacit reliance on a fundamental natural right to equality of concern and respect, he shrugs the whole exercise aside, for it is no more than temporary scaffolding: "All this," he pointedly warns, "is, of course, superficial and trivial as ideological sociology" (p. 173).

In short, the idea that rights and duties are somehow fundamentally at loggerheads gets no support at all from Dworkin. He is keenly aware that rights for some ordinarily entail duties for others. Indeed, equality of concern and respect, the natural right that he would make the sine qua non of a sound liberal political system, splendidly exemplifies the intimacy of the alliance between rights and duties that I have been arguing for. It condemns failures to render aid to suffering strangers like Kitty Genovese every bit as vigorously as any duty-based system would.

To sum up, although I acknowledge the hegemony of rights talk in this country and concede that that rhetorical imbalance has, in itself, some regrettable consequences, I cannot concur with some of the premises set forth in the introductory chapter to this volume. Anyone who, like Finkel and Moghaddam, senses a deep tension between rights and duties and yearns to shift the balance away from rights toward duties might do well to grapple with this question: "How exactly would a duty-based analysis of the Kitty Genovese case differ from an analysis based on her equal right to the concern and respect of her neighbors?" Dworkin's paramount right is explicitly a duty-generating right. Kitty Genovese's neighbors flagrantly failed to live up to the duties it generates. What would be gained by treating duty as primary, right as secondary?

As I see it, the duties that rights create need not be inferior to or any less constraining than duties formulated simply as top-down dictates of the state (or moral law, divine will, etc.). Whether the duties a right creates take the merely negative form of forbearance or go beyond that to require active manifestations of concern for the well-being of others, as Dworkin's paramount right does, they need not lack force. In fact, there seems little reason to expect that they would be behaviorally or psychologically distinguishable from duties formulated in a more authoritarian manner except possibly in their greater palatability in the eyes of those who are constrained by them. That, I suppose, would count in their favor and reinforce the widely shared assumption that a rights-based political system is well suited to people who conceive of themselves as more-or-less autonomous individuals and think of the state as an instrument of their collective well-being, not a master to whom they owe reverence or fealty.

REFERENCES

Dworkin, R. (1977). *Taking rights seriously*. Cambridge, England: Cambridge University Press.

Dworkin, R. (2000). *Sovereign virtue: The theory and practice of equality*. Cambridge, England: Cambridge University Press.

Feinberg, J. (1970). The nature and value of rights. *Journal of Value Inquiry, 4*, 243–257.

Haskell, T. L. (1998). *Objectivity is not neutrality: Explanatory schemes in history*. Baltimore: Johns Hopkins University Press.

Laslett, P. (1971). *The world we have lost*. London: Methuen.

Macfarlane, A. (1987). *The culture of capitalism*. London: Blackwell Science.

Rabban, D. (1997). *Free speech in its forgotten years*. Cambridge, England: Cambridge University Press.

Rosenthal, A. M. (1999). *Thirty-eight witnesses*. Berkeley: University of California Press.

Rutman, D. B. (1970). *American Puritanism: Faith and practice*. New York: Lippincott.

12

THEORIES OF JUSTICE, RIGHTS, AND DUTIES: NEGOTIATING THE INTERFACE BETWEEN NORMATIVE AND EMPIRICAL INQUIRY

THOMAS A. SPRAGENS JR.

Count me among the firm believers in the great value—nay, the necessity—of cohabitation and cross-fertilization between normative political theory and empirical social science, for conceptions of justice are an important subject of moral deliberation and assessment, and they play an important role in real-world political events. Philosophers and social scientists who deal with issues of justice can learn useful things from each other but only if they understand the porous boundary between prescription and explanation in social theory. Despite the logical gap between *is* and *ought*, empirical findings can provide a prima facie case for theories of justice and can illuminate whether they pass the test of feasibility. And normative analysis can provide relevant ideal-type models to guide empirical inquiry and can help resolve conceptual problems that may distort empirical interpretation and explanation.

Issues of justice, rights, and duties certainly represent one area in which empirical and normative inquiry can overlap and interact very profitably. Justice is not the only norm that concerns political theorists, but it clearly is one of the most inescapable considerations for them. Prescriptive theories of politics essentially seek to ascertain those social practices and institutions that can, under the prevailing circumstances, permit the society's members to lead flourishing lives consonant with the constraints of justice. Madison (Hamilton, Madison, & Jay, 1787–1788/1961, p. 324) wrote in Federalist 51 that "justice is the end of government. It is the end of civil society. It ever has been and ever will be pursued until obtained, or until liberty is lost in the pursuit." And more recently, John Rawls (1999, p. 3) has insisted in parallel fashion that "justice is the first virtue of social institutions." So every attempt to produce a comprehensive normative conception of politics has to attend carefully to canons of right and justice.

Conceptions of right and justice, however, are not only theoretical notions deployed by philosophical onlookers. Such conceptions inform the behavior, the commitments, and the attitudes of most of those who live in a society and participate in its politics. These conceptions are, in short, empirical forces that play an important part in shaping political events in the real world. Empirical political scientists, sociologists, and psychologists, therefore, have to attend to these conceptions in their descriptions and explanations of social behavior. And here then, surely, is a place where the essential concerns of normative and empirical analysts converge and where the insights and findings of each can be useful to the other.

Interchange across the boundary between empirical and normative inquiry into conceptions of justice, rights, and duties needs to take place, then. But it needs to be done right. If what is possible and proper in this context is not appreciated, the result can be confusion and ill-based claims on both sides. One has to understand what each enterprise can do for the other, and equally important, what each cannot do for the other. And to reach this understanding of the proper way to negotiate the interface between facts and norms when it comes to conceptions of right and justice one needs, or so I argue here, to escape the long shadow of David Hume.

Hume's Shadow: The Gap Between *Is* and *Ought*

Writing in the 18th century, Hume made two famous arguments regarding the relationship between empirical findings and normative conclusions. As it happens, these two arguments do not cohere very well with each other, and they both have led to misunderstandings and misconceptions that have impeded or distorted the interface between social science and social ethics. One of these arguments has been, unsurprisingly, misread as prohibiting any legitimate use of empirical data by normative theorists in the development or justification of their arguments. The other, paradoxically, seems to dissolve the independent status of moral theory and social ethics altogether, reducing these normative enterprises into a subspecies of empirical science. The first argument seems on its face to render social scientific findings altogether irrelevant to normative theory; the second argument seems to accredit scientific inquiry with the capacity to generate dispositive normative standards for social practice. Each of these arguments contains an important truth, but each is also seriously misleading. To negotiate the interface between normative and empirical inquiry into the meaning, functions, and validity of moral conceptions like justice, rights, and duties, one needs to identify and exorcise the faulty inferences that Hume's arguments have generated; it is likewise necessary to recognize the genuine insights in these arguments and to reconcile them with each other.

The first of Hume's (1739/1948) arguments is his famous insistence on what gets characterized as "the gap between is and ought." At the outset of Book 3 of his *Treatise of Human Nature*, Hume offers the following observation (Part I, Section I):

> In every system of morality which I have hitherto met with, I have always remarked that the author proceeds for some time in the ordinary way of reasoning, and establishes the being of a God, or makes observations concerning human affairs; when of a sudden I am surprised to find, that instead of the usual copulations of propositions, *is*, and *is not*, I meet with no proposition that is not connected with an *ought* or *ought not*. This change is imperceptible; but is, however, of the last consequence. For as this *ought* or *ought not* expresses some new relation or affirmation, it is necessary that it should be observed and explained; and at the same time that a reason should be given for what seems altogether inconceivable, how this new relation can be a deduction from others which are entirely different from it. (p. 43)

There is an important truth in this passage relevant to the interface of concern here, and that truth centers around the word *deduction*. As a purely logical matter, it is in fact impossible to produce a valid prescriptive inference from premises that are entirely descriptive. All the indicative proportions in the world cannot generate a logically compelling imperative conclusion. So if I want to make a logically compelling argument on behalf of a moral or prescriptive claim, I cannot piece together my justification for that claim entirely from *is* and *is not* propositions. At least one of my premises must itself be a moral premise. To take a simple example, I cannot as a purely logical matter fully justify an assertion to you that you should give me $10 by reminding you that you borrowed that amount from me recently and promised to pay me back. To complete my case syllogistically, I would need to add the stipulation that as a moral matter one should keep one's promises.

Bridging the Gap: Counsels of Prudence

What is misleading about Hume's argument, however, turns about the words *inconceivable* and *entirely different*. These terms seem to imply that normative and empirical discourse are so utterly remote and distinct that they can have no relevance to each other. And that misleading implication has been acted on both by crude meta-ethical theories such as the "emotive theory of ethics,"[1] which depicted moral claims as cognitively empty expressions of feeling, and by equally crude conceptions of *wertfrei* social science,[2] which insisted that social scientific findings had no practical bearing on questions of social policy and social morality.

Now if all propositions that come packaged in the indicative language of *is* and *is not* referred solely to static and discrete states of affairs such as the "red, here, now" description that Bertrand Russell offered as the paradigmatic data report, the belief that logical distinctness implied mutual irrelevance might be justified. That conclusion would seem especially reasonable if all *ought* and *ought not* propositions represented moral stipulations such as Kant's imperatives of pure practical reason and never represented what the user of such language sees as peculiarly compelling words to the wise such as the counsels of Aristotelian *phronesis*.

When we consider, however, that the propositions of empirical social science are not simply and entirely bald descriptions of static and discrete facts such as "40% of Catholic voters in Detroit are registered Democrats" or "20% of North Carolina's industrial output is in textiles" and when we recognize that many of the most important propositions of normative social theory are not stipulative moral imperatives but what J. W. N. Watkins, characterizing Hobbes's "laws of nature," called "doctor's orders of a peculiarly compelling kind," it turns out that it is not at all "inconceivable" as Hume insists but instead rather obvious how moral theorists can move without impropriety from the indicative to the prescriptive mode in their arguments. This is especially unmysterious when we recall that some of the common indicative propositions are, as Hume noted, assertions about "human nature." For human beings are not merely pieces of flotsam and jetsam that drift passively through life in mute and unresisting acquiescence to external forces. They are, instead, somewhat teleological organisms whose actions are motivated in large part by natural and socially conditioned desires, needs, and passionately sought goals. And these human beings are not only the subject matter of social scientific propositions but also the makers and the audience of these propositions.

---

[1]The central claim of the emotivist theory of ethics is that ethical propositions are not genuinely cognitive claims about a reality external to the one who utters them but that they are instead expressions of the emotions of approval or disapproval, of liking and abhorrence, aroused in the utterer by the state of affairs he or she is calling good or bad, right or wrong. The classic statement of this viewpoint is perhaps that found in Ayer's (1936) *Language, Truth, and Logic*, and the best secondary account is Urmson's (1968) *The Emotive Theory of Ethics*.

[2]Advocates of the *wertfrei* ideal of social science sought a body of empirical knowledge about human and social phenomena that had been scrupulously cleansed of normative bias, moral assumptions, or ideological influence. Max Weber gave one of the paradigmatic expressions of this ideal in his essays on "The Meaning of Ethical Neutrality in Sociology and Economics" and "Objectivity in Social Science and Social Policy." These essays are translated and edited by Edward Shils and Henry Finch in Max Weber's (1949) *The Methodology of the Social Sciences*.

If doctors tells patients that they ought to quit smoking two packs a day and give as the basis for their imperative claims the purely indicative assertions that heavy smokers are three times more likely than nonsmokers to develop lung cancer and that lung cancer leads in a high percentage of cases to pain, debility, and death, they have committed the logical fallacy Hume deplores in the famous passage I quoted above. But few patients would in an instance like this chastise their physicians for violating the canons of logic. And they would refrain from such objections not because they are themselves logical incompetents but because they understand the tacit normative premise at work here. The physicians could complete their logical cases and close the syllogistic gap by saying that patients ought to prefer a healthy life to a miserable death. Physicians do not do so, though, because it seems a waste of breath; they simply assume that "normal" and "rational" people have the desires physicians take for granted. Logically, of course, patients could dismiss their doctors' strong counsel, expressed in the imperative language of *ought*, by allowing that they were indifferent about life and death or wanted to die or loved high-stakes gambling. But most patients would not avow such unusual preference orderings and would accordingly understand and accept without objection the normative import of their doctors' indicative references.

Now normative social theory is replete with important instances of cases logically parallel to this homely example. One perennial normative issue that Aristotle argued about with Plato, an issue that was central to ideological disputation during the Cold War and that still provides one important axis of partisan division within advanced industrial societies, concerns the best way to institutionalize a society's economic activities. Should these be left to private exchanges in the free marketplace, or should public agencies plan and regulate these activities by law? Part of this issue is a freestanding moral issue about the preinstitutional moral desert and about the nature and extent of moral entitlements to property. But much of the battle turns about empirical questions. Do unregulated market economies produce the most efficient allocation of resources and hence the highest possible gross domestic product (GDP), a full employment equilibrium, and innovations in productive technology? Or do they lead to chronic instability, underemployment, structural poverty, and warfare among stratified social classes? The way that normative theorists depict the structural features of the good society will depend on the answers they endorse to these empirical questions, not because *ought* follows deductively from *is* but because a good society is one in which human lives can flourish and because human lives can flourish better in peaceful and prosperous settings than in poor and acrimonious ones.

Moreover, as a philosophical maxim goes, "ought implies can." That is, no valid obligation can be imposed on anyone to do something that is impossible. And although empirical social science cannot definitively establish on the basis of its evidentiary base what are the limits of the possible (e.g., even if all swans are found by empirical investigation to be white, that in itself does not prove that a black swan is an impossibility, and even if history provides no known instances of classless societies, that does not prove that it could never be done), nevertheless one's best assessments of the limits of social possibility have to be based on one's best understanding of the structural features and dynamics of the real world that we can know only by empirical inquiry. Therefore, when sociologists like Roberto Michels began making arguments about an "iron law of oligarchy" and when political scientists studying public opinion and voting behavior documented a considerable gap between the knowledge and competencies of the electorate and the requisites placed on the citizens of the idealized democratic polity, these empirical findings tended to cut the props out from under or at least to complicate and compromise the normative claims of populist and participatory democratic theory (e.g., Kariel, 1970).

One final significant bridge from *is* to *ought* is worth noting here, particularly in the context of this edited volume and its topical focus. Normative theory is concerned with the human good, and one standard definition of the human good is "the object of rational desire." To the extent that is so, it clearly seems relevant to know what people out there in the world actually desire and consider to be good for them. And that information can only be provided by empirical investigation, canvasing a range of respondents to find out what people in fact accredit as good and whether their responses are largely convergent or instead marked by disagreement. The empirical data here cannot definitively adjudicate normative issues, but they at least shift the burden of proof toward those theorists who insist on establishing standards most of their fellow human beings reject.

Empirical Beliefs and Moral Validity

This logic provides the opening wedge for the second Humean argument that needs considered criticism. This is his avowed intention and recommendation "to introduce the experimental method of reasoning into moral subjects." (This language comes from the subtitle Hume, 1739/1948, gave to his *A Treatise of Human Nature*.) On its face, such an attempt seems to violate Hume's own admonition against moralists who move from *is* to *ought*. But his thinking ran as follows. The good, he argued (Hume, 1751/1948, Part I, Section IX, p. 249), is that which people find to be "useful or agreeable to themselves or others." (It is not entirely clear whether this represents a stipulative endorsement of a utilitarian conception of the good like Mill's statement of the creed in his essay on Utilitarianism or whether it is offered as a kind of Wittgensteinian endorsement of the meaning of terms as grounded in their ordinary use as he understands it or whether it is some combination of moral assertion and acquiescence in prevalent conventions.) Accordingly, to determine what the human good is in concrete terms, one needs to proceed "experimentally," that is, empirically, to determine what it is that people find to be in fact useful and agreeable.

But this proposal, which would seem to turn over to empirical social science the task and the power to settle normative questions, runs into difficulties of both principle and execution. The problem of principle is that some widely held views about what is right or good may be repugnant to many people's moral intuitions. In these cases, one would and should hesitate to accredit such views simply because of their empirically ascertained acceptability to large numbers of people in certain settings. Just because large sectors of the German populace endorsed or acquiesced in Hitler's genocidal anti-Semitism certainly does not provide moral validity for the Holocaust. Or to take a similar more recent case, the fact that many Iraqis see nothing amiss with Saddam's use of poison gas on the Kurdish population does not make such a policy morally licit. (A recent critique of American propaganda efforts used the denunciations of Saddam for human rights violations on radio messages broadcast into Iraq as one example of the propagandists' ineptitude because they failed to understand that many of the targets of the propaganda would not find these actions improper and delegitimating, as they assumed would be the case.)

As for the practical problem of carrying out Hume's proposed project, the phenomenon of moral disagreement poses serious difficulties. Either empirical inquiry must be taken as leading to moral cynicism or to a debilitating relativism—not what Hume intended—or else large blocks of respondents have to be disqualified in their judgment on the grounds that they are in some sense not adequately rational. Hume (1751/1948) resorted to the latter strategy of selective data counting to save his project, discrediting as deluded and hence discountable the moral judgments of those he mocked as "delirious and dismal hair-brained enthusiasts" (p. 251). In his *Enquiry Concerning the Principles of Morals* (Part I, Section IX), Hume proposed to include only the responses of "men of sense" who based their judgments about the human good on "their natural unprejudiced reason without the delusive glosses of superstition and false religion." The problem with this strategy of disqualification of respondents, however sincere though it may be, is that it undercuts the ostensive authority of the empirical evidence: Whether the evidence is to count or not is decided by the application of a priori philosophical standards, and if we can accredit these standards on the basis of philosophical judgments about what is rational, we could just as well proceed to our substantive conclusions directly from these judgments without taking what turns out to be a contingent and qualified detour through a gerrymandered body of "evidence."

Hume thus offers us a pair of apparently incompatible arguments about the relationship of the empirical and the normative, both of which turn out on critical examination to be seriously misleading. He insists on the logical gulf between empirical findings and normative judgments, but in the process leaves us with the misleading implication that facts about the world are not importantly relevant to nonnative claims on that world; he leaves mysterious and unacknowledged the way that our understanding of the limits of what is possible, the direction and force of human desires, and the causal relationships governing the attainment of various goods all create what Charles Taylor has called a "value slope" that goes a long way toward determining what practical political goals and policies seem reasonable and proper to pursue. Then he counsels people to reach their moral conclusions through an "experimental method" to determine what is right and good by canvasing public opinion. In doing so, however, he fails to make clear the way that any conclusions so derived are contingent on prior normative judgments of his own about what the human good in the abstract consists of (i.e., that the good is the useful and agreeable) and about what opinions out there are to be accredited as sensible and reasonable. Where does this leave one, then, with regard to negotiating the interface between normative and empirical inquiry into subjects such as justice, rights, and duties?

WHAT PHILOSOPHERS CAN LEARN FROM EMPIRICAL STUDIES OF JUSTICE

It leaves one, in the first place, telling normative theorists that they have much to learn from empirical studies of the kind included in this volume, for these findings are important to their enterprise. But second, it leaves one telling the normative theorists that they cannot expect to find their questions answered there and that they should resist any intimations to the contrary. In trying to ascertain what is right and good to do, it seems reasonable to acknowledge that what empirical social scientists discover about "commonsense justice" and conventional beliefs about what is humanly desirable add up to a prima facie case but by no means a dispositive case on behalf of those moral beliefs that they find to be widely endorsed.

Widespread endorsement of certain elements or standards of fairness, rights, and justice, such as what Stuart Hampshire (2000) has argued, is the almost universal acceptance of procedural norms of adversarial deliberative argumentation and constitutes a prima facie case on behalf of these standards for three basic reasons. The first of these reasons is found in the logic underlying the venerable notion of the *ius gentium*. The concept of *ius gentium* originated with Roman law, and it referred to the settled customary rules of peoples with whom the Romans had contact. Roman law gave recognition and accorded legitimacy to these rules when they did not conflict with provisions of Roman law itself. That notion later evolved into the idea, as in Grotius, that those customary norms widely endorsed by civilized peoples should be honored as the fruit of the moral sense or natural reason shared by all rational human beings. In the present context, then, the idea is that norms of justice and fairness widely embodied in the customs and conventions of peoples must be seen as carrying a presumption on their behalf by virtue of this empirically ascertained breadth of their acceptance. Second, a similar presumption would seem to follow from the liberal and democratic principles that ground legitimacy in the consent of the governed. And third, to the extent that people are willing to accord consideration to the moral judgment of their fellow creatures, it seems proper to respect, as Jefferson put it in the Declaration of Independence, the "decent opinion of mankind."

This prima facie case can, however, be overridden for legitimate and compelling reasons. What people generally believe is not always right, both as to fact and as to morality. Because people in Salem believed in witchcraft did not mean that anyone there was really a witch. Because most American colonists condoned the prevailing institutions of personal bondage did not mean that slavery was a morally acceptable practice. And just because it is a democratic principle that the people have the right, as Justice Holmes once wrote, to "go to hell in a handbasket if they so choose," does not mean that moral theorists, even those who recognize the legitimacy of democratic procedures, are obliged to acquiesce in making the lineaments of hell normative. Normative theorists cannot get lazy and simply count votes or test public sentiments. They are both entitled and obligated to deploy their powers of reasoning and their own critically examined moral intuitions in developing their conceptions of social justice and the public good. Thus normative theorists need to resist any intimations, some of which appear in places in the empirical chapters of this volume, that the absence of unanimity across cultures about principles of human rights means that belief in universally applicable principles of human rights is ipso facto untenable, or conversely, that the empirical finding that most people endorse certain ideas of rightness (e.g., meritocracy) validates such ideas and insulates them from critical attack. The finding, for example, that something like 75% of the American public endorses distributive norms at odds with Rawls's difference principle does not mean that Rawls's argument in *A Theory of Justice* (Klosko, 2000) must be abandoned. Likewise, if jurors are widely inclined to ignore judicial norms of evidence or standards for judgments of guilt or criteria for the definition of particular crimes, that does not mean that these standards are somehow wrong or inappropriate: The "common sense" of the jurors may be well intentioned but erroneous judgment produced by inexperience and a lack of understanding.

Another reason for normative theorists to attend to empirical studies of existing moral sensibilities is that normative theories depend for their purchase not only on claims of moral validity but also on considerations of practical feasibility and efficacy. Persuasive normative ideals have to be plausibly attainable and not merely morally attractive. For that reason, they come trailing empirical strings, as it were, to functional anchoring points that are needed to make them workable. Normative theorists usually recognize these necessities, but they tend to treat them too summarily or speculatively. At this juncture, their empirically oriented colleagues could help them out.

Two relevant examples of this nexus between empirical findings and normative force arise in the context of John Rawls's project of grounding democratic practices on moral foundations provided by the sense of justice. As Rawls has emphasized in his later work, his aspiration is not simply to provide our democratic society with compelling moral ideas but also to establish for it an axis of political stability. He has practical prudential hopes for his theory, not purely idealistic ones. Here the crucial claim is that contemporary pluralistic democratic societies cannot establish their legitimacy (in the empirical Weberian sense of that term) by reference to a common conception of the human good (e.g., as Aristotle proposed) because these societies are home to multiple and incompatible conceptions of the good life. But that inability, he insists, does not doom these societies to become mere pacts among citizens animated solely by self-interest, a situation that he argues is dangerously unstable because its bases of social cohesion are so fragile and problematic to sustain. Instead, contemporary democracies like the United States can ground their moral legitimacy and political cohesion in a broad "overlapping consensus" on particular principles of social justice that he specifies. His account of this putative consensus, however, is essentially speculative and impressionistic, an abstract model offered without much in the way of evidentiary warrants. Clearly, here is an open invitation and need for some empirical investigation. What evidence, if any, is out there to support the claim that such a consensus currently exists among the democratic populace or that, alternatively, some forces are visible that could reasonably be expected to create such a consensus in the foreseeable future (e.g., Klosko, 2000)?

The other important empirical question that is directly pertinent not only to the practical aspirations Rawls has for his theory but also to all arguments regarding the best strategies for creating and sustaining the legitimacy of democratic regimes concerns the nature and power of moral motives in determining human behavior. The empirical question here is this: "What is the strength and the basis of moral motives as compared with self-interested motives in human behavior?" And if moral considerations in fact have motivational power, can this power derive from adherence to abstract principles of justice or are moral motives derived from this source relatively weak by comparison with those that flow from communal solidarity and devotion to public good? Here, surely, is an area of empirical investigation within the provenance of social psychology that carries vast implications for democratic theory in general and for the persuasiveness of the practical claims advanced on behalf of Rawlsian "political liberalism" in particular.

To sharpen this point a bit and to clarify its theoretical significance, consider Patrick Neal's (1997, pp. 195–196) critical observations on the logic of what he calls the "stability arguments" of political liberals like Rawls and Charles Larmore. He wrote that these arguments

> assume not simply a link, but an extremely powerful one, between moral belief and motivation, one sufficient to override the force of whatever non-moral motivations move us. In the absence of an explanation of the assumed link between moral belief and motivated behavior, I cannot see why there is any reason to accept the argument of Rawls and Larmore that their . . . accounts are superior to a modus vivendi account . . . in terms of stability.

But, he continued, despite this need neither of them

> actually gives an account of moral motivation, though each seems to assume himself to have done so. . . . The link between belief and motivation is simply assumed on their account; they give an account of belief, but treat it as if it were an account of motivation.

To supply evidence on behalf of the crucial link between belief and motivation—and perhaps for explanatory theory as to why that evidence either is or is not forthcoming—one has to make recourse to the methods, the findings, and the theoretical arguments of empirical psychology. Do deontological political liberals like Rawls and Larmore have the stronger case when it comes to the requisites of political stability in contemporary democratic regimes? Or do modus vivendi liberals like Neal and David Gauthier (1986) have the better case? For the life of me I cannot see how these arguments can be assessed and adjudicated without making some serious forays into the vineyards of empirical social psychology.

WHAT SOCIAL SCIENTISTS CAN LEARN FROM MORAL PHILOSOPHY

In these several ways, then, normative theorists of politics need to attend carefully to what empirical social scientists can tell them about social dynamics and human behavior. Without solid anchoring in social reality, normative theories become adrift and ineffectual or positively misleading. The wisdom and prudence of phronesis cannot come about by immaculate conception. What, however, of the reciprocal relationship? Can social scientists learn anything useful from normative theory? Can the analytical methods or substantive arguments of political philosophy contribute to the clarity and relevance of empirical inquiry into social behavior? My own sense is that normative theorists have less to teach our empirically oriented colleagues than they have to teach us. Nonetheless, there are a few ways in which it can be profitable for social scientists to attend to the work of normative theorists or to collaborate with them. Let me conclude this chapter by specifying three of these.

First, normative theory can provide those who seek to investigate and understand "commonsense" moral beliefs and attitudes with empirical models, categories, and paradigms to guide their inquiry. The normative disputation that takes place among moral philosophers and social theorists is an excellent source to use in seeking to identify the most important moral orientations available to those who seek moral reference points for their actions. These orientations can then serve as Weberian "ideal types" by reference to which questions posed to experimental participants can be formulated, data can be gathered, and analytical categories can be deployed to set up empirical descriptions and explanations. Philosophers are human beings, too, and their models tend to embody intellectually refined versions of moral intuitions that arise and function among the general populace. If philosophers debate the relative merits of deontological and utilitarian and eudaemonistic and conventionalist theories of justice, therefore, it is reasonable to expect that "commonsense" conceptions of justice will tend to be somewhat cruder and less articulate versions of those positions. Some people out there will be commonsense deontologists who approach questions of distributive justice and social policy first and foremost in terms of what rights they claim for themselves and attribute to others. Others reason in terms of what they see as the common good. Others repair to customary rules and standards, and so on. Empirical students of everyday moral beliefs and their influence on behavior, therefore, are likely to find in normative literature one of the best possible sources of the categories and frameworks they need to help them sort through the booming and buzzing confusion of their nearly infinite potential data sets. Several of the empirical contributors to this volume exhibit an awareness of this relevance of normative categories to their analytical work, as do other practitioners of this craft like the political scientist Jennifer Hochschild (1981) and the experimental social psychologists Norman Frolich and Joe Oppenheimer (1990). All other things being equal, it can be expected that the more detailed and refined the knowledge of normative theoretical arguments possessed by empirical social scientists, the better their analytical categories are likely to be.

Normative theorists can also contribute to understanding some of the issues examined in the kinds of empirical investigation contained in this volume by drawing upon their own "empirical" knowledge base, which is their familiarity with both contemporary and historical arguments regarding justice or rights and with the political and ideological uses of those arguments. These contributions can in some instances add clarity to the discussion and in others may complicate it in useful ways. Let me give two examples.

The first example regards the apparent perplexity occasioned by Jefferson's language in the Declaration that "it is their right, it is their duty" to throw off the yoke of British rule. This claim seems puzzling if the languages of duties and rights are compatible only correlatively and not through overlap or identity because the one references a permissive claim and the other an obligation. In this instance, however, the widespread belief among the colonists, as seen in the sermonic literature of the day that sought to provide exegeses of scriptural doctrine concerning legitimate power, was that they were both entitled to throw off British rule on the grounds that their rights had been violated and also under a positive obligation to do so because of a divine imperative to resist tyrants (who violated God's mandate by arrogating to themselves an absolute power that was properly God's alone). This piece of intellectual history helps not only to resolve the apparent puzzle of the particular text but also to indicate that any attempt to understand the empirical functioning of discourses of rights and duties cannot proceed on the assumption that these discourses represent *either–or* alternatives that may not in some instances be embraced simultaneously by political actors.

The second example concerns the claim made in one of the empirical contributions to this volume to the effect that "the prevalence of rights talk may be a sign of relative empowerment" of disadvantaged or subordinate groups in society, whereas "duties talk may be characteristic of advantaged-group discourse" (see Louis & Taylor, chap. 5, this volume, p. 116). The logic here is that dominant groups characteristically talk of the duties of obedience to them and of the constituted authority that sustains their privileges, whereas groups that are trod on invoke rights claims to validate their attempts to get their oppressors' boots off their necks. Certainly there are examples that comport with that logic, as in what we often refer to as the civil rights revolution in this country.

However, the record of normative theories of rights and duties and the political uses of these arguments provides some evidence to the contrary and suggests that the attempt to align rights appeals with subordinate groups and appeals to duties with dominant groups may be too hasty and potentially misleading. As Mary Ann Glendon (1991, p. 24) argued in *Rights Talk*, the pivotal and decisive paradigm for rights discourse in this country was Blackstone's absolute and unnuanced defense of property rights in his *Commentaries*. The classes most attracted to the discourse of rights, then, were property-owning classes that are not subordinate groups. Rights discourse could be used as a fence to shelter property owners from the reach of the state (which can be "liberal" or "conservative", I suppose, depending on whether that state is a monarchy wanting to levy taxes without consent or a democratic government wanting to redistribute economic resources), but it also could be used and was used to defend the established property rights and possessions of better off groups against the design of have-nots against these holdings— against, as Locke (1690/1924) put it in *Second Treatise of Civil Government* (Chap. V, Section 34, p. 133), "the fancy or covetousness of the quarrelsome and contentious." Both of these uses were accepted as legitimate by the Founders, and both are on display in Madison's deployment of rights language in Federalist 10.

The contemporary analogue of this deployment of rights discourse on behalf of the self-protective claims of property holders is found in conservative and libertarian arguments such as those of Richard Epstein (1985) and Robert Nozick (1971). Nozick began his argument with the words "Individuals have rights, and there are things no person or group may do to them without violating their rights," (p. ix) and these rights, he asserted, include an absolute entitlement to any property honestly gained or freely given. This is not the discourse of the disenfranchised. Contemporary arguments over affirmative action, to take another example, also seem to confute the claim that subordinate groups invoke rights, whereas dominant groups invoke duties. Here it is the critics of state action to privilege historically subordinate groups who build their case around claims of rights infringement, whereas the principal arguments in defense of such policies are currently grounded in social utility and the social values of inclusiveness and "diversity." The general conclusion to be drawn from these examples taken from intellectual history and recent moral philosophy is this: One cannot be entirely comfortable with any claim made on the basis of particular empirical examples to the effect that one can reliably associate rights claims with subordinate groups or assume that dominant groups are somehow likely to abandon invocations of rights and repair to insistence on duties. That is not logically necessary, and there are too many examples that confute this alleged relationship of social status and moral languages.

CONCEPTUAL CLARITY AND EMPIRICAL INVESTIGATION

A last way in which social scientists who study the role of moral beliefs and political ideals in shaping political behavior can benefit from collaboration with normative theorists involves the research component that Siegfried Hoppe-Graff and Hye-On Kim (chap. 3, this volume) refer to as "conceptual work." Useful empirical investigation and explanation of social behavior cannot proceed by a random compilation of facts and observations. The strategy of data collection is driven by a conceptual framework of some sort that directs the attention of researchers and suggests to them what they need to look for. And the role of concepts is even more fundamental than that, for as philosophers of science have taken pains in recent decades to remind us, the observations that produce research data are themselves in some inescapable ways "theory laden."

So the "conceptual work" aspect of empirical social science is fundamental to its success. Fuzzy or inappropriate or incoherent concepts will corrupt and disable at its base our understanding of what is going on in the social phenomena we are examining. In Wittgenstein's view, indeed, this problem was what accounted for the difficulties and explanatory incapacities of the social sciences by comparison with the natural sciences. From Comte and

Mill on to the present day, the relative weakness of the social sciences has been attributed to their relative newness and immaturity. They are, as the recurrent phrase goes, "infant sciences." But that argument has, some two centuries later, worn thin and unconvincing, Wittgenstein insisted. The problems of the social sciences will not be solved by time and the aggregation of ever more data. The deeper problems of the social sciences result from difficulties in formulating concepts and relating them to data. Psychology, Wittgenstein (1958, p. 232) wrote, and he could have said the same thing of the other social sciences, is not an infant science; instead, the problem is that conceptual difficulties cause "problem and method [to] pass one another by."

To deal with the difficulties of good concept formation and the apposite linking of concepts and data, social scientists can make collaborative efforts with normative social theorists that can be useful and productive—especially concerning some of the concepts that are specifically normative ones like rights and duties. Normative theorists have experience not only in dealing with these concepts but also in the whole process of sorting through concepts, clarifying them, and seeking to minimize linguistic confusion, as these are standard tasks of the trade. This kind of clearing of conceptual underbrush is what Locke referred to as "under laborer" work, and philosophical students of politics and society engage in it continually, even if not always terribly effectively.

Political philosophers have the methodological tools and the background, therefore, to serve as useful interlocutors and critics of the concepts that empirical students of social behavior seek to deploy in the context of their investigations. No doubt the queries and objections that we are likely to raise in this context will at times be experienced as an irritating impediment to moving ahead on the empirical front, but confronting these conceptual issues can nonetheless be very helpful in heading off fruitless lines of inquiry and preventing research from bogging down in conceptual quagmires. In the context of the empirical research agenda of the contributors to this volume, normative analysts might raise cautionary queries and challenges in a number of ways. Consider a few examples for purposes of illustration.

Political philosophers can be useful, first, in helping to sort out and distinguish issues that are empirical and those that are conceptual. This is not always an easy thing to do in the social sciences because human actions possessed of meaning and intentionality can be said to be "lived concepts." As Peter Winch (1958, p. 23) has put it, "social relations are expressions of ideas about reality." Hence, the empirical and the conceptual overlap and intermingle in social scientific descriptions and explanations: They are, as it were, the internal and external faces of the same "event" or social "phenomenon." The logical distinction still remains, however, and it is important methodologically. One problem that arises here is that social scientists have a tendency at times to construe conceptual issues as though they were empirical questions to be adjudicated by gathering relevant observations when in fact these issues are impervious to "external" evidence of this sort and can only be addressed by an "internal" analysis of the logic of the concept and the language game in which it plays. The result is misguided effort and in some instances conceptual confusion and misleading claims.

In the present volume, for example, most philosophers would surely be inclined to say that it is an example of this confusion of the relative functions of concepts and data to pose as an empirical question: "How is it that rights need not be exercised or can be waived whereas waiving duties is not so easily done?" This in fact is not an empirical question at all but one that can be answered and can only be answered by explicating the meaning and use of the concepts involved. It is internal to the concept of rights, part of their logic, that they can be foregone, just as it is internal to the logic of duties that they cannot be ignored on one's own choosing. Rights are entitlements and permissions and protections—goods owned by the holder for his or her own benefit. Hence the holder can without objection opt to waive or give away rights he or she possesses because doing so can only be at the holder's expense and not at cost to some other party. And such charity is permitted us or at least no moral objection can be raised against it. It is part of the very meaning of duties, conversely, that they are binding on those subject to them. They are constraints on people's range of action, social obligations imposed for the benefit of others. (The etymological stem of the word *obligation* comes from *ligare*, which means "to bind.") Strictly speaking, then, empirical investigation is irrelevant to answering the question cited above as it is posed. That question can be addressed only and fully by the tools of conceptual analysis, and the energies of empirical inquiries can be directed toward puzzles amenable to the kind of evidence only they can provide.

Social scientists are also prone to construing as technical problems issues that arise in the context of "operationalizing" concepts and "coding" responses when these issues have conceptual and philosophical dimensions that technical virtuosity alone cannot settle. Is it appropriate, for example, to categorize as duty based the act of feeding the parking meters of other people's cars when they are about to be ticketed? In part, this is an empirical question, albeit not one that can be adjudicated by purely external observation of the acts in question. We have to know the actor's state of mind or motives. We would, therefore, have to interrogate the person who did this to know why he or she fed the meters. And then the philosophical or conceptual question would come into play: Is this behavior properly construable as a response to a sense of duty? All morally driven acts, after all, do not have to be pushed into one of two boxes: rights or duties. Perhaps this was understood by the actor as, and hence was in fact, an act of "random kindness," that is, a morally noncompulsory act of charity or superogatory virtue. Or possibly it was an action taken simply to impede and frustrate the punitive exactions of authority figures, a thumb to the eye of the officer poised to write the traffic ticket. There is in fact important empirical work to be done here, but we also need to keep our concepts clear and refined in order to reach appropriate conclusions about the role that notions of rights and duties (and other moral notions, perhaps) play in shaping human behavior.

There are two final conceptual observations. The first of these is that it is important not to conflate the notions of something that is right to do and something that you have a right to do (e.g., see chap. 3, this volume, for two such locutions). As my political theory colleague William Galston never tires of reminding us, we may very well have a right to do something that may nonetheless not be the right thing to do. We have the right to waste our natural talent, to engage in political demagoguery, and to stand idly by and watch someone drown. But it is not right to do any these things. The second conceptual observation is that it is potentially misleading to deploy the terms *individualism* and *collectivism* uncritically. These are at best rather crude and conceptually fuzzy ideal-type constructs. It is difficult to specify exactly what these terms mean in a concrete and specific sense; also, real-world societies embody a great multiplicity of patterns of relating people to families, groups, institutions of civil society, and the state. If theoretical distinctions are to be invoked to characterize and distinguish among the possibilities in this respect, they will have to be nuanced and numerous rather than simple and dichotomous.

CONCLUSION

In the many ways and for the many reasons canvased above, then, all of us who seek to understand moral ideas and how these bear on social behavior both as legitimate standards and as causal determinants have much to learn from those who labor on the other side of the divide between philosophy and science, between the normative and the empirical. Those of us on the side of philosophy need to attend carefully to the findings of our empirically oriented colleagues to know which of our ideals and aspirations can reasonably hope to achieve the grounding within and the purchase on the world we live in that they require to be effective and which of our philosophically generated moral claims and aspirations are destined to flit uselessly about as mere ghostly phantasmagoria of the academic imagination. Conversely, our familiarity with normative argumentation and its history can provide useful assistance to empirical social scientists as they seek to give their inquiries theoretical sophistication and practical relevance. The kind of interdisciplinary engagement the editors of this volume have sought to create is, therefore, as welcome as it is rare. We can hope that others will follow their lead and be motivated to contribute from their own resources to the intellectual cross-fertilization that can benefit us all.

REFERENCES

Ayer, A. J. (1936). *Language, truth, and logic.* London: Gollancz.

Epstein, R. (1985). *Takings: Private property and the power of eminent domain.* Cambridge, MA: Harvard University Press.

Frolich, N., & Oppenheimer, J. (1990). Choosing justice in experimental democracies with production. *American Political Science Review, 84,* 461–480.

Gauthier, D. (1986). *Morals by agreement.* Oxford, England: Oxford University Press.

Glendon, M. A. (1991). *Rights talk.* New York: Free Press.

Hamilton, A., Madison, J., & Jay, J. (1961). *The federalist papers.* New York: New American Library. (Original work published 1787–1788)

Hampshire, S. (2000). *Justice is conflict.* Princeton, NJ: Princeton University Press.

Hochschild, J. (1981). *What's fair? American beliefs about distributive justice.* Cambridge, MA: Harvard University Press.

Hume, D. (1948). A treatise of human nature. In H. D. Aiken (Ed.), *Hume's moral and political philosophy* (pp. 1–169). New York: MacMillan. (Original work published 1739)

Hume, D. (1948). Enquiry concerning the principles of morals. In H. D. Aiken (Ed.), *Hume's moral and political philosophy* (pp. 173–291). New York: MacMillan. (Original work published 1751)

Kariel, H. (Ed.). (1970). *Frontiers of democratic theory.* New York: Random House.

Klosko, G. (2000). *Democratic procedures and liberal consensus.* Oxford, England: Oxford University Press.

Locke, J. (1924). *Second treatise of civil government.* London: J. M. Dent and Sons. (Original work published 1690)

Neal, P. (1997). *Liberalism and its discontents.* New York: New York University Press.

Nozick, R. (1971). *Anarchy, state, and utopia.* New York: Basic Books.

Rawls, J. (1999). *A theory of justice* (Rev. ed.). Cambridge, MA: Harvard University Press.

Urmson, J. O. (1968). *The emotive theory of ethics.* New York: Oxford University Press.

Weber, M. (1949). *The methodology of the social sciences.* (E. Shils & H. Finch, Eds. & Trans.). New York: Free Press.

Winch, P. (1958). *The idea of a social science.* London: Routledge & Kegan Paul.

Wittgenstein, L. (1958). *Philosophical investigations.* (3rd ed., G. E. M. Anscombe, Trans.). New York: Macmillan.

13

RIGHTS AND DUTIES: PSYCHOLOGY'S CONTRIBUTIONS, NORMATIVE ASSESSMENTS, AND FUTURE RESEARCH

FATHALI M. MOGHADDAM AND NORMAN J. FINKEL

> "Then felt I like some watcher of the skies
> When a new planet swims into his ken;"
> —John Keats, *On First Looking Into Chapman's Homer*

A new planet came into our horizon during the course of developing this book, bringing the exciting vision of increased communications and collaboration across disciplines toward better understanding human rights and duties. Even within the discipline of psychology, scholars have had few communications with one another on the topic because in most cases their research has been formulated in the terminology of subdisciplines and published in different specialized journals that are rarely read by those outside a particular, narrow field. Bringing psychologists and their empirical research together to discuss these sets of questions concerning rights and duties has itself proved to be a constructive and instructive step. The addition of a philosopher, a historian, and a political scientist provided a critical and in-depth assessment of psychology's contribution both as it is and as it could be.

In chapter 1, we introduced 19 focal questions, most of which were addressed in Part II within the chapters by our contributing psychologists. In this final chapter, we focus our attention on three themes that emerge from psychology's contributions and from the assessments by our normative scholars. These three themes underlie the 19 questions posed in chapter 1 and serve to focus future research directions. The three themes concern (a) the question of universals in human rights and duties, (b) the relationship between rights and duties, and (c) the research methods used in the study of rights and duties. At the conclusion of each of these sections, we highlight a research area that we believe deserves special attention on the part of psychologists in the future.

ARE THERE UNIVERSALS IN THE DOMAIN OF RIGHTS AND DUTIES?

The question of whether there are universal rights and duties may appear to refer to an already closed issue because the United Nations Universal Declaration of Human Rights (see Appendix for full text) and other such documents seem to proclaim that there are universals, at least in the domain of rights. However, such declarations are merely affirmations of "what should be," in the eyes of many, rather than "what is"; thus, they reflect aspirations rather than the actual state of affairs. A review of Amnesty International's annual reports makes it clear that each year scores of governments, including those of Western nations, are alleged to trample on the rights of their own citizens, oftentimes trampling on just those rights that are specified in the United Nations Declaration. In acknowledgment of the rift between ideals and actualities, the question we posed can be restated as two questions: (a) Are there universals in the attitudes people have toward rights and duties? and (b) Are there universals in actual behavior in the domain of rights and duties? The first question concerns rhetoric, whereas the second concerns actual practices.

Spini and Doise (chap. 2, this volume) provide the clearest evidence in support of the view that there are universals in the rhetoric of human rights, for they show strong patterns of attitudinal similarities across the scores of cultures they investigate. Discussions by Hoppe-Graff and Kim (chap. 3, this volume) and Moghaddam and Riley (chap. 4, this volume) also present tentative support for some universals in attitudes toward human rights, and Moghaddam and Riley present support for the view that this occurs in the area of duties as well. This evidence involves attitudinal similarities in some domains, although these researchers survey a smaller number of cultures than Spini and Doise. Yet Hoppe-Graff and Kim show rather striking differences between German and Korean adolescents in regard to duties in both their ontology and ontogeny, whereas Finkel's (chap. 7, this volume) results are from cases in which rights and duties clash and reveal no universal winner across cases. To the contrary, his results reveal that citizens use a moral analysis in which rights and duties are grounded in particular unfairnesses and measured by moral principles that consider how far and fairly these rights and duties are extended and whether the underlying motives that propel these competing claims deserve moral support.

However, with respect to behavior in the domain of rights and duties, there is far less evidence pointing our way. For example, Moghaddam and Riley (chap. 4, this volume) argue from a cultural evolutionary perspective that the challenges common to human groups have created certain universals in behavior in rights and duties in which the evolutionary advantages of more advanced communications systems and the limitations of the means through which humans can communicate gave rise to turn-taking practices common to all societies. Still, it becomes clear that one area of research needing the increased attention of psychologists is actual behavior (as opposed to mere attitudes, rhetoric, and discourse) in the domain of rights and duties, a point that both Harré (chap. 10, this volume) and Haskell (chap.11, this volume) accent in their commentaries. A central unanswered question, then, concerns the extent to which behavioral patterns will correspond to the attitudinal universals identified so far.

On the other side of the debate, the idea of universals per se is vigorously attacked by Louis and Taylor (chap. 5, this volume), and Worchel (chap. 9, this volume), and their rebuttals are similar. These authors evaluate rights and duties in terms of power relations, arguing that both rights and duties are highly influenced by majority groups who possess the resources necessary to influence the legal and political systems that legislate and put to practice interpretations of rights and duties. Second, they assume that each group will discuss rights and duties from the perspective of its self-interest; whereas minorities give priority to rights, majority groups give priority to duties because it serves their different and often competing interests to do so. Thus, for example, the rich owners of capital focus on the duty of citizens to put maximum effort into their jobs, but the workers give priority to their right to a better wage and better living conditions. To use another example from Moghaddam and Riley's work (chap. 4, this volume), during parent–child interactions, parents, a majority group, give priority to the duties of children (e.g., "It's your job to clean your room, why haven't you done it?"), whereas children give priority to their alleged rights (e.g., "I have a right to go out and play with my friends").

The proposition that majority groups give priority to duties and minority groups give priority to rights implies that rights and duties are defined locally. That is, groups define and give priority to rights and duties as it suits their particular interests and accords with local norms. If a group loses or gains power or if change occurs in the power status of other groups in that context, then rights and duties will probably come to be defined and prioritized differently by that group. For example, a group that opposed labor unions yesterday may support them today because of a change in its own status vis-à-vis managers, owners, and other power groups. This argument leads to the conclusion that universals do not exist in the domain of rights and duties.

But in chapter 4, Moghaddam and Riley propose that there is an implied underlying universal rule to this scenario: Minority groups always give priority to rights, it is claimed, whereas majority groups always give priority to duties. Thus, the very idea that majority groups give priority to duties and minority groups to rights is endorsing a pattern that they see as universal. This proposition does not go unchallenged from normative scholars.

The political scientist Spragens (chap. 12, this volume) admonishes psychologists for ignoring the historical examples in which majority groups give priority to rights rather than duties and minority groups give priority to duties rather than rights. For example, Spragens reminds us of "affirmative rights" confrontations that typically feature minorities accenting the duty of the majority to be inclusive and promote diversity and the now-excluded majority members arguing for their rights. And in a second example from Spragens's chapter, British property owners, who are in terms of power relations the majority group, cite their property rights, whereas common citizens holding no land, in terms of power relations the minority group, cite duties to all. Spragens's contrary examples rebut the arguments made by Louis and Taylor (chap. 5, this volume) and Worchel (chap. 9, this volume) along with the underlying universal pattern proposed by Moghaddam and Riley. It is noteworthy that Spragens offers empirical examples rather than normative arguments to make his point and that his current and historic instances add nuance and correction to generalized assertions that, in the light of these facts, seem too sweeping.

Empirical facts can also liberate us from certain conceptual and normative snares. For example, when we look closely rather than abstractly, we may find that in most cases in which a majority is giving priority to the rights of minorities, it is actually a vanguard within the majority group taking this action. The role of such a vanguard has been seen by intergroup theorists to be absolutely essential for revolutionary and reform movements. A review of major reform movements, including the important emancipation movements of the 19th century and the feminist, ethnic, and gay movements of the 20th century, all reveal an important role for such a vanguard arising from the majority group but most directly serving the interests of the minority group. However, it could be argued that this vanguard, derived from the majority group and focused on minority rights, is actually a power minority. For example, in a contemporary case that is far from settled, those members of the Catholic church who support and agitate for gay rights or for women priests are a power minority, and if they win the day at some future point, this will likely result because this vanguard persuaded the authorities and the rest of the Church to take this path. Moreover, this persuasive message, according to Louis and Taylor in chapter 5, will likely remind the majority of its duties to all, and thus the realignment of rights, if it occurs, is likely to result from this rhetorical change regarding the concept of duties such that the concept dilates from a narrow construction to one that is broader and more embracing.

The same point can be made regarding the case of property owners who at various times have claimed rights that protect them against excessive taxation and other types of government intervention. For example, White farm owners in Zimbabwe and South Africa, particularly since the early 1990s, have cited their rights as property owners against government plans to redistribute land so that more arable land falls into the hands of Blacks. But, again, the issue of definitions arises: Surely these Whites can be considered to be a power minority because they no longer control the central governments in their societies.

This hand-in-hand change between rights and duties, as the historian Haskell (chap. 11, this volume) reminds us, may be much more visible on the rights side of things, for rights seem to march down the center of the street to drums and cymbals, whereas the less visible and less vocal duties walk in parallel down the crowded sidewalk. Haskell would be quick to point out that if gay rights and women priests did result, they would result because the majority authority had come to accept the correlative duty (Feinberg, 1969). Still, Feinberg makes the "doctrine of the logic of correlativity" a small point within his larger aim to illustrate the separability of rights and duties and discuss its consequences. Feinberg's article details a "thought experiment" about a hypothetical Nowheresville community where a beneficent Kantian world is imagined to exist and where duties are all and rights are nowhere to be found. This contemplated Nowheresville illustrates that a fissure between rights and duties can certainly be contemplated.

But we do not have to venture into the make-believe Nowheresville world to infer that independence is possible; we can simply cite, as Harré does (chap. 10, this volume), historical exemplars of duty-based societies. If we stand back, though, we once again see that the argument is being fought through empirical examples rather than normative formulations. Taken together, Harré and Spragens (chap. 12, this volume) cite archival historical examples, noting facts, peoples, and societies "as they have been," to paraphrase Rousseau's words, Rawls's argument, and the point we made in our introductory chapter, whereas psychologists typically cite aggregate findings from more controlled studies that sometimes reveal correlativity, independence, and relationships in between. The examples cited by Harré and Spragens derive from different empirical methods, but they are empirical nonetheless.

In terms of implications for research, the realization of a "global village" through vastly expanded and improved international communications, transportation, and trade as well as increased cross-national movements of human populations has led to an urgent need for further psychological research on the universality of human rights and duties. Human beings from different cultural and ideological backgrounds are coming in contact with one another far more frequently, and we need to know more about their similarities and differences with respect to rights and duties. Psychological research in this domain should benefit from and link with research in comparative law on legal traditions across cultures. However, there is a need to attend to behavior as it is in practice as well as what is espoused in rhetoric. So far, research in psychology and in comparative law has focused on rights and duties as reflected in attitudes and in written law and not enough on actual practices. It is particularly important to unravel how rights and duties relate to one another in everyday life. This leads us toward the second of our three questions in which we take up the relationship between rights and duties.

THE RELATIONSHIP BETWEEN RIGHTS AND DUTIES

In considering the relationship between rights and duties, we give particular importance to two issues. A first issue concerns the extent to which either rights or duties are replaceable by the other as opposed to being fixed and separate, and a second related issue concerns the extent to which rights and duties are compatible or antagonistic; the alternative approaches can be conceived as lying at some point in a space delimited by two vectors (see Figure 13.1). The first vector has as its polar extremes *completely replaceable* (i.e., where the same behavior can be described as a right or a duty depending on circumstances) and *completely fixed* (i.e., where the rights and duties have set meanings that are stable across situations and time). The extreme poles of the second vector are *completely compatible* (i.e., where rights and duties can exist side by side without competition) and *completely antagonistic* (i.e., where rights and duties are inevitably in direct conflict with one another). This creates four types of possible relationships between rights and duties, from the most to the least fluid (see Figure 13.1): Rights and duties are (a) replaceable and compatible, (b) replaceable but antagonistic, (c) compatible but fixed, and (d) antagonistic and fixed.

It is in relation to these four possibilities that we should consider the issue of balance between rights and duties. How we conceptualize balance depends in large part on the assumptions we make about the validity of each of these four possibilities. For example, if our assumption is that rights and duties are replaceable and compatible (Possibility 1 in Figure 13.1), then there should be a great deal of room for manipulating the stipulated rights and duties to achieve an acceptable balance. However, if we assume that rights and duties are antagonistic and fixed (Possibility 4 in Figure 13.1), then presumably we can change far less to achieve a balance. This continuum from least to most fluid is also in an important way relevant to the basis on which we assume people make decisions and take actions on rights and duties: Is this done on the basis of stable and fundamental principles or on the

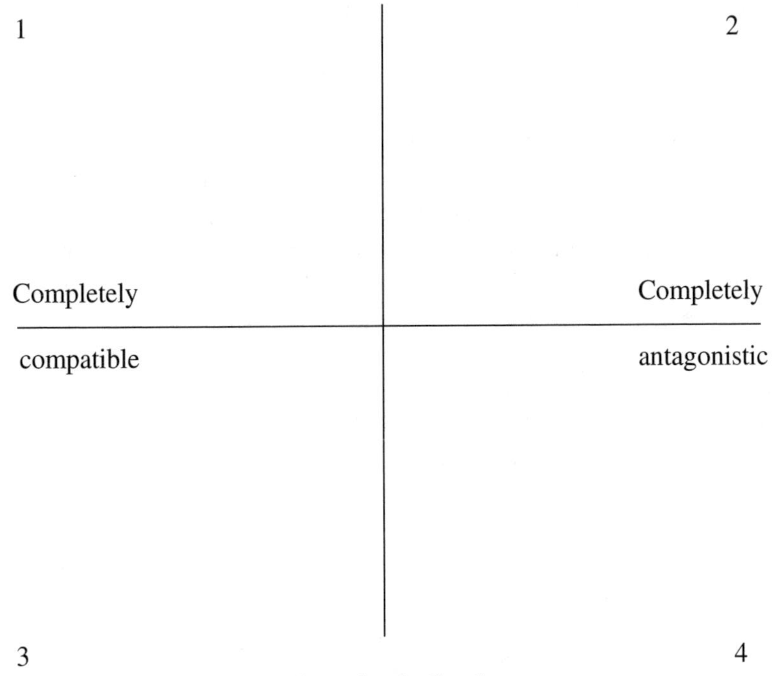

Figure 13.1. Diagrammatical representation of alternative approaches to describing rights and duties.

basis of changes in circumstances? If we recall the findings from Finkel's work (chap. 7, this volume), abstract principles accounted for very little of the variance explained when looking at participants' decisions and reasons, whereas circumstantial factors did predict well.

If behavior in the domain of rights and duties is based on certain overarching principles, then we should find consistency of behavior across contexts. For example, a government that has expressed a principled leaning in favor of certain interpretations of rights and duties should not alter its interpretation as circumstances change. In Kohlberg's (1976) terms, if behavior in the domain of rights and duties is at the principled or postconventional stage, then the context should not alter the interpretation of rights and duties. However, both experimental evidence (Finkel, chap. 7, this volume; Moghaddam & Vuksanovic, 1990) and life experience argue against such principled consistency.

In the context of these vectors, consider the actions of President George W. Bush's administration after the tragedy of September 11, 2001. This is a historically important example because September 11th and the events that have followed have had a dramatic impact on both the United States and the rest of the world, something akin to the Japanese attack on Pearl Harbor in 1941. Thus, we are interested in this crisis because of its monumental importance and because the way it was handled by the government can inform us about actual behavior in the domain of rights and duties. We are not interested in the political aspects of the September 11 tragedy and the government's response to it.

The rhetoric of the Bush administration when it first came into power indicated that priority would be given to individual rights with a promise to diminish the size and reach of the federal government. In Finkel's terms (chap. 7, this volume), this administration came to power questioning the reach and motive of the rights and duties claimed by the federal government; in terms of Moore, Spernak, and Chung (chap. 8, this volume), this indicated a shift toward greater power in the hands of consumers of government services, "the we the people"; in Worchel's terms (chap. 9, this volume), this is a shift in favor of the individual rather than the group.

But in the changed, post-September 11 context, there was a dramatic shift in the Bush administration's rhetoric and behavior in the domain of rights and duties: There was a sharp rise in "government interests" (Gottlieb, 1993) or what Karen Orren (2000) called "officers' rights," in which the administration claims a right to promote and protect the safety of the public. In times past, however, this interest would have typically been expressed as a duty on the government's part to promote and protect the safety of the citizens. Thus we seem to have an example of replaceability. Whether the use of the rhetoric of rights as opposed to the rhetoric of duties conveys a stronger force in this culture is another unanswered question, one deserving further empirical testing.

The shift in emphasis on the part of the Bush administration is most clearly reflected in the Justice Department's handling of José Padilla, also known as Abdullah al Muhajir, who is a United States citizen accused of being part of a plot to make and explode a dirty bomb and to commit other crimes, and in the case of Yaser Esam Hamdi, a Louisiana-born man who was declared an enemy combatant by the Justice Department. Both men were held in military brigs without charge and without access to lawyers. In a series of editorials in *The Washington Post,* it was alleged that Padilla's and Hamdi's rights under the First, Fourth, Fifth, Sixth, Eighth, and Fourteenth Amendments had been violated (e.g., "Civics Lessons for Prosecutors," 2002; "Dying Behind Closed Doors," 2002; "Still No Lawyers," 2002; "The Case Against Mr. Hamdi," 2002; "The I-Said-So Test," 2002) and that the administration's duty to citizens had either been forgotten or had been replaced by its rights claim.

Such cases highlight the variability, and perhaps flexibility, of how rights and duties are interpreted and implemented in practice. For example, a simple statement such as "Mr. Padilla has a right to speak" can be interpreted as "Mr. Padilla has the right to speak to an attorney, to tell his story, and to seek legal counsel." But it may also be interpreted as "Mr. Padilla has a right and a duty to speak to the government and tell all he might know about terrorist networks and plots." The ease with which supporters of the government's position move between rights and duties suggests that there is both variation and flexibility in how rights and duties play out in behavior. As Tyler points out (chap. 6, this volume), when a nation's security is at stake, individuals are likely to waive their rights, show deference to the government, and even empower the government to act on citizens' behalf. But citizens often disagree as to the ultimate motives of the political party in power, and they may question whether security issues are being used as a camouflage for limiting the rights of certain individuals while the rights of other individuals are strongly protected. The flexibility and apparent replaceability of rights and duties in actual behavior argue against the validity of a general rule to the effect that rights and duties are antagonistic; rather, it would seem that rights and duties could be either antagonistic or compatible, depending on the context and the interests of the parties involved.

But far more psychological research is needed to try to unravel possible differences between types of rights and duties. For example, supererogatory duties, duties an individual will be praised for performing but not morally blamed for omitting, seem to stem from a personal conviction that "something must be done." For example, in the play *Antigone*, written by Sophocles (442 B.C./1977) almost 2,500 years ago, the king has forbidden that anyone bury Polyneicês, one of Antigone's brothers who was killed in a rebellion against the king. But Antigone feels that she must do her duty and bury her brother even though it means certain death if she is found out and even though her own sister Ismene tells her that they should yield to those in authority. Is there a rights equivalent to supererogatory duties in the everyday practices of people? Perhaps not, but everyday behavior demonstrates types of rights that may not have an equivalent in the realm of duties. For example, we are all familiar with rights that exist on paper but are not realized in practice (violations of the United Nations Universal Declaration of Human Rights reflect this situation), but there are also instances in which individuals have rights on paper that they explicitly choose to forego for the sake of a larger goal. Consider the case of a newspaper editor who chooses not to exercise the right to free speech by voluntarily not publishing a story that could damage national morale during a time of war. Do people perceive an equivalent to this in the realm of duties? Such questions deserve more attention from research psychologists.

The important characteristics of rights and duties, then, including possible degrees of replaceability and compatibility, should become a major focus for psychological research. Again, such research needs to examine both actual behavior and expressed attitudes (practice and theory), rather than just the latter. Experimental methods traditionally used in psychology are well suited to explore the conditions in which rights and duties become more or less replaceable and compatible. Indeed, the four possibilities (1–4) identified in Figure 13.1 involving varying degrees and combinations of compatibility and replaceability seem almost ideally suited for experimental examination. Of course, this does not necessitate an exclusive reliance on traditional experimental methods. Indeed, there are a number of important reasons why alternative, qualitative, and normative approaches should also be used, and we turn to this issue next.

RESEARCH METHODS AND RIGHTS AND DUTIES ACROSS CULTURES

The third and final question we raise concerns the research methodologies used to investigate rights and duties. The studies reported in this book for the most part use traditional survey methodologies and quantitative scaling techniques, in some cases with some experimental or quasi-experimental manipulations. The philosopher of science Harré (chap. 10, this volume) has rightly admonished psychologists for neglecting the deeper flaws of traditional methods. Psychologists see traditional methods as having some advantages, but they may not be appropriate for certain contexts and questions. For example, traditional quantitative methods tend to lack the sensitivity needed to get at the more subtle nuances of cross-cultural differences in rights and duties. In particular, such possible differences concern both the meaning of and importance given to duties. As an example, let us briefly consider the case of duties in the Islamic Republic of Iran.

The 1978–1979 revolution in Iran toppled the Shah and led to the establishment of an Islamic Republic. Iranians are predominantly Shi‘a Muslims, Shi‘a being a minority sect that makes up about 15% of the total world Muslim population with the majority being Sunni Muslims. Rights and duties in Iran must be understood in the context of how Shi‘a Islam is practiced there. Central to this practice is the concept of *marja-i-taqlid*, the source of emulation. Every Shi‘a Muslim has a duty to select from among the *mujtahid* of the day (spiritual leaders recognized as rightful interpreters of holy scripture) a *marja-i-taqlid* to emulate. The follower has a duty to obey the *marja-i-taqlid*.

The balance between rights and duties of the follower becomes clear when we consider how the concept of *marja-i-taqlid* is incorporated into the Constitution of the Islamic Republic of Iran. On the one hand, this Constitution gives citizens the right to vote on many issues. Article 6 states the following:

> In the Islamic Republic of Iran, the affairs of the country must be administered on the basis of public opinion expressed by the means of elections, including the election of the President, the representatives of the

National Consultative Assembly, and the members of the councils, or by means of referenda in matters specified in other articles of this Constitution. (Arjomand, 1988, p. 376)

This basis would seem to give priority to the rights of citizens in these very important matters. However, closer scrutiny reveals that it is duties rather than rights that have the upper hand. Article 4 states, "All civil, penal, financial, economic, administrative, cultural, military, political, and other laws and regulations must be based on Islamic criteria." In the Preamble as well as in Article 5, the Constitution makes clear that what is and what is not correct according to Islamic criteria is to be judged by the one person who from among all of the *mujtahedin* is seen as most worthy to lead. This is what Ayatollah Khomeini argued for under the title *vilayat al-faqih* (Khomeini, 1981). This person basically acts as a *marja-i-taqlid* for the country. If one person is not recognized as being above all others in leadership quality, a group of *mujtaheds* will serve the same function. This Islamic leadership is further buttressed by the Guardian Council (Article 91), which decides whether legislation passed by the representatives of the people meets Islamic criteria.

Thus, the rights of the people (e.g., to vote) are trumped by the duties of the people to follow and obey. The people have a right to vote, but their representatives and the legislation they pass have to be approved by Islamic leaders whom the people are duty bound to follow and obey. The point underlined by this example is that there are certain nuances of the balance between rights and duties that are better assessed through qualitative methods and critical assessment rather than through traditional survey methods. Also, in assessing a given situation, researchers must proceed on the basis of fairly detailed knowledge of local cultural conditions.

This raises major challenges for those who conduct multinational surveys because of the difficulties of developing test instruments that both reflect local needs and characteristics and tap into potential universals. Future research on human rights and duties needs to adopt a more multimethod approach, one involving both qualitative and quantitative techniques. No doubt, greater interactions between psychologists and researchers from other disciplines interested in human rights and duties, such as those in comparative law, could gradually lead to greater appreciation for a range of research methods. In particular, researchers must have available methods that meet the challenge of deception: how to study human rights and duties among a group of people who intentionally try to give misleading answers.

A multimethod approach is also important in exploring the relationship between different types of rights and duties. For example, behavior in the domain of supererogatory duties can be examined using traditional quantitative methods, such as through a survey as conducted by Doise and Spini, or through experimental or quasi-experimental procedures lasting an hour or two as used by Finkel. However, an alternative qualitative approach could involve case studies of the evolution of actual specific supererogatory duties over years or decades. The latter kind of research would fit more with the tradition of comparative law or social aspects of legal history. Similarly, quantitative and qualitative methods would complement one another in exploring aspects of rights that might be unique and nonoverlapping with duties, such as when a person has a right but declines to demand it.

CONCLUDING COMMENT

Harré (chap. 10, this volume), Haskell (chap. 11, this volume), and Spragens (chap. 12, this volume), our normative commentators, all point to and illustrate how heeding long-debated conceptual distinctions can produce better empirical research in the future and less confusion in the present. Their illustrations, citing historic and current empirical facts, also indicate that normative disciplines are not exclusively so. Moreover, when our commentators chide us to get clear about concepts, they remind us that our so-called empirical discipline is, in good part, a conceptual, normative discipline. These commentators argue that by understanding the ontology of the concepts we sometimes invoke uncritically, by appreciating that the facts we accumulate are themselves generated by value-laden methods and implied assumptions, and by heeding the long and deep history that animates rights and duties, psychology's contributions can grow substantively weightier by being conceptually more sophisticated.

At this interface between normative and empirical inquiry, as Kant understood a long time ago, abstractions need solid content and intuitions need clear concepts. We have seen in this volume examples of how this informing function works and goes both ways. Taking people, societies, and culture as they are, with their own conceptualizations of rights, duties, and their relationship, provides conceptualists with substance that can ground airy principles and Platonic ideals in concrete fact. The fact finders, in upholding their end, must ground themselves in the conceptual, lest they generate findings and conclusions that not only miss the mark but also completely fail to make a mark on their own field let alone on the more normative disciplines. It is our hope that this work promotes future collaborations between empirical and normative scholars, for the results of such efforts, as we can attest, can bring far greater clarity and substance to a topic that is foundational and fundamental for many disciplines, for citizens of differing cultures, and for the civics they create.

REFERENCES

Arjomand, A. A. (Ed.). (1988). *Authority and political culture in Shi'ism*. Albany: State University of New York Press.

The case against Mr. Hamdi. (2002, July 28). *The Washington Post*, p. B6.

Civics lessons for prosecutors. (2002, June 1). *The Washington Post*, p. A18.

Dying behind closed doors. (2002, August 28). *The Washington Post*, p. A22.

Feinberg, J. (1969). The nature of the value of rights. *Journal of Value Inquiry, 4*, 243–257.

Gottlieb, S. E. (1993). *Public values in constitutional law*. Ann Arbor: University of Michigan Press.

The I-said-so test. (2002, June 20). *The Washington Post*, p. A22.

Khomeini, R. (1981). *Islam and revolution* (H. Algar, Trans.). Berkeley, CA: Nizan Press.

Kohlberg, L. (1976). Moral stages and moralization: The cognitive–developmental approach. In T. Lickona (Ed.), *Moral development and behavior* (pp. 31–53). New York: Holt.

Moghaddam, F. M., & Vuksanovic, V. (1990). Attitudes and behavior toward human rights across different contexts: The role of right-wing authoritarianism, political ideology, and religiosity. *International Journal of Psychology, 25*, 455–475.

Orren, K. (2000). Officers' rights: Toward a unified theory of American constitutional development. *Law and Society Review, 34*, 873–909.

Sophocles. (1977). *The Oedipus cycle: Oedipus Rex, Oedipus at Colonus, Antigone* (D. Fitts & R. Fitzgerald, Trans.). New York: Harvest/HBJ. (Original work written 442 B.C.)

Still no lawyers. (2002, July 9). *The Washington Post*, p. A20.

APPENDIX: UNITED NATIONS UNIVERSAL DECLARATION OF HUMAN RIGHTS

PREAMBLE

Whereas recognition of the inherent dignity and of the equal and inalienable rights of all members of the human family is the foundation of freedom, justice and peace in the world,

Whereas disregard and contempt for human rights have resulted in barbarous acts which have outraged the conscience of mankind, and the advent of a world in which human beings shall enjoy freedom of speech and belief and freedom from fear and want has been proclaimed as the highest aspiration of the common people,

Whereas it is essential, if man is not to be compelled to have recourse, as a last resort, to rebellion against tyranny and oppression, that human rights should be protected by the rule of law,

Whereas it is essential to promote the development of friendly relations between nations,

Whereas the peoples of the United Nations have in the Charter reaffirmed their faith in fundamental human rights, in the dignity and worth of the human person and in the equal rights of men and women and have determined to promote social progress and better standards of life in larger freedom,

Whereas Member States have pledged themselves to achieve, in co-operation with the United Nations, the promotion of universal respect for and observance of human rights and fundamental freedoms,

Whereas a common understanding of these rights and freedoms is of the greatest importance for the full realization of this pledge,

Now, therefore, the General Assembly proclaims this Universal Declaration of Human Rights as a common standard of achievement for all peoples and all nations, to the end that every individual and every organ of society, keeping this Declaration constantly in mind, shall strive by teaching and education to promote respect for these rights and freedoms and by progressive measures, national and international, to secure their universal and effective recognition and observance, both among the peoples of Member States themselves and among the peoples of territories under their jurisdiction.

Retrieved June 2004 from http://www.unhchr.ch/udhr/index.htm.

Article 1.

All human beings are born free and equal in dignity and rights. They are endowed with reason and conscience and should act towards one another in a spirit of brotherhood.

Article 2.

Everyone is entitled to all the rights and freedoms set forth in this Declaration, without distinction of any kind, such as race, colour, sex, language, religion, political or other opinion, national or social origin, property, birth or other status. Furthermore, no distinction shall be made on the basis of the political, jurisdictional or international status of the country or territory to which a person belongs, whether it be independent, trust, non-self-governing or under any other limitation of sovereignty.

Article 3.

Everyone has the right to life, liberty and security of person.

Article 4.

No one shall be held in slavery or servitude; slavery and the slave trade shall be prohibited in all their forms.

Article 5.

No one shall be subjected to torture or to cruel, inhuman or degrading treatment or punishment.

Article 6.

Everyone has the right to recognition everywhere as a person before the law.

Article 7.

All are equal before the law and are entitled without any discrimination to equal protection of the law. All are entitled to equal protection against any discrimination in violation of this Declaration and against any incitement to such discrimination.

Article 8.

Everyone has the right to an effective remedy by the competent national tribunals for acts violating the fundamental rights granted him by the constitution or by law.

Article 9.

No one shall be subjected to arbitrary arrest, detention or exile.

Article 10.

Everyone is entitled in full equality to a fair and public hearing by an independent and impartial tribunal, in the determination of his rights and obligations and of any criminal charge against him.

Article 11.

(1) Everyone charged with a penal offence has the right to be presumed innocent until proved guilty according to law in a public trial at which he has had all the guarantees necessary for his defence.

(2) No one shall be held guilty of any penal offence on account of any act or omission which did not constitute a penal offence, under national or international law, at the time when it was committed. Nor shall a heavier penalty be imposed than the one that was applicable at the time the penal offence was committed.

Article 12.

No one shall be subjected to arbitrary interference with his privacy, family, home or correspondence, nor to attacks upon his honour and reputation. Everyone has the right to the protection of the law against such interference or attacks.

Article 13.

(1) Everyone has the right to freedom of movement and residence within the borders of each state.

(2) Everyone has the right to leave any country, including his own, and to return to his country.

Article 14.

(1) Everyone has the right to seek and to enjoy in other countries asylum from persecution.

(2) This right may not be invoked in the case of prosecutions genuinely arising from non-political crimes or from acts contrary to the purposes and principles of the United Nations.

Article 15.

(1) Everyone has the right to a nationality.

(2) No one shall be arbitrarily deprived of his nationality nor denied the right to change his nationality.

Article 16.

(1) Men and women of full age, without any limitation due to race, nationality or religion, have the right to marry and to found a family. They are entitled to equal rights as to marriage, during marriage and at its dissolution.

(2) Marriage shall be entered into only with the free and full consent of the intending spouses.

(3) The family is the natural and fundamental group unit of society and is entitled to protection by society and the State.

Article 17.

(1) Everyone has the right to own property alone as well as in association with others.

(2) No one shall be arbitrarily deprived of his property.

Article 18.

Everyone has the right to freedom of thought, conscience and religion; this right includes freedom to change his religion or belief, and freedom, either alone or in community with others and in public or private, to manifest his religion or belief in teaching, practice, worship and observance.

Article 19.

Everyone has the right to freedom of opinion and expression; this right includes freedom to hold opinions without interference and to seek, receive and impart information and ideas through any media and regardless of frontiers.

Article 20.

(1) Everyone has the right to freedom of peaceful assembly and association.

(2) No one may be compelled to belong to an association.

Article 21.

(1) Everyone has the right to take part in the government of his country, directly or through freely chosen representatives.

(2) Everyone has the right of equal access to public service in his country.

(3) The will of the people shall be the basis of the authority of government; this will shall be expressed in periodic and genuine elections which shall be by universal and equal suffrage and shall be held by secret vote or by equivalent free voting procedures.

Article 22.

Everyone, as a member of society, has the right to social security and is entitled to realization, through national effort and international co-operation and in accordance with the organization and resources of each State, of the economic, social and cultural rights indispensable for his dignity and the free development of his personality.

Article 23.

(1) Everyone has the right to work, to free choice of employment, to just and favourable conditions of work and to protection against unemployment.

(2) Everyone, without any discrimination, has the right to equal pay for equal work.

(3) Everyone who works has the right to just and favourable remuneration ensuring for himself and his family an existence worthy of human dignity, and supplemented, if necessary, by other means of social protection.

(4) Everyone has the right to form and to join trade unions for the protection of his interests.

Article 24.

Everyone has the right to rest and leisure, including reasonable limitation of working hours and periodic holidays with pay.

Article 25.

(1) Everyone has the right to a standard of living adequate for the health and well-being of himself and of his family, including food, clothing, housing and medical care and necessary social services, and the right to security in the event of unemployment, sickness, disability, widowhood, old age or other lack of livelihood in circumstances beyond his control.

(2) Motherhood and childhood are entitled to special care and assistance. All children, whether born in or out of wedlock, shall enjoy the same social protection.

Article 26.

(1) Everyone has the right to education. Education shall be free, at least in the elementary and fundamental stages. Elementary education shall be compulsory. Technical and professional education shall be made gener-

ally available and higher education shall be equally accessible to all on the basis of merit.

(2) Education shall be directed to the full development of the human personality and to the strengthening of respect for human rights and fundamental freedoms. It shall promote understanding, tolerance and friendship among all nations, racial or religious groups, and shall further the activities of the United Nations for the maintenance of peace.

(3) Parents have a prior right to choose the kind of education that shall be given to their children.

Article 27.

(1) Everyone has the right freely to participate in the cultural life of the community, to enjoy the arts and to share in scientific advancement and its benefits.

(2) Everyone has the right to the protection of the moral and material interests resulting from any scientific, literary or artistic production of which he is the author.

Article 28.

Everyone is entitled to a social and international order in which the rights and freedoms set forth in this Declaration can be fully realized.

Article 29.

(1) Everyone has duties to the community in which alone the free and full development of his personality is possible.

(2) In the exercise of rights and freedoms, everyone shall be subject only to such limitations as are determined by law solely for the purpose of securing due recognition and respect for the rights and freedoms of others and of meeting the just requirements of morality, public order and the general welfare in a democratic society.

(3) These rights and freedoms may in no case be exercised contrary to the purposes and principles of the United Nations.

Article 30.

Nothing in this Declaration may be interpreted as implying for any State, group or person any right to engage in any activity or to perform any act aimed at the destruction of any of the rights and freedoms set forth herein.

INDEX

ABOUT THE EDITORS

Norman J. Finkel, PhD, is a professor of psychology at Georgetown University in Washington, DC. He received his PhD in clinical psychology from the University of Rochester in 1971 and has been in private practice for 20 years. Since coming to Georgetown, he has served as director of undergraduate studies, director of graduate studies, and chair of the psychology department. He is a coeditor of the Law and Public Policy: Psychology and the Social Sciences (Forensic Studies) book series published by the American Psychological Association (APA) and has served on the editorial boards of various journals, such as *Psychology, Public Policy, and Law*; *Law and Human Behavior*; and *Behavioral Sciences and the Law*. He is currently an at-large member of the American Psychology–Law Society (Division 41 of the APA). Some of his other books include *Insanity of Trial; Therapy and Ethics* (1988): *The Courtship of Law and Psychology* (1980); *Mental Illness and Health: Its Legacy, Tensions, and Changes* (1976); and *Not Fair! The Typology of Commonsense Unfairness* (APA, 2001).

Fathali M. Moghaddam, PhD, was born in Iran and educated in England from an early age. He returned to Iran after the 1979 revolution to work in various universities there and then took up posts with the United Nations and McGill University in Canada before moving to his present position as a professor of psychology at Georgetown University in 1990. His current research focuses mainly on culture and justice and particularly on the identification of universal conceptions of rights and duties. His most recent books are *The Individual and Society: A Cultural Integration* (2002); *The Self and Others* (2003, with Rom Harré); *The Psychology of Ethnic and Cultural Conflict* (2004, with Y. T. Lee, C. McCauley, & S. Worchel); and *Understanding Terrorism: Psychosocial Roots, Consequences, and Interventions* (APA, 2004, with A. J. Marsella). Dr. Moghaddam's hobby is reading classic literature, which he enjoys incorporating into his psychology lectures.